United States Edition

2020

Workbook for **Lectors**, **Gospel Readers**, and **Proclaimers** of the **Word**®

Elizabeth M. Nagel, SSL, SSD

Elaine Park, SSL, STD

Mary Pat Haley

LTP
LITURGY
TRAINING
PUBLICATIONS

CONTENTS

WORKBOOK FOR LECTORS, GOSPEL READERS, AND PROCLAIMERS OF THE WORD® 2020, United States Edition © 2019 Archdiocese of Chicago. All rights reserved.

Liturgy Training Publications, 3949 South Racine Avenue, Chicago, IL 60609, 800-933-1800, fax: 800-933-7094, orders@ltp.org, www.LTP.org.

Cover art: Barbara Simcoe

This book was edited by Victoria M. Tufano. Christian Rocha was the production editor, Anna Manhart was the designer, and Luis Leal was the production artist.

Printed in the United States of America

ISBN: 978-1-61671-473-4
WL20

Ordinary Time

In accordance with c. 827, permission to publish was granted on March 29, 2019, by Most Reverend Ronald A. Hicks, Vicar General of the Archdiocese of Chicago. Permission to publish is an official declaration of ecclesiastical authority that the material is free from doctrinal and moral error. No legal responsibility is assumed by the grant of this permission.

(see endnotes on page x)

The Authors

Elizabeth M. Nagel is a professor emerita of biblical exegesis at the University of Saint Mary of the Lake / Mundelein Seminary and a retired president of its Pontifical Faculty of Theology. She earned the licentiate (SSL) and doctorate (SSD) in Sacred Scripture at the Pontifical Biblical Institute and is the author of *Be a Blessing: A Spring of Refreshment on the Road of Daily Life* and a contributor to *The Paulist Biblical Commentary* (2018).

Elaine Park has a licentiate in Sacred Scripture (SSL) from the Pontifical Biblical Institute and a sacred theology doctorate (SSD) from the Gregorian University. She has been a professor of biblical studies and academic dean at Mt. Angel Seminary in St. Benedict, Oregon. Currently she is a pastoral associate at Christ the King parish in Milwaukie, Oregon.

Mary Pat Haley wrote the introduction and margin notes for the readings. She received a BA in speech and drama from St. Mary -of-the-Woods College, and an MA in theatre from Roosevelt University. She taught speech and drama for many years at St. Ignatius College Prep in Chicago and still serves on the staff for theatre productions.

MINISTRY OF THE WORD BASICS

The Word of God in the Liturgy

The Word of God proclaimed in the liturgy is a living Word with power to nourish and transform both those who proclaim it and those who hear it. In the words of the Second Vatican Council's *Constitution on Divine Revelation* (*Dei Verbum*), "The Church has always venerated the divine Scriptures just as she venerates the body of the Lord, since, especially in the sacred liturgy, she unceasingly receives and offers to the faithful the bread of life from the table both of God's word and of Christ's body" (DV, 21).

Throughout its history, the Church has affirmed over and over the close tie between the Word proclaimed in the liturgy and the Word made flesh received in the Eucharist, recognizing both as Christ present to give himself as food. Pope Francis, in his apostolic exhortation *Evangelii gaudium*, writes that the hearts of the faithful who gather on the Lord's Day are nourished both by his Word and by the bread of eternal life (EG, 15). He emphasizes as well that being fed at both tables gives strength for the whole journey: "God's word, listened to and celebrated, above all in the Eucharist, nourishes and inwardly strengthens Christians, enabling them to offer an authentic witness to the Gospel in daily life. . . . The preaching of the word, living and effective, prepares for the reception of the sacrament, and in the sacrament that word attains its maximum efficacy" (EG, 174).

The image of food to refer to God's Word has a strong foundation in the Hebrew Scriptures. Moses tells the people prior to their entering the land, "it is not by bread alone that people live, but by all that comes forth from the mouth of the Lord" (Deuteronomy 8:3). The prophet Jeremiah, commanded to proclaim God's Word, cried out, "When I found your words, I devoured them; your words were my joy, the happiness of my heart" (Jeremiah 15:16). And God later instructed Ezekiel to open his mouth and eat the scroll. Ezekiel recounts the episode: "Feed your stomach and fill your belly with this scroll I am giving you. I ate it, and it was as sweet as honey in my mouth" (Ezekiel 3:1–3). Each of these passages, and many more, highlight God's gift of satisfying our deepest hungers with a Word that is life giving.

How does this Word of God actually feed us with joy, happiness, sweetness, and an abundance of life? Think of what goes into a lavishly prepared feast that gives delight and nourishment to guests. In the same way, the Word of God proclaimed in the liturgy also requires careful selection and preparation. Those proclaiming the Word are like good chefs who have done everything needed to present a nourishing meal. The lectionary provides the selection of the food set at the table of the Word. Its

In the beginning was the Word, and the Word was with God, and the Word was God.

design offers a rich variety, much like a well-chosen menu. The variety of fare means that the readings provide, as fully as possible, an overview of the biblical story and its great themes, even when they might not be people's favorite menu items. Although it isn't the role of the reader to make the selection, it is important for those who proclaim to see where particular texts fit into the broad sweep of the biblical story (our salvation history), how it harmonizes with the season or feast we are celebrating, and how it can offer insights for their particular community at this particular moment. Some questions we might ask are: Why was this text selected? How does it relate to the other readings of the day? How does it provide the variety of nourishment essential for a mature faith? Was the passage selected because of the season or feast, or as part of a continuous reading of a book, letter, or Gospel? How do we hear it echoed in the images and words of the prayers, music, liturgical environment, and ritual actions of this specific liturgy?

In addition to being nourishing food, the Word in the liturgy is also a very personal communication from God to his people: "When the Sacred Scriptures are read in the Church, God himself speaks to his people, and Christ, present in his word, proclaims the Gospel," (*General Instruction of the Roman Missal*, 29). Proclaimers of the Word, then, lend their voices for this personal communication, preparing themselves with sincere humility, through prayer, study, and practice to faithfully convey to the people what God intends.

Understanding the Word We Proclaim

Preparation for reading at the table of the Word can be just as multifaceted as preparing for a family feast. Consider the story of Philip and the Ethiopian eunuch, in which Philip asked the eunuch who was reading from Isaiah, "Do you understand what you are reading?" (Acts 8:30), a question that we should ask ourselves in preparing for liturgical proclamation. If we who proclaim do not understand our reading, how can we help the assembly understand it? In his apostolic exhortation *Verbum Domini*, Pope Benedict XVI commented: "Word and Eucharist are so deeply bound together that we cannot understand one without the other: the word of God sacramentally takes flesh in the event of the Eucharist. The Eucharist opens us to an understanding of Scripture, just as Scripture for its part illumines and explains the mystery of the Eucharist" (VD, 55).

Understanding Word and Sacrament comes partly through research that draws on the wisdom of others, and also through prayer that relies on the inspiration of the Holy Spirit. The wisdom of others may be both from written sources and from discussion and prayer flowing from the readings, perhaps with people from the parish. The biblical texts themselves, as well as prayers used in the liturgy of the day, are rich sources that can prepare one's mind and heart. Such careful reading, research, and prayer constitute the preparation we do in the days prior to our proclamation. Some additional quiet reflection immediately before the celebration of the liturgy is the final preparation.

Good preparation for proclamation aims at unleashing the power of the Word for the whole assembly. As at a festive meal, a hospitable attitude welcomes all who are gathered and also welcomes the Word that will be proclaimed. We taste, we chew, we savor, we digest and absorb the Word so that it becomes a part of us, going forth with the energy of the Holy Spirit. It is most particularly in the liturgy that God's Word becomes bread plentiful enough to feed five thousand and more, becoming an abundant source of nourishment. This is beautifully expressed by St. Ambrose: "This bread which Jesus breaks is, according to the mystery, the Word of God and a teaching about Christ. When this bread is distributed, it multiplies. . . . Jesus gives his words as bread" (*Treatise on Luke's Gospel*, 6:86).

Elaine Park

The Minister of God's Word in the Liturgy

Throughout the Scriptures, God calls individuals to carry out his will in a particular way: kings, queens, prophets, and apostles, among others. God chose to reveal his Word to Israel through their history, their writings, and, finally, through his Son. From among the people of Israel, God chose Mary, through whom God's Word became flesh. In him, Jesus Christ, God chose us to be his own through Baptism and to proclaim the Word of God to the ends of the earth. Christians are called to proclaim God's Word in many ways, through words, actions, and attitudes, in every aspect of their lives, to every person they encounter.

We who are lectors, readers, deacons, and priests are also messengers of that Word at liturgy, particularly the Mass. There believers are reminded once again of God's great love for them, deepening their resolve to live according to God's Word.

This is my commandment: love one another as I love you.

There may also be catechumens present who are in the process of deepening their faith in Jesus Christ in preparation for receiving the sacraments of initiation. In addition, there may be people who are seeking God for the first time.

Listening

Those who face us as we proclaim God's Word must always be our first concern. Our proclamation is for them. God has something to say to them and is using our voice to say it. We must do everything we can to engage them.

Listening is not a simple task. When the assembly is seated for the Liturgy of the Word, they must accomplish several things.

First, they must select to listen. Even at Mass, a number of things are competing for their attention. They may be concerned about something that happened before Mass or what they must do after. There may be troubles or joys that occupy their minds. The phone in their pocket may be vibrating. Or their minds may simply be wandering. They may have to select to listen several times during the Liturgy of the Word.

Second, they must focus on what is being said. Listening is an activity, not a passive stance. They must be open to receiving what is being given, not merely allow the words to wash over them.

Third, they must understand the reading. That means they must be able to hear, to comprehend the words, to follow the line of thought, and to interpret its meaning.

Finally, they must remember the message and carry it with them into their lives.

As proclaimers, we can assist the members of the assembly in participating in the Liturgy of the Word. How? By preparing ourselves, first by getting to know and understand the Scriptures that we will proclaim and then by preparing how we will proclaim them.

Getting to Know the Scriptures

Why do we proclaim God's Word at Mass? To inform? To persuade? To inspire? To comfort? To challenge? It is all of the above at one time or another. Sometimes it can be several in one reading!

It is important to know the purpose and meaning of the reading. It will determine everything! Our tone, delivery, and our understanding all play a part in conveying the message we are proclaiming.

Sometimes we will be reading one of the great stories of the Jewish people from the Old Testament. Other times we speak the words of a prophet as he admonishes the people for being unfaithful to God's covenant or assures them that God is still with them in their time of suffering. Sometimes we are proclaiming from a letter of St. Paul scolding his flock for bad behavior or instructing them how they (and we) should live as followers of Christ. Deacons and priests have the privilege of telling the same parables that Jesus told and conveying his preaching in his own words.

How can we know the purpose of a particular reading? First, just read it. Listen to it as you read it. What does it say to you? Is it telling a story or teaching or giving direction? Is it encouraging or warning? Giving information or telling someone (us) to do something? The first read-through may reveal the reading's purpose, or you may still need more information.

Next, read the commentary. A commentary is provided for every Scripture reading in this book, on the same page as the reading. It will give you context and an explanation of the reading. You may also want to go to your Bible and read the section just before and just after your reading to give you the context in which it was written.

Finally, read your reading in the context of the other readings for the same Mass. Read the Gospel first; it determines the direction of the entire Liturgy of the Word. Then read the first reading next; it is always chosen in light of the Gospel reading. What similarities do you notice between the first reading and the Gospel? If you are assigned the first reading, it may help you decide how to proclaim it. You might also read the responsorial psalm even though it will be sung. It was chosen in light of the first reading and may highlight elements of the first reading for you. Then read the second reading. During Lent, Easter, Advent, and Christmas Time, the second readings coordinate with the other readings. During Ordinary Time, however, second readings are not chosen to coordinate with the other two. We read from one epistle for several weeks in a row and then begin with another epistle. If you are assigned the second reading, it may help you to look at the previous week's second reading.

Now that you have a whole picture of the Liturgy of the Word you are preparing for, you will certainly want to read the commentaries of the readings that you will not be proclaiming. They will greatly enrich your experience of the Liturgy of the Word.

Preparing to Proclaim

In addition to understanding the reading, a strong delivery is key to an effective proclamation. No matter how experienced we are as lectors, we must rehearse every time we are to proclaim. Rehearsal requires attention to several aspects of proclamation.

Volume. Quite simply, the assembly has to hear us. Although most lectors will proclaim with a microphone, the lector's voice must be focused on the assembly, not the microphone. Proclaim to the whole assembly. The microphone is an aid; the voice should do most of the work. Proclamation begins with the lungs and the diaphragm; take a breath before you begin and at each major pause so you have enough air to sustain your volume.

It is important, however, that you know how to use the microphone. It takes practice to know how close to the microphone you should be. If the church is large and has many hard surfaces, it is likely the sound will reverberate more than in a small church or one with softer surfaces, such as carpeting or cushions. You may need to adjust your pace or your volume.

Facial expression. Proclaiming the Word of God is not acting, but it is conveying content and meaning. Part of that meaning is emotion and attitude. After you have done the work to understand your reading, you know what the tone of the reading is: joyful, sorrowful, angry, impatient, confident, serious, or reflective, for example. Respond to the attitude and emotion in your reading by letting it show naturally on your face. It adds to the assembly's understanding of what they are hearing.

Magnify the LORD with me; let us exalt his name together.

Eye contact. When we say something important to someone, we look them in the eye. Look the assembly in the eye when you proclaim so they understand that you are speaking to them, individually and collectively. It takes some practice to do it. You have to know the reading well enough to look up from the text occasionally and then return to the right place. Subtly moving your thumb down the edge of the page as you read might help. Even if you have not yet mastered looking up during the reading, you can look at the assembly when you say the introductory and closing statements: "A reading from . . . " and "The word of the Lord." Keep looking at them until they respond, "Thanks be God."

Vocal variety. When we speak, we naturally raise and lower our voice, pause for emphasis or to change subjects, and talk slower or faster as the content demands. Apply that to the reading. For example, if someone in the reading is calling out or speaking to a crowd, a slightly higher pitch might be called for. Some of the long, complicated sentences from St. Paul might require a slower pace and careful phrasing to help the meaning come through. Dropping your voice at the end of a sentence and raising it at the end of a question is essential for the hearer to interpret what you are saying. A pause after an important point or before a new thought begins may help the hearers absorb what you are saying.

Articulation. Each syllable must be spoken clearly, with appropriate emphasis, but not overemphasis. What you are saying should be clear, but natural sounding. Know how to pronounce each word (there are clues to pronouncing many names in this book). Pay special attention to the ends of words; don't cut them off or swallow them. Moving your lips and showing your teeth will help you enunciate and project your words.

Rehearse

You understand the reading. You know how to pronounce the words, where to raise and lower your voice, where to pause. Now you have to practice. Out loud. Maybe with someone listening. You can't just go over it in your head; you have to use your mouth. Only then will you know how it sounds. When you practice, determine when to pause and when to look up at the assembly. Practicing aloud helps us become comfortable with speaking a bit more slowly than we normally do. We shouldn't rush God's Word.

Overcoming Nervousness

Most readers, even experienced ones, feel a bit of nervousness before we proclaim. This is normal. We understand how important what we are doing is and we all want to do it well!

It may help to remind ourselves that this is about God speaking to his people. We are God's instrument. We have been blessed in so many ways, including our talent as lectors. We have been chosen, and we are prepared. Now we must disappear and let God speak. What better way to give back to God for all that he has given us.

Mary Pat Haley

An Option to Consider

The third edition of *The Roman Missal* encourages ministers of the Word to chant the introduction and conclusion to the readings ("A reading from . . . "; "The word of the Lord"). For those parishes wishing to use these chants, they are demonstrated in audio files that may be accessed either through the QR codes given here (with a smartphone) or through the URL indicated beneath the code. This URL is case sensitive, so be careful to distinguish between the letter l (lowercase L) and the numeral 1.

The first QR code contains the tones for the first reading in both a male and a female voice.

http://bit.ly/l2mjeG

The second QR code contains the tones for the second reading in both a male and a female voice.

http://bit.ly/krwEYy

The third QR code contains the simple tone for the Gospel.

http://bit.ly/iZZvSg

The fourth QR code contains the solemn tone for the Gospel.

http://bit.ly/lwf6Hh

Recommended Works

Find a list of recommended reading and assistance in considering and implementing chanted introductions and conclusions to the readings in downloadable PDF files at http://www.ltp.org/products/details/WL19.

Pronunciation Key

bait = bayt	thin = thin
cat = kat	vision = VIZH*n
sang = sang	ship = ship
father = FAH-<u>th</u>er	sir = ser
care = kayr	gloat = gloht
paw = paw	cot = kot
jar = jahr	noise = noyz
easy = EE-zee	poison = POY-z*n
her = her	plow = plow
let = let	although = ahl-<u>TH</u>OH
queen = kween	church = cherch
delude = deh-L<u>OO</u>D	fun = fuhn
when = hwen	fur = fer
ice = īs	flute = fl<u>oo</u>t
if = if	foot = foot
finesse = fih-NES	

Shorter Readings

In the Scripture readings reproduced in this book, shorter readings are indicated by brackets and also by a citation given at the end of the reading.

Endnotes

(continued from page ii)

Quotations from *Verbum Domini* by Pope Benedict XVI and from *Evangelii gaudium* by Pope Francis, © Libreria Editrice Vaticana.

Excerpts from the English translation of the Introduction from *Lectionary for Mass* © 1969, 1981, 1997, International Commission on English in the Liturgy Corporation (ICEL); excerpts from the English translation of *The Roman Missal* © 2010, ICEL. All rights reserved.

FIRST SUNDAY OF ADVENT

LECTIONARY #1

READING I   Isaiah 2:1–5

A reading from the Book of the Prophet Isaiah

This is what Isaiah, son of **Amoz**,
  saw concerning Judah and Jerusalem.
  In **days to come**,
the mountain of the Lᴏʀᴅ's house
  shall be **established** as the highest **mountain**
  and raised above the hills.
All nations shall **stream** toward it;
  many **peoples** shall come and say:
"**Come**, let us climb the Lᴏʀᴅ's mountain,
  to the **house** of the God of Jacob,
that he may **instruct us** in his ways,
  and we may walk in his paths."
For from **Zion** shall go forth instruction,
  and the word of the Lᴏʀᴅ from Jerusalem.
He shall judge between the nations,
  and **impose** terms on many **peoples**.
They shall **beat** their **swords** into plowshares
  and their **spears** into **pruning hooks**;
one nation shall **not raise** the **sword against** another,
  nor shall they train for war again.
O house of Jacob, come,
  let us walk in the light of the Lᴏʀᴅ!

Sidebar notes (left margin):

Isaiah = Ī-ZAY-uh
Amoz = AY-muhz
Judah = JOO-duh

Pause and build energy.

Take your time.

Keep your energy up.
Zion = ZĪ-uhn or ZĪ-ahn

Articulate word endings.

Proclaim with intensity. The stakes are high.

Transition to a tone of rejoicing in the light.
Smile.

READING I Isaiah's opening prophecies concern Judah and Jerusalem. Prophesying in the last half of the eighth century ʙᴄ, Isaiah knew well of the power of the Assyrian empire, and the threat to Solomon's magnificent temple in Jerusalem. While the intimidating military might of Assyria looms on the present horizon, Isaiah sees an ideal Judah and Jerusalem "in days to come." Isaiah's vision reveals a future time of peace and security founded on the presence of the Lord on the heights of Jerusalem.

In Isaiah's day, mountains and high places were typically considered to be the dwelling places of gods. Jerusalem itself was built on a hill, perhaps for security, although its height is symbolic and theological. Isaiah's vision emphasizes the height of the mountain of the Lord's house, established by God as the highest mountain, raised above the hills. It will be a place to which all nations will stream. The people climbing up to the Lord's own mountain creates a picture of energy and determination, as nations are inspired to come to the Lord's dwelling place. Even those who had

been enemies of Judah will want to be instructed by the Lord, the God of Jacob. God's Word, proclaimed from the height of the temple, will be available to all people.

Isaiah's prophecy suggests that conflicts between nations will continue, but God will be the one who will judge and impose terms. If opposing nations have come with swords, they will beat them into plowshares, and turn their spears into pruning hooks. Ultimately, "walking in the light of the Lord" means God's people, gathered from all nations, will live in accord with God's Word.

1

For meditation and context:

RESPONSORIAL PSALM   Psalm 122:1–2, 3–4, 4–5, 6–7, 8–9

R. Let us go rejoicing to the house of the Lord.

I rejoiced because they said to me,
    "We will go up to the house of the LORD."
And now we have set foot
    within your gates, O Jerusalem.

Jerusalem, built as a city
    with compact unity.
To it the tribes go up,
    the tribes of the LORD.

According to the decree for Israel,
    to give thanks to the name of the LORD.
In it are set up judgment seats,
    seats for the house of David.

Pray for the peace of Jerusalem!
    May those who love you prosper!
May peace be within your walls,
    prosperity in your buildings.

Because of my brothers and friends
    I will say, "Peace be within you!"
Because of the house of the LORD, our God,
    I will pray for your good.

READING II   Romans 13:11–14

A reading from the Letter of Saint Paul to the Romans

Pause after "Brothers and Sisters:"

Brothers and sisters:
You **know** the time;
    it is the **hour now** for you to awake from sleep.

More intense. You are giving a command.

For our **salvation** is **nearer** now than when we **first** believed;
    the **night** is **advanced**, the **day** is at **hand**.
Let us then **throw off** the works of **darkness**

Take your time. Proclaim with boldness how we are to act.

    and **put on** the armor of **light**;
    let us **conduct** ourselves **properly** as in the **day**,
    not in **orgies** and **drunkenness**,
    not in **promiscuity** and **lust**,
    not in rivalry and jealousy.
But put on the Lord Jesus **Christ**,

Pause and say in a tone of conviction.

    and make **no provision** for the **desires** of the **flesh**.

READING II In the reading from Romans, Paul uses familiar human experiences and images to delve into the unseen mysteries of faith. Everyone knows the moment of awaking from sleep and of the darkness of night giving way to the brightness of day. Writing to a community in Rome, Paul urges them wake from slumber, and to live in the light of the day, casting off the deeds of darkness.

The imagery has a certain paradox about it, because the death and Resurrection of Jesus has already inaugurated the new age, the dawning of the day of sal-vation. Believers are therefore already living in the light of day. However, like the early believers in Rome, we are still awaiting Christ's coming again in glory, his *parousia*. A common way of referring to this paradoxical tension is *the already-and-not-yet of salvation*.

In much of this letter, Paul develops significant theological insights, the core of Christian faith much discussed and debated throughout history. In this part of the letter Paul urges the Christians in Rome to live in light of what they believe. Continuing the image of darkness and light, he says believ-ers should take off the clothing of darkness and put on the armor of light. Then, properly clothed for the daylight, they are to conduct themselves properly, with dignity and decorum.

The deeds of darkness that Paul lists are similar to others in Paul's letters (e.g., Galatians 5:19–21). Broadly, the vices can be grouped into acts of drunkenness, sexual impropriety, and community discord. All of these are works of the flesh, whereas Christians are to live according to the spirit. Paul returns to the image of clothing, with

GOSPEL   Matthew 24:37–44

A reading from the holy Gospel according to Matthew

Proclaim in an authoritative tone.

Jesus said to his disciples:
"As it was in the days of Noah,
   so it will be at the coming of the **Son of Man**.

Use an informative tone.

In those days before the **flood**,
   they were eating and drinking,
   marrying and **giving** in marriage,
   up to the day that **Noah entered** the **ark**.
They **did** not **know** until the **flood** came and **carried** them
    all **away**.
So will it be also at the coming of the **Son of Man**.

Proclaim with energy.

Two men will be out in the field;
   one will be taken, and one will be left.
Two **women** will be grinding at the mill;
   one will be taken, and one will be left.

Proclaim with intensity.
Speak slowly with eye contact.
Look at your audience and articulate your words.

Therefore, **stay awake!**
For you **do** not **know** on which **day** your **Lord** will come.
Be sure of **this**: if the master of the house
   had **known** the hour of night when the thief was coming,
   he **would** have stayed awake
   and not let his house be broken into.

Proclaim slowly.

So too, **you also must be** prepared,
   for at an hour you do **not expect**, the **Son of Man** will **come**."

TO KEEP IN MIND
The words in bold are suggestions for ways to express the meaning of the reading. Consider using them as you practice the reading, then choose to stress them or to find your own way of proclaiming.

---

the most important and encompassing garment being the Lord Jesus Christ himself.

GOSPEL   The Gospel from Matthew is part of Jesus' last address to his disciples before his passion. Throughout the discourse, Jesus speaks of what will happen in the future, at the end of the age. Today's reading opens and closes with reference to the coming (*parousia*) of the Son of Man, an end-time event when God will manifest ultimate salvific power. Although the *parousia* of the Son of Man is certain, when it will happen is

unknown. Therefore, Jesus' disciples must always be prepared and vigilant.

In order to instruct his disciples on the necessity of being ever alert, Jesus makes a graphic comparison between the flood in the days of Noah and the coming of the Son of Man. People were eating, drinking, and marrying, oblivious of the flood that was about to come and carry them away. Similarly, when the Son of Man comes, as people continue ordinary activities such as grinding at the mill, one will be taken away while another will be left. In another analogy, Jesus tells of the master of a house

who would stay awake if he knew when a thief would come to break into his house. Both analogies emphasize the suddenness and unknown time of a startling event.

Each of the readings on this First Sunday of Advent have a twofold focus. As they look to the future, whether described as *days to come* or *parousia*, they are also instructing people how to live in the present: walk in the light of the Lord; put on the Lord Jesus Christ; stay awake and be prepared. E.P.

SECOND SUNDAY OF ADVENT

LECTIONARY #4

READING I   Isaiah 11:1–10

Isaiah = ī-ZAY-uh

What a beautiful reading from Isaiah! Take your time and build with excitement.

Jesse = JES-ee

Proclaim in a gentle tone and build energy.

Say firmly.

Keep up the energy.

Gently proclaim "Then the wolf shall be a guest" until you finish with "and the child lay his hand on the adder's lair" (next page).

A reading from the Book of the Prophet Isaiah

> **On that day**, a **shoot** shall **sprout** from the **stump of Jesse**,
>   and from his roots a **bud** shall blossom.
> The spirit of the Lord shall rest upon him:
>   a spirit of **wisdom and of** understanding,
> a spirit of counsel and of strength,
>   a spirit of knowledge and of fear of the Lord,
>   and his delight shall be the **fear** of the Lord.
> Not by appearance shall he **judge**,
>   nor by **hearsay** shall he decide,
> but he shall **judge** the **poor** with **justice**,
>   and **decide aright** for the land's **afflicted**.
> He shall **strike** the **ruthless** with the rod of his mouth,
>   and with the **breath** of his lips he shall **slay** the wicked.
> Justice shall be the band around his waist,
>   and faithfulness a belt upon his hips.
> Then the wolf shall be a **guest** of the lamb,
>   and the leopard shall **lie down** with the kid;
> the calf and the **young** lion shall browse together,
>   with a **little** child to guide them.

READING I Isaiah's vision of a world transformed "on that day," was written when the kingly descendants of David were weak, unjust, and lacking in knowledge. The eighth-century BC Davidic kings were a mere "stump" of the tree that grew from the root of Jesse, the father of King David. Today's reading opens and closes with a promise that new life will arise from that stump, blossoming anew from the roots, and will be a signal for the nations.

Isaiah begins his description of the future Davidic descendant by announcing that the spirit of the Lord will rest upon him; he emphasizes the spirit-bestowed gifts by repeating the word *spirit* three more times. The spirit is God's own life-giving breath that will be the source of wisdom, understanding, counsel, strength, knowledge, and fear of the Lord. These gifts are essential for the king to rule wisely, as did his ancestor David.

Filled with the spirit at the core of his being, the king will not only imitate David, but he will also act as the Lord does in governing the earth. Unlike earthly kings, who are concerned with appearances and make decisions based on hearsay, the spirit-filled king will make judgments based on justice: right relationships in every dimension. The king will rule like the Lord God of Israel, who showed justice particularly to the poor and afflicted. Justice will be so important that the king will be clothed in it, with a band of justice around his waist.

The effects of such spirit-endowed governance will extend beyond the people of his kingdom. Nature itself will be transformed. Animals that ordinarily relate as predator and prey will live in harmony. Their new relationship will be more than avoiding conflict, but will involve intimacy.

The cow and the bear shall be **neighbors**,
  together their young shall rest;
  the lion shall **eat hay** like the **ox**.
The **baby** shall **play** by the **cobra's** den,
  and the child lay his hand on the **adder's** lair.
There shall be **no harm** or **ruin** on all **my holy mountain**;
  for the earth shall be filled with **knowledge** of the LORD,
  as **water** covers the **sea**.
On that day, the root **of Jesse**,
  set up as a **signal** for the nations,
  the Gentiles shall **seek out**,
  for his **dwelling** shall be glorious.

Proclaim in a tone of expectation. Smile.

Gentiles = JEN-tĭls

For meditation and context:

RESPONSORIAL PSALM Psalm 72:1–2, 7–8, 12–13, 17 (7)

R. Justice shall flourish in his time, and fullness of peace forever.

O God, with your judgment endow the king,
  and with your justice, the king's son;
he shall govern your people with justice
  and your afflicted ones with judgment.

Justice shall flower in his days,
  and profound peace, till the moon be
  no more.
May he rule from sea to sea,
  and from the River to the ends of
  the earth.

For he shall rescue the poor when he
  cries out,
  and the afflicted when he has no one
  to help him.
He shall have pity for the lowly and the poor;
  the lives of the poor he shall save.

May his name be blessed forever;
  as long as the sun his name shall remain.
In him shall all the tribes of the earth
  be blessed;
  all the nations shall proclaim
  his happiness.

> **TO KEEP IN MIND**
> Read the Scripture passage and its commentary in *Workbook*. Then read it from your Bible, including what comes before and after it, so that you understand the context.

Being a guest, lying down and browsing together, and being neighbor create a hopeful scenario for the future. The peace of the animal kingdom reaches also to humanity, for the whole earth will be filled with the knowledge of the Lord. Like the new harmony in the animal kingdom, there will be harmony between the house of David and the Gentiles in the glorious dwelling "on that day."

 READING II Two themes tie the first and second readings together: hope and harmony. The hopeful vision in

Isaiah's peaceable kingdom had not yet been brought to fulfillment when Paul wrote his letters. Jews and Gentiles could not even eat together, and there was dissention among the many factions within Judaism. In the Christian community in Rome, there appeared to be rivalry between Gentile and Jewish believers, and those who considered themselves strong looked down on those they regarded as weak. Isaiah's vision of harmony remained a distant hope.

Paul uses several methods to promote the hoped-for unity and understanding in

the community: instruction, prayer, and exhortation. He begins by reminding his audience of the teaching they have received from the Scriptures. Believers who live in a state of endurance in the face of trials receive encouragement and hope from the Word of God. Although the tradition is ancient, it is relevant to their contemporary situation.

Paul inserts a brief prayer between instruction and exhortation. Echoing his description of the believers in Rome, Paul asks that the God of endurance and encouragement will inspire them, both in

READING II   Romans 15:4–9

A reading from the Letter of Saint Paul to the Romans

Pause after "Brothers and sisters."
Use a tone of authority.

Brothers and sisters:
Whatever was written **previously** was written for our instruction,
    that by **endurance** and by the **encouragement** of the Scriptures
    we might have hope.

Proclaim as if you are praying.

May the God of endurance and encouragement
    grant you to think in harmony with one another,
    in **keeping** with Christ **Jesus**,
    that with **one accord** you may with one **voice**
    glorify the **God and Father** of our Lord Jesus Christ.

Read with energy.

circumcised = SER-kuhm-sīz*d
patriarchs = PAY-tree-ahrks
Gentiles = JEN-tīls
Proclaim with gratefulness in your voice.
Pause.
Proclaim with enthusiasm.

Welcome one another, then, as Christ **welcomed you**,
    for the glory of God.
For **I** say that Christ became a **minister** of the **circumcised**
    to show God's **truthfulness**,
    to confirm the promises of the patriarchs,
    but so that the Gentiles might **glorify** God for his mercy.
As it is written:
    Therefore, I will praise you among the Gentiles
        *and **sing praises** to your name.*

GOSPEL   Matthew 3:1–12

A reading from the holy Gospel according to Matthew

Proclaim with vocal variety and facial expression.
Judea = joo-DEE-uh

Isaiah = ī-ZAY-uh

John the **Baptist appeared**, preaching in the desert of Judea
    and saying, "**Repent**, for the kingdom of **heaven** is at **hand**!"
It was of him that the prophet **Isaiah** had spoken when he said:
    *A voice of one **crying out** in the desert,*
    Prepare the way of the Lord,
        make straight his paths.

---

their thinking and their acting, to live in harmony with one another, with one accord and one voice. Exhibiting such internal unity is in keeping with Christ Jesus, who is the exemplar of the unity for which Paul prays. Harmony in the community is a way of glorifying God.

Paul's exhortation to "welcome one another" implies more than abiding by the cultural norms of hospitality. He gives his audience a clear pattern of how they are to welcome one another: as Christ has welcomed them. Christ's ministry to the circumcised, the Jewish people, showed God's truthfulness and fidelity to the promises made to their ancestors. His welcome of them was a manifestation of God's endurance and encouragement. In addition, Christ's ministry to the Jews was not for them alone. It was also for the Gentiles who, seeing God's mercy manifest to the Jews, would also praise God's mercy. God's plan, and Paul's hope, is that Jews and Gentiles, living in harmony, would sing praise to God's name.

GOSPEL | The first two chapters of the Gospel according to Matthew tell of the announcement of Jesus' birth, the birth itself, and events surrounding it. After these two chapters, Matthew jumps forward to the adult Jesus, his ministry, passion, death, and Resurrection.

Before saying anything about the adult Jesus, though, Matthew gives an account of John the Baptist, the precursor who prepared "the way of the Lord." John appears as a prophet in the Jewish tradition, like Elijah and Isaiah, calling the people to repentance. His strange clothing, desert diet, and demanding message, rather than keeping the city inhabitants away, attract

Pharisees = FAYR-uh-seez

Sadducees = SAD-yoo-seez

John wore clothing made of **camel's hair**
    and had **a leather belt** around his waist.
His food was **locusts** and wild **honey**.
At that time **Jerusalem**, **all** Judea,
    and the whole region around the Jordan
    were going **out** to **him**
    and were being baptized by him in the Jordan River
    as they acknowledged their sins.

Build to anger as you say, "You brood
of vipers!"

When he **saw** many of the Pharisees and Sadducees
    coming to his **baptism**, he said to them, "You brood of **vipers**!
Who **warned** you to flee from the coming wrath?
Produce good fruit as evidence of your repentance.
And do not **presume** to say to yourselves,
    'We have **Abraham** as our father.'
For I tell **you**,
    God can **raise up** children to Abraham from these **stones**.
Even **now** the **ax** lies at the **root** of the trees.
Therefore every tree that does **not** bear **good** fruit
    will be cut **down** and **thrown** into the **fire**.

Transition your tone to one of humility as you
proclaim, "I am baptizing you with water . . ."

I am **baptizing** you with **water**, for repentance,
    but the one who is coming after me is mightier than I.
I am not worthy to carry his **sandals**.
He will baptize **you** with the **Holy** Spirit and fire.
His **winnowing fan** is **in his hand**.

Proclaim with a tone of authority. Articulate
your words. Take your time.

He will **clear** his threshing floor
    and gather his **wheat** into his barn,
    but the **chaff** he will **burn** with **unquenchable fire**."

them in large numbers. Crowds from Jerusalem, including Pharisees and Sadducees, come to him for baptism. His words to them are sharp and severe: "You brood of vipers!" Having Abraham for their father, the root of their tradition, is not enough. An ax lies at the very root, ready to cut down the tree if it does not bear good fruit. John's preaching is a forceful call to repentance (*metanoia*) that entails changes of thinking, attitudes, behavior, and relationships.

John's baptism is a symbolic action. In Judaism, there were other symbolic acts involving water, such as ritual cleansings and ceremonial washings. Those actions were meant to be repeated, while John's baptism was a one-time event of repentance and forgiveness. It signifies a deep and abiding *metanoia*. John declares that those immersed into the baptismal waters must produce good fruit as evidence that they have truly changed.

The final part of the account changes focus from those being baptized by John to "the one who is coming after me." Without naming Jesus, John exercises his role of preparing the way of the Lord by speaking enigmatically of the one who is mightier. John is so much lower than this mighty one that he cannot even perform the slave's task of carrying his sandals. John baptized with water for repentance and forgiveness, but the mighty one will baptize with the Holy Spirit and fire. Repentance and forgiveness prepare for God's definitive rule in the future, while the Holy Spirit and fire signify the very presence of God here and now. E.P.

THE IMMACULATE CONCEPTION OF THE BLESSED VIRGIN MARY

LECTIONARY #689

READING I Genesis 3:9–15, 20

A reading from the Book of Genesis

Genesis = JEN-uh-sihs

After the **man**, Adam, had **eaten** of the **tree**,
the Lord God **called** to the man and **asked** him,
"**Where are you**?"

The congregation must hear fear in your voice.

He answered, "I **heard** you in the garden;
but I was afraid, because I was **naked**,
so I **hid** myself."

Proclaim slowly, with authority.

Then he asked, **"Who told you** that you were naked?
You have eaten, then,
from the **tree** of which I had forbidden **you** to eat!"
The man replied, "The woman whom you put here with me—
she gave **me** fruit from the tree, and so **I** ate **it**."
The Lord God then asked the woman,

Ask this question slowly, with authority.

"Why did you **do such** a **thing**?"
The woman answered, "The **serpent tricked me** into it,
so I **ate** it."

Pause.
Transition your tone to reflect God's anger.

Then the Lord God said to the **serpent**:
"Because you have done this, **you** shall be banned
from all **the** animals
and from all the **wild creatures;**
on your belly shall you crawl,
and dirt shall you eat
all the days of your *life*.

READING I The reading from Genesis is part of a longer narrative that stretches from Genesis 2:25 through 3:24. It begins by stating that the man and his wife were naked, but that they felt no shame. Their nakedness signifies both their innocence and their ignorance. They seem easy prey for the serpent, whose temptation leads them to eat of the forbidden fruit. Today's reading begins after their eating from the tree, with God's call to them, "Where are you?" Adam and his wife Eve are hiding, attempting to evade God and hide their nakedness, which they have cov-

ered with fig leaves. They have lost their innocence and their ignorance of sin. God continues to ask questions of the couple: "Who told you that you were naked?" and "Why did you do such a thing?"—queries for which God already knows the answer. The questions provide the opportunity for the man and woman to admit what they have done, even as they attempt to place the blame on someone else, from wife to serpent. Adam even tries to blame God, since God put the woman in the garden with him. The blaming does not fool God, who delineates the consequences for all

the characters in the story, beginning with the serpent. Cursed and banned from being with other animals, the serpent will be forced to crawl on his belly. The punishment suggests that the serpent formerly had legs like other wild creatures, but will now be demeaned, forced to crawl and eat the dirt of the earth. No longer will the serpent be able to tempt the woman, for there will be an eternal enmity between the serpent's offspring and those of the woman. The punishment meted out to the couple is described in verses just after the reading, including the pain of childbirth for the

8

enmity = EN-mih-tee (mutual hatred)

Pause and proclaim slowly.

Build energy as you read.

Say this last line in an informative tone.

I will put **enmity** between you and the **woman**,
   and between your **offspring** and hers;
he will strike at **your head**,
   while you **strike** at **his heel**."

The **man** called his wife **Eve**,
   because **she** became the mother of **all** the **living**.

For meditation and context:

RESPONSORIAL PSALM   Psalm 98:1, 2–3ab, 3cd–4 (1)

R. Sing to the Lord a new song, for he has done marvelous deeds.

Sing to the LORD a new song,
   for he has done wondrous deeds;
His right hand has won victory for him,
   his holy arm.

The LORD has made his salvation known:
   in the sight of the nations he has revealed
     his justice.
He has remembered his kindness and
   his faithfulness
   toward the house of Israel.

All the ends of the earth have seen
   the salvation by our God.
Sing joyfully to the LORD, all you lands;
   break into song; sing praise.

READING II   Ephesians 1:3–6, 11–12

Ephesians = ee-FEE-zhuhnz

Your tone throughout this reading is one of joy.

Blessed – BLES-uhd

blessed = blesd

Smile as you proclaim.

A reading from the Letter of Saint Paul to the Ephesians

Brothers and sisters:
Blessed be the God and Father of our Lord Jesus Christ,
   who has blessed us in **Christ**
   with **every** spiritual **blessing** in the heavens,
   as he chose us **in him**, **before** the foundation of the **world**,
   to be holy and without blemish before him.
In love he destined us **for** adoption to himself
   through Jesus **Christ**,
   in accord with the **favor** of his will,
   for the praise of the glory of his **grace**
   that he granted **us** in the beloved. »

woman, and being ruled by her husband. The punishment for the man is his toiling over land that is cursed—filled with thorns and thistles. And both of them are expelled from the garden.

This ancient story describes original relationships fractured by sin, and the ongoing consequences. Questions and answers, along with consequences of sin, are intended to draw readers into the story. The questions are addressed to everyone who hears the account: "Where are you?" "Why did you (you who hear this story) do such a thing?" Admission of guilt, accepting

the consequences, and hope for newness are part of our human story, beginning with this account from Genesis.

READING II It is appropriate that this reading from Ephesians be used in the liturgy, since its original use was likely liturgical, proclaimed when the nascent Christian communities gathered for worship or Baptism. Such blessings of God, called *berakah*, were hymns of extended praise in the Jewish tradition (for example, Psalms 41:13; 72:18, 19). The early Church adapted these praises, transform-

ing them by emphasizing God's salvific work in Christ (2 Corinthians 1:3–5; 1 Peter 1:3–12). In this blessing, we praise God who has extended blessings to embrace all who are "in Christ," a shorthand phrase to refer to the baptized. Paul's use of "us" and "we" as recipients of God's saving blessings connects his own life with the community of believers.

The focus of the hymn is on blessings given through the myriad actions of God that reach through all times and places, as far as the heavens and begun before the foundation of the world. "Every spiritual

Take your time as you read. Articulate your words. You are giving praise to God!

In him we were **also** chosen,
   destined in accord with the purpose of the One
   who accomplishes all **things** according to the **intention**
      of **his** will,
   so that we **might exist for the** praise **of** his glory,
   we who first hoped in Christ.

GOSPEL   Luke 1:26–38

A reading from the holy Gospel according to Luke

Take your time with this well-loved Gospel passage. Articulate your words.

The angel **Gabriel** was sent from God
   to a town of **Galilee** called **Nazareth**,
   to a **virgin betrothed** to a man named Joseph,
   of the house of David,
   and the virgin's **name** was Mary.
And coming to her, he said,
   "**Hail, full of grace!** The **Lord** is **with you.**"
But she was greatly troubled at what was said
   and pondered what sort of **greeting** this might be.

The angel speaks gently. Use vocal variety and eye contact to convey the dialogue.

Then the angel **said** to her,
   "**Do** not **be** afraid, Mary,
   for **you** have found **favor** with **God.**
Behold, you will conceive **in your womb** and bear a son,
   and you shall **name** him **Jesus.**
He will be **great** and will be called Son of the Most High,
   and the **Lord God** will **give** him the **throne** of **David** his **father,**
   and he will **rule** over the house of **Jacob** forever,
   and of **his Kingdom there will** be no end."
But **Mary** said to the angel,
   "**How can this be,**
   since I have **no relations** with a **man?**"

Pause. Build energy with the angel's words.

blessing" is best understood as the power and presence of the Holy Spirit in each of the blessings. The first blessing is God's choosing of us, announced two times in the reading. Associated with God's choice or election in Christ is that of being destined in accord with God's purpose. Predestination occurs in other places in Paul's writings as well (for example, 1 Corinthians 2:7 and Romans 8:29–30), and has given rise to the notion of some people being predestined for salvation and others for damnation. Paul's view of predestination, however, is that blessing, not condem-

nation, has been God's plan from the beginning, a plan flowing from his love. The intention of choosing us is to make us holy so we may live as God's beloved adopted children, beloved as Christ himself is. Being chosen, or elected, by God is not based on any prior good deeds, but simply because of God's abiding love. The final words of the reading highlight the very purpose of our existence: that we who have hoped in Christ might praise God's glory. This liturgical hymn thus begins and ends with praise of God, as do all of our liturgical gatherings.

GOSPEL In the first reading we heard a story of the first acts of disobedience, followed by a proclamation of God's blessings given in love. Here in the Gospel we hear a contrasting story of perfect obedience and the fulfillment of God's promise of divine blessings, now bestowed on God's chosen one, the mother of Jesus. Her portrait is beautifully and skillfully drawn. She is a virgin named Mary, or Miriam, after her Jewish ancestor. All that she does and says in the opening chapters of Luke's Gospel show her as a woman steeped in the Jewish tradition.

The angel speaks in an informative tone.

And the angel said to her in **reply**,
   "The Holy Spirit will come **upon you**,
   and the **power** of the Most High will **overshadow you**.
Therefore the **child** to be **born**
   will be called holy, the Son of God.
And **behold**, **Elizabeth**, your relative,
   has also conceived a **son** in her **old age**,
   and this is the **sixth month** for her who was called barren;
   for nothing will be impossible for **God**."

Use a tone of humble acceptance.

Mary said, "Behold, **I am the handmaid of the Lord**.
May it be done to me **according to your** word."
Then the angel departed from her.

THE **4** STEPS OF *LECTIO DIVINA* OR PRAYERFUL READING

1. *Lectio:* Read a Scripture passage aloud slowly. Notice what phrase captures your attention and be attentive to its meaning. Silent pause.

2. *Meditatio:* Read the passage aloud slowly again, reflecting on the passage, allowing God to speak to you through it. Silent pause.

3. *Oratio:* Read it aloud slowly a third time, allowing it to be your prayer or response to God's gift of insight to you. Silent pause.

4. *Contemplatio:* Read it aloud slowly a fourth time, now resting in God's word.

This scene even echoes other stories from the Old Testament in which an angel announces a coming birth through the power of God (for example, Judges 13:2–7). Gabriel addresses the young woman from Nazareth as "full of grace," almost as if that were her name. Based on the root word for "grace," her new name is *kecharitomene*, indicating that she has been exceedingly favored, or abundantly graced. The grace, given long ago, is God's freely bestowed blessing, assured by the divine presence: "the Lord is with you." The angel promises Mary that, though a virgin, she will con-ceive and bear a son. Her child will be great, will be given the throne of his ancestor David, will be holy, and will be the Son of God. The identity of Mary in this scene is intimately connected with the identity of her son.

Although Mary questions, "How can this be?" her response is an unequivocal yes to whatever God asks of her. She identifies herself as a "handmaid of the Lord," perhaps better translated as "slave (*doule*) of the Lord," the same designation that St. Paul uses for himself. With her self-identification, Mary states both her humility before God, and that she is in God's service without reservation. She promises not only obedience to what God asks of her through the angel, but also yes to whatever God may ask in the future. Far from being a passive acceptance, Mary's answer is a courageous, freely exercised eagerness. E.P.

THIRD SUNDAY
OF ADVENT

LECTIONARY #7

READING I   Isaiah 35:1–6a, 10

Isaiah = ī-ZAY-uh

Smile as you proclaim this reading. Articulate your words.

Lebanon = LEB-uh-nuhn

Carmel = KAHR-m*l

Sharon = SHAYR-uhn

Let the congregation hear strength in your voice. "Be strong, fear not!"

Proclaim slowly.

Read with joy. Build intensity.

A reading from the Book of the Prophet Isaiah

The desert and the parched land will exult;
    the steppe will rejoice and bloom.
They will **bloom** with abundant **flowers**,
    and **rejoice** with joyful **song**.
The **glory** of Lebanon will be given to them,
    the **splendor** of Carmel and Sharon;
they will see the glory of the Lᴏʀᴅ,
    the splendor of our God.
Strengthen the hands that are **feeble**,
    make firm the knees that are **weak**,
say to those whose hearts are **frightened**:
    Be **strong**, **fear** not!
Here is your God,
    he comes with vindication;
with divine **recompense**
    he comes to save you.
Then will the eyes of the **blind** be opened,
    the ears of the **deaf** be cleared;
then will the lame leap like a stag,
    then the **tongue** of the mute will **sing**. »

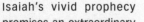 **READING I**   Isaiah's vivid prophecy promises an extraordinary renewal of land and people. In the preceding chapter, Isaiah describes the fruitful land of Israel's enemy turned into a desert wasteland; in today's reading, he presents an opposite scenario: the parched land becoming fruitful. Isaiah develops this prophecy in three stages: image of a desert transformed; direct address to God; direct address to the people, with promise of human restoration.

The opening imagery is of a desert personified: the parched land will exult, the steppe will rejoice, and the desert will rejoice with joyful song. Isaiah's promise of the earth itself participating in praising God has psalm-like poetry: "Let the rivers clap their hands, the mountains shout with them for joy" (Psalm 98:8). The land has great cause for such rejoicing, for the southern desert will receive the abundant growth associated with the northern fruitfulness of Lebanon, Carmel, and Sharon. The land will see God's own glory, the tangible weight of God's power and presence.

Having described a fecund transformation of the desert, Isaiah then speaks directly to God, or perhaps a divine messenger. Knowing the suffering of the people, Isaiah asks that God strengthen their feeble hands and weakened knees. The God who can bring about life in the desert is also able to heal whatever suffering afflicts God's own people. Asking that God say to frightened hearts "Be strong, fear not," has a twofold significance: the people themselves must be strong in the face of adversity, and they should know well that God abides with them, "Fear not, I am with you" (Isaiah 41:10).

12

Those whom the LORD has ransomed **will** return
   and enter Zion **singing**,
   crowned with everlasting joy;
they will meet with joy **and** gladness,
   sorrow **and** mourning will **flee**.

Smile as you read this last sentence. Take your time. Wonderful news!

Zion = Zī-uhn or Zī-ahn

For meditation and context:

RESPONSORIAL PSALM   Psalm 146:6–7, 8–9, 9–10 (Isaiah 35:4)

R. Lord, come and save us.
   or
   R. Alleluia.

The LORD God keeps faith forever,
   secures justice for the oppressed,
   gives food to the hungry.
The LORD sets captives free.

The LORD gives sight to the blind;
   the LORD raises up those who were
   bowed down.
The LORD loves the just;
   the LORD protects strangers.

The fatherless and the widow he sustains,
   but the way of the wicked he thwarts.
The LORD shall reign forever;
   your God, O Zion, through all generations.

READING II   James 5:7–10

A reading from the Letter of Saint James

Be patient, brothers and sisters,
   until the **coming** of the Lord.
See how the **farmer waits** for the **precious fruit** of the earth,
   being **patient** with it
   until it receives the early and the late rains.
You too must be **patient**.
Make your hearts firm,
   because the **coming** of the Lord is **at hand**.

Pause after "Be patient."

Continue to read as one sentence.

Say this line firmly with good eye contact.

Proclaim slowly.

In the third movement of his prophecy, Isaiah announces that God does indeed come to save the people. The future will bring an opening of the eyes of the blind, a clearing of the ears of the deaf, and an empowering of the lame to leap. Along with the land that will sing, the mute too will sing. In verses omitted from today's reading, Isaiah returns to the image of the transformed earth, where God will open a highway through the desert for the redeemed to walk. Transformed people will walk on transformed land, as those ransomed by the Lord will enter Zion with joy and gladness.

READING II The Letter of James is an extended exhortation, reading like a lengthy sermon that urges believers to persevere in the face of trials and testing. The audience, identified as "the twelve tribes of the dispersion," may refer to Jewish believers scattered throughout the Mediterranean world. More broadly, the audience includes all Christians who strive to live in patient fidel-ity to the belief they profess, whether in the first century or today.

The overarching theme of today's reading is patience. James urges patience specifically "until the coming (*parousia*) of the Lord." From the beginning, Christians have believed in Christ's coming again in glory, his *parousia*. While there is certainty in Christ's future coming, there has never been certainty as to when it will happen. Because the *parousia* may be soon, or may be in the far distant future, James urges the community to wait in patience.

A command on how we should act. Proclaim with firmness.

Do not complain, brothers and sisters, about one another,
   that **you** may **not** be **judged**.
Behold, the Judge is standing before the gates.
Take as an example of hardship **and** patience, brothers and sisters,
   the prophets who spoke in the **name of the Lord**.

GOSPEL   Matthew 11:2–11

A reading from the holy Gospel according to Matthew

Proclaim in an authoritative tone.

When **John the** Baptist heard in **prison** of the **works** of the Christ,
   he sent his disciples to Jesus with this question,
   "Are **you** the one who is to come,
   or should we look for **another**?"
Jesus said to them in reply,

Use a firm but gentle tone. Take your time.

   "**Go** and tell John what you **hear** and **see**:
   the **blind** regain their **sight**,
   the **lame walk**,
   lepers are **cleansed**,
   the **deaf hear**,
   the dead are **raised**,
   and the poor have the good news proclaimed to them.
And blessed is the one who takes no **offense** at me."

Blessed = BLES-uhd

As they were going off,
   Jesus began to speak to the crowds about **John**,
   "What did you go out to the desert to see?

Pause after each question and use strong eye contact.

A **reed** swayed by the wind?
Then **what** did **you** go out to see?
Someone dressed in fine **clothing**?
Those who wear **fine clothing** are in royal **palaces**. »

In using the analogy of the farmer, the only actions that James mentions are waiting and being patient. Yet the farmer's unspoken actions are also important. The farmer works diligently in preparing the soil, sowing the seed, and tending the crop all season long. For the coming rains to be effective, the ground must be ready to receive it. So too those who wait patiently are to be actively engaged in living in accord with the faith they profess. Present actions prepare the person to be ready for the Lord's future coming. James' entire letter advises such active and ethical living. In

this reading, he looks at relationships within the community: "Do not complain about one another." Patience with one another is another way of being patient for the Lord's coming.

Along with the farmer as an image of patience, James sees the Hebrew prophets as an example both of hardship and patience. They waited long years for God to intervene. In the verse after today's reading, James adds Job as another example of perseverance. Since even God is steadfast and patient according to the Bible, (e.g.,

Romans 15:5; 1 Peter 3:20), Christian patience is modeled after God's own.

GOSPEL While John the Baptist was imprisoned, he heard about Jesus' activities throughout Galilee. Although Matthew identified Jesus as "the Christ" in his first verse, John himself wants to know if Jesus is indeed the "one who is to come." John had earlier described the one coming after him in graphic imagery: he would gather wheat into his barn and burn the chaff with unquenchable fire (3:12). This expectation of the coming one

Read this slowly and with certainty.

Articulate your words. Proclaim with strength in your voice.

> TO KEEP IN MIND
> Smile when you share good news in a reading. Nonverbal cues like a smile help your assembly better understand your reading.

Then why did you **go out**? To see a prophet?
Yes, I tell you, and more than a prophet.
This is the **one** about whom it is written:
 *Behold, I am sending my **messenger** ahead of you;*
  *he will prepare your **way** before you.*
Amen, I say to you,
 among those born of **women**
  there has been none **greater** than **John the** Baptist;
  yet the least in the kingdom of heaven is greater **than he**."

as a severe judge seems at odds with what John is hearing of Jesus' teaching, healing, and mercy. Thus he sends his disciples to Jesus for a direct answer to his puzzlement.

In addition to John's notion of the messiah as a judge, there were other views in Judaism of what God's anointed one would be; some expected a political or military ruler, and others hoped for a priestly messiah. Jesus' answer to the Baptist's query presents another view. Combining prophecies from Isaiah that looked toward the messianic age, Jesus reviews what the crowds have heard and seen from him: giv-ing sight to the blind, cure of lameness, and other works of healing and wholeness. Jesus then adds a beatitude to the ones he had proclaimed in his Sermon on the Mount. Those who do not take offense in him (literally, who are not scandalized) are the recipients of God's freely given blessing.

Having replied to John's emissaries, Jesus then speaks about John to the crowds. The Baptist is no mere reed, easily swayed by the wind. He is a desert prophet, fearless and forceful. He is the fulfillment of Malachi's ancient prophecy, the messenger who prepared the way. Jesus prefaces his next statement with "Amen," giving it solemnity and significance. John is the greatest of those born of women, praising him as the greatest of those born on the earth. Great as John is, even the least of those born into the kingdom of heaven are greater than John is. Jesus' teaching has thus moved from speaking about himself, to speaking about John, to speaking about his audience. Even though they may count themselves as insignificant when compared to Jesus or to the great John the Baptist, they can be great in the kingdom of heaven. E.P.

FOURTH SUNDAY
OF ADVENT

LECTIONARY #10

READING I Isaiah 7:10–14

Isaiah = Ī-ZAY-uh

A reading from the Book of the Prophet Isaiah

Ahaz = AY-haz

Proclaim in a clear, authoritative tone.

Read with firmness and energy.

The LORD **spoke** to Ahaz, saying:
   Ask for a **sign** from the **Lord**, **your GOD**;
   let it be deep as the netherworld, or high as the sky!
But **Ahaz** answered,
   "I will not ask! I will **not tempt** the LORD!"
Then **Isaiah** said:
   Listen, **O** house of David!

Say as if you are scolding a child.

Use a tone of frustration.

Is it **not** enough for you to weary **people**,
   must you **also** weary my **God**?

Pause and project your voice.

Pause and emphasize the words in bold.

Emmanuel = ee-MAN-yoo-el

Therefore the Lord himself will give you **this sign**:
   the virgin shall **conceive**, and bear a son,
   and shall name him Emmanuel.

For meditation and context:

RESPONSORIAL PSALM Psalm 24:1–2, 3–4, 5–6 (7c, 10b)

R. Let the Lord enter; he is king of glory.

The LORD's are the earth and its fullness;
   the world and those who dwell in it.
For he founded it upon the seas
   and established it upon the rivers.

Who can ascend the mountain of the LORD?
   or who may stand in his holy place?
One whose hands are sinless, whose heart
    is clean,
   who desires not what is vain.

He shall receive a blessing from the LORD,
   a reward from God his savior.
Such is the race that seeks for him,
   that seeks the face of the God of Jacob.

READING I Isaiah's prophecy from the eighth century BC is set in the context of the powerful and brutal Assyrian empire, and a coalition of smaller nations against it. When Ahaz, ruler of the kingdom of Judah, refused to join the coalition, some of the neighboring kingdoms marched against him. In the face of Ahaz's wavering, Isaiah assured him that the coalition would not prevail, that he should stop being afraid, and should put his faith in the Lord.

After foretelling the fall of Judah's enemies, Isaiah tells Ahaz to ask for a sign from the Lord. In an expression of pseudo-piety, Ahaz asserts that he will not tempt the Lord by asking for a sign. Seeing through Ahaz' hypocritical words, Isaiah sounds exasperated. Not only has Ahaz wearied the people, he has also wearied God! Even if Ahaz will not ask for a sign, God will give one anyway.

The exact meaning of the sign is unclear, and has been interpreted in a variety of ways. The one who will give birth is understood in Hebrew as any young woman of marriageable age. The unknown woman may refer to the wife of Ahaz or Isaiah, or she could be any young woman of Judah. The focus is on the child born to her who will be a sign of God's presence during this time of turmoil.

As we hear the prophecy given to Ahaz during the Advent season, we see it fulfilled in a surprising way as the virgin Mary gives birth to a Son who is indeed Emmanuel, the presence of God among us.

READING II Paul begins his letter to the Romans by introducing himself and his Gospel. Similar to numerous Hebrew ancestors, from patriarchs to kings

READING II   Romans 1:1–7

A reading from the Letter of Saint Paul to the Romans

In this reading, we are called to be holy. Start proclaiming in an informative tone.

Paul, a slave of Christ **Jesus**,
    called to be an apostle and **set** apart for the gospel of God,
    which he **promised previously** through his prophets in the
        holy Scriptures,
    the **gospel** about his **Son**, descended from **David** according
        to the flesh,
    but **established** as Son of God in power
    according to the Spirit of holiness
    through **resurrection** from the dead, **Jesus Christ our** Lord.
Through **him** we have received the **grace** of **apostleship**,
    to bring about the obedience of faith,
    for the **sake** of **his** name, among **all** the **Gentiles**,
    among whom are you also, who are **called** to belong
        to Jesus Christ;
    to **all** the beloved of **God** in **Rome**, called to be **holy**.
Grace to you and peace from **God** our Father
    and the **Lord Jesus** Christ.

Take your time and articulate your words.

Transition your tone to one of warmth.

Pause before you say the last line. A greeting of peace is given in love.

and prophets who were regarded as slaves of the Lord, Paul is a slave of Jesus Christ. To be a slave in the biblical context of relationship with God signifies total, unwavering obedience. Secondly, Paul identifies himself as an apostle, one sent out as an authoritative representative of the one who sends him. The third way that Paul identifies himself, "set apart for the gospel of God," moves seamlessly into a summary of the Gospel.

The Good News that Paul proclaims was promised long ago through the prophets. Throughout the New Testament, we see new, unexpected fulfillment of the Jewish tradition that can be understood only in light of the story of Jesus Christ. The content of the Gospel of God, most succinctly, is "about his Son." Everything that Paul and the other early evangelists write concerns Jesus Christ, Son of God, and long-awaited son of David. As the Davidic descendant, Jesus has a human origin, for he was born "according to the flesh."

Not only is Jesus son of David, he is also Son of God, revealed through his Resurrection from the dead. In just a few words, Paul has announced the heart of the Good News of Jesus: Son of David, Son of God, born in the flesh, risen in power.

As Paul completes his introduction, he explains that the Good News about Jesus has far-reaching effects. Paul's own apostleship flows from Jesus Christ. He is sent to bring the Gospel to the Roman audience and to all who are called to belong to Jesus Christ. They are God's beloved, called to be holy, and to all of them Paul extends God's grace and peace.

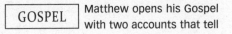 GOSPEL   Matthew opens his Gospel with two accounts that tell

GOSPEL   Matthew 1:18–24

A reading from the holy Gospel according to Matthew

Pause before you begin. Proclaim in a formal voice.

This is how the birth of **Jesus Christ** came about.
When his mother Mary was betrothed to Joseph,
    but **before** they lived together,
    she was found **with** child through the **Holy** Spirit.
Joseph her husband, since he was a righteous man,
    yet unwilling to expose her to **shame**,
    decided to **divorce** her **quietly**.
Such was his **intention** when, **behold**,
    the **angel** of the Lord **appeared** to him in a **dream** and said,
    "Joseph, son of David,
    do not be afraid to take Mary your wife into your home.
For it is through the Holy Spirit
    that this child has been conceived in her.
She will **bear** a **son** and you are to **name** him Jesus,
    because he will **save** his people from their **sins**."
All this took place to fulfill what the Lord had said through
        the **prophet**:
    Behold, *the **virgin** shall **conceive** and bear a **son**,
    *and they shall **name** him Emmanuel,*
    which means "God is **with** us."
When Joseph awoke,
    he **did** as the angel of the Lord had commanded him
    and **took** his wife into his **home**.

(Margin notes:)

Pause before you begin. Proclaim in a
formal voice.

Transition to a gentler tone when the
angel speaks.

Pause and speak slowly.

Emmanuel = ee-MAN-yoo-el

---

of Jesus' origins. The first is a long genealogy (*genesis*) telling of Jesus' human ancestry. Using the same word, today's Gospel describes Jesus' birth (*genesis*). The two segments complement one another by looking first at Jesus' Jewish lineage, and then at the immediate circumstances of his birth. In the genealogy as well as the birth, Matthew identifies Jesus as the Messiah or Christ, God's promised anointed one.

Matthew begins the story of Jesus' birth by telling of Mary's betrothal to Joseph. The Jewish custom of betrothal is not the same as the contemporary under-

standing of betrothal or engagement. In the marriage customs of the time, Mary and Joseph had completed the first stage of marriage, and were considered husband and wife though not yet living together. Often because of her youth, the woman remained in the home of her parents until the public ceremony took place. When Mary was found to be pregnant before she and Joseph were living together, he faced a sad dilemma. According to the law, Mary was guilty of adultery and was thus subject to stoning.

After Joseph decides to take the quietest, most merciful path, an angel appears in a dream. Like the dreams of his predecessor Joseph, the dreams of this later Joseph point to the divine plan. Although the child was conceived through the Holy Spirit, Joseph himself is to name the child, thereby accepting him as his legal offspring. Isaiah's ancient prophecy to Ahab is brought to fulfillment in a totally unexpected way. When the righteous Joseph acts exactly as commanded in the angelic message, the virgin gives birth to Emmanuel, God with us. E.P.

THE NATIVITY OF THE LORD (CHRISTMAS): VIGIL

LECTIONARY #13

READING I   Isaiah 62:1–5

A reading from the Book of the Prophet Isaiah

Isaiah = Ī-ZAY-uh

Zion = ZĪ-uhn or ZĪ-ahn

Transition to a gentler tone when the angel speaks.

The tone transitions to excitement as you begin. Take your time. Continue to build energy.

Proclaim in a gentler tone. Articulate word endings. Smile.

For Zion's **sake** I will not be **silent**,
   for Jerusalem's **sake** I will **not** be **quiet**,
until her vindication **shines** forth like the **dawn**
   and her victory like a **burning** torch.

Nations shall **behold** your vindication,
   and **all** the **kings** your glory;
you shall be called by a new name
   pronounced by the mouth of the LORD.
You shall be a **glorious crown** in the hand of the LORD,
   a **royal** diadem held by your God.
No more shall people call you "Forsaken,"
   or your land "Desolate,"
but you shall be called "**My** Delight,"
   and your land "Espoused."
For the LORD delights in you
   and makes your land his **spouse**.
As a young **man** marries a virgin,
   your **Builder** shall marry **you**;
and as a bridegroom **rejoices** in his bride
   so shall your **God rejoice** in **you**.

READING I The short poem we hear from Isaiah is part of an extended prophecy (from Isaiah 60 to 62) proclaiming the Lord's new creative action about to unfold. The precise situation of the prophecy is uncertain, perhaps occurring just before the end of the exile in Babylon, or at the beginning of the postexilic period (ca. 539–520 BC). Isaiah announces that God's saving action is at hand. In earlier parts of Isaiah, the prophet frequently called the people to repentance, announced judgment and issued warnings. We hear none of his stern language in this poem, but only words of newness and rejoicing.

Whatever its original context, the poem was probably sung by later Jews as they made their way to Jerusalem on pilgrimage. They looked to the city as a tangible symbol of God's promise of restoration of land and people. In verses shortly after today's reading, the prophet acclaims, "Say to daughter Zion, your savior comes!" (62:10). Isaiah's hopeful prophecy heard on this Christmas Vigil has yet another significance; it is brought to fulfillment in the long-awaited savior's coming into the world, creating uniMagined newness and cause for rejoicing.

Zion's vindication and victory will be observed far and wide, witnessed by nations and kings. Such widespread knowledge of God's saving actions for Jerusalem hints at the universalism seen throughout this part of Isaiah: "Nations shall walk by your light, and kings by your shining splendor" (Isaiah 60:3). Isaiah adds to the imagery of visible splendor by envisioning the people as "a glorious crown" and "a royal diadem," held closely by their God.

For meditation and context:

RESPONSORIAL PSALM   Psalm 89:4–5, 16–17, 27, 29 (2a)

R. For ever I will sing the goodness of the Lord.

I have made a covenant with my chosen one,
    I have sworn to David my servant:
forever will I confirm your posterity
    and establish your throne for all
        generations.

Blessed the people who know the
    joyful shout;
    in the light of your countenance, O LORD,
        they walk.
At your name they rejoice all the day,
    and through your justice they are exalted.

He shall say of me, "You are my father,
    my God, the rock, my savior."
Forever I will maintain my kindness
    toward him,
    and my covenant with him stands firm.

READING II   Acts of the Apostles 13:16–17, 22–25

A reading from the Acts of the Apostles

When **Paul** reached **Antioch** in Pisidia and entered the **synagogue**,
    he **stood** up, motioned with his hand, and said,
    "Fellow Israelites and you others who are God-fearing, listen.
The God of this people Israel chose our **ancestors**
    and exalted the people during their sojourn in the land
        of **Egypt**.
With **uplifted arm** he led them **out** of it.
Then he removed Saul and **raised** up **David** as **king**;
    of him he **testified**,
    'I have found **David**, son of Jesse, a man after my own **heart**;
    he will carry out my every **wish**.' »

Antioch = AN-tee-ahk

Pisidia = pih-SID-ee-uh

Pause before you begin. Use an authoritative tone.

sojourn = SOH-jern (exile)

Pause.

Jesse = JES-ee

Foreign nations who had once called the exiles "forsaken" and their land "desolate" will hear their new name. God gives them this name, as he had done throughout their history; Abram became Abraham, and Jacob became Israel. The new names signify a radically new identity. The people will become "My Delight," and their land will be "Espoused." By using marriage imagery, as found elsewhere in Isaiah (e.g., 54:5–6; 61:10), the prophet announces for everyone that God has once again taken the forsaken people into a covenant relationship comparable to a marriage. Not

only will the people be gladdened by the restored relationship, but God also will rejoice as does a bridegroom in his bride.

READING II   The story from Acts of the Apostles takes place during Paul's first missionary journey. Along with his coworker Barnabas, Paul proclaimed the Good News beginning in Cyprus, preaching in synagogue after synagogue. In Pisidian Antioch, one of the most important cities in their missionary endeavors, Paul preaches in their synagogue on the Sabbath. He addresses an

audience that includes Jews and "others who are God-fearing," probably referring to Gentiles who frequent the synagogue, though they have not fully converted to Judaism. Paul's actions of standing, gesturing, and calling his audience to listen give his sermon solemnity and importance before this diverse audience.

After his opening injunction to listen, Paul gives total attention to "the God of this people." Our reading omits several verses in which Paul uses forceful verbs to describe God's actions for the people. God chose ancestors, exalted the people, led

From this man's **descendants** God, according to his **promise**,
    has **brought** to Israel a savior, Jesus.
John **heralded** his coming by proclaiming a baptism of **repentance**
    to **all** the people of **Israel**;
    and as John was **completing** his course, he would say,
    'What do you suppose that **I am**? I am **not** he.
Behold, one is coming after me;
    I am not worthy to unfasten the **sandals** of his feet.'"

Transition your tone to one who is humble.

GOSPEL   Matthew 1:1–25

A reading from the holy Gospel according to Matthew

The book of the genealogy of **Jesus** Christ,
    the son of David, the son of Abraham.

Abraham became the father of **Isaac**,
    Isaac the father of **Jacob**,
    Jacob the father of **Judah** and his brothers.
Judah became the father of **Perez** and **Zerah**,
    whose **mother** was **Tamar**.
Perez became the father of **Hezron**,
    Hezron the father of **Ram**,
    Ram the father of **Amminadab**.
Amminadab became the father of **Nahshon**,
    Nahshon the father of **Salmon**,
    Salmon the father of **Boaz**,
    whose **mother** was **Rahab**.
Boaz became the father of **Obed**,
    whose **mother** was **Ruth**.
Obed became the father of **Jesse**,
    Jesse the father of **David** the **king**.

genealogy = jee-nee-OL-uh-jee
Abraham = AY-bruh-ham; Isaac = Ī-zik

Pause before you begin the genealogy. Read it like a story, not a list. Use eye contact to stay connected to the assembly.

Judah = JOO-duh

Tamar = TAY-mahr

Perez = PAYR-ez; Zerah = ZEE-rah

Hezron = HEZ-ruhn

Ram = ram

Amminadab = uh-MIN-uh-dab

Nashon = NAH-shun

Salmon = SAL-muhn

Rahab = RAY-hab

Boaz = BOH-az

Obed = OH-bed

Jesse = JES-ee

---

them out of Egypt, put up with them in the desert, destroyed seven nations, gave them their land as an inheritance, provided judges, and gave them Saul as their king. The removal of Saul from kingship was God's action as well, as was raising up David as king. God's actions throughout Jewish history seem to be leading up to David, a man after God's own heart.

David had hoped to build a house for the Lord, a temple that would be worthy of the God who had acted so powerfully throughout their history. Using a clever play on words, the Lord reverses David's hopes by stating that the Lord would build a house for David rather than David building a house for him (2 Samuel 7:11). As in English, "house" (*bayit*) in Hebrew may refer either to a physical dwelling place or to descendants. God promises to make firm the kingdom of a Davidic descendant, building a house for his name, and making his royal throne firm forever. The kings who followed David did not fulfill the divine promise, ruling unjustly. King Abijam, for example, was a typical Davidic ruler: "He imitated all the sins his father had committed before him, and his heart was not entirely with the Lord, his God, like the heart of his grandfather David" (1 Kings 15:3).

Yet, since God had made the promise of a descendant who would make the throne firm forever, the people continued to hope for its fulfillment. Paul tells those gathered in the synagogue that Jesus is the promised Davidic descendant, and is a savior to Israel. John, the last of the prophets, heralded his coming. As people came to him for baptism, they asked John if could he be the promised one. In response, John steadfastly declared that he was not the one they were awaiting. Another one is

Uriah = yoo-RĪ-uh

Rehoboam = ree-huh-BOH-uhm

Abijah = uh-BĪ-juh

Asaph = AY-saf

Asaph = AY-saf

Jehoshaphat = jeh-HOH-shuh-fat

Joram = JOHR-uhm

Uzziah = yuh-ZĪ-uh

Jotham = JOH-thuhm

Ahaz = AY-haz

Hezekiah = hez-eh-KĪH-uh

Manasseh = muh-NAS-uh

Amos = AY-m*s

Josiah = joh-SĪuh

Jechoniah = jek-oh-NĪ-uh

Keep up your energy.

Shealtiel = shee-AL-tee-uhl

Zerubbabel = zuh-ROOB-uh-b*l

Abiud = uh-BĪ-uhd

Eliakim = ee-LĪ-uh-kim

Azor = AY-sohr

Zadok = ZAD-uhk

Achim = AH-kim

Eliud = ee-LĪ-uhd

Eleazar = el-ee-AY-zer

Matthan = MATH-uhn

Babylonian = bab-uh-LOH-nee-uhn

David became the father of **Solomon,**
     whose **mother** had been the wife of **Uriah.**
Solomon became the father of **Rehoboam,**
     Rehoboam the father of **Abijah,**
     Abijah the father of **Asaph.**
Asaph became the father of **Jehoshaphat,**
     Jehoshaphat the father of **Joram,**
     Joram the father of **Uzziah.**
Uzziah became the father of **Jotham,**
     Jotham the father of **Ahaz,**
     Ahaz the father of **Hezekiah.**
Hezekiah became the father of **Manasseh,**
     Manasseh the father of **Amos,**
     Amos the father of **Josiah.**
Josiah became the father of **Jechoniah** and his brothers
     at the time of the **Babylonian exile.**

After the Babylonian exile,
     Jechoniah became the father of **Shealtiel,**
     Shealtiel the father of **Zerubbabel,**
     Zerubbabel the father of **Abiud.**
Abiud became the father of **Eliakim,**
     Eliakim the father of **Azor,**
     Azor the father of **Zadok.**
Zadok became the father of **Achim,**
     Achim the father of **Eliud,**
     Eliud the father of **Eleazar.**
Eleazar became the father of **Matthan,**
     Matthan the father of **Jacob,**
     Jacob the father of **Joseph,** the husband of **Mary.**
Of her was born **Jesus** who is called the **Christ.**

Thus the total number of **generations**
     from Abraham to David
     is **fourteen** generations;
     from David to the **Babylonian** exile, »

coming after him, mysteriously unnamed by John. Paul, however, has already named Jesus as David's offspring. As great as the Baptist was, he is not even worthy to take on the role of a slave in unfastening the sandals on his feet.

 GOSPEL From the opening words of his Gospel, Matthew presents Jesus as thoroughly immersed in the Jewish tradition. Writing for an audience of Jewish Christians, Matthew showed that Jesus was the fulfillment of God's promises and purpose, overcoming seemingly impos-

sible obstacles, as God had done so often throughout their history. As he tells the story of Jesus, Matthew uses ancient biblical symbolism and texts both by direct citation and by allusion, even as he shows how God is doing something extraordinarily new in Jesus. Throughout his Gospel, the evangelist is like the scribe instructed in the kingdom of heaven who brings out of his storeroom both the new and the old (Matthew 13:52).

In the genealogy or origin of Jesus Christ, Matthew interweaves the old and new. As in the Hebrew Bible, Matthew uses

the genealogy as a means of showing relationships and continuity. In describing the continuity from one generation to the next, Matthew likely draws on genealogies in 1 Chronicles 2–3 as well as Ruth 4:18–22, though bringing in new names and features. By stating that the genealogy is the record of Jesus Christ, Son of David and Son of Abraham, Matthew is already hinting that Jesus' ancestry places him solidly in relationship with the Jewish people and as fulfillment of God's promise to David.

A new feature in Matthew's genealogy is the inclusion of four women. While each

fourteen generations;
from the **Babylonian exile** to the Christ,
fourteen generations.

[**Now** this is how the birth **of Jesus Christ** came about.
When his mother **Mary** was betrothed to Joseph,
     but before they **lived** together,
     she was found with **child** through the **Holy** Spirit.
Joseph her husband, since he was a righteous man,
     yet **unwilling** to expose her to shame,
     decided **to divorce** her quietly.
Such was his **intention** when, **behold,**
     the angel **of the Lord appeared** to him in a dream and said,
     "**Joseph**, son of **David,**
     do not be afraid to take Mary your wife into your **home.**
For it is **through** the **Holy** Spirit
     that this **child** has been **conceived** in her.
She will bear a **son** and you are to name him **Jesus,**
     because he will save his people from their sins."
All this took place to **fulfill**
     what the **Lord** had said through the prophet:
          Behold, the virgin shall **conceive** *and bear a son,*
               and they shall name him Emmanuel,
          which means "God **is with us.**"
When **Joseph awoke,**
     he **did** as the **angel of the Lord** had **commanded** him
     and took his wife into his home.
He had no relations with her until she bore a son,
     and he **named** him Jesus.]

[Shorter: Matthew 1:18–25 (see brackets)]

Pause before you begin to proclaim the story. Build energy as you read.

Transition to a gentle tone as the angel speaks to Joseph.

Pause. Take your time. Keep your volume up. Smile.

Emmanuel = ee-MAN-yoo-el

Speak in a reverent tone as you conclude.

---

of the women appeared in far different contexts, each of them gave birth to sons in extraordinary, sometimes scandalous, circumstances. They also show the inclusion of Gentiles in Jesus' ancestry, an important newness even in the midst of the old traditions. These women ancestors exhibited courage and determination as they brought forth descendants of Abraham and David, preparing the way for Jesus the Christ. The fifth and final woman in the genealogy is Mary, whose pregnancy is accomplished through the power of the Holy Spirit. In changing the format of the genealogy by describing Joseph as the husband of Mary, from whom Jesus was born, Matthew does not identify Joseph as Jesus' physical father. Jesus' birth was far more extraordinary than that of any of his ancestors.

The second part of today's Gospel, heard also on the Fourth Sunday of Advent, tells about the birth or origin of Jesus. Like the genealogy, the account of Jesus' birth is steeped in a Jewish atmosphere: Jewish marriage customs; echoes of the patriarch Joseph in the portrait and dreams of the husband of Mary; fulfillment of Isaiah's prophecy to Ahaz. God's intervention, which was assumed in the genealogy, is explicit in the account of Jesus' birth. The creative action of the Holy Spirit and the appearance of an angel in Joseph's dream reveal God's power and presence in Jesus' origins, as was evident throughout the history of his ancestors. E.P.

THE NATIVITY OF THE LORD (CHRISTMAS): NIGHT

LECTIONARY #14

READING I   Isaiah 9:1–6

Isaiah = Ī-ZAY-uh
Midian = MID-ee-uhn

This reading is joyful! Take the congregation from darkness to light. Your voice must sound full of happiness.

A reading from the Book of the Prophet Isaiah

The people who walked in darkness
    have seen a **great** light;
upon those who dwelt in the land of gloom
    a light has shone.
You have **brought** them **abundant** joy
    and **great** rejoicing,
as they rejoice before you as at the **harvest**,
    as people make merry when dividing **spoils**.
For the yoke that **burdened** them,
    the pole on their **shoulder**,
and the rod of their **taskmaster**
    you have smashed, as on the day of **Midian**.

Many hardships have been overcome. Let the assembly hear the trials in your voice.

For every **boot** that tramped in battle,
    every **cloak rolled** in **blood**,
    will be burned as fuel for **flames**.
For a **child** is born to us, a **son** is given us;
    upon his shoulder dominion **rests**.
They name him Wonder-Counselor, God-Hero,
    Father-Forever, Prince of Peace. »

Take your time. Articulate your words. Use vocal variety with this beautiful reading.

Pause after each name with a smile.

There are options for readings today. Ask your parish staff which ones will be used.

READING I   Being enshrouded in darkness and gloom was a situation well understood in Isaiah's eighth-century BC world. Not only did Assyria to the north threaten the kingdoms of Israel and Judah, but other, smaller nations put Judah in close and immediate danger. While the threat still looms, Isaiah announces that the people have seen the light of dawn. The verbs that specify that the light has already transformed the darkness are often regarded as "prophetic past," indicating that divinely-inspired prophecies about the future that are so certain that they are as good as already completed.

After announcing the new dawn, Isaiah speaks directly and exuberantly to God, who has brought about joy to the people. In the past, God had defeated Midian in a display of miraculous power. The people who have experienced darkness in the form of military defeat and continuing menace have also experienced times of rejoicing. By using the imagery of a merry harvest, Isaiah creates a scenario of a peaceful land devoid of enemy conflict. Situations that seem to be brought about by the people's own actions occur in reality only because of God's deeds. God has taken away the yoke that burdened them and the rod of their taskmasters. Just as God had acted so decisively in the past, so is God doing now. Throughout his prophecy, both in his words to the people and in this address to God, Isaiah seamlessly weaves together past, present, and future in telling of God's timeless saving deeds.

Build excitement in your voice.

His dominion is vast
    and forever peaceful,
from David's **throne**, and **over** his kingdom,
    which he confirms and sustains
by judgment and justice,
    both now and forever.
The zeal **of the Lord of hosts will** do **this!**

End strongly with a firm belief in the Lord!

For meditation and context:

RESPONSORIAL PSALM   Psalm 96:1–2, 2–3, 11–12, 13 (Luke 2:11)

R. Today is born our Savior, Christ the Lord.

Sing to the LORD a new song;
    sing to the LORD, all you lands.
Sing to the LORD; bless his name.

Announce his salvation, day after day.
    Tell his glory among the nations;
    among all peoples, his wondrous deeds.

Let the heavens be glad and the earth rejoice;
    let the sea and what fills it resound;
    let the plains be joyful and all that is
        in them!
Then shall all the trees of the forest exult.

They shall exult before the LORD,
    for he comes;
    for he comes to rule the earth.
He shall rule the world with justice
    and the peoples with his constancy.

READING II   Titus 2:11–14

Titus = TĪ-tuhs

A reading from the Letter of Saint Paul to Titus

Notice that this reading is one long sentence. Take your time. Pause at the commas and keep your energy up.

Beloved:
The grace of God has appeared, saving all
    and training us to reject godless ways and worldly desires
    and to live temperately, justly, and devoutly in this age,
    as we **await** the blessed hope,

blessed = BLES-uhd
Say this line and the next as one thought.

    the appearance of the **glory** of our great **God**
    and savior Jesus **Christ**,

Pause and slowly proclaim the words in bold.

    who **gave** himself **for us** to **deliver** us from all **lawlessness**
    and to cleanse for **himself** a people as his own,

Smile as the reading ends.

    eager to do what is **good.**

As the distressed people long for God to fulfill the promise to raise up a righteous Davidic descendant, Isaiah assures them of the birth of a royal son. The child that God is giving "to us" will be even more than an ideal ruler. His name, "Wonder-Counselor, God-hero, Father-Forever, Prince of Peace," expresses his intimate connection with God and people. His kingship for the sake of the people will be like God's own. He will rule as an ever-present father, establish peace over a vast dominion, and reign with judgment and justice. Having described the child's rule in terms reflective of God's own

kingship, Isaiah concludes that the Lord's zeal will accomplish this.

READING II Along with the two letters to Timothy, the letter to Titus is a pastoral epistle that instructs and exhorts Church leaders and their communities. The structure and richness of today's short reading from Titus sounds like a biblically based liturgical hymn that may have been part of early Church worship. Through this hymn, believers confess their faith in God's saving actions, including how God assists them to live in light of their faith. By

using the pronouns "us" and "we," Paul includes himself and believers of later ages in this profession of faith.

God's grace has already appeared, and is thus already effective, even as we await the appearance of God's future glory. In this state of already-and-not-yet, God's grace is active, training us to live rightly. The verb "to train" (*paideuein*) refers to the rearing and education of a child, consisting of intellectual, cultural, religious, and ethical dimensions. Such training aims at forming an ideal person to live well in society; from a religious perspective, this entails

GOSPEL   Luke 2:1–14

A reading from the holy Gospel according to Luke

In those days a decree went out from Caesar Augustus
     that the **whole** world should be enrolled.
This was the **first** enrollment,
     when **Quirinius** was governor of **Syria**.
So all went to be enrolled, **each** to his own town.
And Joseph too went up from Galilee from the town of **Nazareth**
     to **Judea**, to the **city of David** that is called **Bethlehem**,
     because he was of the house and family of **David**,
     to be enrolled with Mary, his betrothed, who was with **child**.
While they were there,
     the time **came** for her to have her **child**,
     and she **gave** birth to her **firstborn** son.
She wrapped him in **swaddling clothes** and **laid** him in a manger,
     because there was **no** room for them in the inn.

Now there were shepherds in that region living in the **fields**
     and keeping the night watch over their **flock**.
The angel of the Lord **appeared** to them
     and the glory of the **Lord shone** around them,
     and they were **struck** with **great** fear.
The **angel** said to them,
     "Do **not** be **afraid**;
     for **behold**, I **proclaim** to you **good** news **of great** joy
     that will be for all **the people**.
For today in the city of David
     a savior has been **born** for you who is Christ **and** Lord.
And **this** will be a sign for you:
     you will find an infant wrapped in **swaddling** clothes
     and lying in a **manger**." »

Your tone is one of authority.

Caesar = SEE-zer

Augustus = aw-GUHS-tuhs

Quirinius = kwih-RIN-ee-uhs

Galilee = GAL-ih-lee

Judea = joo-DEE-uh

Transition to a tone of gentleness.

Slowly build the angel's words to a joyful tone.

---

right relationship with God and other people. The grace of God training children in the present age is akin to God's action in bringing up the children of Israel in the past, sometimes by correcting and disciplining them when they rebelled.

According to this passage from Titus, grace guides believers in living rightly in this age by avoiding godless ways. More than simply training to avoid evil, grace also moves us to act justly and devoutly, to live in a godly way. An important virtue in the pastoral letters, godliness is rooted in awe of God. It includes religious devotion and respect, with outward manifestations flowing from a profound inner devotion. Justice, temperance, and devout living are expected of anyone who is living in a godly way.

After beginning with confessing that the grace of God has already appeared, the hymn then says that we await the appearance of future divine glory. Christ's first appearance, beginning with his birth and culminating in his Resurrection, gives us a blessed hope for his coming again in glory. He has given himself to deliver us, to cleanse us, and to make us his own people. With grace bestowed on us, we are eager to do what is good, living in a godly way.

GOSPEL   The angelic announcement to Mary described the son to be born to her as great, Son of the Most High, who will be given the throne of David his father. He will rule over a kingdom that will have no end. Surely such an exalted child will be surrounded by wealth, comfort, and nobility at his birth. Surely his kingdom that will last forever will surpass the temporary kingdom of Caesar.

Proclaim this line with a burst of energy.

And suddenly there was a **multitude** of the **heavenly host** with
the **angel**,
praising **God** and saying:
"Glory **to God in the** highest
and on earth peace **to those on whom his** favor **rests.**"

Proclaim the last sentence with a smile and good volume.

> **TO KEEP IN MIND**
> Always pause at the end of the reading, before you proclaim the closing dialogue ("The Word of the Lord" or "The Gospel of the Lord").

How unexpected and shocking, then, is the account of the child's birth. Augustus had decreed an enrollment of the "whole world," to which the child's parents, as the emperor's subjects, respond. They make the difficult journey to Bethlehem without any word of the greatness of the soon-to-be-born child. In Bethlehem, no royal lodgings await them, as Mary gives birth to her son in the lowliest and most inhospitable of circumstances. As Luke narrates the account, he weaves in a major theme that he will develop throughout his Gospel: reversal of expectation and status.

Rather than the presence of wealthy attendants, the child's first visitors are shepherds who were keeping night watch over their flocks. In spite of the well-known image of the Lord as shepherd in Psalm 23, in the culture of Jesus' day shepherds were considered unclean and unworthy. Yet they are the unlikely recipients of news of great joy: they will find a savior who is Christ and Lord. The manger in which they will find the child could well describe the sleeping place for their own children. They will find the savior and Lord as poor as the shepherds

themselves, a scandalous reversal of both expectation and status.

Luke began his account of Jesus' birth with well-known people and places: Caesar Augustus, Quirinius, Nazareth, and Bethlehem. He uses these details not to give a history lesson, but to serve a theological purpose. Jesus came into the world in historical circumstances that turned around perceptions of power and worthiness. The humble birth of the savior reveals God's extraordinary action within ordinary human history. E.P.

THE NATIVITY OF THE LORD (CHRISTMAS): DAWN

LECTIONARY #15

READING I   Isaiah 62:11–12

A reading from the Book of the Prophet Isaiah

See, the LORD **proclaims**
   to the ends of the earth:
say to daughter Zion,
   your **savior comes**!
Here is his **reward** with him,
   his recompense before him.
They shall be called the holy **people**,
   the redeemed of the LORD,
and **you** shall be called "Frequented,"
   a city that is not **forsaken**.

Isaiah = Ī-ZAY-uh

This reading is joyful! Keep your energy level up while you are proclaiming.

Zion = ZĪ-uhn or ZĪ-ahn
Pause.
recompense = REK-uhm-pens
Proclaim slowly. Articulate your words and word endings.

Frequented = FREE-kwen-t*d

This is great news! Smile.

For meditation and context:

RESPONSORIAL PSALM   Psalm 97:1, 6, 11–12

R. A light will shine on us this day: the Lord is born for us.

The LORD is king; let the earth rejoice;
   let the many isles be glad.
The heavens proclaim his justice,
   and all peoples see his glory.

Light dawns for the just;
   and gladness, for the upright of heart.
Be glad in the LORD, you just,
   and give thanks to his holy name.

There are options for readings today. Ask your parish staff which ones will be used.

READING I Prophetic proclamations are more than human words. Our first reading begins with a strong affirmation of this biblical belief: "See, the Lord proclaims." By beginning with the word "see," or "behold" (*hinneh*), Isaiah tells his audience to pay close attention because he is speaking what the Lord has commanded. Further, the announce-ment is not only for daughter Zion, but is to be proclaimed to the ends of the earth.

Isaiah is to tell daughter Zion, Jerusalem, "Your savior comes." In announc-ing that the Lord will come with reward and recompense, Isaiah is reiterating an earlier promise of the Lord's coming (40:10). Today's promise has an immediacy about it: the Lord's rescue will not be accomplished in some unknown future, but is already bringing about a new reality for the belea-guered people.

In the readings that we hear from Isaiah in this season, as well as those from the Gospels of Matthew and Luke, there is a repeated reference to names given and names changed. In both the Old and New Testaments, a person's name expresses something essential about his or her iden-tity. The name that God gives, whether the name is for an individual or a group, indi-cates the relationship between God and the named one. Isaiah proclaims that God is now giving the people a new name, "redeemed of the Lord," indicating that God will act as their nearest kinsman in rescu-ing and restoring them. The former name of the city will also be changed; "Forsaken"

READING II   Titus 3:4–7

A reading from the Letter of Saint Paul to Titus

Beloved:
When the kindness and **generous love**
    of **God** our savior **appeared**,
not because of any **righteous deeds** we had done
    but because of **his** mercy,
he **saved** us through the **bath** of rebirth
    and renewal by the **Holy** Spirit,
whom he **richly poured** out on **us**
    through **Jesus Christ** our **savior**,
so that **we** might be justified by **his grace**
    and become heirs in **hope** of **eternal** life.

Titus = Tī-tuhs
This is a beautiful little reading. Proclaim it slowly so that nothing is lost.
Pause.

Say this line slowly and continue to read the next line as one.

Smile at this great news!

Pause for emphasis before you end the reading.

---

will become "Frequented," for Jerusalem will be inhabited by numerous people who are holy and redeemed.

READING II In the letter to Titus, Paul addresses believers who live between the first appearing (epiphany) of Christ at his birth and his future appearing in glory. Expanding on the proclamation that "the grace of God appeared," heard at the Christmas Mass during the night, this reading at dawn announces the appearance of the kindness and generous love of God. Both of these appearances have already

happened in the birth of Christ. A first-century audience hearing of the "kindness" (*chrestotes*) of God would likely link this to Christ (*christos*), since the pronunciations of the two words are nearly identical: Christ is the manifestation of God's kindness.

The beginning and end of this hymn, probably part of a baptismal liturgy, refers to "God our savior" and "Christ our savior." Through the renewing action of the Holy Spirit, God the savior has saved us through Christ the savior. With the language of salvation applied without distinction to God and to Christ, along with the action

of the Holy Spirit, the Trinitarian theology developed in later centuries has a rudimentary foundation.

The rebirth through Baptism is something totally new. God's new saving action appears so that believers might be justified, not by righteous deeds but through the outpouring of freely given grace. This present reality has a future dimension: hope of eternal life. In the opening of this letter, Paul also wrote of his hope of eternal life, as he had earlier done while in prison (Philippians 1:2). The manifestations of God's saving love in the present, whether experienced in

GOSPEL   Luke 2:15–20

A reading from the holy Gospel according to Luke

When the **angels** went away from them to heaven,
    the shepherds said to one another,
    "Let us **go**, then, to **Bethlehem**
    to see this thing that has taken place,
    which the **Lord** has made **known** to us."
So they went in **haste** and found Mary **and** Joseph,
    and the infant lying in the manger.
When they **saw** this,
    they made known the **message**
    that had been **told** them about this child.
All who heard it were amazed
    by what had been told them by the **shepherds**.
And **Mary kept** all these things,
    reflecting on them in her **heart**.
Then the shepherds returned,
    glorifying and praising God
    for all they had heard and seen,
    just as it had been told to them.

Proclaim with excitement.

Keep your voice and face expressive so that the congregation can easily visualize the moment.

manger = MAYN-jer

Pause.

Proclaim with energy and good volume.

difficult or easy circumstances, are a first installment of eternal life.

GOSPEL The account of the shepherds' multifaceted response to the angelic message has echoes of the earlier account of the angelic annunciation to Mary. Like Mary, the shepherds are far removed from the elite in Jerusalem, and are counted among the lowly and the poor; the shepherds are even considered sinful and unclean. After hearing the angel's message, both Mary and the shepherds go "in haste" where they will see the signs that the angel foretold: Mary to the barren Elizabeth in the sixth month of her pregnancy and the shepherds to the infant lying in a manger. Their journeys each express belief in the angel's words and an eager readiness to respond, resulting in their meeting others who share in the revelatory experience. What they hear and see, they proclaim: Mary in her poetic canticle, and then the shepherds, who make known the message that had been told to them. Mary's Magnificat can be summed up in the shepherds' glorifying and praising God. The beautifully drawn portraits of Mary and the shepherds present people from ordinary circumstances becoming the bearers of the extraordinary good news.

The similarities of the two events point to several important themes that Luke develops throughout his Gospel: good news to the poor; journeys of faith; prophecy and fulfillment; belief and response. At the heart of the story and themes is the Savior who is Christ and Lord, the one who is both Son of David and Son of God. He brings good news to the poor, makes his own journey of faith to Jerusalem, is the personal fulfillment of God's promises, and responds in perfect obedience to his Father's will. E.P.

THE NATIVITY OF THE LORD (CHRISTMAS): DAY

LECTIONARY #16

READING I   Isaiah 52:7–10

A reading from the Book of the Prophet Isaiah

How beautiful upon the mountains
　　are the **feet** of him who brings glad **tidings**,
announcing peace, bearing **good** news,
　　announcing **salvation**, and saying to **Zion**,
"Your God is King!"

Hark! Your sentinels raise a cry,
　　together they **shout** for **joy**,
for they see directly, before their eyes,
　　the Lord restoring **Zion**.
Break out **together** in **song**,
　　O ruins of Jerusalem!
For the Lord **comforts** his people,
　　he redeems **Jerusalem**.
The Lord has **bared** his holy arm
　　in the sight of **all** the nations;
all the ends of the **earth** will **behold**
　　the **salvation** of our God.

Isaiah = Ī-ZAY-uh

Zion = Zī-uhn or Zī-ahn

Sound exuberant during this reading.

With good volume. Smile.

Slowly proclaim as you build excitement in your voice. Articulate the words.

Keep your energy up. Smile as you proclaim with good eye contact and volume.

There are options for readings today. Ask your parish staff which ones will be used.

READING I Each of the three readings for Christmas day announces the good news in poetic language. Filled with imagery that appeals to the senses, the biblical poems draw those who hear them into the experience of wonder and awe. In the first reading, signs of restoration that can be seen and heard would have been important for the exiles in Babylon, who longed to see their home-land. Along with the restoration of Jerusalem is the restoration of hope for despondent exiles.

In the beginning, center, and conclusion of his poem, Isaiah presents hope-filled sights. The first image, observed from Jerusalem's heights, is that of a herald with feet hurriedly running to bring the good news. Like the words of a prophet, the words of the herald are effective, for the sentinels "see, directly, before their eyes" the Lord restoring Zion. Not only do the observers from the mountain see the herald and signs of restoration, but also the Lord's holy arm is bared in the sight of the nations. The power of God's arm is reminiscent of the power that God displayed in freeing the people from Egypt and bringing them to their own land. Today's responsorial psalm echoes, "his right hand has won victory for him, his holy arm." The people can see God again acting for the sake of the chosen people. So extensive is divine salvation for Zion that all the ends of the earth will behold it.

Interspersed between the visible sights of the arrival of the good news are exuberant sounds. The herald's announcement is

For meditation and context:

RESPONSORIAL PSALM Psalm 98:1, 2–3, 3–4, 5–6 (3c)

R. All the ends of the earth have seen the saving power of God.

Sing to the LORD a new song,
  for he has done wondrous deeds;
his right hand has won victory for him,
  his holy arm.

The LORD has made his salvation known:
  in the sight of the nations he has revealed
    his justice.
He has remembered his kindness and
    his faithfulness
  toward the house of Israel.

All the ends of the earth have seen
  the salvation by our God.
Sing joyfully to the LORD, all you lands;
  break into song; sing praise.

Sing praise to the LORD with the harp,
  with the harp and melodious song.
With trumpets and the sound of the horn
  sing joyfully before the King, the LORD.

READING II Hebrews 1:1–6

A reading from the Letter to the Hebrews

Brothers and sisters:

Pause. Use an informative tone.

In times **past**, God spoke in partial and various ways
  to our **ancestors** through the prophets;

Use strong eye contact.

  in these **last** days, **he** has **spoken** to **us** through the Son,
  whom **he** made **heir** of **all** things
  and through whom **he created** the **universe**,

Use strong eye contact.

  who is the refulgence of his glory, the very imprint of his being,
  and who **sustains** all things by his mighty **word**.

refulgence = rih-FUHL-j*nts (radiance or brilliance)

  When he had **accomplished** purification from sins,
  he took his seat at the right **hand** of the **Majesty** on **high**,
  as far superior to the angels
  as the **name he** has inherited is more **excellent** than **theirs**.

Energy needed. Pause before you ask God's questions.

For to **which** of the angels did God **ever say**:
  You are my son; this day I have begotten you?
Or again:
  I will be a father to him, and he shall be a son to me?
And again, when he **leads** the firstborn into the world, he says:
  Let all the angels of God worship him.

---

totally positive as he proclaims peace, salvation, and "Your God is King." Neither Babylon nor any other earthly empire rules over Zion, for the Lord is their King. As the sentinels themselves shout with joy when they hear the good news, we can easily iMagine them using the psalms to express their joy. "The Lord is king; let the earth rejoice" (Psalm 97:1). Even the ruins of Jerusalem will join in singing. Sights and sounds together give witness to God's action; comfort, redemption, and salvation express a powerful and intimate relation-

ship of the Lord with Zion, past, present, and future.

READING II   The letter to the Hebrews opens with a hymn, probably sung in early liturgies, that ponders the mystery of Christ. Like Isaiah's prophecy, the poem is filled with auditory and visual imagery. God's own voice resounds from times past to these last days in which God has spoken through his Son. As varied and insistent as was God's voice in the past, the revelation was only partial. The prophet Isaiah's proclamation in the first reading was a semi-

nal revelation that announced the good news of peace, salvation, and the Lord's kingship. In unfolding the mystery of Jesus, the author will draw on the ancient and partial revelation and give it new meaning.

Because the spoken word was incomplete, God spoke in these last days in a visible and personal way through his own Son. Although the word spoken through God's Son is astonishingly new, there is continuity and resonance with God's partial word from the past. In particular, the portrait of God's Son bears striking resemblance to Wisdom personified. A mysterious figure of

GOSPEL   John 1:1–18

A reading from the holy Gospel according to John

[In the **beginning** was the Word,
    and the Word was with **God**,
    and the Word was God.
He was in the beginning with God.
All things **came to be through** him,
    and without him nothing came to be.
What came to be **through** him was life,
    and this **life** was the light of the human race;
the light **shines** in the darkness,
    and the darkness has **not overcome** it.]
A man named John was sent from God.
He came for testimony, to testify to the light,
    so that **all** might believe through him.
He was not the light,
    but came to testify to the light.
[The true **light**, which enlightens **everyone**,
    was coming **into the world**.
He was in the world,
    and the world came to **be through** him,
    but the world did **not know** him.
He **came** to what was **his own**,
    but his own people did **not** accept him.

But to those who did accept him
    he gave power to become children of **God**,
    to those who believe in his name,
    who were born **not** by **natural** generation
    nor by human **choice** nor by a man's decision
    but of God.

Lady Wisdom appears in several books of wisdom literature. Like Lady Wisdom, the Son of God was involved in the creation of the universe and reflects the glory of God, the tangible, weighty manifestation of divine presence. Though distinct from God, the Son is the very imprint or stamp of the divine being. In the Hebrew Scriptures, God cannot be seen, but now, in these last days, we can see the visible imprint of God's own being, and hear God's Word in the person of the Son.

To this exalted portrait of the Son reflecting the image of the Father, the poem develops the Father-Son relationship further. Not even to the angels did God say, "You are my son" (Psalm 2:7). In the original context of the psalm, God is saying "my son" to an earthly king, whether David or one of his descendants. Reinterpreting the original meaning, the hymn in Hebrews sees in Jesus the exalted Son of God, kingly descendant of David, the firstborn worshiped even by angels.

GOSPEL "In the beginning." With a phrase that echoes the opening words of Genesis, John introduces the mystery of Christ as the Word present with God in the beginning, and even identified with God. John's majestic hymn initiates the portrait of Jesus that he will develop throughout his Gospel. In both hymn and narrative, John draws on themes and motifs from the Hebrew Scriptures and gives them a new, unexpected meaning. He does so in the prologue where he alludes further to the first chapter of Genesis, in which God began with the creation of light, and culminated by bringing life into being. Like the God of creation, the Word is also the source of light and life. Everything that

Transition to a tone of happiness.

Proclaim John's excitement.

Let the congregation hear thankfulness in your voice.

Pause and say this line slowly.

And the Word became flesh
   and made his dwelling among **us**,
   and we saw his glory,
   the glory as of the Father's only Son,
   full of grace **and** truth.]
John testified to him and **cried** out, saying,
   "**This** was **he** of whom I said,
   'The one who is coming **after** me ranks ahead of me
   because he existed before me.'"
From his fullness we have all received,
   grace in place of grace,
   because while the law was given through Moses,
   grace and truth came **through Jesus** Christ.
No one has ever seen God.
The only Son, God, who is at the Father's side,
   has revealed him.

[Shorter: John 1:1–5, 9–14 (see brackets)]

can be said of God and God's work of creation known through the Old Testament can also be said of the Word.

After the soaring, cosmic, and primordial imagery of the opening verses, the evangelist brings the poem down to earth by describing John the Baptist. Although timeless, the Word came into the world in a specific time and place, and lived among real people. By giving witness to the light, the Baptist points to the Word's presence in concrete, historic circumstances. The world into which the Word came had (and continues to have) opportunities to know

him or not to know him, to accept him or to reject him. To each of those who accept him, the Word gives power to become God's own children.

On this Christmas day, as we celebrate Jesus' Incarnation, one verse from this hymn sums up this core mystery of faith: "The Word became flesh and made his dwelling among us." To become flesh (*sarx*) in the Greek of the New Testament means to live in the bodily existence and mortality in which we all share. "Dwelling among us," or more literally "pitching his tent among us" means also that the Word has made a home

in the midst of all the joys and sorrows, light and darkness, of the human condition.

The Word enfleshed in Christ is not only a Word that is heard, but is also a Word that is seen. We have seen his glory, the visible manifestation of God's own weighty presence. Besides seeing his glory, we have also received from his fullness the plenitude of God's grace and truth. John concludes his hymn by telling us that no one has ever seen God. Yet, the only Son, the Word-made-flesh who is God among us, has shown the unseen God to us. E.P.

THE HOLY FAMILY OF JESUS, MARY, AND JOSEPH

LECTIONARY #17

READING I   Sirach 3:2–6, 12–14

A reading from the Book of Sirach

Sirach = SEER-ak

Slowly articulate your words in a gentle tone.

God sets a **father** in honor over his **children**;
   a **mother's authority** he **confirms** over her sons.
Whoever **honors** his **father atones** for **sins**,
   and preserves himself from them.
When he prays, he is heard;
   he stores up riches who **reveres** his **mother**.
Whoever honors his father is **gladdened** by children,
   and, when **he prays**, is **heard**.
Whoever **reveres** his father will **live** a long **life**;
   he who **o**beys his father brings comfort to his **mother**.

Imagine you are speaking to a child. Be kind in explaining how you would like to be treated as a parent.

My son, take **care** of your **father** when he is old;
   grieve him not as **long** as he **lives**.
Even if his mind fail, be considerate of him;
   revile him not all the **days** of his life;
kindness to a father will **not** be **forgotten**,
   firmly planted against the debt of your sins
   —a house **raised** in justice to **you**.

Pause before you say this last line. Keep up the energy. Be firm.

READING I Jesus Ben Sira was a Jewish wisdom teacher writing around 200 BC who provided instruction on how to live wisely in society. His advice includes an array of topics ranging from how to use money, to the evils of gossip, to how to deal with fools. Underlying such seemingly mundane advice is Sirach's overarching theme: fear of the Lord. While the phrase often conjures up the notion of cringing dread, Sirach explains that fear of the Lord means love, hope, trust, and humility before God, keeping God's law, and seeking to please the Lord who acts

with mercy, compassion, and forgiveness. Today's reading expresses how the honoring of one's father and mother is a living, observable example of fear of the Lord.

The first word today, "God," places everything that Sirach says about family relationships in the context of God's power and purpose. Sirach teaches how to live in fear of the Lord within family life. Most of his instruction is about the honor due to the father, a perspective consistent with the patriarchal society of the era. Along with the honor due to the father, Sirach states clearly that the mother has God-

given authority over her sons (and daughters). Today, we aptly apply the instruction about honor to the father equally to both father and mother.

The honor due to parents, like fear of the Lord, implies respect and obedience. Particularly when parents are old and unable to care for themselves, children honor them by kindness, attentiveness, and understanding. In contrast, grieving a father or mother in their older years may be from neglect or even from insulting them in their frailty. The Lord, who is also a father (23:1), will remember how children treat

For meditation and context:

RESPONSORIAL PSALM   Psalm 128:1–2, 3, 4–5 (1)

R. Blessed are those who fear the Lord and walk in his ways.

Blessed is everyone who fears the LORD,
  who walks in his ways!
For you shall eat the fruit of your handiwork;
  blessed shall you be, and favored.

Your wife shall be like a fruitful vine
  in the recesses of your home;
your children like olive plants
  around your table.

Behold, thus is the man blessed
  who fears the LORD.
The LORD bless you from Zion:
  may you see the prosperity of Jerusalem
  all the days of your life.

READING II   Colossians 3:12–21

A reading from the Letter of Saint Paul to the Colossians

[Brothers and sisters:
Put **on**, as **God's chosen** ones, holy and beloved,
  heartfelt compassion, kindness, humility, gentleness,
    and patience,
  bearing with one another and forgiving one another,
  if one has a grievance against another;
  as the Lord has forgiven **you**, so must you **also** do.
And over **all** these put on love,
  that is, the **bond** of **perfection**.
And let the peace of Christ **control** your **hearts**,
  the **peace** into which **you** were **also** called in **one** body.
And be thankful.
Let the word of **Christ dwell** in you **richly**,
  as in all wisdom you teach and admonish one another,
  singing psalms, hymns, and spiritual songs
  with gratitude in your hearts to **God**.
And **whatever** you do, in word or in deed,
  do everything in the **name** of the **Lord** Jesus,
  giving thanks to **God** the Father through him.]

A call to action. Pause before you begin.

Take your time as you proclaim these wonderful words: compassion, kindness, humility.

Let the congregation hear love and thankfulness in your voice. Smile.

---

their parents. Throughout his wisdom teaching, Sirach shows that genuine fear of the Lord must include right relationships in day-to-day living.

For their part, children benefit by honoring their parents. Sirach writes extensively about the results of fulfilling the commandment of honoring father and mother: atonement for sins; prayers that are heard; lives gladdened by children; length of life; the canceling of debt for sin. The blessing given by honoring parents results in blessing received from God.

READING II   Paul addresses his letter to the Colossians to "the holy ones and faithful brethren in Christ in Colossae" (1:2). In today's reading, he expands on this initial identity. They are "God's chosen ones, holy and beloved." In both verses, Paul regards the Colossians as "holy," his most common designation for the family of believers (e.g., Romans 1:7; 1 Corinthians 1:2). Their holiness signifies being set apart by God's call, establishing them as God's own people. Being chosen and beloved further express the commu-

nity as belonging to God, having been immersed into Christ at Baptism.

Paul then explains to the whole community the lived implications of being chosen, holy, and beloved. As God has poured out love on them, they must pour out love in their own relationships. And as Christ was compassionate, kind, humble, and gentle, so too must be those who live in him. Because they are clothed in Christ, both their inner dispositions and outward actions should express their unity and transformation, for they have been formed into a single body.

Pause. Transition to a different tone as you address wives, husbands, children, and fathers.

Wives, be subordinate to your **husbands**,
    as is proper in the **Lord**.
Husbands, love your wives,
    and **avoid** any bitterness toward them.
Children, obey your parents in **everything**,
    for this is **pleasing** to the **Lord**.
Fathers, do **not** provoke your children,
    so they may **not** become discouraged.

[Shorter: Colossians 3:12–17]

GOSPEL   Matthew 2:13–15, 19–23

Your tone is one of firmness. Pause before you proclaim the angel's words.

As you lead the assembly through the journey, make sure you read with good eye contact and volume.

Herod = HAYR-uhd

A reading from the holy Gospel according to Matthew

When the magi had departed, behold,
    the angel of the Lord appeared to Joseph in a **dream** and said,
    "Rise, take the child and his mother, **flee** to **Egypt**,
    and **stay** there until I **tell** you.
Herod is going to search for the child to destroy him."
Joseph **rose** and **took** the child and his mother by night
    and **departed** for Egypt.
He stayed there until the **death** of Herod,
    that what the **Lord** had said through the **prophet** might
      be fulfilled,
    *Out of **Egypt I called** my son.*

When Herod had died, behold,
    the angel of the Lord appeared in a dream
    to **Joseph** in **Egypt** and said,
    "Rise, take the child and his mother and **go** to the land
      of **Israel**,
    for those who sought the child's **life** are dead."

Paul's exhortation to them, "be thankful," is the expected response of the community life in Christ. With the Word of Christ making a rich home in them, the family of believers ought together to offer prayers and sing hymns that overflow with gratitude.

After exhorting the whole community, Paul gives specific advice to husbands, wives, and children. While such household codes were common in the first-century milieu, Paul gives the code a baptismal interpretation. Having been plunged into Christ, each of them live in the Lord. Even

with the mutuality because of their common Baptism, Paul's injunction to women to be subordinate to their husbands reflects the cultural expectation in a patriarchal society. Yet with this traditional view of the role of wives, Paul is more revolutionary in what he says about husbands. In the Greco-Roman world, husbands could exercise complete control over their wives, but because of their relationship in Christ, husbands are to show the same love already recommended to the whole community. The obedience expected of chil-

dren is accompanied by a loving tolerance of parents toward them.

GOSPEL Before the birth of Jesus, an angel appeared to Joseph in a dream. In today's Gospel, Joseph receives two more revelatory dreams. The pattern of the two dreams today continues the pattern established in the first dream: the angel directs Joseph how to act, and Joseph responds obediently. Throughout Matthew's opening chapters, Joseph is a righteous man who readily accepts the revelations that God gives him.

Proclaim clearly and be firm.
Archelaus = ahr-kuh-LAY-uhs
Galilee = GAL-ih-lee
Slowly articulate your words.

Nazorean = naz-uh-REE-uhn

> TO KEEP IN MIND
> Read the Scripture passage and its commentary in *Workbook*. Then read it from your Bible, including what comes before and after it so that you understand the context.

He **rose**, **took** the child and his **mother**,
    and went to the land of Israel.
But when he heard that Archelaus was ruling over **Judea**
    in **place** of his father **Herod**,
    he was afraid to go back there.
And because he had been warned in a **dream**,
    he **departed** for the region of Galilee.
He went and **dwelt** in a town called Nazareth,
    so that what had been spoken through the **prophets** might be
        fulfilled,
    He shall be called a Nazorean.

In all three dream scenes, allusions to the Hebrew Scriptures create continuity with the past even as God is doing something new in the present.

The first scene begins when the Magi departed. Though the Magi had thwarted Herod's plans, the angel reveals that Herod is still seeking to destroy the child. Like his ancestor Joseph, the new Joseph is to flee to Egypt for refuge. Unlike the Joseph of old who interpreted Pharaoh's dreams, Joseph's dreams in Matthew need no interpretation. The Lord's directions to him are clear, and Joseph does exactly as

the Lord says. The final verse in this episode is from the prophet Hosea, fulfilled in a new and unexpected way, a prominent theme in Matthew's Gospel. In Hosea, Israel is God's son, called from Egypt to return to their own land; now Jesus, God's own son, is called from Egypt to return to his homeland, where he will minister to his people.

The second scene continues the pattern as the angel of the Lord again appears in a dream. Again, Joseph is to rise and take the child and his mother where the angel commands him. This time, they are to go to

the land of Israel, recalling Hosea's prophecy. They return, not to Judea where Herod's son is wreaking havoc on the people, but to Nazareth in Galilee. The reference to Nazareth gives rise to yet another prophecy, one that is actually not found in the Hebrew Scriptures. The meaning of the prophecy is interpreted in various ways: it may also derive from the term *nazir*, signifying one devoted to God, or from *neser*, meaning a branch in reference to the Messiah; in the context of this scene, it likely refers to Jesus' hometown of Nazareth. E.P.

MARY, THE HOLY MOTHER OF GOD

LECTIONARY #18

READING I   Numbers 6:22–27

A reading from the Book of Numbers

Pause. Proclaim with authority.

Aaron = AYR-uhn

The Lord said to Moses:
  "Speak to Aaron and his sons and **tell** them:
  This is how you shall bless the **Israelites**.
Say to them:

The tone in your voice is one of joy. Let the congregation see happiness in your face. Smile.

  The Lord bless you and keep you!
  The Lord let his face shine upon
    you, and be gracious to you!
  The Lord look upon you kindly and
    give you peace!
So shall they invoke my name upon the Israelites,
  and I will bless them."

For meditation and context:

RESPONSORIAL PSALM   Psalm 67:2–3, 5, 6, 8 (2a)

R. May God bless us in his mercy.

May God have pity on us and bless us;
  may he let his face shine upon us.
So may your way be known upon earth;
  among all nations, your salvation.

May the nations be glad and exult
  because you rule the peoples in equity;
  the nations on the earth you guide.

May the peoples praise you, O God;
  may all the peoples praise you!
May God bless us,
  and may all the ends of the earth
    fear him!

READING I   Embedded in the story of the Lord's saving actions, divine commands, and instructions is God's instruction to Moses to teach the priests how to bless Israel. Likely one of the oldest poetic texts in the Old Testament, it retains a freshness and lasting appeal. The prayer is both individual and universal; the "you" as recipient of the blessing is singular, given to each person individually, as well as to the whole nation regarded as a single person.

The phrasing of the blessing is solemn as well as tender, announcing the Lord's imparting of abundant favor that overflows on those so blessed. Each time the name "Lord" (Yahweh) is mentioned, the people are reminded that it is the God of the covenant who blesses them, the God who acted with power in rescuing them from Egypt. After the verb that promises blessing, the next verb proclaims *how* God blesses: by the abiding action of guarding and protecting Israel. Since the people have already experienced God's protective action in their desert sojourn, they can be confident that it will continue in the present and future.

The second line of the blessing, typical of Hebrew poetry, is almost synonymous with the first. The image of God's face shining upon the people portrays God's blessing as personally enveloping them with radiant divine presence. God's graciousness is the bestowal of abiding favor, and a sign of God's fidelity. In looking kindly on Israel, the Lord will grant the gift of peace, *shalom*, the blessing of well-being in every dimension of life.

After the blessing prayer, God tells the priests to "invoke my name upon the Israelites." With God's name upon them, the people are to be identified as God's

Galatians = guh-LAY-shuhnz

Pause after you proclaim, "Brothers and sisters." How blessed we are to be God's children! The tone in this reading is one of simple gratitude.

Keep up your energy.

Abba = AH-bah

Pause before you say "Abba, Father!" Use good eye contact as you end the reading.

READING II   Galatians 4:4–7

A reading from the Letter of Saint Paul to the Galatians

Brothers and sisters:
When the **fullness** of time had come, **God** sent his Son,
    born of a **woman**, **born** under the **law**,
    to ransom those under the law,
    so that we might **receive adoption** as **sons**.
As proof that you are sons,
    God sent the Spirit of his Son into our hearts,
    crying out, "Abba, Father!"
So you are **no** longer a **slave** but a **son**,
    and if a **son** then also an heir, through God.

Proclaim with energy in your voice.

Say this quietly.

GOSPEL   Luke 2:16–21

A reading from the holy Gospel according to Luke

The **shepherds** went in **haste** to **Bethlehem** and found Mary
    and Joseph,
    and the infant lying in the manger.
When they **saw** this,
    they made **known** the message
    that had been told them about this **child**.
All who heard it were amazed
    by what had been told them by the **shepherds**.
And **Mary kept** all these things,
    reflecting on them in her heart. »

---

own possession, blessed, guarded, favored, and given the Lord's own peace.

READING II The context of the reading from Galatians is Paul's explanation that humanity had not yet reached adulthood. As minors, they were no better than slaves and remained under guardianship until the proper time. Then Paul announces the good news that the designated time has come. In the fullness of time, predetermined by God, humanity has come of age; they are no longer slaves but fully grown children.

This new status has come about because God sent his Son, born of a woman, into the world. In a few words, Paul proclaims the profound mystery of Jesus' identity as the divine Son of God and the fully human son of Mary. As one intimately related both to God and to humanity, Jesus' mission is to bring the immature, enslaved human race into mature relationship with God and into freedom. He does this by rescuing or redeeming us, and making us adopted sons and daughters. Like the designated redeemer in ancient Israel, Jesus acts as the closest relative with the

task of freeing family members from poverty, imprisonment, or slavery.

Having become adopted children through Jesus' redeeming action, we have received the gift of Christ's Spirit that God has sent into our hearts. Earlier in Galatians, Paul wrote that Christ lives in him (2:20). Whether speaking about Christ or the Spirit, Paul repeatedly affirms the divine indwelling in his very being and in that of believers. Because of that profound relationship that makes us God's sons and daughters, we can address God as did Jesus, "Abba." God is our ever-present

Transition to excitement in your reading.

circumcision = ser-kuhm-SI-zhuhn
Use strong eye contact as you conclude.

> **TO KEEP IN MIND**
> Words in bold are significant words about which you must make a choice to help their meaning stand out. You may (or may not) choose to stress them.

Then the **shepherds** returned,
    glorifying and praising God
    for **all** they had heard and seen,
    just as it had been told to them.

When eight days were completed for his circumcision,
    he was named Jesus, the name given him by the angel
    before he was conceived in the womb.

Father who has made us heirs of the promise in the fullness of time.

GOSPEL Today we hear again the account of the shepherds finding the infant Jesus in Bethlehem, along with Mary and Joseph. On this feast of Mary, the Mother of God, we turn our attention to her. Beginning with the angel's annunciation to her, Mary responded with obedience to God's Word, eagerly visited her cousin Elizabeth, and joyfully proclaimed God's saving deeds in the Magnificat. Then, having made the journey to Bethlehem with Joseph, she gave birth to her son in fulfillment of the angel's message. There she hears the shepherds tell of their own angelic message that elicits amazement from all who hear their news.

For her part, Mary "kept (*synterei*) all these things, reflecting (*symballousa*) on them in her heart." Two verbs express how she responded to all that she has heard, seen, and experienced. The first verb that tells of Mary's response indicates that she treasured and held everything in her memory. The second verb describes an active reflecting as she turns around in her mind and heart the great mystery in which she is an integral participant. Both verbs indicate not a brief meditation but a continuous, contemplative immersion in the events.

As a faithful Jewish woman, Mary is obedient to the laws and customs of her people. Thus, eight days after Jesus' birth, Mary and Joseph keep the laws regarding circumcision. Further, in compliance with the angel's message, they name the child Jesus, "God saves," his name pointing to his mission of being a savior. E.P.

THE EPIPHANY OF THE LORD

LECTIONARY #20

READING I   Isaiah 60:1–6

A reading from the Book of the Prophet Isaiah

Isaiah = ī-ZAY-uh

Begin with high energy and enthusiasm.

Rise **up** in **splendor**, **Jerusalem**! Your light has come,
    the glory of the Lord shines upon **you**.

Use less intensity with this line, but continue to build and sound joyous.

See, **darkness covers** the earth,
    and thick clouds **cover** the peoples;

Pause. Proclaim this line slowly, emphasizing the words in bold. Smile.

but upon you the Lord shines,
    and **over** you **appears** his glory.
Nations shall **walk** by your light,
    and kings by your **shining** radiance.
Raise your **eyes** and look about;
    they **all gather** and **come** to **you**:
your sons come from **afar**,
    and your daughters in the arms of their **nurses**.

Keep up your energy with a smile!

Then you shall be radiant at what you **see**,
    your **heart** shall throb and overflow,
for the riches of the sea shall be emptied out before you,
    the wealth of **nations** shall be brought to you.
Caravans of camels shall **fill you**,

dromedaries = DRAH-muh-dayr-eez
(single-humped camels)

Midian = MID-ee-uhn

Ephah = EE-fuh

Sheba = SHEE-buh

    dromedaries from **Midian** and **Ephah**;
all from Sheba shall come
    bearing gold and frankincense,
    and **proclaiming** the praises of the LORD.

READING I   Isaiah addresses his prophecy to Jerusalem, a city personified, symbolizing the whole people. The prophecy was probably written around the end of the exile in Babylon (586 BC), when the first Israelites returned, finding their beloved city Jerusalem devastated. The temple was gone, the city walls were in ruins, the economic conditions were dire, and there was no Davidic king to rule over them. In this context, Isaiah offers a vision of the city and people transformed. Not only is this a portrait of future renewal, it also announces a dramatic transformation

that is happening in their midst. Isaiah tells the people to rise up, to let their light shine, to raise their eyes and look around them to see what the Lord is already doing.

At the heart of Isaiah's promise is the glory of the Lord. A unifying theme in this section of Isaiah, divine glory is a weighty manifestation of God's power and presence. Isaiah uses imagery of light and shining radiance to announce how visible God's glory is, if only the people will look around them. God's luminous glory is so powerful that the divine light will shine forth from the people themselves. Even foreign

nations and kings will walk by the light that flows forth from Jerusalem.

For the newly returned exiles, the image of wealthy nations streaming toward their city would present a sharp contrast with their memories of impoverished Jerusalemites trudging into exile. With God's radiance shining from the inhabitants of Jerusalem, foreigners will arrive with riches, coming on caravans of camels, bringing gold and frankincense. Along with Isaiah, the prophet Haggai offered a similar vision of hope. Through him, the Lord told the people, "the treasures of all the nations

For meditation and context:

RESPONSORIAL PSALM   Psalm 72:1–2, 7–8, 10–11, 12–13 (11)

R. Lord, every nation on earth will adore you.

O God, with your judgment endow the king,
   and with your justice, the king's son;
he shall govern your people with justice
   and your afflicted ones with judgment.

Justice shall flower in his days,
   and profound peace, till the moon be
     no more.
May he rule from sea to sea,
   and from the River to the ends of
     the earth.

The kings of Tarshish and the Isles shall
   offer gifts;
the kings of Arabia and Seba shall
   bring tribute.
All kings shall pay him homage,
   all nations shall serve him.

For he shall rescue the poor when he cries out,
   and the afflicted when he has no one to
     help him.
He shall have pity for the lowly and the poor;
   the lives of the poor he shall save.

READING II   Ephesians 3:2–3a, 5–6

Ephesians = ee-FEE-zhuhnz

A reading from the Letter of Saint Paul to the Ephesians

Your tone is one of clarity and firmness. Pause before you begin.

Brothers and sisters:
You have heard of the **stewardship** of God's grace
   that was given to me for your **benefit**,
   namely, that the mystery was made known to me
     by revelation.
It was **not** made known to people in **other** generations
   as it has now been revealed
   to his holy apostles and prophets by the Spirit:
   that the Gentiles are coheirs, members of the **same** body,
   and copartners in the **promise** in **Christ Jesus** through
     the **gospel**.

Be careful of your pace. Take your time. Use strong eye contact throughout the reading.

---

will come in, and I will fill this house with glory" (Haggai 2:7). For long centuries, the glory of Jerusalem and the inclusion of Gentiles envisioned by Isaiah, Haggai, and other post-exilic prophets did not find fulfillment. On this feast of the Epiphany, we celebrate prophetic fulfillment with a new manifestation of God's glory to foreigners, represented by the Magi.

READING II In the verse immediately preceding today's reading from Ephesians, Paul identifies himself as "a prisoner of Christ for you Gentiles." He continues addressing Gentile believers, reminding them of the stewardship of God's grace given to him for their benefit. As a steward, Paul is responsible for overseeing the household of believers, comparable to a steward who manages a family household. While there are many facets to Paul's stewardship, God called him specifically to proclaim Christ to the Gentiles (Galatians 1:16).

Earlier in Ephesians, Paul had reminded his Gentile audience that they were at one time without Christ and alienated from the community of Israel. Now, however, they are fellow citizens with them in the household of God (see Ephesians 2:12–22). For their benefit, God revealed the mystery to Paul. Like the Gospel that Paul proclaims, mystery has a cognitive content, something long hidden that has been unveiled by divine revelation. Both Gospel and mystery center on the unifying and saving plan of God brought to fulfillment in Christ. Unknown to earlier generations, the Spirit of God has revealed the mystery to Paul, and through him, also to those in God's household.

GOSPEL   Matthew 2:1–12

A reading from the holy Gospel according to Matthew

When **Jesus** was born in **Bethlehem** of **Judea**,
    in the **days** of **King Herod**,
    behold, **magi** from the east arrived in Jerusalem, saying,
    "**Where** is the **newborn king** of the **Jews**?
We saw his star at its rising
    and have come to do him homage."
When King Herod heard this,
    he was greatly troubled,
    and **all Jerusalem** with him.
Assembling all the **chief priests** and the scribes of the people,
    he **inquired** of them where the Christ was to be **born**.
They said to him, "**In** Bethlehem **of** Judea,
    for thus it has been written through the prophet:
        *And **you**, Bethlehem, land of Judah,*
            *are **by** no **means** least among the **rulers** of Judah;*
        *since **from you** shall come a ruler,*
            who is to shepherd my people Israel."
Then Herod called the magi secretly
    and ascertained from them the time of the star's appearance.
He sent them to Bethlehem and said,
    "Go and **search diligently** for the child.
When you have found him, **bring** me **word**,
    that I too may **go** and **do** him homage."
After their audience with the king they **set out**. »

Judea = joo-DEE-uh;

Herod = HAYR-uhd.

You are setting the stage for what is to come. Proclaim in an informative tone.

Pause.

homage = HOM-ij

The assembly must hear intensity in King Herod's actions.

Pause for emphasis before you proclaim this line.

Say firmly.

In addition to the intellectual dimension of mystery, it also has a relational aspect. Sacred mysteries draw believers to ever-deeper participation into Christ. The mysteries revealed and proclaimed are transformative. Thus the Gentiles, who were once alienated and far off, have become coheirs, members of the one body, and copartners with Jewish believers. Paul's stewardship not only announces this mystery to others, but he is immersed in it himself, transformed by grace. He too is recipient of the promise in Christ Jesus through the Gospel.

GOSPEL Writing for a Jewish-Christian audience, the evangelist Matthew weaves their Scriptures, symbols, and allusions to their ancestors into his Gospel. He gives their Hebrew texts new meaning, showing fulfillment in unforeseen ways in light of Jesus, the Messiah. As we listen to Matthew's account of the Magi, we can hear echoes both of the Jewish tradition and of the first two readings today. Each reading on this feast of Epiphany presents a manifestation of God's inclusion of Gentiles into the plan of salvation: distant nations see divine glory flowing from Jerusalem; Gentiles learn that they are one body with Jewish believers; and now Gentile astrologers from the east see the newborn king of the Jews.

The Gospel opens with reference to two kings: King Herod in Jerusalem, and the newborn king of the Jews in Bethlehem. Beginning with these two brief introductions, Matthew sets up contrasts that he will develop throughout the narrative. Herod is a tyrannical ruler, obsessed with power, reminiscent of the Pharaoh of Egypt. Herod was so threatened by possible rivals that he even put family members

Proclaim with good volume and use facial expression.

prostrated = PROS-trayt*d

Proclaim with a tone of resolution.

And **behold**, the **star** that they had **seen** at its rising
 preceded them,
 until it **came** and **stopped** over the **place** where the child **was**.
They were overjoyed at seeing the star,
 and on **entering** the house
 they **saw** the **child** with **Mary** his mother.
They prostrated themselves and did him homage.
Then they **opened** their **treasures**
 and offered him gifts of gold, frankincense, and myrrh.
And having been warned in a **dream not** to return to **Herod**,
 they departed for their country **by another** way.

to death. Jerusalem is his capital, the city where he displayed his wealth and life of luxury. The temple he built was as much to honor himself as to honor the Lord God of Israel. The infant king in contrast has no display of wealth or power. He is found not in a palace in Jerusalem surrounded by attendants, but in a house with his mother in the small village of Bethlehem. Tiny in size, Bethlehem's significance arises from the prophecy of a ruler who will be born there, one who like King David would shepherd the people of Israel.

Another contrast is between the Gentile Magi and the Jewish chief priests and scribes. Having no knowledge of the Hebrew Scriptures, the Magi rely on their study of heavenly signs to discover meaning for the earth. They make a journey from the east and continue their diligent searching until they find the child. On the other hand, the Jewish scholars rely on their Scriptures, knowing their tradition well. While the scholars could readily quote the ancient biblical prophecies, they did not understand their meaning for the present. Nor did they make a journey or search for

the child, even though the prophecy should have inspired them to do so. They seem incurious, while the Magi are open to learning something new. In hearing this account, Matthew's audience of first-century Jewish Christians would be nudged to look anew at the Word of God, seeking to find how it must be reinterpreted in light of Jesus. E.P.

THE BAPTISM OF THE LORD

LECTIONARY #21

READING I Isaiah 42:1–4, 6–7

A reading from the Book of the Prophet Isaiah

Thus says the LORD:
Here is my **servant** whom **I** uphold,
  my chosen one with whom I am pleased,
upon whom I have **put** my spirit;
  he shall **bring** forth justice to the nations,
not crying out, **not shouting**,
  not making his **voice** heard in the **street**.
A **bruised** reed he shall **not break**,
  and a smoldering **wick** he shall **not quench**,
until he **establishes** justice on the **earth**;
  the **coastlands** will wait for his teaching.

I, the LORD, have called you for the victory of justice,
  I have grasped you by the **hand**;
I formed you, and **set** you
  as a covenant of the people,
  a light for the nations,
to open the eyes of the blind,
  to **bring** out prisoners from confinement,
  and from the dungeon, those who **live** in darkness.

Isaiah = ī-ZAY-uh

Proclaim in an authoritative voice.
Pause and do not rush your words.
Use facial expression. Smile!

Emphasize the words in bold.

This reading is an important reminder of how we are to live. It is a call to action. Proclaim slowly and firmly. Pause after commas. Inspire the congregation with your energy.

READING I In four beautiful poems, the prophet Isaiah describes a mysterious servant whom God choses and sustains. The identity of the servant at times seems to be an individual, perhaps Isaiah himself, or the Messiah to come; at other times it appears to refer to the people as a whole. Whoever the servant may be, he will be the instrument of bringing God's justice to the earth.

Today's reading is the first of these servant songs. Well pleased with the servant, God has put the divine spirit upon him, thereby endowing him with the power to accomplish the designated mission. In the first part of the poem, God presents the servant to an audience that may include both the exiles and the oppressor nations. Though the nations had treated God's people with harsh injustice, the servant will bring about justice in a gentle way. He will act patiently, neither breaking those who are bruised, nor quenching the faint light of those barely surviving. Even the distant coastlands will await the servant's life-giving teaching.

Having described the servant to exiles and nations, God addresses the servant directly. The divine actions of calling, grasping by the hand, and forming the servant are deliberate, intimate, and done for a specific purpose. The servant is to be a living sign of God's covenant to Israel and at the same time be a light to the nations. The justice and light that the servant will bring will be directed particularly to the blind, imprisoned, and those in darkness. The servant's actions will thus be like God's own in caring for those most in need.

READING II The story of Peter and the Roman centurion Cornelius

46

For meditation and context:

RESPONSORIAL PSALM   Psalm 29:1–2, 3–4, 3, 9–10 (11b)

R. The Lord will bless his people with peace.

Give to the LORD, you sons of God,
   give to the LORD glory and praise,
Give to the LORD the glory due his name;
   adore the LORD in holy attire.

The voice of the LORD is over the waters,
   the LORD, over vast waters.
The voice of the LORD is mighty;
   the voice of the LORD is majestic.

The God of glory thunders,
   and in his temple all say, "Glory!"
The LORD is enthroned above the flood;
   the LORD is enthroned as king forever.

READING II   Acts of the Apostles 10:34–38

A reading from the Acts of the Apostles

Cornelius = kohr-NEEL-yuhs

Use an informative tone.

Peter proceeded to **speak** to those gathered
   in the house of Cornelius, saying:
   "In truth, I **see** that God shows no partiality.
Rather, in every nation whoever **fears** him and acts **uprightly**
   is acceptable to him.
You **know** the word that he sent to the **Israelites**
   as he proclaimed peace through Jesus Christ, who is Lord of all,
   what has happened **all** over Judea,
   beginning in **Galilee after** the baptism
   that **John** preached,
   how God **anointed Jesus** of **Nazareth**
   with the Holy Spirit and power.
He went about **doing** good
   and healing all those **oppressed** by the **devil**,
   for God was **with him**."

Take your time. When commas are omitted at the end of a line, continue reading. The reading won't be as choppy and will be easier to understand.

Judea = joo-DEE-uh
Galilee = GAL-ih-lee

Say this last line slowly and with a smile.

---

is a multi-scene drama that begins with Cornelius' vision in Caesarea, followed by Peter's vision in Joppa. Today's reading is from the next scene in which Peter, having gone to Caesarea, enters Cornelius' house. That Peter, a faithful Jew, would enter the house of the Gentile Cornelius is surprising and unlawful for him. Thus Peter explains the new insight that arose from his vision: "God has shown me that I should not call any person profane or unclean."

In the Gentile house, after a brief dialogue with Cornelius, Peter addresses all those gathered there. In telling them "I see

that God shows no partiality," Peter is relating his own changed understanding and behavior. He realizes that these Gentiles whom Peter had formerly regarded as unclean are included among those acceptable to God.

Peter's new comprehension is actually rooted in Jewish history. God had initially sent word to the Israelites, Peter's own ancestors, from whom came Jesus Christ, who is Lord of all. Lord of all! That is at the heart of Peter's new insight. He explains that after John's preaching of baptism, Jesus himself was baptized, anointed with

the Holy Spirit and power. Peter's reference to Baptism is the springboard for what will happen next in the drama. The two visions, Peter's journey to Caesarea, and the encounter in Cornelius' house where Peter gives his discourse each prepare the way for the Baptism of Cornelius' Gentile household, for Jesus is Lord of all.

 **GOSPEL** The first scene in which the adult Jesus appears in Matthew's Gospel is at the Jordan River. Crowds from Jerusalem were coming there to John for baptism. After chastising and

GOSPEL   Matthew 3:13–17

A reading from the holy Gospel according to Matthew

Jesus came from **Galilee** to John at the **Jordan**
 to be baptized **by** him.
John tried to prevent him, saying,
 "**I** need to be baptized by **you**,
 and yet you are coming to me?"
Jesus said to him in reply,
 "Allow it now, for thus it is fitting for us
 to fulfill all righteousness."
Then he allowed him.
After Jesus was baptized,
 he came up from the **water** and **behold**,
 the **heavens** were opened for him,
 and he saw the Spirit **of God** descending like a **dove**
 and coming upon **him**.
And a voice came from the **heavens**, saying,
 "This is my beloved Son, with whom I am **well** pleased."

Use a gentle tone.

As you proclaim the dialogue between John and Jesus, use vocal variety and facial expression.

Pause and say slowly.

Proclaim with a tone of reverence.

Pause and smile.

calling them to repentance, John changes his tone to tell them of a mightier one coming after him; though John baptizes with water, the one coming after him will baptize with the Holy Spirit and fire.

At this point in the drama, Jesus comes to John to be baptized. Having just spoken about the mightier one, John immediately recognizes that this man is the one he had just described. Stunned at Jesus' intention, John refuses, going so far as to say Jesus should instead baptize John himself. Since Jesus has no need to repent, why should he be baptized?

In Jesus' first words in Matthew's Gospel, he answers the unspoken question. His baptism is "to fulfill all righteousness." Two of Jesus' words, *fulfill* and *righteousness*, are thematic in Matthew's Gospel. The entirety of Jesus' life is a fulfillment of God's plan revealed in the Old Testament. Only in Jesus' story can the ancient story be understood as fulfilled. His baptism will fulfill all righteousness, meaning that it will manifest the right relationship between God and humanity. Though Jesus has no need of repentance, he stands in solidarity with all humanity that does need to repent.

As the scene continues, Matthew reveals Jesus' identity as the beloved Son of God. The opening of the heavens, descent of God's Spirit, and the heavenly voice emphasize divine presence. The words of the voice recall Isaac, David, and Isaiah's suffering servant. These figures were glimpses that foreshadow God's beloved Son, who will fulfill the right relationship between God and humanity. E.P.

SECOND SUNDAY IN ORDINARY TIME

LECTIONARY #64

READING I   Isaiah 49:3, 5–6

A reading from the Book of the Prophet Isaiah

> The LORD said to me: **You** are my servant,
>   **Israel**, through whom **I** show my glory.
> Now the LORD has spoken
>   who formed me as his **servant** from the womb,
> that Jacob may be **brought back** to him
>   and Israel gathered to him;
> and I am **made glorious** in the sight of the LORD,
>   and **my God** is now my strength!
> It is too little, the LORD says, for **you** to be my servant,
>   to **raise** up the **tribes** of **Jacob**,
>   and **restore** the **survivors** of Israel;
> I will make **you** a light to the nations,
>   that my salvation may **reach** to the ends of the **earth**.

Isaiah = ī-ZAY-uh

Begin with a humble tone. Pause before you say, "You are my servant."

Proclaim with energy. Keep building energy and end with excitement: "My God is now my strength!"

Pause.

End the reading with a tone of joy.

READING I The reading from Isaiah is the second of four poems traditionally referred to as "servant songs." Each of these poems describes a mysterious servant that sometimes seems to be Isaiah himself and at other times, Israel. An enigmatic figure, the servant can be viewed both as an individual and as a community, with the description aptly applied in one verse to the prophet and in the next to the nation as a whole. Whether describing Isaiah, the people of Israel, or an unnamed ideal servant of God, the portrait presents someone intimately involved in God's plan.

Such a servant obediently fulfills the will of the master: the Lord God.

After the first words, in which the Lord says, "You are my servant," the servant himself speaks, telling of God's words, actions, and purpose. The reason that God formed the servant even from the womb is so that the people—referred to either as Jacob or Israel—may be brought back to God. To be brought back has a twofold meaning; it can indicate being brought back from the land of exile or brought back from sinfulness and idolatry. The servant sees God's plan of bringing Israel back both from exile and from sin, fulfilled only because God is the servant's strength.

In the final verses, the Lord again speaks. God has formed the servant not for the sake of Israel alone, but also for the nations. God will make the servant become a light to the nations so that salvation will reach to the most distant parts of the earth. From beginning to end, the abiding presence and powerful action of God, working in the servant, fulfills the divine intention.

READING II The first way that Paul identifies himself for the

For meditation and context:

RESPONSORIAL PSALM   Psalm 40:2, 4, 7–8, 8–9, 10 (8a, 9a)

R. Here am I, Lord; I come to do your will.

I have waited, waited for the LORD,
    and he stooped toward me and heard
    my cry.
And he put a new song into my mouth,
    a hymn to our God.

Sacrifice or offering you wished not,
    but ears open to obedience you gave me.
Holocausts or sin-offerings you sought not;
    then said I, "Behold I come."

"In the written scroll it is prescribed for me,
to do your will, O my God, is my delight,
    and your law is within my heart!"

I announced your justice in the vast assembly;
    I did not restrain my lips, as you,
        O LORD, know.

READING II   1 Corinthians 1:1–3

Corinthians = kohr-IN-thee-uhnz

Proclaim slowly. Articulate your words.

Sosthenes = SOS-thuh-neez

Address each group in a different tone:
Sosthenes (gently), the Church (formal),
you (personal), all (broadly).

Smile and say warmly.

A reading from the first Letter of Saint Paul to the Corinthians

Paul, **called** to be an apostle of Christ Jesus by the **will** of **God**,
    and Sosthenes our brother,
    to the **church** of God that is in Corinth,
    to you who have been sanctified in Christ Jesus,
        called to be holy,
    with **all** those everywhere who **call** upon the name of our
        Lord Jesus Christ, **their** Lord and ours.
Grace to you and peace from God our Father
    and the **Lord** Jesus **Christ**.

church in Corinth is "called to be an apostle of Christ Jesus." Both his call and his apostleship signify that Paul has a commission based on his God-given vocation. As an apostle of Christ, Paul is sent forth to proclaim him and to act as his authoritative representative, much like the followers sent forth by Jewish rabbis of the period. Paul does not fulfill his task as an independent missionary, but does so along with others. In addition to Sosthenes in this letter, Paul names numerous coworkers who share in the mission of Christ Jesus in other letters.

Paul and Sosthenes write to the young Corinthian church. Like the Israelite assembly in the desert, the church (*ekklesia*) is chosen to be God's own people. Though there is continuity with God's people of old, there is something new in the church Paul addresses. They have been sanctified in Christ Jesus. Their identity is thus shaped by Christ who sanctifies them, making them holy, set apart by God and for God.

Paul himself and the church in Corinth are in union with believers everywhere who call on the name of the Lord Jesus. If they are united with the church all around

the Mediterranean, they must first be united with the believers in their own city. Paul seems to be subtly reminding the Corinthian church, fractured by divisions, that they must embody the oneness of the whole body of believers. Paul extends to them the grace and peace that is their gift from the Father and the Lord Jesus Christ.

GOSPEL From the opening words of his Gospel, John the evangelist creates a multifaceted portrait of Jesus. In today's Gospel, John the Baptist adds features to this developing picture.

GOSPEL John 1:29–34

A reading from the holy Gospel according to John

Proclaim with good volume and energy.

Pause.

Proclaim with reverence.

End with a firmness in your voice. Speak slowly and emphasize the words in bold.

John the Baptist saw **Jesus** coming toward him and said,
   "**Behold**, the Lamb **of** God, who **takes** away the sin
      of the world.
He is the **one** of whom I said,
   'A man is coming after me who ranks ahead of me
   because he existed before me.'
I did **not know** him,
   but the **reason** why I came **baptizing** with **water**
   was that **he** might be **made known** to Israel."
John testified **further**, saying,
   "I saw the Spirit come down like a **dove** from **heaven**
   and remain upon him.
I did **not know** him,
   but the one who sent me to **baptize** with water told me,
   'On whomever you **see** the **Spirit** come down and remain,
   he is the one **who** will baptize with the **Holy** Spirit.'
Now I have seen and testified that he is the Son **of** God."

Telling his audience "Behold, the Lamb of God," the Baptist focuses attention on Jesus, referring to him with a metaphor stemming from the Jewish tradition. The lamb was an essential part of the account of the Passover, when its blood on the doorposts preserved the homes of the Hebrews as the family shared in a meal (Exodus 12:7). Further, the lamb is a symbol for the Suffering Servant of Isaiah who bore the sufferings of others, and was led like a lamb to the slaughter (Isaiah 53:7, 11). The Jewish traditions contribute to an image of the lamb as profoundly involved in the suf-fering of the people, offering its life for them. Jesus' death on the cross will reveal him as the perfect lamb of sacrifice, led silently to the slaughter, bringing John's words to startling fulfillment.

The Baptist acknowledges that he did not know Jesus, although his role was to make Jesus known to Israel. Ultimately, a revelatory vision opened John's eyes to Jesus' identity. When he saw the Spirit come down and remain on Jesus, John recognized Jesus as the one who would baptize with the Holy Spirit. The evangelist uses the word "remain" (*meno*) here to sig-nify the Spirit's presence in Jesus, intimate and permanent. With the Holy Spirit abiding in him, Jesus will baptize others, immersing them in the same Spirit.

John the Baptist's vision makes him an authentic witness to Jesus as the Lamb of God, Son of God, one filled with the Spirit, ranking before John and even existing before him. E.P.

THIRD SUNDAY
IN ORDINARY TIME

LECTIONARY #67

READING I   Isaiah 8:23—9:3

A reading from the Book of the Prophet Isaiah

Proclaim in an informative tone.
Isaiah = ī-ZAY-uh
Zebulun = ZEB-yoo-luhn
Naphtali = NAF-tuh-li

First the LORD degraded the land of Zebulun
    and the land of **Naphtali**;
    but in the end he has glorified the seaward road,
    the land **west** of the **Jordan**,
    the **District** of the Gentiles.

Gentiles = JEN-tīls

Proclaim with more intensity.

Anguish has taken **wing**, dispelled is **darkness**:
    for there is **no** gloom where but **now** there was distress.
The people who **walked** in darkness
    have **seen** a great light;
    upon those who **dwelt** in the land of gloom
    a light has **shone**.

Transition your tone to one of hope.
Great news! Let the assembly hear happiness in your voice.

You have brought them **abundant** joy
    and great **rejoicing**,
    as they rejoice before you as at the harvest,
    as people make **merry** when **dividing** spoils.
For the yoke that **burdened** them,

Take your time and clearly proclaim your word endings.

    the pole on their **shoulder**,
    and the rod of their **taskmaster**
    you have smashed, as on the **day** of Midian.

Midian = MID-ee-uhn

READING I   In the eighth century BC, the ever-expanding and brutal Assyrian empire invaded the northern kingdom of Israel, beginning with the conquest of the territories of Zebulon and Naphtali. The Assyrian military brought such devastation to land and people that darkness seemed to enshroud everything. Yet in that time of darkness Isaiah announces that the gloom will be transformed to light. Though the people are still suffering, Isaiah uses verbs that sound as if the darkness has already been dispelled. So certain is the promise of God's saving action that Isaiah

and other prophets frequently speak as if it were already accomplished.

The first biblical reference to darkness occurs in the creation account when darkness covers the abyss. God's word, "Let there be light," was the first act of creation. In another manifestation of divine creative power, God will dispel all the darkness, gloom, and distress in which war-torn Israel dwells. The darkness is both individual and universal, for war has brought chaos to family life, the trampling of crops, political and societal upheaval, and feeling abandoned by God. Isaiah's hopeful words seem to suggest

that God's voice will again be heard in the darkness, "Let there be light," assuring that the dawn of a new day has come.

In the second part of Isaiah's prophecy, he speaks directly to the Lord who is the source of light. God's gift of light brings such abundant joy that Isaiah uses three images to describe it. First, the people's joy is comparable to the rejoicing at harvest time. When the land has been crushed by war, its restored fruitfulness brings great celebration. In a second image, the people make merry in dividing spoils. Rather than being plunged into the darkness of defeat,

For meditation and context:

RESPONSORIAL PSALM Psalm 27:1, 4, 13–14 (1a)

R. The Lord is my light and my salvation.

The LORD is my light and my salvation;
　whom should I fear?
The LORD is my life's refuge;
　of whom should I be afraid?

One thing I ask of the LORD;
　this I seek:
to dwell in the house of the LORD
　all the days of my life,
that I may gaze on the loveliness of the LORD
　and contemplate his temple.

I believe that I shall see the bounty
　of the LORD
　in the land of the living.
Wait for the LORD with courage;
　be stouthearted, and wait for the LORD.

READING II 1 Corinthians 1:10–13, 17

A reading from the first Letter of Saint Paul to the Corinthians

I urge you, brothers and sisters, in the **name** of our
　Lord Jesus **Christ**,
　that **all** of you agree in what you say,
　and that there be **no** divisions among you,
　but that you be **united** in the **same mind** and in the
　　same purpose.
For it has been reported to **me** about you, my brothers and sisters,
　by Chloe's people, that there are **rivalries** among you.
I **mean** that each of you is saying,
　"I belong to Paul," or "I belong to Apollos,"
　or "I belong to Cephas," or "I belong to Christ."
Is Christ divided?
Was **Paul crucified** for you?
Or were you **baptized** in the **name** of **Paul**?
For Christ did **not** send me to baptize but to **preach** the **gospel**,
　and **not** with the wisdom of human **eloquence**,
　so that the cross of Christ might **not** be emptied of its meaning.

Corinthians = kohr-IN-thee-uhnz

Proclaim St. Paul's letter with a sense of urgency. There are rivalries brewing.

Chloe = KLOH-ee
Choose a different inflection with each name.
Apollos = uh-POL-uhs
Cephas = SEE-fuhs
Pause for emphasis after each question.

Proclaim with a tone of firmness and authority.

---

they rejoice in the rewards of victory. The final image for rejoicing is the relief of being freed from the weight of yoke, pole, and rod, all instruments of servitude and oppression. Just as God had freed their ancestors from Midian long ago, in the time of the judge Gideon, God will again rescue Israel from whatever and whoever may oppress them.

READING II Beginning with the opening chapter of his first letter to the Corinthians, Paul addresses a major problem in the Corinthian community: lack of unity. He uses both positive and negative terminology, seeming to nudge the community to look at the situation from multiple angles. Paul summarized the positive perspective in the verse just before today's reading, telling the church that they have been called into fellowship (*koinonia*) with Christ. Since communion with Christ is at the heart of their faith, believers should agree in what they say, and be united in mind and purpose. The unity of speech, mind, and purpose that Paul is promoting is not referring to agreement of nonessential aspects of life, where individual prefer-

ences and insights add to the rich fabric of the community. Rather, Paul is writing about oneness rooted in their common faith in Christ and manifest in their loving, respectful relationships with one another.

Paul has learned of the opposite, negative speech and behavior from Chloe's people. Only in this text do we hear of Chloe who was probably the head of one of the house churches in Corinth. Members of her household inform Paul of the divisions (*schismata*) and rivalries among believers. They may be telling him about divisions in their own small community or

GOSPEL   Matthew 4:12–23

A reading from the holy Gospel according to Matthew

[When **Jesus heard** that **John** had been arrested,
    he **withdrew** to **Galilee**.
He left **Nazareth** and went to **live** in **Capernaum** by the sea,
    in the region of Zebulun and Naphtali,
    that **what** had been said **through Isaiah** the prophet
    might be fulfilled:
    Land of Zebulun *and* **land of** *Naphtali,*
        the way to the sea, beyond the Jordan,
            Galilee *of the* **Gentiles,**
        the **people** *who sit in darkness have* **seen** *a great light,*
    on those dwelling in a land **overshadowed** *by death*
        light has **arisen.**
From **that** time on, Jesus began to preach and **say,**
    "Repent, for the **kingdom** of heaven is at hand."]

As he was **walking** by the Sea of **Galilee**, he saw two **brothers,**
    Simon who is called Peter, and his brother Andrew,
    casting a **net** into the sea; they were fishermen.
He **said** to them,
    "**Come after** me, and I will make you **fishers of** men."
At **once** they left their nets and followed him.
He walked along from there and saw **two other brothers,**
    James, the son of **Zebedee**, and his brother John.
They were in a **boat**, with their **father** Zebedee, mending
        their **nets.**

Begin with an informative tone.

Capernaum = kuh-PER-nee-*m/
kuh-PER-nay-*m/ kuh-PER-n*m
Zebulun = ZEB-yoo-luhn
Naphtali = NAF-tuh-lī

Transition your voice to excitement.

Pause. There is an urgency in Jesus' words.

Jesus' tone is calm and inviting.

Zebedee = ZEB-uh-dee

---

about rivalries among the different house churches. Later in the letter, Paul chastises the Corinthians because these schisms are evident even when the assembly gathers for the Eucharist.

When some people seem to place their faith in Paul, Apollos, or Cephas, Paul poses questions that can only be answered with an emphatic "no." The positive answers to Paul's questions are that Christ is not divided, but is the visible embodiment of unity as well as its source. Only Christ, in whose name believers have been baptized, has been crucified for them.

Paul's apostolic mission is to preach the Gospel of Christ; the Good News does not rest on wisdom or human eloquence, whether from Apollos, Cephas, or Paul, but on Christ, the one who gave his life on the cross for all.

GOSPEL | After his baptism by John and his temptations in the wilderness, Jesus begins his public ministry in Galilee. The region was sometimes called "Galilee of the Gentiles" because of the large Gentile population there, dating back to the time of the Assyrian conquest and

resettling of foreigners. In Jesus' day, the area was under the political control of Herod Antipas, who had already arrested John the Baptist. According to Matthew, Jesus' reason for withdrawing to this territory of Zebulun and Naphtali was to fulfill Isaiah's prophecy heard in today's first reading. Those dwelling in darkness for long centuries have at last seen a great light, Jesus himself.

Jesus chooses as his home base the city of Capernaum, a fishing village on the shore of the Sea of Galilee. To the mixed population of Jews and Gentiles there,

Proclaim with energy. Smile.

He called them, and **immediately** they **left** their **boat**
and their father
and **followed** him.
He went around **all** of **Galilee**,
teaching in their synagogues, **proclaiming** the **gospel**
of the **kingdom**,
and curing every **disease** and **illness** among the people.

[Shorter: Matthew 4:12–17 (see brackets)]

Jesus begins his preaching by calling for repentance for the kingdom of heaven is at hand, the same message that the Baptist preached (3:2), each urging a repentance that entails a turning away from sin and reorienting one's life to embrace God's reign.

In the next scene, Jesus encounters the brothers Simon and Andrew, casting a net into the sea. Because Capernaum was a bustling fishing village, the brothers were probably among a large number of fishermen. From that crowd, Jesus sees and calls the two he wants to be his disciples. Not saying whether Jesus had met Simon and Andrew previously, nor whether they had heard his preaching, Matthew draws our attention to the power of Jesus' word and the ideal immediacy of response. Simon and Andrew will continue to be fishermen, Jesus tells them, only their catch from now on will be people. Jesus' words to them are both an invitation and a promise of a new life's work. The next two brothers, James and John, similarly leave everything, even their father Zebedee, again showing the ideal response to Jesus. The four fishermen are leaving all security to follow the uncertain travels of an itinerant rabbi.

The brief summary of Jesus' ministry in the concluding verse tells how he brought light to those dwelling in darkness. His teaching and ministry transformed the darkness of ignorance, the darkness of despair, and the darkness of broken bodies. E.P.

THE PRESENTATION OF THE LORD

LECTIONARY #524

READING I   Malachi 3:1–4

A reading from the Book of the Prophet Malachi

Thus says the **Lord** God:
Lo, I am **sending** my messenger
   to **prepare** the **way** before me;
And **suddenly** there will **come** to the temple
   the LORD whom you seek,
And the **messenger** of the covenant whom you **desire**.
   Yes, he is coming, says the LORD of hosts.
But who will endure the day of his **coming**?
   And who can stand when he **appears**?
For he is like the **refiner's** fire,
   or like the **fuller's** lye.
He will sit refining **and** purifying silver,
   and he will **purify** the **sons** of **Levi**,
Refining them like **gold** or like **silver**
   that they may **offer** due sacrifice to the LORD.
Then the **sacrifice** of Judah and Jerusalem
   will please the LORD,
   as in the **days** of **old**, as in years gone **by**.

Malachi = MAL-uh-kī

Proclaim in an authoritative tone.

As you proclaim the Lord's coming, the assembly must hear excitement in your voice.

Smile on this line.
Pause after each question for emphasis.

Read slowly and say clearly each word and word ending.

Levi = LEE-vī

Smile.

READING I   Malachi, one of the last of the Hebrew prophets, wrote during the Persian period, when the temple was rebuilt and worship resumed after the exile. The name Malachi means "my messenger," and may either be the personal name of the prophet or a designation of his role to be God's messenger. There is a future orientation to his prophecy, looking toward the day of the Lord when God will act as a powerful judge. Even as he looks toward the future, the prophet is also urging righteous behavior in the present time.

The messenger that the Lord will send to prepare the way may be Malachi himself, Elijah, or another prophet or leader. The messenger's unknown identity has led to a history of varied interpretation, with the New Testament ultimately seeing John the Baptist as the long-awaited one preparing the way. Whatever his identity, in both the original context and later interpretations, he will act powerfully and decisively, like fire that refines ore and lye that whitens cloth.

In preparing the way of the Lord, he will be the messenger of the covenant, indicating that underlying his role is the ancient covenant, always to be renewed. Every act of purification, though sometimes harshly painful like fire and lye, is intended to restore the covenant relationship between God and Israel. In particular, the messenger will purify the priests, the sons of Levi. Not only must abuses in worship be corrected, but even more importantly, purification will entail reform of the conduct of priests and

For meditation and context:

RESPONSORIAL PSALM   Psalm 24:7, 8, 9, 10 (8)

R. Who is this king of glory? It is the Lord!

Lift up, O gates, your lintels;
    reach up, you ancient portals,
    that the king of glory may come in!

Who is this king of glory?
    The Lord, strong and mighty,
    the Lord, mighty in battle.

Lift up, O gates, your lintels;
    reach up, you ancient portals,
    that the king of glory may come in!

Who is this king of glory?
    The Lord of hosts; he is the king of glory.

READING II   Hebrews 2:14–18

A reading from the Letter to the Hebrews

Since the children **share** in **blood** and **flesh**,
    Jesus likewise shared **in** them,
    that through **death** he might destroy the one
    who has the power of **death**, that is, the **devil**,
    and free those who through fear of death
    had been subject to slavery **all** their **life**.
Surely he did **not** help **angels**
    but rather the **descendants** of **Abraham**;
    therefore, he had to become **like** his brothers and sisters
    in **every way**,
    that he might be a merciful and faithful high priest before God
    to **expiate** the sins of the people.
Because he **himself** was **tested** through what he suffered,
    he is able to help those who are being tested.

Use an informative tone as you proclaim. Take your time and articulate your words and word endings.

Keep your energy up.

Read in a deliberate tone.

---

people alike. Only then will their sacrifices be pleasing to the Lord.

READING II Today's reading from Hebrews presents Jesus from two distinct yet interrelated perspectives: he is fully human and he is a high priest. He shares in "blood and flesh," a common idiom for a human being. Jesus thus shares in the limitations and capacities of other humans. Because angels do not share in these experiences, Jesus did not come for them, but for humanity, with whom he is in solidarity. Even as he endured death, as do all human persons, Jesus had power over it and over the devil. In some Jewish traditions, the devil was believed to be in control of death and was even thought to be the cause of bringing death into the world (see, for example, Wisdom 2:24).

Jesus' power over the devil and over death itself frees his brothers and sisters from the fear of physical death at the end of life. This is so because Jesus is the source of life beyond death. From another angle, existence outside the faith community and alienation from God because of sin is tantamount to being dead. Jesus also frees his brothers and sisters from such a moral death.

Jesus' role as high priest flows from his humanity. He must be one of the human community to serve as their high priest. In addition to his being one with humanity, Jesus is also a part of the Jewish community, from whom the high priest must come. Not every high priest was worthy or righteous, as was seen in today's reading

GOSPEL Luke 2:22–40

A reading from the holy Gospel according to Luke

Read in an informative tone.

[When the **days** were completed for their purification
  according to the law of **Moses**,
    Mary and **Joseph** took **Jesus** up to **Jerusalem**
  to **present** him to the **Lord**,
  just as it is written in the **law** of the Lord,
  Every **male** *that opens the womb shall be consecrated
    to the Lord*,
  and to offer the sacrifice of
  a pair of **turtledoves** *or two young* **pigeons**,
  in accordance with the **dictate** in the law of the Lord.

Pause before you say this line.

Now there was a man in Jerusalem whose name was Simeon.
This man was righteous and devout,
  awaiting the consolation of Israel,
  and the Holy **Spirit** was **upon** him.
It had been revealed to him by the **Holy Spirit**
  that he should **not** see **death**
  before he had **seen** the **Christ** of the Lord.
He came in the Spirit into the temple;
  and when the parents brought in the **child** Jesus
  to perform the **custom** of the **law** in regard to him,
  He took him into his arms and blessed God, saying:

As you proclaim, continue to tell the story in a calm, informative tone.

Simeon = SIM-ee-uhn

  "**Now**, Master, you may let your servant go
    in peace, according to your **word**,
  for my eyes have seen your salvation,
    which you prepared in the sight of **all** the **peoples**:
  a light for revelation to the **Gentiles**,
    and glory for your people **Israel**."]

Say these lines as if you are praying.

---

from Malachi. But Jesus is the perfect high priest, merciful and faithful, whose sacrifice expiated the sins of the people. Jesus' testing and suffering gave him a profound understanding of the experiences of his brothers and sisters.

 GOSPEL When Mary and Joseph bring Jesus to the temple to present him to the Lord, they simultaneously present him to the world. The righteous, devout Simeon is the first of Spirit-filled prophetic figures

to present Jesus to both Jews and Gentiles. Before his proclamation of the universal significance of the child, Simeon gratefully acknowledges the personal favor God has shown him. With the child in his arms, Simeon prays with a profound sense of peace.

The scene is filled with visual imagery and terminology. God had promised that Simeon would not see death until he had seen God's anointed one, and now his eyes have seen God's salvation in the infant he is holding. Simeon rec-

ognizes that what he has seen is not for his eyes alone, but is prepared in the sight of all people, bringing light to the Gentiles. For Israel, the child is a manifestation of God's glory, a visible sign of God's saving presence.

After such a joyous revelation, Simeon's words to Mary offer a glimpse of future sorrow. Prophesying that her child is destined for the fall and rise of many in Israel, Simeon foretells the opposition he will face. He tells the child's mother that she will experience

Focus on being deliberate in saying Simeon's words.

The child's father and mother were amazed at what was **said**
    about him;
    and Simeon **blessed** them and said to Mary his **mother**,
    "**Behold**, this child is **destined**
    for the **fall** and **rise** of many in Israel,
    and to be a **sign** that will be contradicted
    —and you **yourself** a **sword** will **pierce**—
    so that the thoughts of many **hearts** may be revealed."

Pause. Keep your energy up as you tell us the story of Anna.

There was also a **prophetess**, Anna,
    the daughter of **Phanuel**, of the tribe of **Asher**.

Phanuel = FAN-yoo-ehl

Asher = ASH-ehr

She was advanced in years,
    having lived seven years with her **husband** after her marriage,
    and then as a **widow** until she was eighty-four.
She **never left** the temple,
    but **worshiped night** and **day** with fasting and prayer.
And coming forward at that **very time**,
    she gave thanks to God and **spoke** about the child
    to all who were **awaiting** the redemption of **Jerusalem**.

Proclaim in a tone of resolution.

When they had **fulfilled** all the prescriptions
    of the law of the Lord,
    they returned to Galilee, to their own town of **Nazareth**.

Galilee = GAL-ih-lee

Say in a gentle tone.

The child grew and became strong, filled with wisdom;
    and the **favor** of **God** was upon him.

[Shorter: Luke 2:22–32 (see brackets)]

grief so great that it will pierce her very being. As if to counterbalance Simeon's prophecy, the prophetess Anna approaches at that very moment. She gives thanks for the child and speaks of him to all awaiting Jerusalem's redemption, thereby presenting him to his own people. After the multiple revelations, the scene ends quietly with the family returning to Nazareth, where Jesus will grow with God's favor ever upon him. E.P.

FIFTH SUNDAY IN ORDINARY TIME

LECTIONARY #73

READING I Isaiah 58:7–10

Isaiah = Ī-ZAY-uh

This reading challenges the congregation to act. Proclaim with intensity and urgency. Emphasize the words in bold.

A reading from the Book of the Prophet Isaiah

Thus says the LORD:
  Share your bread with the **hungry**,
    shelter the **oppressed** and the **homeless**;
  clothe the naked when you **see** them,
    and do **not** turn your back on your own.
  Then your light shall **break forth** like the **dawn**,
    and your wound shall quickly be healed;
  your vindication shall go before you,
    and the glory of the LORD shall be your **rear** guard.

Proclaim with excitement.

  Then you shall call, and the LORD will answer;
    you shall cry for help, and he will say: **Here I** am!
  If you remove from your midst

Another action for the assembly. Pause for emphasis. Read slowly and deliberately. Use strong eye contact.

    oppression, **false accusation** and **malicious speech**;
  if you bestow your bread on the **hungry**
    and satisfy the **afflicted**;
  then light shall rise for you in the **darkness**,

Use facial expression. Smile. There is hope!

    and the **gloom** shall become for **you** like **midday**.

READING I The final chapters of Isaiah (56–66) were likely addressed to Judeans recently returned from exile in Babylon. A prophet, often referred to as Third Isaiah, wrote to them in the spirit of Isaiah, who had prophesied before the exile. Now that they are again in the land God had given them, this later prophet urges them to be faithful to the covenant by obeying all that God commanded, both religious and social practices. They do seem to observe religious rituals such as fasting, donning sackcloth, and lying down in ashes, but the prophet focuses on their obligation to care for one another.

Today's reading follows his warning that pious acts are empty of meaning if they are disconnected from deeds of compassion. He tells them, in fact, that feeding, sheltering, and clothing those in need are the kinds of fasting the Lord desires. These actions reinforce the bond they have with one another. Feeding, sheltering, and clothing are not done from a distance, but imply the intimacy of eating together and bringing the homeless brother or sister into one's own home. Regarding the naked, the Hebrew text says literally, "Do not hide yourself from your own flesh." Those who are naked are of the same flesh as those who will clothe them.

When people concretely demonstrate such kinship, God's saving actions will follow. Light will break forth, wounds will be healed, there will be vindication and glory, answers to pleas, and removing of oppression. Those who have given and those who have received will together experience God's bounty, for light and glory will transform darkness and gloom for all.

For meditation and context:

RESPONSORIAL PSALM   Psalm 112:4–5, 6–7, 8–9 (4a)

R. The just man is a light in darkness to the upright.
or R. Alleluia.

Light shines through the darkness for
　　the upright;
　he is gracious and merciful and just.
Well for the man who is gracious and lends,
　who conducts his affairs with justice.

He shall never be moved;
　the just one shall be in everlasting
　　remembrance.
An evil report he shall not fear;
　his heart is firm, trusting in the Lord.

His heart is steadfast; he shall not fear.
　Lavishly he gives to the poor;
his justice shall endure forever;
　his horn shall be exalted in glory.

READING II   1 Corinthians 2:1–5

Corinthians = kohr-IN-thee-uhnz

Proclaim in a tone of firm purpose. Read for clarity. Do not rush.

sublimity = suhb-LIM-ih-tee

The congregation must hear St. Paul's growth in his preaching—from weakness and fear to strength. Your energy must build as you proclaim.

Pause. Say this line slowly. Emphasize words in bold.

Pause. Smile as you say this last line.

A reading from the first Letter of Saint Paul to the Corinthians

When I **came** to you, brothers and sisters,
　proclaiming the **mystery** of God,
　I did **not** come with **sublimity** of words or of wisdom.
For I **resolved** to **know** nothing while I was with you
　except Jesus Christ, and him **crucified**.
I **came** to you in weakness and fear and much trembling,
　and my message and my proclamation
　were **not** with **persuasive** words of wisdom,
　but with a **demonstration** of Spirit and power,
　so that your **faith** might rest **not** on human wisdom
　but on the power **of** God.

Early in his first letter to the Corinthians, Paul explains how his proclamation of the mystery of God contrasts dramatically with the so-called wisdom of Greek orators. On the one hand, orators with whom the people were familiar were known for their eloquence and human wisdom. Schooled in persuasive techniques, they had learned a wide variety of strategies to influence both the beliefs and behaviors of their audiences. Paul describes their words as sublime and persuasive, the precise characteristics that people expected and clamored for. Even

Apollos, who preached the Christian message, seemed well versed in such methods, and was welcomed by people captivated by his rhetorical abilities.

On the other hand, Paul presents himself as coming in weakness, fear, and trembling. By downplaying himself, Paul focuses on the message and not the messenger. Paul himself is weak, but the message is powerful and a manifestation of God's Spirit. Yet even the message of Christ crucified seems devoid of wisdom. How could a crucified messiah be a manifestation of power? Paul himself, as well as the Gospel

he preaches, is paradoxical; both message and messenger show forth the power of God in humility, weakness, scandal, and apparent foolishness. In these verses, Paul lays the foundation for his further unfolding of the mystery of Christ crucified, a mystery that displays the stark contrast between divine and human wisdom.

In a long and complicated sentence, Paul tells the believers in Corinth why he has come to them in such weakness. He wants them to base their faith not on the cleverness and sophistication of human wisdom, but on the power of God.

This teaches us how we are to live as disciples of Christ. Begin with good volume and energy. Continue to build with enthusiasm.

Pause.

Use facial expression. Smile.

TO KEEP IN MIND

Pause to break up separate thoughts, set apart significant statements, or indicate major shifts. Never pause in the middle of a single thought. Your primary guide for pauses is punctuation.

GOSPEL   Matthew 5:13–16

A reading from the holy Gospel according to Matthew

Jesus said to his **disciples**:
   "You are the salt of the **earth**.
But if salt loses its taste, with what can it be seasoned?
It is no **longer** good for **anything**
   but to be thrown out and **trampled** underfoot.
You are the light of the **world**.
A city set on a **mountain cannot** be hidden.
Nor do they light a **lamp** and then put it under a bushel basket;
   it is **set on** a lampstand,
   where it gives light to **all** in the house.
Just so, **your light** must shine before **others**,
   that they may see your **good deeds**
   and glorify your heavenly Father."

GOSPEL Today's reading from Matthew, taken from the Sermon on the Mount, follows the listing of beatitudes with Jesus beginning the sermon. Having described the characteristics of those who are blessed, Jesus then portrays his disciples through two images: salt and light. Coming right after the beatitudes, the images suggest further blessing, "Blessed are you who are the salt of the earth; blessed are you who are light for the world." God's blessing is not for the disciples alone, but so that they will be instrumental in bringing it to others.

The first image, salt, presents Jesus' disciples as providing flavor and preservative for the community. Without salt, food will lose its taste and become spoiled. The Bible also describes the sharing of salt as a sign of friendship (Leviticus 2:13) and as a means of purifying sacrifices (Exodus 30:35). Given the elasticity of the salt metaphor, any or all of the symbols can be applied to the disciples. Wherever they are present, so is the savory goodness of the Gospel, preserved and purified; the disciples are signs of friendship between God and humanity, and among the members of the community.

The second image for disciples is light, another multifaceted symbol. It evokes divine creative power that guides the footsteps of God's people, enlightens their minds, and gives them comfort and warmth. Neither hiding nor fearful, the disciples radiate this light for the benefit of others. Seeing the good deeds of Jesus' followers, those they encounter will join them in glorifying their heavenly Father. E.P.

SIXTH SUNDAY IN ORDINARY TIME

LECTIONARY #76

READING I   Sirach 15:15–20

Sirach = SEER-ak

Pause after the word *choose*. Proclaim slowly and deliberately.

Keep up your volume. For emphasis, pause after the word *death* in this line.

Transition your tone to one of gentleness and kindness.

A reading from the Book of Sirach

If you choose you **can** keep the commandments, they will
    save you;
  if you trust in God, you too shall live;
he has set before you fire and water;
    to whichever you **choose**, stretch forth your **hand**.
Before man are life and death, good and evil,
    whichever he **chooses** shall be given him.
Immense is the **wisdom** of the LORD;
  he is **mighty** in **power**, and **all**-seeing.
The eyes **of God** are on those who **fear** him;
  he understands man's every deed.
No one does he command to **act** unjustly,
    to **none** does he **give** license to **sin**.

For meditation and context:

RESPONSORIAL PSALM   Psalm 119:1–2, 4–5, 17–18, 33–34 (1b)

R. Blessed are they who follow the law of the Lord!

Blessed are they whose way is blameless,
  who walk in the law of the LORD.
Blessed are they who observe his decrees,
  who seek him with all their heart.

You have commanded that your precepts
  be diligently kept.
Oh, that I might be firm in the ways
  of keeping your statutes!

Be good to your servant, that I may live
  and keep your words.
Open my eyes, that I may consider
  the wonders of your law.

Instruct me, O LORD, in the way of
    your statutes,
  that I may exactly observe them.
Give me discernment, that I may observe
    your law
  and keep it with all my heart.

READING I In a long speech to Israel before they entered the Promised Land, Moses told the people that if they obeyed God's commandments, they would live and God would bless them. If they turned away and did not listen, they would perish. He emphasized the decision each one must make: "Choose life, that you may live" (Deuteronomy 30:15–20). Centuries later (about 180 BC), a wisdom teacher named Jesus Ben Sira gave similar advice to young men in Jerusalem aspiring to be scribes. Adding to the traditions of his ancestors, Ben Sira teaches about wisdom, popular in the culture of his day. Sirach's underlying belief was that God was the source of human wisdom, as he states in the first words of his book, "All wisdom comes from the Lord and with him it remains forever."

Both Moses and Ben Sira teach that keeping God's commandments is a choice that people can freely exercise. They have free will to choose between fire and water, life and death, good and evil, and they face the consequences of their choices. In wisdom, God sets before all humanity such decisions, and promises life for making right choices. For Moses and Sirach, *life* refers to the life that each person experiences on this earth, daily life with all the mundane ups and downs in which the mighty and all-seeing God is always present.

Throughout Sirach's teaching, similar to that of other sages, is the emphasis on fear of the Lord. Those who fear God act with awe and reverence, and they recognize their dependence on God. They are trusting and humble, and are thus inclined to choose obedience to God's commandments, resulting in God's gift of life.

READING II   1 Corinthians 2:6–10

A reading from the first Letter of Saint Paul to the Corinthians

Brothers and sisters:
We **speak** a wisdom to those who are mature,
 not a wisdom of **this** age,
 nor of the rulers of this age who are passing away.

Rather, we speak God's wisdom, **mysterious**, **hidden**,
 which God **predetermined** before the ages for **our glory**,
 and which **none** of the rulers of this age **knew**;
 or, if they had known it,
 they would **not** have **crucified** the **Lord** of glory.
But as it is written:

 *What **eye** has not seen, and **ear** has not heard,*
 *and what has **not entered** the **human** heart,*
 what God has prepared for those who love him,
 ***this God** has revealed to **us** through the **Spirit**.*

For the Spirit **scrutinizes everything**, even the depths of **God**.

GOSPEL   Matthew 5:17–37

A reading from the holy Gospel according to Matthew

[Jesus said to his disciples:]
 "Do **not think** that I have come to abolish the law
 or the prophets.
I have come **not** to abolish but to fulfill.
Amen, I say to you, until **heaven** and **earth** pass away,
 not the smallest **letter** or the smallest **part** of a letter
 will **pass** from the law,
 until all **things** have taken place. »

READING II In his two letters to the Corinthians, Paul addresses an audience apparently attracted to the human wisdom promoted by skilled orators. Paul warns the young Christian community that both the wisdom and the rulers of this age are passing away, powerful and permanent as they appear. Another wisdom—hidden, mysterious, and predetermined by God—was unknown by the deluded rulers who crucified the Lord of glory. This is the wisdom that Paul preaches.

As he writes about the ignorance of those who crucified Christ, Paul declares that if they had known, they would not have crucified him. Similarly, in a speech attributed to Paul in Acts of the Apostles, he says that the Jerusalem rulers did not understand the prophets read to them every Sabbath (Acts 13:27). And from the cross, Jesus himself asks for forgiveness for them, "for they do not know what they do" (Luke 23:34). Relying on human wisdom, the rulers and those who followed them did not see or understand the divine wisdom revealed in Jesus crucified.

On their own, people lack the capacity to comprehend this paradoxical mystery. Only God's revelation, poured out through the Spirit, opens eyes, ears, and hearts. This revealed wisdom is so new and contrary to common perceptions that Paul will continue to expound on it in the verses following today's reading. He explains that what he preaches has not been taught by human wisdom, but was given to him by the Spirit of God. What he preaches appears as foolishness to those without the Spirit, but Paul is preaching "the mind of Christ."

Stress the bold words.

Therefore, whoever breaks one of the **least** of these
      commandments
   and **teaches others** to do so
   will be called least in the **kingdom** of heaven.
But whoever obeys and teaches these commandments
   will be called greatest in the kingdom of heaven.
[**I tell** you, unless your **righteousness** surpasses
   that of the **scribes and Pharisees**,
   you will not enter the kingdom of heaven.

Pause before you say this line.
Proclaim these lines clearly and firmly.
Pause for emphasis after each semicolon.

Raqa = RAH-kah (an insult; exact meaning uncertain)
Sanhedrin = san-HEE-druhn

Gehenna = geh-HEN-nah
Keep up the energy. Use expression in your reading.

"You have heard that it was said to your ancestors,
   You shall not **kill***; and whoever kills will be liable to* **judgment***.*
But I say to you,
   whoever is angry with his brother
   will be **liable** to judgment;]
   and whoever says to his brother, 'Raqa,'
   will be **answerable** to the **Sanhedrin**;
   and whoever says, '**You** fool,'
   will be liable to fiery **Gehenna**.
Therefore, if you **bring** your **gift** to the altar,
   and there recall that your **brother**
   has anything against you,
   leave your gift **there** at the altar,
   go first and be reconciled with your brother,
   and then come and **offer** your gift.
Settle with your opponent quickly while on the way to court.
Otherwise your **opponent** will hand you over to the **judge**,
   and the **judge** will hand you over to the **guard**,
   and you will be thrown into **prison**.
Amen, I say to you,
   you will not be released until you have **paid** the **last penny**.

Pause before you say this line.

Proclaim with good volume.

["You have heard that it was said,
   You shall not commit **adultery***.*

GOSPEL After Jesus describes his disciples as salt and light, he continues his sermon by explaining how they are to understand his teaching. He has come not to abolish the law but to bring it to fulfillment. Jesus could well reiterate this statement when his later actions seem to negate the convictions of his Jewish contemporaries on keeping God's law. He eats with sinners (9:11), cures on the Sabbath (12:7–13), and does not enforce the traditions of the elders on his disciples (12:1–8; 15:2). Yet Jesus' words and his actions

show that he is not in conflict with the law itself, but with how it is being interpreted.

The law, understood and lived correctly, guides people in living righteously, or in right relationships, a virtue emphasized throughout Matthew's Gospel. Though external manifestations of righteousness are important, Jesus goes beyond external actions to consider the interior dispositions. Later in Matthew's Gospel, as Jesus' passion draws near, he explains the "weightier things of the law: judgment and mercy and fidelity" (23:23). These are the interior dispo-

sitions of righteousness that are the foundational for Jesus' view of the law.

Jesus teaches through a series of antitheses, or contrasts, the difference between his teaching about the law and what people have heard about the law. Far from abolishing the law, Jesus' teaching goes deeper, moving from external behavior to the righteous heart that motivates action. In the first antithesis, Jesus states the law against killing. He regards anger and contemptible speech as already making a person guilty of transgressing the commandment. Therefore, Jesus' disciples

Pause. Pay attention to the words in bold.
Read with a tone of urgency.

But I **say to you,**
   everyone who looks at a woman with **lust**
   has already committed adultery **with** her in his **heart**.]
If your **right eye** causes you to sin,
   tear it out and throw it away.
It is better for you to lose one of your **members**
   than to have your **whole** body **thrown** into Gehenna.
And if your right **hand** causes you to sin,
   cut it off and throw it away.
It is **better** for you to **lose** one of your members
   than to have your **whole** body go into **Gehenna**.

"It was **also said,**
   Whoever divorces his wife *must **give** her a bill of divorce.*
But I **say to you,**
   whoever divorces his wife—**unless** the marriage is unlawful—
   causes her to **commit** adultery,
   and whoever **marries** a **divorced** woman commits adultery.

["Again you have heard that it was said to your ancestors,
   Do not take a false oath,
   but make good to the Lord all that you vow.
But I say to you, do **not** swear **at all**;
   not by **heaven**, for it is God's throne;
   nor by the **earth**, for it is his footstool;
   nor by **Jerusalem**, for it is the **city** of the great King.
Do not swear by your **head**,
   for you cannot make a single hair white or black.
Let your **'Yes' mean** 'Yes,' and your **'No' mean 'No.'**
Anything more is from the evil one."]

[Shorter: Matthew 5:20–22a, 27–28, 33–34a, 37 (see brackets)]

Pause before you begin, and use an
informative tone.

Say with authority.

Read slowly. Be clear and firm.

Pause. Emphasize the words in bold. These
are strong words. Increase your volume.

should forgive from their hearts any wrongs against them and be reconciled with one another before bringing their gifts to the altar of worship. When Jesus describes an image of the courtroom, he suggests a scene of the final judgment before God, who alone is able to judge a person's heart.

Jesus' second antithesis again goes beyond the external keeping of the law. Like the anger and contempt, which transgress the commandment against murder, lustful thoughts are sins against adultery. Jesus' interpretation of the prohibition against adultery includes guarding one's

thoughts and senses that cause one to sin (*skandilizo*), literally making a person stumble. Jesus warns his disciples to avoid whatever is a source of stumbling.

Jesus also holds higher standards regarding divorce and taking of oaths. The Torah allowed divorce (Deuteronomy 24:1), initiated by the husband, and interpreted broadly to allow divorce for quite trivial reasons. Even with the exception of some sexual sin (*porneia*, variously interpreted), Jesus' teaching is more demanding than that of his contemporaries. (Jesus teaches more fully on divorce in a later response to

the Pharisees testing of him at 19:1–12.) The fourth antithesis goes farther than the law that prohibits taking of false oaths (Exodus 20:16). Not only should Jesus' disciples avoid false oaths, they should not take an oath at all. Sworn testimony that calls upon God to witness is unnecessary because a simple yes or no should express the truth of a disciple's word, like that of Jesus himself (2 Corinthians 1:18). E.P.

SEVENTH SUNDAY IN ORDINARY TIME

LECTIONARY #79

READING I   Leviticus 19:1–2, 17–18

Leviticus = lih-VIT-ih-kuhs

Proclaim in a tone of clear purpose and authority. Pause before you read the Lord's words.

Read slowly with a tone of firmness.

A reading from the Book of Leviticus

The LORD said to **Moses**,
   "**Speak** to the whole Israelite community and tell them:
   Be holy, for **I**, the LORD, your God, am holy.

"You shall **not** bear hatred for your brother or sister in your **heart**.
Though you may have to reprove your fellow citizen,
   do **not incur** sin because of him.
Take **no revenge** and cherish **no grudge** against any of your people.
You shall love your neighbor as yourself.
I am the LORD."

For meditation and context:

RESPONSORIAL PSALM   Psalm 103:1–2, 3–4, 8, 10, 12–13 (8a)

R. The Lord is kind and merciful.

Bless the LORD, O my soul;
  and all my being, bless his holy name.
Bless the LORD, O my soul,
  and forget not all his benefits.

He pardons all your iniquities,
  heals all your ills.
He redeems your life from destruction,
  crowns you with kindness and compassion.

Merciful and gracious is the LORD,
  slow to anger and abounding in kindness.
Not according to our sins does he deal
  with us,
nor does he requite us according to
  our crimes.

As far as the east is from the west,
  so far has he put our transgressions
   from us.
As a father has compassion on his children,
  so the LORD has compassion on those who
   fear him.

READING I   Of the many characteristics that Israel came to understand about the Lord God, holiness is foundational for their experience of God. God's holiness signifies divine otherness, God's being different, separate, and set apart from anything evil. The holy God is pure, clean, and strong. Though holiness does connote separateness, the holy God is deeply relational and is involved with the created world through acts of compassion, abiding guardianship, restoration of brokenness, and power that sustains the universe.

The holy God is transcendent, even while remaining unexpectedly near.

In today's reading, the Lord commands that the community of Israel be holy because their God is holy. A long section in Leviticus, from which today's reading is taken, is called the Holiness Code, a collection of numerous directives that explain how people are to live in holiness. Underlying all the commandments is the core belief that human persons are holy because they belong to God. As well as relating to God with awe, reverence, and right worship, God's holy people are also to

care for one another. Not only are they to avoid such negative actions as deep-seated hatred, taking vengeance or bearing a grudge, they are also to love their neighbors as they love themselves. As they take responsibility for the well-being of others who belong to God, the holy people of God strengthen the bonds of community, so that all of them might live in holiness. The concluding verse, "I am the Lord (Yahweh)" is an emphatic statement of the identity of the holy God.

READING II   1 Corinthians 3:16–23

A reading from the first Letter of Saint Paul to the Corinthians

Brothers and sisters:
Do **you not** know that **you** are the **temple** of **God**,
    and that the **Spirit of God** dwells in **you**?
If anyone destroys God's temple, God will **destroy** that **person**;
    for the temple of God, which **you** are, is holy.

Let **no one deceive** himself.
If any one among you considers himself wise in this age,
    let him become a fool, so as to become wise.
For the wisdom of this world is foolishness in the **eyes** of God,
    for it is written:
        God *catches the wise in their own* **ruses**,
    and again:
        The Lord **knows** *the thoughts of the wise,*
            that they are vain.
So let **no one boast** about human beings, for everything **belongs**
        to **you**,
    Paul or Apollos or Cephas,
    or the **world** or **life** or **death**,
    or the **present** or the **future**:
    all belong to you, and you to Christ, and **Christ to** God.

Corinthians = kohr-IN-thee-uhns

Pause after the greeting.
Proclaim slowly with good volume.

Emphasize the words in bold.

Pause.
St. Paul's words are strong. Be firm in your reading.

Pause.

Keep up your energy. Articulate your words.

Apollos = uh-POL-uhs
Cephas = SEE-fuhs

Pause before you say this line. Smile as you conclude.

READING II "Temple of God" is the third image Paul uses to promote unity in the fractured Corinthian community. First he told them they are the field belonging to God, suggesting the many seeds, grains, and plantings needed for a rich harvest. Next, they are God's building, where each member builds on the foundation laid by Paul. In today's reading, they are a particular building: God's temple.

The Jerusalem temple, a structure made of inanimate stones, is the dwelling place of God; Paul tells the Corinthians to see themselves as a living temple in Corinth. God's own Spirit has made a home within them, enlivening, empowering, and uniting the divided community. Similar to the Jerusalem temple as a holy place, the Corinthian temple is a holy people, set apart as God's dwelling place. Paul's warning about destroying the temple likely refers to damage or corruption of the structure. Those who corrupt the temple by false behaviors and beliefs will be brought to ruin themselves.

The next topic, wisdom, seems at first to be unrelated to the temple image. Yet those who consider themselves wise in this age and rely on the wisdom of this world are the ones who are destroying the temple. As he often does in his letters, Paul supports his argument here by using Scripture. He links two texts (Job 5:13 and Psalm 94:11), associated by their common reference to "the wise." Together, they tell of the futility of human wisdom, judged as vain and deceptive by God. Those who boast about belonging to Paul or Apollos or Cephas are tangible examples of accepting the wisdom of this age. These leaders belong to the community, and all of them belong to Christ, who belongs to God.

GOSPEL   Matthew 5:38–48

A reading from the holy Gospel according to Matthew

Jesus said to his disciples:
"You have **heard** that it was said,
An eye for an eye and a tooth for a tooth.
But I say to you, offer no resistance to **one** who is **evil**.
When someone strikes you on your right **cheek**,
    turn the other one as well.
If anyone wants to go to law with you over your **tunic**,
    hand over your **cloak** as well.
Should anyone **press** you into service for **one** mile,
    go for two **miles**.
Give to the one who **asks** of you,
    and do **not** turn your back on one who **wants** to **borrow**.

"You have heard that it was said,
You shall love your neighbor and hate your enemy.
But I say to you, love your enemies
    and pray for those who **persecute** you,
    that you may be children of your heavenly Father,
    for he makes his sun **rise** on the **bad and** the **good**,
    and causes rain to fall on the **just and** the **unjust**.
For if you **love** those who **love you**, what recompense will
        you have?
Do **not** the **tax collectors** do the same?
And if you **greet** your brothers only,
    what is unusual about that?
Do not the pagans do the same?
So be perfect, just as your heavenly **Father** is perfect."

Proclaim with authority.

Pause.
A call to act in a different way. Proclaim in a tone of clear purpose. Take your time.

Increase your volume. Be direct with your assembly. Articulate your words.

Smile as you conclude the reading.

GOSPEL In Jesus' day, the laws and religious traditions of Judaism were subject to widely diverse interpretations. Not only was there controversy between Pharisees and Sadducees, but also among Pharisees themselves. For example, the followers of the teachings of two wise men, Hillel and Shammai (who was stricter in his teachings), differed on matters of ethics and how Jews should relate to their Roman oppressors. As Jesus continues his Sermon on the Mount, he joins in the conversation by offering his own interpretation on how to live faithfully to God.

The taking of an eye for an eye (Exodus 21:24), as harsh as it sounds, was an advance over the practice of sevenfold vengeance. Jesus' teaching goes far beyond "getting even"; there is to be no retaliation at all. Rather, respond to insults with nonviolence; when paying debts, give back more than required; when pressed into service, like that demanded by Roman soldiers, go twice as far. In each case, Jesus' disciples are to do more than what is asked for or required.

Jesus' teaching on love of neighbor is another new interpretation of the law. Today's reading from Leviticus commanded Israelites to love their fellow Israelites. Such a law brought about stability and harmony in the community. But the God of creation acts for the benefit of everyone. Similarly, like the sun and rain that God provides equally for the good and the bad, Jesus' disciples are to show love equally for enemies and neighbors. In acting toward others as their heavenly Father acts, they will become perfect (*teleios*), attaining completeness, by acting toward others as their heavenly Father does. E.P.

ASH WEDNESDAY

LECTIONARY #219

READING I   Joel 2:12–18

A reading from the Book of the Prophet Joel

Even now, says the LORD,
 return to me with your **whole** heart,
 with **fasting**, and **weeping**, and **mourning**;
Rend your **hearts**, **not** your garments,
 and return to the LORD, your **God**.
For gracious and merciful is he,
 slow to anger, rich in kindness,
 and relenting in punishment.
Perhaps he will again relent
 and leave behind him a blessing,
Offerings and libations
 for the LORD, **your** God.

Blow the **trumpet** in **Zion**!
 proclaim a **fast**,
 call an assembly;
Gather the people,
 notify the congregation;
Assemble the elders,
 gather the children
 and the **infants** at the breast;
Let the **bridegroom** quit his room
 and the **bride** her chamber.

Joel = JOH-*l

The Lord loves us and wants us back. Proclaim with tenderness.

Our God is a good God. Let us hear kindness as you describe him. Use strong eye contact.

Zion = ZĪ-uhn or ZĪ-ahn

The stakes are high. Put more intensity and energy in your voice.

READING I Joel addresses the entire community in his prophetic call to repentance. The prophecy begins with the Lord saying to the people, "Return to me with your whole heart." The whole heart refers not only to the entire heart of each individual, but even more to the heart of the people as a whole. Israel's heart is the living, beating center of the people, their emotions, their thinking and choosing, their collective sin. Returning to the Lord with their whole heart means a complete transformation of their lives.

After the Lord's opening plea, the prophet expands on the call to repentance, and simultaneously reminds the people of the Lord's identity. The people of Israel know the visible signs of repentance, since they were commonly practiced. Their external acts such as fasting, mourning, weeping, and rending of garments are symbolic of their interior contrition. But externals are not enough. When people rend their hearts, they are turning their emotions, thoughts, and actions toward the generous and merciful God who long ago had spoken to Moses. In fact, Joel's description of God echoes that

of Moses, as both patriarch and prophet reveal that the God of the covenant is slow to anger, rich in kindness, and turns away from punishment. In a twofold movement that reestablishes the covenant relationship, the people turn away from sin, and the merciful God turns away from punishing them.

A few verses before today's reading, Joel had commanded, "Blow the trumpet in Zion," telling the sentinels on the wall to raise the alarm for war. The ram's horn would announce God's punishment on the sinful people. Now Joel issues the same command, "Blow the trumpet in Zion," this

Pause before you proclaim "Spare, O LORD," and use good volume.

Between the **porch** and the **altar**
  let the **priests**, the **ministers** of the LORD, weep,
And say, "Spare, **O** LORD, your people,
  and make not your heritage a reproach,
  with the nations **ruling** over them!
Why should they say among the peoples,
  '**Where** is their **God**?' "

Use a gentler tone.

Then the LORD was stirred to **concern** for his land
  and took pity on his people.

For meditation and context:

RESPONSORIAL PSALM   Psalm 51:3–4, 5–6ab, 12–13, 14 and 17 (3a)

R. Be merciful, O Lord, for we have sinned.

Have mercy on me, O God, in your goodness;
  in the greatness of your compassion wipe
    out my offense.
Thoroughly wash me from my guilt
  and of my sin cleanse me.

For I acknowledge my offense,
  and my sin is before me always:
"Against you only have I sinned,
  and done what is evil in your sight."

A clean heart create for me, O God,
  and a steadfast spirit renew within me.
Cast me not out from your presence,
  and your Holy Spirit take not from me.

Give me back the joy of your salvation,
  and a willing spirit sustain in me.
O Lord, open my lips,
  and my mouth shall proclaim your praise.

READING II   2 Corinthians 5:20—6:2

Corinthians = kohr-IN-thee-uhnz

A reading from the second Letter of Saint Paul to the Corinthians

Brothers and sisters:

Proclaim with authority.

We are ambassadors for **Christ**,
  as if God were appealing through us.

Make your voice stronger on these lines.

We implore you on behalf of **Christ**,
  be reconciled to **God**.
For **our** sake he made him to **be sin** who did **not** know sin,
  so that **we** might become the righteousness of God **in** him. »

---

time for the people to announce their repentance. The communal nature of their repentance means the participation of everyone: elders and children, bride and bridegroom, priests and assembly. Together they chant, "Spare, O Lord, your people." Because God's compassion is greater than the people's sin, the Lord takes pity on them, transforming their repentant heart. True to the divine nature, the Lord acts with graciousness and mercy.

READING II   "Paul, an apostle of Christ Jesus by the will of God,

and Timothy our brother." In these opening words of Paul's second letter to the Corinthians, he presents himself and his coworker Timothy as apostles of Christ Jesus. In today's reading, he adds a complementary designation: ambassador of Christ. Apostles and ambassadors act with authority and as representatives of the one who sent them, Christ himself. Commissioned by God, they speak in Christ's name (2:13), the mercy of God sustains their ministry (4:1), and they are impelled by the love of Christ (5:14).

Their ministry as ambassadors acting in and for Christ is to continue Christ's own mission of reconciling the world to himself. Used in the military sphere, the term *reconciliation* implies that the fighting between armies and nations has ended with the possibility of a new positive relationship. Reconciliation in Christ likewise brings about an end to divisions and fractured relationships. Yet reconciliation in Christ is far greater than that seen in a military or political context. There, reconciliation can stop wars or conflict, but doesn't imply transformation of the enemies' hearts, and

Use good eye contact.

Working together, then,
　　we appeal to you not to receive the grace of God in vain.
For he **says**:

> *In an acceptable time I heard you,*
> 　*and on the day of salvation **I** helped you.*

Proclaim with urgency in your tone.

Behold, now is a very acceptable time;
　　behold, now is the day of **salvation**.

GOSPEL　Matthew 6:1–6, 16–18

A reading from the holy Gospel according to Matthew

Jesus said to his **disciples**:

Jesus is telling us how to act. Take your time and articulate the words in bold.

　　"Take **care not** to perform righteous deeds
　　in order that people may **see** them;
　　otherwise, you will have **no** recompense from your
　　　　heavenly **Father**.
When you **give alms**,
　　do **not blow** a **trumpet before** you,
　　as the hypocrites do in the synagogues and in the streets
　　to win the praise of **others**.
Amen, **I** say to you,
　　they have received their reward.
But when you give alms,
　　do **not** let your left hand know what your right is doing,
　　so that **your** almsgiving may be secret.
And your Father who sees in secret will repay you.

This is how we are to pray. Do not rush your words. Use strong volume.

"When you **pray**,
　　do **not** be like the hypocrites,
　　who love to stand and **pray** in the synagogues and on street
　　　　corners
　　so that others may **see** them.

---

wars often break out again. By reconciliation in Christ, the people become a new creation, and the old things have passed away (5:17). With their sins forgiven, reconciled people now have a renewed, transformed relationship with God and with one another.

　　How is such reconciliation accomplished? One verse provides at least a partial answer to this question. God "made him to be sin who did not know sin so that we might become the righteousness of God in him." Christ, fully human and sinless himself, has taken the place of sinful humanity. His death on the cross is a sacrificial act

that reconciles, transforms, and restores the fractured relationship between God and humanity. This past deed has present implications. The saving death of Christ is "so that we might become the righteousness of God," with each believer continuing Christ's ministry of reconciliation, living in and empowered by the grace of God.

GOSPEL　Today's Gospel is taken from the central section of Jesus' Sermon on the Mount, the first of his five sermons in Matthew's Gospel. From the mountain, Jesus presents his authorita-

tive interpretation of the law he came to fulfill, and explains how his disciples are to live in light of his teaching. In this part of the sermon, he instructs them about the Jewish practices of almsgiving, prayer, and fasting, and warns against performing them in order to gain human honor and reward.

　　The first deed Jesus describes is giving alms to those in need, as commanded in the Torah and reinforced by the prophets and sages: "Happy those who are kind to the poor" (Proverbs 15:21). While almsgiving is clearly commendable, those who "blow the trumpet," whether literally or

Amen, **I** say to you,
> they have received their reward.
But when you pray, **go** to your inner room,
> **close** the door, and **pray** to your **Father** in secret.
And your Father who sees in secret will repay **you**.

"When you fast,
> do **not look gloomy** like the **hypocrites**.
They **neglect** their appearance,
> so that they may **appear** to **others** to be **fasting**.
Amen, **I** say to you, they have received their reward.
But when you fast,
> anoint your head and wash your face,
> so that you may not **appear** to be fasting,
> **except** to your **Father** who is hidden.
And **your** Father who sees what is hidden will repay you."

Pause before "But when you fast." Speak with authority.

figuratively, when they give alms do so in order to earn human praise. Jesus calls them hypocrites, depicting them as actors who perform for the public, wearing a mask of righteousness. They put on a show rather than giving in secret where only God observes and rewards them.

Next, Jesus designates as hypocrites those who make prayer a performance for their own benefit. They love public places where they can parade their prayer "so that others may see them." Jesus' further teaching on prayer, omitted from the lectionary, explains for his disciples how they should pray, not like the pagans or the hypocrites, but as he teaches them: "This is how you are to pray: Our Father . . . " The third group of hypocrites are those who ostentatiously display signs of their fasting for all to see. Instead of looking gloomy and unkempt, those who fast should anoint their heads and wash their faces, so people will not suspect they are fasting.

Jesus' warnings and criticisms are not aimed at the acts of almsgiving, prayer, and fasting, since they are important dimensions of Israel's law and practice. A shared commitment to give to those in need, to pray together, and to participate in the community acts of repentance enhance the faith of the people and express their common fidelity to God. In that context, Jesus' repetition of the words "secret" and "hidden" emphasize the interior disposition and motive that should underlie eternal acts. E.P.

FIRST SUNDAY OF LENT

LECTIONARY #22

READING I Genesis 2:7–9; 3:1–7

A reading from the Book of Genesis

The LORD GOD formed man out of the clay of the ground
  and blew into his nostrils the breath of life,
  and so man became a living being.

Then the LORD God **planted** a garden in Eden, in the east,
  and placed **there** the man whom he had formed.
Out of the ground the LORD GOD made various **trees grow**
  that were delightful to look at and **good** for **food**,
  with the tree of life in the middle of the garden
  and the tree of the knowledge of good **and** evil.

Now the serpent was the most cunning of all the animals
  that the LORD GOD had **made**.
The **serpent** asked the **woman**,
  "Did **GOD** really tell you **not** to eat
  from any of the trees in the garden?"
The **woman** answered the serpent:
  "We may eat of the fruit of the trees in the garden;
  it is **only** about the fruit of the tree
  in the middle of the garden that **GOD** said,
  'You shall **not eat** it or even touch **it**, lest you die.'"
But the **serpent** said to the woman:
  "You **certainly** will not **die**!
No, **God** knows **well** that the moment you **eat** of it

Genesis = JEN-uh-sihs

Begin with a tone of awe and wonder. Do not rush this reading. Take your time.

Eden = EE-d*n

Pause before you begin the words of the serpent and the woman. You must use facial expression and vocal variety as you proclaim the story.

READING I The book of Genesis, as its name implies, is about origins. It begins with a poetic description of the origin of time and space brought about by God's Word. On the sixth day, God creates humanity in the divine image and gives them responsibility over the land and beasts. After this poetic account of the earth's origin in which everything is good, the next chapters are a narrative account of the origin of sin. The goodness of creation has become disordered.

Our reading today begins with Genesis' second view of human origins. First described as made in the divine image, the human being is now described in more earthy terms. God forms the man (*'adam*) out of clay of the ground (*'adamah*), and breathes life into him. From the same ground from which *'adam* is formed, God makes various trees grow, with special mention given to the tree of life and the tree of the knowledge of good and evil. The lectionary omits God's command to *'adam*, in which the Lord tells him he can eat from any tree of the garden except from the tree of knowledge. "The moment you eat from it you are surely doomed to die." Another

omission from the lectionary is the creation of woman. Since it is not good for *'adam* to be alone, God creates one who is a fitting helper for him. She is called Eve, her name derived from the word for "life," because she is mother of all the living (3:20).

With the man and woman placed in the garden, another character, the serpent, enters the story that unfolds the origin of sin. The cunning serpent uses a shrewd question and deceitful answers to tempt the woman. Though the word "sin" does not appear in the story, we can see a common experience of the movement from tempta-

your eyes will be opened and you will be like gods
who know what is **good** and what is **evil**."
The woman saw that the tree was good for **food**,
pleasing to the eyes, and desirable for gaining wisdom.
So she **took** some of its fruit and ate it;
and she **also** gave some to her **husband**, who was **with** her,
and **he ate** it.
Then the **eyes** of both of them were opened,
and they **realized** that they were **naked**;
so they sewed fig leaves together
and **made loincloths** for themselves.

Pause before you say this last paragraph. Emphasize the words in bold.

For meditation and context:

RESPONSORIAL PSALM   Psalm 51:3–4, 5–6, 12–13, 17 (3a)

R. Be merciful, O Lord, for we have sinned.

Have mercy on me, O God, in your goodness;
in the greatness of your compassion wipe
out my offense.
Thoroughly wash me from my guilt
and of my sin cleanse me.

For I acknowledge my offense,
and my sin is before me always:
"Against you only have I sinned,
and done what is evil in your sight."

A clean heart create for me, O God,
and a steadfast spirit renew within me.
Cast me not out from your presence,
and your Holy Spirit take not from me.

Give me back the joy of your salvation,
and a willing spirit sustain in me.
O Lord, open my lips,
and my mouth shall proclaim your praise.

READING II   Romans 5:12–19

A reading from the Letter of Saint Paul to the Romans

[Brothers and sisters:
Through **one** man sin entered the world,
and through sin, death,
and thus death came to all men, inasmuch as **all** sinned]—
for **up** to the time of the law, **sin** was in the world,
though sin is **not** accounted when there is **no** law. »

You are setting the stage for the one who is to come, the one who will take us from sin and death to life. Speak with authority.

tion, to sin, to consequences, and the underlying rationalization and motivations.

The temptation begins with the serpent suggesting how unreasonable God must be to deny the fruits of all the trees. The woman's response, as often happens when temptations are dangled, is not entirely truthful. She claims that God has forbidden even touching the tree, or face death. The serpent now has an opening to further temptation, suggesting that God does not want humanity to be like gods; God is unfair! For the woman, the food of the tree now looks good, pleasing, and

desirable, illustrating how attractive sin can be to both the mind and the senses. When 'adam also eats of the forbidden fruit, their eyes are opened; they have indeed gained knowledge of good and evil. Recognizing their nakedness, feeling shame and vulnerability, they clothe themselves, beginning to hide even from God.

The engaging details of the story, rich in iMagination and symbolism, invite audiences to reflect on their relationship with God, and how the loving bond can be strained or even broken. Yet even with the consequences of the couple's disobedience

and hubris, the loving, forgiving God will remain ever present as the story continues.

READING II Throughout the reading from Romans, Paul writes as a Jew who knows the tradition well, including the account of Adam and Eve in today's first reading. He employs several methods of argumentation, using strategies employed in Judaism as well as those of Greek rhetoric. Paul presumes that his audience knows both the story of Adam's sin and that of Christ's saving death on the cross. In the verses just before today's

St. Paul is a teacher in this letter. You are teaching and proclaiming about "the gift" we have been given through Jesus Christ. Read with clarity. Articulate your words.

Pause before you conclude.

But **death reigned** from Adam **to** Moses,
    even **over** those who did not sin
    after the pattern of the **trespass** of Adam,
    who is the type of the **one** who **was** to come.

But the gift is **not** like the transgression.
For **if** by the transgression of the one, the **many died**,
    how much more did the grace of God
    and the **gracious** gift of the **one** man **Jesus** Christ
    overflow for the many.
And the gift is **not** like the result of the **one** who **sinned**.
For after one sin there was the judgment that **brought**
        condemnation;
    but the gift, after many transgressions, brought acquittal.
[For **if**, by the transgression of the one,
    death came to **reign** through that **one**,
    how much more will those who receive the **abundance**
        of **grace**
    and of the **gift** of justification
    come to reign **in life** through the **one Jesus** Christ.
In conclusion, just as through **one transgression**
    condemnation came upon all,
    so, through **one righteous** act,
    acquittal and life came to all.
For just as through the disobedience of the **one** man
    the **many** were made **sinners**,
    so, through the obedience of the **one**,
    the **many** will be made righteous.]

[Shorter: Romans 5:12, 17–19 (see brackets)]

reading, he wrote about the effects of Christ's death: justification, peace, access to grace. He continues to unfold the meaning of this extraordinary manifestation of God's love even for sinners.

Paul refers to Adam as "a type of the one who was to come." In biblical interpretation, a "type" is a person, event, or object that precedes or foreshadows a later one, resembling the later figure in some way. The type is both alike and unlike the one that follows, and the later figure is always greater than the initial type. (For example, the sacrificial lamb at Passover is a type of

Christ, the sacrificial lamb on the cross, who is far greater than the original.) Adam is a type of Christ because his transgression had a far-reaching effect on the human race, resulting in death, while Christ's death on the cross had an even greater effect on the human race, bringing the gift of life. They are alike in that both Adam and Christ are in solidarity with humanity. Yet Paul develops the unlikeness between Adam and Christ much more than their likeness.

In a sustained comparison, Paul presents Adam as the type, and Christ as the one who is greater in every way. On Adam's

side are sin, transgression, disobedience, judgment, condemnation, and death. The death resulting from Adam's sin is so powerful and pervasive that Paul personifies it; death "reigned," acting as a tyrant over humanity, even over those who did not sin.

On Christ's side, the repetition of "how much more," along with the words "abundance" and "overflow," make it clear that Christ is greater than the ancient type, Adam. Christ, obedient and righteous, brings grace, justification, acquittal, and life. Paul uses the word "gift" over and over, sometimes to refer to a specific effect of the

GOSPEL   Matthew 4:1–11

A reading from the holy Gospel according to Matthew

At that time Jesus **was led** by the Spirit into the desert
    to be tempted by the devil.
He fasted for **forty** days and **forty** nights,
    and afterwards he was hungry.
The **tempter approached** and said to him,
    "**If you are** the **Son** of **God**,
    command that these **stones** become loaves of **bread**."
He said in reply,
    "It is written:
    One does **not live** on bread **alone**,
        but on **every word** that comes forth
        from the **mouth of God**."

Then the devil took him to the **holy city**,
    and **made** him stand on the **parapet** of the temple,
    and said to him, "If **you** are the Son of God, throw
        yourself down.
For it is written:
    He will command his **angels** concerning you
        and with their **hands** they will **support** you,
    lest you **dash** your **foot** against a **stone**."
Jesus answered him,
    "Again it is **written**,
    You shall not put the Lord, your God, to the **test**." »

Use an informative tone as you proclaim the tempting of Jesus in the desert.

Speak with more intensity as you say the tempter's words.

Pause before you begin. Remember to build the intensity each time the devil tempts Jesus.

parapet = PAYR-uh-puht

Christ-event (such as justification), and also to refer to Christ himself. Christ is the gift of God whose saving grace overflows to all. Christ transforms the universality of sin and death resulting from Adam's transgression to the abundance of life and grace for all.

GOSPEL Matthew's Gospel, written for an audience of Jews who believed in Jesus as their messiah, shows how Jesus fulfills their prophecies and hopes. In solidarity with the Jewish people, Jesus' story continues the story of his ancestors. Also in solidarity with the human race, Jesus "has similarly been tested in every way, yet without sin" (Hebrews 4:15); he undergoes the full range of human experiences. In today's Gospel, we see him both as fully human and fully Jewish in his threefold temptations.

The account of Israel's forty years in the desert, particularly in chapters 6 through 8 of Deuteronomy, is the background for Jesus' forty days in the desert. In the wilderness, God had tested Israel to determine if they would keep God's commandments (Deuteronomy 8:2), a test that they repeatedly failed. God had made a covenant with them, establishing such an intimate relationship that the nation itself was called God's son (e.g., Exodus 4:22). The devil's taunt to Jesus, "If you are God's Son," unites him with the people of Israel in their identity as God's son. In the context of Matthew's Gospel, Jesus' title "Son of God" takes on an added meaning of Jesus in a unique filial relationship with God his Father.

The agent of Jesus' testing is the devil, also called the "tempter" and "Satan." In the first test, the devil uses Jesus' hunger as a way of ensnaring him. Because God had fed Israel with manna in the desert, the

Keep up your energy and volume.

Jesus is angry. Let the congregation hear that.

Pause before you say the last line.

> TO KEEP IN MIND
> Making eye contact with the assembly connects you with them and connects them to the reading more deeply than using your voice alone. This helps the assembly stay with the story and keeps them engaged.

Then the devil took him up to a very **high** mountain,
    and showed him all the kingdoms of the world in their
        magnificence,
    and he said to him, "All these I shall give to you,
    if you will **prostrate** yourself and **worship** me."
At this, Jesus said to him,
    "Get away, Satan!
It is written:
    The Lord, your *God,* ***shall you worship***
        and him *alone* ***shall you*** *serve."*

Then the devil **left** him and, **behold**,
    angels came and ministered to him.

tempter challenges Jesus to provide bread for himself, thereby taking on God's own power. Satan is, in effect, testing Jesus' trust that God will provide for him. Jesus' response is taken from Deuteronomy 8:3. The reason for God feeding the people with manna was so that they would understand that the real source of life and nourishment is God's Word.

Unsuccessful in the first temptation, the devil takes Jesus to the temple, again prefacing his challenge with "If you are the Son of God." This time, the devil cites Scripture (Psalm 91), misusing the life-giv-

ing word Jesus had just affirmed. If Jesus were to give in to the temptation to throw himself down, he would be putting God to the test, as Israel had done in the wilderness (Deuteronomy 6:16).

The place of the third temptation is a high mountain where Jesus could see the magnificent kingdoms of the world. To gain power over all these kingdoms, Jesus would prostrate himself and worship the devil, as the Magi had earlier done to Jesus. Only God is worthy of worship, another faith statement taken from Deuteronomy (6:13). Always faithful to his Father, Jesus

will proclaim his power from a mountaintop only after his death and Resurrection: "All power in heaven and on earth has been given to me" (28:18). E.P.

SECOND SUNDAY OF LENT

LECTIONARY #25

Genesis = JEN-uh-sihs

READING I   Genesis 12:1–4a

A reading from the Book of Genesis

Abram = AY-br*m
Speak with authority.

The Lord said to **Abram**:
   "Go forth from the land of your **kinsfolk**
   and **from** your **father's** house to a land that **I** will **show you**.

Proclaim with a smile. This is wonderful news!

   "**I** will make of **you** a great nation,
      and I will bless **you**;
   I will make your **name** great,
      so that you will be a blessing.
   I will **bless** those who bless **you**
      and curse those who curse **you**.
   All the communities of the earth
      shall find **blessing in you**."

Pause before you say this last line.

Abram went as the Lord **directed him**.

TO KEEP IN MIND
Repetition of the same word or phrase over the course of a reading emphasizes a point. Make each instance distinct, and build your intensity with each repetition.

READING I The saga of Abram (whose name is changed to Abraham at Genesis 17) begins with the Lord's command and promises, followed by Abram's unquestioning obedience. Genesis tells his story in thirteen chapters in which his faith in God and the divine promises are tested over and over. Though Abram is the main human character in the story, it is God who takes the initiative, makes promises, acts decisively, and is always faithful.

Prior to the story of Abram's call, Genesis tells the story of widespread disobedience and its consequences. Because of repeated sin, God had pronounced curses (3:14, 17; 4:11; 9:25), maledictions that carried harsh effects of loss and alienation. The opposite of a curse is a blessing, by which God imparts goodness, strength, and grace. Using the term "blessed" or "blessing" five times in the scene we read today, God announces a new bestowal of divine favor, a new stage in divine/human relationship.

To receive God's blessing, Abram must go forth from his land and from all that is familiar, prosperous, and secure, without knowing where God will lead him. Along with this life-changing command, God makes seemingly impossible promises to the seventy-five-year-old Abram, who had no heir. More than assuring a single heir, God promises to make of Abram a great nation, later telling him that his descendants will be as countless as the stars of the sky (Genesis 22:17). Abram's belief in God's promise of blessing and his obedience even in the face of uniMaginable testing present him as a model of faith. Receiving blessing not only for himself, Abram becomes a source of blessing to others.

RESPONSORIAL PSALM   Psalm 33:4–5, 18–19, 20, 22 (22)

R. Lord, let your mercy be on us, as we place our trust in you.

Upright is the word of the LORD,
   and all his works are trustworthy.
He loves justice and right;
   of the kindness of the LORD the earth
      is full.

See, the eyes of the LORD are upon those
      who fear him,
   upon those who hope for his kindness,
to deliver them from death
   and preserve them in spite of famine.

Our soul waits for the LORD,
   who is our help and our shield.
May your kindness, O LORD, be upon us
   who have put our hope in you.

READING II   2 Timothy 1:8b–10

A reading from the second Letter of Saint Paul to Timothy

Beloved:
Bear your share of **hardship** for the **gospel**
   with the strength that comes from God.

He saved us and called us to a **holy** life,
   not according to our **works**
   but according to his own **design**
   and the grace bestowed on **us** in **Christ Jesus before** time began,
   but now made **manifest**
   through the appearance of our savior Christ Jesus,
   who destroyed death and brought life and immortality
   to light through the gospel.

Sound strong as you proclaim. Be clear with good volume.

This letter from St. Paul is all good news! Pay attention to the words in bold and use facial expression. Be gentle in tone.

READING II The letters to Timothy and Titus offer guidance to Church leaders as well as to their communities. These letters present a picture of Church belief, behaviors, relationships, and structure in the late first century. In the greeting, Paul addresses Timothy as "my dear child," a designation used by a rabbi of Paul's day to a disciple. Like a rabbi, Paul is a father to Timothy because he was a teacher and guide to his younger disciple.

Paul himself had endured suffering for the Gospel, and his "dear child" Timothy must share in such hardships. Though suf-fering is expected, Paul assures Timothy that God provides the strength to live in fidelity to the Gospel. After the exhortation to Timothy, Paul moves to a poetic procla-mation for the whole community. Similar to other New Testament hymns, Paul's hymn reveals God's saving actions and the grace bestowed "on us" in Christ. The first two divine actions, "save" and "call," focus on God's power and purpose. God has saved us from sin so that we can live a holy life. This is accomplished according to God's own design and manifests God's grace bestowed on us in Christ. Christ our savior has appeared to us at his Incarnation, and we anticipate his future appearance to us when he comes again in glory.

The mystery of God's abundant grace extends through every age: the past, "before time began"; the present, "now"; and into the future, with the promise of "life and immortality." The Gospel, accord-ing to Paul, is more than words, but is the active and effective graciousness of God.

GOSPEL A theophany is a mysteri-ous, divine appearance that includes a revelation, such as that

GOSPEL   Matthew 17:1–9

A reading from the holy Gospel according to Matthew

Jesus took Peter, James, and **John** his brother,
   and **led them** up a **high mountain** by themselves.
And he was transfigured before them;
   his face shone like the **sun**
   and his clothes became white as light.
And **behold**, Moses and Elijah appeared to them,
   conversing with him.
Then **Peter** said to Jesus in reply,
   "Lord, it is good that we are **here**.
If you wish, I will make three **tents** here,
   one for you, one for Moses, and one for Elijah."
While he was still **speaking**, **behold**,
   a bright cloud **cast** a **shadow** over them,
   then from the cloud came a **voice** that said,
   "**This** is my beloved **Son**, with whom I am well pleased;
   listen to him."
When the disciples **heard** this, they fell prostrate
   and were **very** much afraid.
But Jesus came and **touched** them, saying,
   "**Rise**, and **do not** be **afraid**."
And when the disciples **raised** their **eyes**,
   they saw no one **else** but **Jesus** alone.

As they were coming **down** from the mountain,
   Jesus **charged** them,
   "**Do not** tell the vision to **anyone**
   until the **Son of Man** has been raised from the dead."

Proclaim with authority and with clarity. Use good eye contact as you read to your assembly about the Transfiguration.

Moses = MOH-ziz; MOH-zi
Elijah = ee-LĪ-juh

Pause before God speaks.

Pause for emphasis.

Be firm when you proclaim the words of Jesus.

---

given to Moses at the burning bush (Exodus 3:2–6). The scene in today's Gospel of Jesus with his three disciples on a mountaintop is a theophany that reveals Jesus' hidden identity, both through his transfigured appearance and through God's Word to the disciples. As in other passages in Matthew's Gospel, this scene shows continuity with the Jewish tradition, important for Matthew's audience of Christian Jews. Moses and Elijah, representative of the law and prophets, are signs of continuity. Both of them had ascended a mountain and wit-

nessed a theophany in which God spoke to them (Exodus 24:12–18; 1 Kings 19:8–18).

In addition to continuity, Matthew highlights the extraordinary newness evident in Jesus. When he ascends a mountain, Jesus himself radiates a divine presence that his disciples witness. A voice from the cloud utters the same message to them as heard at Jesus' baptism: he is God's beloved Son to whom his disciples must listen. Shortly before his transfiguration, Jesus had told them about his coming passion and death, a teaching that they neither understood nor accepted. Now they must

listen to Jesus' teaching, just as Moses and Elijah had listened to the voice of God. Jesus then tells them they must leave the shining glory of the mountain and continue the journey that will take them to Jerusalem and all that he had foretold. E.P.

THIRD SUNDAY
OF LENT

LECTIONARY #28

READING I   Exodus 17:3–7

A reading from the Book of Exodus

Exodus = EK-suh-duhs
Moses = MOH-zis

The people are complaining. Let the assembly hear complaining in your voice.

In **those** days, in their thirst for water,
    the people grumbled against **Moses**,
    saying, "**Why** did you **ever** make us **leave** Egypt?
Was it just to have us die here of thirst
    with **our** children and **our** livestock?"
So Moses cried **out** to the LORD,

Moses is frustrated. Sound more intense when you are saying "What shall I do . . . ?"

    "What shall I do with this people?
A little more and they will stone me!"
The LORD **answered** Moses,

Pause before the Lord's answer. Proclaim his words in an informative tone.

    "**Go** over there in front of the people,
    along with some of the elders of Israel,
    holding in your hand, as you go,
    the staff with which you **struck** the **river**.

Horeb = HOHR-eb

I will be standing there in **front** of you on the **rock** in **Horeb**.
Strike the rock, and the **water** will **flow** from it
    for the people to **drink**."
This Moses did, in the presence of the elders of Israel.
The place was called Massah and Meribah,

Massah = MAS-uh
Meribah = MAYR-ih-bah

    because the Israelites quarreled there
    and tested the LORD, saying,
    "Is the LORD in our **midst** or not?"

READING I Grumbling, questioning, quarreling, and testing the Lord—Israel's repeated complaining against Moses is actually a lack of trust, indicative of their rebellion against God. They doubted God and Moses, even though Israel had already experienced God coming to their rescue by freeing them from Egypt, opening a dry passage through the sea, and feeding them with manna in the wilderness. Throughout their journey, Moses has been their leader and mediator; now he is the target of their complaint. Psalm 106 paints a memorable picture of this people:

"They did not believe the promises; in their tents they complained" (verses 24–25).

The scene of Israel's grumbling begins with questions, the first two built on accusations against Moses, followed by Moses' own pleading question to God. The people's questions assign blame to Moses for bringing them into the desert, and even imply that his motive was to make them die of thirst. Moses' question to God expresses his own exasperation. The people's grumbling seems to have put Moses' faith to the test and even raised his fear that they might stone him. The series of questions is a liter-

ary means of drawing the biblical audience into the story by eliciting their own questions and reflecting on their answers.

Similar to other events in Israel's desert sojourn, this one recounts familiar human experiences that also have a symbolic meaning. Like physical hunger and thirst that is assuaged by food and water, so are spiritual and emotional hungers and thirsts assuaged by God's presence and attentiveness. Underlying the thirst for water, so scarce in the desert environs, is the people's thirst for God's saving presence.

For meditation and context:

RESPONSORIAL PSALM   Psalm 95:1–2, 6–7, 8–9 (8)

R. If today you hear his voice, harden not your hearts.

Come, let us sing joyfully to the LORD;
    let us acclaim the Rock of our salvation.
Let us come into his presence
        with thanksgiving;
    let us joyfully sing psalms to him.

Come, let us bow down in worship;
    let us kneel before the LORD who made us.
For he is our God,
    and we are the people he shepherds,
        the flock he guides.

Oh, that today you would hear his voice:
    "Harden not your hearts as at Meribah,
        as in the day of Massah in the desert,
    where your fathers tempted me;
        they tested me though they had seen
            my works."

READING II   Romans 5:1–2, 5–8

A reading from the Letter of Saint Paul to the Romans

Brothers and sisters:
Since we have been **justified** by **faith**,
    we have peace with **God** through our **Lord Jesus** Christ,
    through whom we have gained access by faith
    to this grace in which we **stand**,
    and we **boast** in hope of the **glory** of God.

And **hope** does **not** disappoint,
    because the **love** of God has been poured out into our **hearts**
        through the **Holy Spirit** who has been given to us.
For **Christ**, while we were still helpless,
    died at the appointed time for the ungodly.
Indeed, only with **difficulty** does one die for a just person,
    though perhaps for a good person one might even find **courage**
        to die.
But God **proves** his love **for us**
    in that while we were **still** sinners Christ died for us.

This wonderful letter from St. Paul gives us hope and proves God's love for us. Proclaim with firmness and clarity.

Use a gentler tone.

This last line is important. Pause before you proclaim it and say it slowly.

Rather than punishing the ungrateful and rebellious people, the Lord directs Moses to take some of the elders and set out for Mount Horeb (also called Sinai), the Mountain of God (3:1). The Lord promises to be standing in front of Moses at the rock in Horeb, subtly and symbolically fulfilling the people's unspoken thirst for God's presence. When Moses strikes with his authoritative staff, water will flow from it for the people to drink. Surprisingly, the place is named not for the wondrous water that flows from the rock, but for the people's persistent complaining. Massah means "the

place of testing," and Meribah is "the place of quarreling." Psalm 95, today's responsorial, uses the scene to remind later generations not to repeat their ancestors' testing and quarreling against the Lord.

The reading ends with yet another question: "Is the Lord in our midst or not?" Whether the question is asked by Moses or by the people, the answer, based on what the Lord has just done, must be "Yes! Amen!"

READING II   Paul is writing to Christians in Rome, "who believe in

the one who raised Jesus our Lord from the dead" (Romans 4:24). God's past action of raising Jesus from the dead has an ongoing effect in the present and gives believers hope of future sharing in God's glory. Throughout today's reading, Paul weaves together divine action and human benefit, past, present, and future.

Four references to God, three to Christ, and one to the Holy Spirit in these few verses contribute to Paul's proclamation of "the power of God for salvation" (Romans 1:15). Christ's death for us in the past is a manifestation of God's salvific

Samaria = suh-MAYR-ee-uh
Sychar = SĪ-kahr

You are proclaiming context for this Gospel. Use an informative tone with good volume.

Pause for emphasis before Jesus and the Samaritan woman speak.

Samaritan = suh-MAYR-uh-tuhn

A teaching moment for Jesus and the stakes are high. Make sure you take your time and articulate every syllable and word ending with good volume.

The woman is sincere and innocent in her questioning.

cistern = SIS-tern

GOSPEL   John 4:5–42

A reading from the holy Gospel according to John

[**Jesus** came to a town of Samaria **called Sychar**,
   near the plot of land that Jacob had **given** to his son **Joseph**.
Jacob's **well** was there.
Jesus, tired from his journey, **sat down** there at the **well**.
It was about **noon**.

A woman of Samaria came to draw **water**.
Jesus said to her,
   "Give me a **drink**."
His disciples had gone into the town to buy food.
The Samaritan woman said to him,
   "How can you, a **Jew**, **ask** me, a Samaritan **woman**, for a **drink**?"
—For Jews use **nothing** in common with Samaritans.—
Jesus answered and said to her,
   "If you **knew** the **gift of God**
   and who is saying to you, 'Give me a drink,'
   you would have **asked him**
   and he would have **given** you living **water**."
The woman said to him,
   "Sir, you do **not** even have a **bucket** and the cistern is **deep**;
   where then can you get this living water?
Are you greater than our **father** Jacob,
   who **gave** us this cistern and drank from it **himself**
   with his children and his flocks?"
Jesus **answered** and said to her,
   "Everyone who drinks **this** water will be thirsty **again**;
   but whoever drinks the water I shall give will never **thirst**;
   the water I shall give will become in him
   a **spring** of water **welling** up to **eternal** life."

power, which continues to be effective in the present. God also reveals saving power through the love that has been poured out on us through the Holy Spirit. Although Paul never uses the word "Trinity" to refer to God, his teaching about God is clearly that of God/Father, Son/Christ, and Holy Spirit, as seen in this passage. When he writes about Jesus *Christ*, Paul is implicitly referring to God as well, since *Christ*, in Hebrew *Messiah*, identifies Jesus as God's anointed one, through whom God fulfills the divine redemptive work.

Paul describes the state of humanity prior to Christ's death as helpless, ungodly, and unjust. But Christ's death has brought a transformation, first described as justification. To be justified in Pauline theology is to be brought into right relationship with God, a process that has already begun in the present, and will be brought to fullness in the future. The most complete understanding of justification includes right relationship not only with God, but also with one another. The believing community is to be characterized by living in relationships that reflect God's own generosity and

mercy toward them. Accompanying justification are other effects of God's saving action: peace with God, access to grace, and hope of God's glory.

Besides the triad of God, Christ, and Holy Spirit in this reading, Paul has another important triad: faith, hope, and love. These three virtues originate in, from, and through God. Paul says specifically that the love of God has been poured into our hearts. We can also say that faith and hope have been poured into our hearts, signs of God's powerful grace that flows from the past, into the present, and will be brought to fullness

The woman said to him,
  "Sir, give me this water, so that I may **not** be **thirsty**
  or have to **keep** coming here to draw water."]

Jesus said to her,
  "**Go call** your **husband** and come back."
The woman answered and said to him,
  "I do **not have** a husband."
Jesus answered her,
  "You are right in saying, 'I do not have a husband.'
For you have had five husbands,
  and the one you have **now** is **not** your husband.
What you have said is **true**."
The woman said to him,
  "Sir, [I can see that you are a prophet.
Our ancestors **worshiped** on this **mountain**;
  but **you** people say that the place to worship is in Jerusalem."
Jesus said to her,
  "**Believe me**, woman, the **hour** is coming
  when you will worship the Father
  neither on this **mountain nor** in **Jerusalem**.
You people worship what you do not understand;
  we worship what we **understand**,
  because salvation is from the **Jews**.
But the **hour** is coming, and is **now** here,
  when true worshipers will **worship** the **Father in** Spirit
    and truth;
  and indeed the Father seeks such people to worship him.
God is Spirit, and those who worship him
  must worship in Spirit **and** truth." »

Start with a tone of informing and build the intensity of Jesus' words.

in the future. Believers respond to the grace that God has given to them by living in fidelity to these God-given gifts.

GOSPEL   John the evangelist uses conversations, sometimes developed into lengthy dialogues between Jesus and another person, to reveal Jesus' identity gradually. Individuals often misinterpret what Jesus is saying, thereby offering Jesus the opportunity to correct them and lead them to a deeper insight. One of the reasons people so often misunderstand Jesus is because of the layers of meaning in what he says. Sometimes there is a symbolism underlying his words, and at other times the words themselves have more than one meaning. Another reason for misunderstanding Jesus is that his teaching often turns around cherished beliefs and behaviors, making a new belief difficult to accept. He crosses boundaries that shock both his disciples and his adversaries. Along with Jesus' words and actions, the narratives in which they are placed can also be filled with symbolism and multiple meanings. All of these features, so typical of the fourth Gospel, are found in today's reading.

John begins the story of Jesus and the Samaritan woman by noting that Jesus "had to pass through Samaria" (4:4). There is no geographical necessity of passing through Samaria. Jews could cross the Jordan to avoid going through Samaria, the territory of their centuries-long enemy. The necessity for Jesus seems rather to have a divine motivation. Jesus must move beyond the confines of Judaism, bringing his good news even to Samaritans.

The woman said to him,
  "I know that the Messiah is **coming**, the **one** called
    the **Christ**;
  when he **comes**, he will tell us **everything**."
Jesus said to her,
  "I **am** he, the one **speaking** with you."]

Say in a humble tone.

At that moment his disciples **returned**,
  and were amazed that he was talking with a woman,
  but still **no** one said, "**What** are you **looking** for?"
  or "**Why** are you **talking** with her?"
The woman **left** her water jar
  and went into the town and said to the people,
  "**Come see** a man who told me everything **I have done**.
Could he **possibly be** the **Christ**?"
They went out of the town and **came** to him.

Proclaim in an excited tone.

Meanwhile, the disciples urged him, "Rabbi, **eat**."
But he said to them,
  "I have **food** to eat of which you do **not know**."
So the disciples said to one another,
  "Could **someone** have brought him something to eat?"
Jesus said to them,
  "**My food** is to do the will of the one who **sent** me
  and to finish his work.

There is an urgency in Jesus' tone.

Do you not say, 'In four months the **harvest** will be here'?
I tell you, look up and **see** the fields ripe for the harvest.
The reaper is already receiving payment
  and gathering crops for **eternal** life,
  so that the **sower** and **reaper** can rejoice **together**.
For **here** the saying is verified that 'One **sows** and another **reaps**.'

Weary from his journey, Jesus sits by Jacob's well at the sixth hour, noon, when both heat and light are at their peak. It is a strange time for anyone to draw water from the well; this is ordinarily done in the coolness of morning or evening. Alone, a woman of Samaria comes to draw water. Jesus too is alone, since his disciples have gone to buy food. Jesus has crossed one boundary in entering Samaria; now he crosses another in asking the woman for a drink. Not only is he speaking alone with an unknown woman, Jews and Samaritans do not drink from a common cup. They use

nothing in common. Even in her isolation, the woman knows well the tradition and expresses her surprise and puzzlement.

Her question to Jesus opens the dialogue between them. Jesus moves the conversation from the tangible, earthly reality of water drawn from a well to unseen, heavenly realities: "gift of God" and "living water." The woman naturally does not understand; she presumes that "living water" refers to flowing water from a spring, not the still water of a cistern. Asking "Are you greater than our father Jacob?" sounds sarcastic, since Jacob was

the great patriarch revered both by Jews and Samaritans. Jesus tells her that those who drink from Jacob's well will indeed thirst again, but the water he will give will become a spring welling up to eternal life. The life (*zoe*) that Jesus promises is not ordinary human life, but God's own life, the "gift of God" that will quench the deepest thirst of humanity. The woman, however, still thinks of the water on a physical level. She has not rejected Jesus or his promises, but she has not understood.

Jesus' next words to her are an abrupt change of subject. We can hear the conver-

I **sent you** to reap what you have **not worked** for;
>   others have **done** the work,
>   and you are sharing the **fruits** of their work."

A change of tone. Speak with resolution and authority.

[**Many** of the **Samaritans** of that town began to believe in him]
>   **because** of the word of the woman who testified,
>   "**He** told me **everything** I have **done**."
[When the Samaritans **came** to him,
>   they **invited** him to **stay** with them;
>   and he stayed there two days.
Many more began to believe in him because of his **word**,
>   and they said to the woman,
>   "We **no** longer **believe** because of your word;
>   for we have heard for ourselves,
>   and we **know** that this is truly the **savior of the world**."]

[Shorter: John 4:5–15, 19b–26, 39a, 40–42 (see brackets)]

TO KEEP IN MIND
Use inflection (the high or low pitch of your voice) to convey attitude and feeling. High pitch expresses intensity and excitement; low pitch expresses sadness, contrition, or solemnity.

---

sation about the Samaritan woman's husbands in two ways, one literal and one symbolic: her own multiple marriages and a symbol for Samaria's acceptance of multiple gods. Samaritan idolatry with the gods of other nations is comparable to marital infidelity. From the second perspective, the woman stands for the Samaritan people, to whom Jesus is offering living water. Jesus' knowledge of her leads her first to see him as a prophet and later to invite the townspeople to come and see a man who could possibly be the Christ.

The motif of misunderstanding continues when the disciples enter the scene. They are not as willing as Jesus to cross the boundary of talking with Samaritans, especially this lone Samaritan women. In a twist of roles, Jesus, who had offered living water to the woman, is now offered ordinary food by his disciples. They too must develop a deeper understanding of Jesus' identity and learn that his food is to do the will of the one who sent him and to finish his work.

The story concludes rapidly. Many Samaritans come to believe in Jesus, no longer because of the woman's testimony, but because of Jesus' own word. Long before Jews believe in Jesus, the Samaritans know that he is savior of the world. E.P.

FOURTH SUNDAY OF LENT

LECTIONARY #31

READING I   1 Samuel 16:1b, 6–7, 10–13a

A reading from the first Book of Samuel

The LORD said to Samuel:
   "**Fill** your horn with **oil**, and be on your **way**.
I am **sending** you to Jesse of **Bethlehem**,
   for I have chosen my **king** from among his **sons**."

As Jesse and his sons came to the **sacrifice**,
   Samuel looked at **Eliab** and **thought**,
   "Surely the LORD's anointed is here before him."
But the LORD said to Samuel:
   "Do **not** judge from his appearance or from his lofty stature,
   because I have rejected him.
Not as **man** sees does **God** see,
   because man **sees** the **appearance**
   but the LORD **looks** into the **heart**."
In the same way Jesse presented **seven** sons before Samuel,
   but Samuel said to Jesse,
   "The LORD has **not** chosen any one of these."
Then Samuel asked Jesse,
   "Are these all the sons you have?"
Jesse replied,
   "There is **still** the **youngest**, who is tending the sheep."
Samuel said to Jesse,
   "Send for him;
   we will **not** begin the sacrificial banquet until he arrives here."

Proclaim in a tone of authority.

Jesse = JES-ee

Read with clarity and purpose.

Eliab = ee-LĪ-uhb

Pause before you say this line.

Use an informative tone.

Remember to use vocal variety and articulation as you proclaim the conversation between Samuel and Jesse.

READING I When the Lord commands Samuel to go to Jesse of Bethlehem to anoint one of his sons king, Samuel is afraid, and asks God, "How can I go? Saul will hear of it and kill me." Even though the Lord had rejected Saul, he remains a powerful king, able to gather military forces and track down those he suspected of treachery. To keep Saul from realizing what Samuel is about to do, the Lord directs Samuel to offer a sacrifice where the elders of Bethlehem, along with Jesse, would join him at a sacrificial banquet.

Obedient to the Lord's command, Samuel meets Jesse and his sons at the sacrifice. As Samuel sees the first son, Eliab, he thinks that he must be the one chosen by the Lord. Consecrated by a ritual of pouring oil from a ram's horn on his head, the future king would thereafter be known as "the Lord's anointed." Like Saul, Eliab has the look of a king, both men being tall. Yet the Lord, who does not judge by appearance, rejects Eliab, just as he had rejected Saul.

One by one, Jesse presents seven sons before Samuel. Seemingly puzzled, Samuel asks Jesse, "Are these all the sons you have?" Since the number seven symbolized completeness, Jesse's seven sons would seem to be the total number. (In a different tradition, 1 Chronicles 2:13–15, names David as the seventh and youngest son of Jesse.) Jesse then acknowledges that he has an eighth son, without naming him, as if he had forgotten him, so far away tending the sheep. Speaking with prophetic authority, Samuel commands Jesse to send for his youngest son, even announcing that the sacrificial banquet would be postponed until his arrival.

Jesse sent and had the young man brought to them.
He was **ruddy**, a youth **handsome** to behold
　　and making a splendid appearance.
The LORD said,
　　"There—anoint him, for this is the **one**!"
Then Samuel, with the horn of **oil** in hand,
　　anointed David in the presence of his brothers;
　　and from that day on, the spirit of the LORD rushed
　　　　upon David.

Make your voice strong as you finish the reading.

For meditation and context:

RESPONSORIAL PSALM　Psalm 23:1–3a, 3b–4, 5, 6 (1)

R. The Lord is my shepherd; there is nothing I shall want.

The LORD is my shepherd; I shall not want.
　In verdant pastures he gives me repose;
beside restful waters he leads me;
　he refreshes my soul.

He guides me in right paths
　for his name's sake.
Even though I walk in the dark valley
　I fear no evil; for you are at my side
with your rod and your staff
　that give me courage.

You spread the table before me
　in the sight of my foes;
you anoint my head with oil;
　my cup overflows.

Only goodness and kindness follow me
　all the days of my life;
and I shall dwell in the house of the LORD
　for years to come.

READING II　Ephesians 5:8–14

Ephesians = ee-FEE-shuhnz

A reading from the Letter of Saint Paul to the Ephesians

Proclaim with a tone of happiness now that "you are light in the Lord."

Brothers and sisters:
You were once darkness,
　but **now** you are light in the Lord.
Live as children of **light**,
　for light produces every kind of goodness
　and righteousness and truth.
Try to **learn** what is pleasing to the Lord. »

When the young man is finally brought before Samuel, the prophet responds immediately to God's command, "There—anoint him, for this is the one!" The anointing of the young David is part of the biblical motif of God's choice of the younger over the elder, beginning with the choice of Abel over Cain, and Jacob over Esau. Being anointed in the presence of his brothers is a sign that the youngest has again taken precedence over the elder. From the moment of his anointing, the spirit of the Lord was with David, signifying God's presence and power with him.

This episode begins the long saga of David's rise to power and of his kingship. Even with his well-known sins and limitations, David was remembered as the ideal king, called God's servant, and God's son, who kept the Lord's statutes and commandments. The Lord who looks into the heart, rather than to the outward appearance, found in David "a man after his own heart" (1 Samuel 13:14).

READING II In the Letter to the Ephesians, Paul, or someone writing in his name, presents teaching and

exhortations that are applicable to all of the baptized. While most of his letters address specific situations of a local church, Ephesians seems to have a more universal audience. Many features of the letter have led some commentators to think that it may have been an early encyclical, with copies sent to various churches, of which Ephesus was the first. Today's reading is a good example of instruction given to those of any community who are "faithful in Christ Jesus" (Ephesians 1:1), both in Paul's day and in our own.

"Do not live in darkness," St. Paul tells us. Use a tone of informing.

Take **no** part in the **fruitless** works of **darkness**;
 rather expose them, for it is **shameful** even to mention
 the things **done** by them in secret;
 but everything **exposed** by the **light** becomes visible,
 for everything that becomes visible is light.
Therefore, it says:

Pause before you say this last line. Read with intensity.

 "**Awake**, O sleeper,
 and arise from the **dead**,
 and **Christ** will **give** you light."

GOSPEL   John 9:1–41

A reading from the holy Gospel according to John

Proclaim with an informative tone.

Rabbi = RAB-Ī

[As **Jesus** passed by he saw a man blind from birth.]
His disciples asked him,
 "**Rabbi**, **who sinned**, **this** man or **his** parents,
 that he was born **blind**?"
Jesus answered,

Pause before you give Jesus' answer. Use a tone of authority.

 "**Neither he** nor his parents sinned;
 it is **so** that the **works** of God might be made visible
 through him.
We have to **do** the works of the **one** who sent **me** while it is day.
Night is coming when **no one** can work.
While **I** am **in** the world, **I** am the light of the **world**."
When he had said this, [he spat on the ground

saliva = suh-LĪ-vuh

Siloam = sih-LOH-uhm

 and made clay with the **saliva**,
 and smeared the clay on his eyes, and said to him,
 "**Go wash** in the **Pool of Siloam**"—which means Sent—.
So he went and **washed**, and came back **able** to **see**.

His neighbors and those who had seen him earlier
 as a **beggar** said,
 "Isn't **this** the **one** who used to sit and **beg**?"

During this conversation, use vocal variety and take your time.

The imagery in this reading draws on biblical tradition as well as common human experience. Light and darkness in the Bible, other literature, and human thought is symbolic of day and night, of good and evil, of knowledge and ignorance, of divine and demonic. Paul's use of the darkness and light metaphor resonates particularly with the creation account in Genesis, when the darkness that covered the abyss is transformed to light at God's command. Those who are "light in the Lord" are also transformed, created anew, as Paul says else-

where, "Whoever is in Christ is a new creation" (2 Corinthians 5:17).

Having been created anew, the baptized are to "live as children of light." The verb Paul uses here (*peripateite*) means "walk," not as a momentary or temporary action, but as a continuous process. The verb in the Bible describes an ongoing way of life, as in God's command to Abram, "Walk in my presence and be blameless" (Genesis 17:1). Similarly, Paul exhorts the Ephesians and the whole church to walk in the light, radiating every kind of goodness, righteousness, and truth. Not intended as

an exhaustive list of what it means to live in the light, these three virtues are representative of a way of life for the faithful. Even though they have already received the light of Christ, they must continue to learn how to walk in the light and do what is pleasing to the Lord.

Having first described the deeds of light, Paul then exhorts his audience to stay away from works of darkness. Because they walk in the light, they unmask darkness by casting light into secret and shadowy places. When Paul tells them to take no part in works of darkness, he is advising

Some said, "It **is**,"
   but others said, "No, he just **looks** like him."
He said, "**I am**."]
So they said to him, "**How** were your eyes opened?"
He replied,
   "The man called Jesus made clay and **anointed** my eyes
      and told me, 'Go to Siloam and **wash**.'
So I went there and washed and was able to **see**."
And they said to him, "**Where is** he?"
He said, "I don't **know**."

Read with an informative tone.

Pharisees = FAYR-uh-seez

[They **brought** the one who was **once** blind to the Pharisees.
Now **Jesus** had made clay and **opened** his eyes on a sabbath.
So **then** the Pharisees also asked him how he was able to see.
He said to them,
   "He put clay on my eyes, and I washed, and now I can see."
So some of the Pharisees said,
   "This man is not from God,
      because he does **not** keep the **sabbath**."
But others said,
   "How can a sinful man **do** such signs?"
And there was a division among them.
So they said to the blind man again,
   "What do you have to say about him,
      since he opened your eyes?"
He said, "He is a prophet."]

The Pharisees are angry. Let the assembly hear this in your voice.

Now the Jews did **not believe**
   that he had been blind and gained his sight
      until they **summoned** the parents of the one who had gained
         his sight.
They asked them,
   "Is this **your** son, who you **say** was born blind?
How does he **now see**?"
His parents answered and said,
   "We know that this **is** our son and that he **was** born **blind**. ❯❯

Change your tone to informative. Pay attention to the words in bold.

them to bring God-given light to expose darkness and sin in their own lives as well as other dark places in the world.

Paul concludes with a baptismal hymn probably well known to the communities he addresses. In the baptismal celebration, a lighted candle signifies the new light of Christ given to believers. No longer asleep in a time of darkness, they are now awake to the light of day. Christ himself is the light in whom they walk and live.

GOSPEL | As today's Gospel from John opens, Jesus has just left

the temple area where the scribes and Pharisees had repeatedly questioned him, showing a contemptuous refusal to accept him, even picking up stones to throw at him. After such a threatening encounter, Jesus appears calm and undisturbed when he sees a man blind from birth. Now it is the disciples who question Jesus. Displaying a lack of understanding, they offer two common reasons in the ancient world that could explain the man's blindness: his own sin or that of his parents. Each option assigns blame to someone and shows a startling lack of compassion for the man.

Jesus does not accept their negative suggestions of assigning blame, offering instead the positive view of the man's blindness as the occasion for divine action. In repeating the word "work," Jesus uses an all-encompassing term for God's deeds of creating, healing, forgiving, and saving, actions in which he shares. Jesus, the One sent by God, is not alone in doing the works of God. Speaking to his disciples, he says *we* must do the works of God, thereby including them in participating in God's saving works.

The first work of God was to create light (Genesis 1:3); now Jesus as the light of

We do not know how he **sees now**,
   nor do we know **who** opened his eyes.
Ask him, he is of age;
   he can **speak** for **himself**."
His parents said **this** because they were afraid of the Jews,
      for the Jews had already agreed
      that if anyone acknowledged him as the Christ,
      he would be expelled from the synagogue.
For this reason his parents said,
   "He is of **age; question him**."

Speak with strength in your voice as you proclaim, "Give God the praise."

So a second time they called the man who had been blind
   and said to him, "Give God the praise!
We know that this man is a **sinner**."
He replied,
   "**If** he is a sinner, **I** do **not** know.
One thing I do know is that I was blind and now I see."
So they said to him,
   "What did he do to you?
   How did he open your eyes?"
He answered them,
   "I told you already and you did **not** listen.
Why do you want to hear it again?
Do **you** want to become his disciples, **too**?"
They ridiculed him and said,

Say in a tone of disgust.

   "You are that man's disciple;
   we are disciples of Moses!
We **know** that **God** spoke to **Moses**,
   but we do **not** know **where this one** is from."
The man answered and said to them,

Read the blind man's words with gentleness.

   "This is what is **so amazing**,
      that you do **not** know where he is from, **yet** he opened my **eyes**.
We know that God does **not** listen to **sinners**,
   but if one is devout and does his **will**, he listens to him.
It is unheard of that anyone ever opened the eyes of a person
      born **blind**.

the world continues to bring divine light into the world. In this scene, he will bring physical light to the blind man, as well as a gradually growing light of understanding. After teaching his disciples through words, Jesus teaches through his work of healing. His words alone could restore health and wholeness, but on this occasion Jesus heals through his own multiple actions, completed by the blind man's washing. Characteristic of John's Gospel, Jesus' actions, as well as that of the blind man, have symbolic value. Many commentators have seen in Jesus' actions an allusion to creation, when the Lord God took clay from the earth and formed the first human. Jesus' using clay for the man's healing brings about a new creation in him. The man's own action of washing in the Pool of Siloam has a baptismal resonance. The evangelist notes that the name *Siloam* means "sent," signifying that the man is washed in Jesus himself, the one already identified as the One who is sent.

After the details of the man's healing, the many questions asked by various characters in the story move the Gospel forward. The man's neighbors wonder if this could be the one who used to sit and beg. In answering their questions, the man knows only that the one who healed him is called Jesus. Next are the Pharisees, whose questions, similar to those they had asked Jesus in the temple, show their unwillingness to see Jesus as a man from God. While the Pharisees are blind to Jesus' identity, the once-blind man now proclaims "He is a prophet." Unsatisfied with the man's answers, the Pharisees summon his parents, badgering them for an answer to their questions. The parents shield themselves from answering by asserting, "He is of age,

If this man were **not** from God,
   he would **not** be able to do **anything**."
[They answered and said to him,
   "**You** were born totally in sin,
   and are you trying to **teach** us?"
Then they threw him out.

When **Jesus** heard that they had thrown him out,
   he found him and said, "Do you believe in the **Son of Man?**"
He answered and said,
   "**Who is** he, sir, that I may believe in him?"
Jesus said to him,
   "You have seen him,
   and the one speaking with you **is** he."
He said,
   "I do believe, Lord," and he **worshiped** him.]
Then **Jesus** said,
   "I came into this world for **judgment**,
   so that those who do not see **might see**,
   and those who do see might become blind."

Some of the Pharisees who were with him heard this
   and said to him, "Surely **we** are **not** also blind, **are** we?"
Jesus said to them,
   "If you were blind, you would have **no sin**;
   but **now** you are saying, 'We **see**,' so your sin remains."

[Shorter: John 9:1, 6–9, 13–17, 34–38 (see brackets)]

A teaching moment for the blind man and the Pharisees. As you proclaim, help the assembly visualize the encounter by using vocal variety and facial expression.

he can speak for himself." Their fear of acknowledging Jesus as the Christ is representative of those in John's audience (as well as today) who do not dare to profess faith in Jesus, lest they be ridiculed and even expelled from society.

The Pharisees again question the man, "What did he do to you?" Now he turns the questions back on the Pharisees, as he challenges them, perhaps sarcastically, if they want to be Jesus' disciples. Their response to him, peppered with the words "know" and "do not know," are further revelation of their own blindness about Jesus. Expressing their stubbornness, the Pharisees throw the man out.

Being thrown out is precisely what the man's parents feared. But for the man himself, being thrown out is the occasion for Jesus to seek him out. Jesus now becomes the questioner as he asks the man, "Do you believe in the Son of Man?" another baptismal allusion. Puzzled by Jesus' question, the man asks one of his own, "Who is he, that I may believe?" Jesus' next words to him, "You have seen him," are a tender reminder that the man can now see. His sight is both physical and one born of faith. He now sees and knows. Addressing Jesus as "Lord," he has arrived at full sight and full faith. His increasing sight is a sharp contrast with the Pharisees' increasing blindness. E.P.

FIFTH SUNDAY
OF LENT

LECTIONARY #34

READING I   Ezekiel 37:12–14

A reading from the Book of the Prophet Ezekiel

Thus says the Lord God:
O my people, I will open your **graves**
and have you rise from them,
and **bring** you **back** to the land of **Israel**.
Then you shall know that I **am** the Lord,
when I open your graves and have you **rise** from them,
O my people!
I will put my spirit **in you** that you may live,
and I will **settle** you upon your **land**;
thus you shall know that I **am** the Lord.
I have promised, and I will do it, says the Lord.

RESPONSORIAL PSALM   Psalm 130:1–2, 3–4, 5–6, 7–8 (7)

R. With the Lord there is mercy and fullness of redemption.

Out of the depths I cry to you, O Lord;
    Lord, hear my voice!
Let your ears be attentive
    to my voice in supplication.

If you, O Lord, mark iniquities,
    Lord, who can stand?
But with you is forgiveness,
    that you may be revered.

I trust in the Lord;
    my soul trusts in his word.
More than sentinels wait for the dawn,
    let Israel wait for the Lord.

For with the Lord is kindness
    and with him is plenteous redemption;
and he will redeem Israel
    from all their iniquities.

Ezekiel = ee-ZEE-kee-uhl

Such good news! Pause before you begin to proclaim. Make your voice strong and take your time. Use good eye contact. Stress the words in bold.

Say this line and the next slowly and with a smile.

For meditation and context:

READING I Ezekiel was a prophet during the exile in Babylon; he was one of the exiled Jerusalemites. As both prophet and priest, his tasks ranged from chastising and correcting to comforting and offering hope. He fills his prophecies with striking imagery and dramatic visions that open up new ways of pondering on the great mysteries of God, life, and the future. His poetic language raises questions about the meaning of his imagery, eliciting a variety of interpretations that often go beyond Ezekiel's intent.

Ezekiel's prophecies begin with divine judgment and end with consolation. In today's reading, God speaks to the humiliated, mournful exiles. The broad valley that Ezekiel sees in his vision is filled with bones, symbolic of the exiles themselves, dried up and without hope. Torn away from their land that was long ago promised to them by God, they seem to be living in the burial ground of Babylon. In the midst of this horrid valley of death, God promises to open up their grave of exile and bring them back to their own land. God promises that they will *rise* from their graves. The same

verb is used to describe the people going up to Jerusalem, the mountain of the Lord (e.g., Psalm 24:3). When the people rise, they will again be able to worship the Lord in the holy city.

God tells the people that when they have been brought back to their land they will "know that I am the Lord." For the people to know the Lord is the reason God is freeing them from their entombment in exile. To know the Lord is to be in a right covenant relationship with God, manifest by attentiveness, obedience, and worship. The opposite of knowing is widespread

READING II   Romans 8:8–11

A reading from the Letter of Saint Paul to the Romans

Brothers and sisters:
Those who are **in** the **flesh cannot** please God.
But you are not in the flesh;
    on the **contrary**, you **are** in the spirit,
    if **only** the **Spirit of God** dwells in you.
Whoever does **not** have the **Spirit of** Christ does **not belong**
      to him.
But if **Christ** is in you,
    although the body is dead because of sin,
    the **spirit** is alive because of righteousness.
If the **Spirit** of the **one** who raised **Jesus** from the dead dwells
    in you,
    the One who raised **Christ** from the dead
    will give life to your mortal **bodies also**,
    through his Spirit dwelling in you.

Pause for emphasis before you say this line. Proclaim with a strong voice. Use good eye contact.

Build with intensity until the end of the reading. Always remember to articulate your words.

> TO KEEP IN MIND
> Be careful not to swallow words by mumbling. Articulate carefully, especially at the end of lines.

rebellious refusal to listen and obey. Their lack of knowing was the reason God sent them into exile in the first place. Yet, they remain God's people. God will create them anew by sending the spirit (*ruah*), imparting to them the Lord's own life-giving breath.

Ezekiel's poetic imagery in this oracle has significance beyond its original meaning. Christians have long seen the promise of rising from the grave as fulfilled in Jesus' Resurrection and assurance of the future resurrection of the dead. The final verse in today's reading that first offered assurance to the exiles in Babylon continues to offer hope-filled assurance today: what God has promised will be fulfilled!

READING II   In the first verse of the reading from Romans, Paul contrasts living in the flesh with living in the spirit. As he juxtaposes flesh (*sarx*) and spirit (*pneuma*), Paul uses terms that have more than one meaning. From one perspective, Jesus is described as being "in the flesh," (Hebrews 5:7), and similarly in John's Gospel, Jesus is the Word who "became flesh" (1:14). In both passages being in the flesh simply means being fully human, one who shares in the human condition. At other times, flesh has a negative connotation, indicative of a person's orientation toward sin. Sins of the flesh, though sometimes misinterpreted to refer only to sins of a physical or sexual nature, are actually much broader. As described by Paul, they include rivalry and jealousy and other selfish actions and attitudes (Galatians 5:19–21). Here in Romans, Paul is using this second meaning of flesh, having already given a brief summary in the verse preceding it, "the concern of the flesh is hostility toward God; it does not submit to the law of God,

GOSPEL   John 11:1–45

A reading from the holy Gospel according to John

Now a man was **ill**, Lazarus from **Bethany**,
    the village of Mary and her sister Martha.
Mary was the one who had anointed the **Lord** with perfumed oil
    and dried his feet with her **hair**;
    it was **her brother Lazarus** who was ill.
So [the sisters **sent** word to **Jesus** saying,
    "**Master**, the one you love is ill."
When **Jesus** heard this he said,
    "This illness is **not** to end in **death**,
    but is for the **glory** of **God**,
    that the **Son of God** may be **glorified through** it."
Now Jesus loved Martha and her sister and Lazarus.
So when he heard that he was ill,
    he remained for two days in the place where he was.
Then after this he said to his disciples,
    "Let us go back to **Judea**."]
The disciples said to him,
    "Rabbi, the Jews were just trying to stone you,
    and you want to go back there?"
Jesus answered,
    "Are there **not** twelve hours in a **day**?
If one walks during the **day**, he does **not stumble**,
    because he **sees** the light of this world.
But if one walks at night, he stumbles,
    because the **light** is **not in** him."
He said this, and then **told** them,
    "Our friend Lazarus is **asleep**,
    but I am going to awaken him."

Marginal notes (left column):

Proclaim with an informative tone.

Lazarus = LAZ-uh-ruhs

Bethany = BETH-uh-nee

Say with a sense of urgency.

Pause before you give Jesus' response.

Judea = joo-DEE-uh

Rabbi = RAB-ī

Use vocal variety as you ask the disciples question.

Stress the words in bold.

Say in a gentler tone.

(Bottom commentary, three columns:)

nor can it." According to today's reading, those who live in the flesh do not belong to Christ, and are dead because of sin.

    Paul also uses spirit in a variety of ways, at times referring to the human spirit and at other times the Spirit of God. From a human perspective, spirit refers to the animating principle that gives a person the capacity to think and to choose between good and evil. A person living in the spirit can also signify being oriented toward God, and being directed by the Spirit of God. Regarding the divine Spirit, Paul writes, apparently without distinction, of the Spirit

of God, the Spirit of Christ, or the Holy Spirit. Each description refers to God's personal presence, who pours the love of God into our hearts (Romans 5:5). In Galatians, after his list of sins of the flesh, Paul lists the nine fruits of the Spirit, closely linking the human spirit with the Spirit of God. The source of the nine fruits is God's own Spirit who empowers people to live and be guided by the Spirit.

    Paul's comparison of those who do not belong to Christ with those in whom Christ lives is akin to what he says about those who are dead because of sin and

those who are alive because of righteousness. Belonging to God and being alive because of righteousness are nearly synonymous ways of describing what it means to live in the spirit/Spirit. Paul's purpose in developing the contrasts in this pericope is to motivate the Christians in Rome to shun life according to the flesh, and to live in communion with the Spirit of God.

GOSPEL The account of Lazarus and his two sisters, beginning with his illness, followed by his death, and culminating with his being brought back to

So the disciples said to him,
      "Master, if he is asleep, he will be saved."
But Jesus was talking about his death,
      while **they** thought that he meant **ordinary** sleep.

Use a more pointed tone as Jesus
explains again.

So then Jesus said to them **clearly**,
      "Lazarus has died.
And I am glad for **you** that I was **not** there,
      that you may believe.
Let us go to him."

Didymus = DID-uh-muhs (meaning "twin")

So **Thomas**, called Didymus, said to his fellow disciples,
      "Let us also go to **die** with him."

John is giving us context for the next
conversation between Martha and Jesus.

[When Jesus arrived, he found that Lazarus
      had **already** been in the tomb for four days.]
Now **Bethany** was near **Jerusalem**, **only** about two miles away.
And many of the Jews had come to Martha and Mary
      to **comfort** them about their brother.
[When Martha heard that **Jesus** was coming,
      she went to meet him;
      but **Mary** sat at home.
Martha said to Jesus,

Martha speaks with urgency. Let us hear this
in your voice.

      "Lord, if you had **been here**,
      my brother would not have died.
But **even now** I know that whatever you **ask** of God,
      God will give you."
Jesus said to her,

Jesus responds calmly with an attitude
of love.

      "Your brother **will** rise."
Martha said to him,
      "I know he will rise,
      in the **resurrection** on the last day."
Jesus told her,

Do not rush Jesus' words.

      "**I am** the resurrection and the life;
      whoever believes in me, even if he dies, will live,
      and everyone who lives and believes in me will never die. »

life, is filled with intense human emotions. Though the story is situated in a first-century Palestine Jewish setting, it portrays familiar experiences, such as loss of a loved one, and the interplay of fear, doubt, faith, and hope that resonate with people living in far different times, places, and situations. In the context of John's Gospel, Jesus' words and actions add to the portrait the evangelist has been drawing. We also see how characters in the story relate to him, with his own disciples misunderstanding him, his friends expressing disappointment and grief

and displaying other attitudes and emotions as the story progresses.

In the first scene, Jesus is at a distance from Bethany, the location of his three friends. When the sisters send him a message about Lazarus' illness, Jesus' first words reveal the divine purpose underlying his friend's illness and death: the glory of God and the glorification of the Son of God. In last Sunday's Gospel, Jesus had similarly seen in a man's blindness God's hidden plan (John 9:3). Both the cure of the blind man and the raising of Lazarus add to the

developing picture of Jesus, his mission, and his intimacy with his Father.

Having delayed his journey to Bethany for two days, Jesus invites his disciples to go with him "back to Judea." Fearful because of recent attempts there to stone Jesus (8:59; 10:31), they try to dissuade him. Undeterred, Jesus again teaches them, drawing on his frequent imagery of day and night, light and darkness. If they walk with him, he will be the light that will prevent them from stumbling. When Jesus tells them the reason for going to Judea is to awaken Lazarus who has fallen asleep, his

Pause before you read Martha's words.

Do **you** believe this?"
She said to him, "Yes, Lord.
I have come to believe that **you are** the Christ, the **Son of God**,
    the one who is **coming** into the world."]

When she had said this,
    she went and **called** her sister Mary secretly, saying,
    "The **teacher** is here and is asking for you."

Say with a sense of urgency.

Take your time in the telling of this story.
Articulate your words. Read with emotion.

As soon as she heard this,
    she **rose quickly** and went to him.
For Jesus had **not** yet come into the village,
    but was still where Martha had met him.
So when the Jews who were with her in the house comforting her
    saw Mary get up quickly and go out,
    they followed her,
    presuming that she was **going** to the tomb to **weep** there.
When Mary came to where **Jesus** was and **saw** him,
    she fell at his feet and said to him,
    "Lord, if you had **been** here,
    my brother would **not** have **died**."
When Jesus saw her **weeping** and the Jews who had come with
        her weeping,

perturbed = per-TERBD (agitated and upset)

    [he became perturbed and deeply troubled, and said,
    "Where have you laid him?"
They said to him, "Sir, come and **see**."

Pause before you say this line.

And Jesus **wept**.
So the Jews said, "See how he loved him."
But some of them said,
    "Could **not** the one who **opened** the **eyes** of the blind man
    have **done something** so that this man would **not** have **died**?"

So Jesus, **perturbed** again, came to the **tomb**.
It was a cave, and a **stone** lay across it.
Jesus said, "Take away the stone."

disciples misunderstand him, as they so often do. As if to teach Jesus, they state that, once awake, Lazarus will be *saved*, using a word that for them means to "to recover," but elsewhere in John's Gospel refers to *salvation* (3:17; 5:34; 10:9). After Jesus' blunt statement, "Lazarus has died," Thomas, in a quick turnaround, jumps in with eager readiness to die with him!

Jesus' next encounter is with Martha, who has gone out to meet him. Addressing him as "Lord," she tells of her severe disappointment that he had not prevented her brother's death, and then professes her confidence that God will do whatever he asks. As she continues, she articulates her belief in the resurrection on the last day, a belief held by some Jews of the time, most notably the Pharisees. Then Jesus offers her a startlingly new revelation about his own identity and the life he promises: "I am the Resurrection and the life." Throughout John's Gospel, Jesus has already presented himself multiple times with "I am" statements, such as "I am the bread of life," and "I am the light of the world." In this "I am" announcement, Jesus expands on what he had earlier told Nicodemus, "God gave his only Son, so that everyone who believes in him might not perish but might have eternal life" (3:16). Martha's next words are a proclamation of faith in Jesus as the Christ, Son of God, the one coming into the world. Since Jesus has not yet acted to bring Lazarus back to life, Martha is a prototype of one who has not seen and has believed (20:29).

Having stated her belief in Jesus, even in the midst of her grief, Martha calls her sister. When Mary sees Jesus, she falls at his feet, an action that can simultaneously express anguish and reverence. Her words are fewer than those of her sister, seem-

Martha, the dead man's sister, said to him,
    "Lord, by now there will be a **stench**;
    he has been **dead** for four **days**."
Jesus said to her,
    "Did **I not** tell you that if you **believe**
    you will **see** the glory **of God?**"
So they took **away** the stone.
And Jesus **raised** his eyes and said,
    "**Father**, **I thank** you for hearing me.
I know that you always hear me;
    but because of the **crowd** here I have said this,
    that **they** may believe that **you sent** me."
And when he had said this,
    he cried out in a loud **voice**,
    "Lazarus, come out!"
The dead man came **out**,
    tied hand and foot with burial bands,
    and his face was wrapped in a cloth.
So Jesus said to them,
    "Untie him and let him go."

Now **many** of the Jews who had come to Mary
    and **seen** what he had done **began** to believe in him.]

[Shorter: John 11:3–7, 17, 20–27, 33b–45 (see brackets)]

Proclaim as if in prayer.

Proclaim in a clear, loud voice.

Say slowly and calmly.

ingly cut short by her tears. Deeply troubled at Mary's weeping, Jesus himself weeps, mentioned only here and in Hebrews (5:7). Jesus finally comes to the tomb where the body of Lazarus has been for four days. First, assuring Mary that if she believes she will see the glory of God, Jesus then gives confident thanks to his Father who always hears his Son. Earlier in the Gospel, Jesus had declared "the hour is coming in which all who are in the tombs will hear his voice and will come out" (5:28–29). Now, fulfilling this promise and also foreshadowing future resurrection, Jesus calls, "Lazarus, come out!" At Jesus' words, Lazarus immediately comes forth, still wrapped in burial cloths. Jesus' command to unbind him and let him go frees Lazarus from the garments of death so he may live again. A fifth-century writer said that Lazarus had taken a sip of the resurrection, while we await drinking the whole draft of universal resurrection. E.P.

PALM SUNDAY OF THE PASSION OF THE LORD

LECTIONARY #37

GOSPEL AT THE PROCESSION   Matthew 21:1–11

A reading from the holy Gospel according to Matthew

Proclaim with authority and purpose. Use good volume. Pause before Jesus' words.
Bethphage = BETH-fuh-jee

When **Jesus** and the disciples drew near **Jerusalem**
  and came to **Bethphage** on the Mount of **Olives**,
  Jesus **sent** two disciples, saying to them,
  "Go into the village opposite you,
  and immediately you will find an **ass** tethered,
  and a **colt** with her.
Untie them and bring them **here** to me.
And if **anyone** should say **anything** to you, reply,
  'The **master** has **need** of them.'
Then he will **send** them at **once**."
This **happened** so that what had been **spoken** through the **prophet**
  might be fulfilled:
  Say *to daughter* **Zion**,
  *"**Behold**, your king **comes** to you,*
    *meek and **riding** on an **ass**,*
    *and on a **colt**, the foal of a beast of burden."*
The disciples went and did as **Jesus** had **ordered** them.
They **brought** the ass and the colt and **laid** their **cloaks** over them,
  and **he** sat upon them.
The very large **crowd spread** their **cloaks** on the **road**,
  while others **cut branches** from the trees
  and strewed them on the road.

Jesus calmly gives them a specific task.

Zion = ZĪ-uhn or ZĪahn

Read in an informative tone. Pause before you begin reading the quote. Articulate.

foal = fohl

strewed = strood (scattered or spread)

PROCESSION GOSPEL When Jesus arrives at the Mount of Olives, he is on the verge of fulfilling his long-planned determination to go to Jerusalem. Up to this time, his ministry had centered in Galilee, where he was "teaching in their synagogues, proclaiming the Gospel of the kingdom, and curing every disease and illness among the people" (4:23). Now, from the Mount of Olives, he would at last be able to see Jerusalem, to observe the palace of Herod with its gardens and wealth from one direction, and

from another direction to see neighborhoods steeped in poverty. Most significantly would be the view of the temple, believed to be the dwelling place of God. In the first century, the Jewish author Josephus maintained that the temple shone at sunrise with such brilliance that no one could look at it directly. Having viewed the city and the glorious temple from the Mount, Jesus and his disciples make their way into the city.

According to the synoptic Gospels, this was Jesus' first visit to Jerusalem. Just

after Peter proclaimed Jesus as the Messiah, the Son of the living God, Jesus had told his disciples that he must go to Jerusalem, where he would suffer, be killed, and be raised on the third day (16:21). Although Peter tried to prevent Jesus' journey, Jesus himself is determined, ultimately leaving Galilee to make his way to the holy city (19:1). All four of the Gospels recount Jesus' entrance into Jerusalem, with each evangelist developing the scene in distinctive ways. Matthew, writing for a primarily Jewish Christian audience, had a particular

100

The crowds **preceding** him and those **following**
    kept crying out and **saying**:
       "Hosanna to the **Son of David**;
          blessed is **he** who comes in the **name** of the Lord;
       hosanna in the highest."
And **when** he **entered** Jerusalem
    the **whole** city was shaken and asked, "**Who is** this?"
And the crowds replied,
    "This is **Jesus** the prophet, from **Nazareth in Galilee**."

READING I   Isaiah 50:4–7

A reading from the Book of the Prophet Isaiah

The **Lord** God has **given** me
    a well-**trained** tongue,
that I might know how to **speak** to the weary
    a word that will rouse them.
Morning after **morning**
    he **opens** my ear that I may hear;
and I have **not** rebelled,
    have not **turned back**.
I gave my back to those who beat **me**,
    my cheeks to those who **plucked** my **beard**;
my **face** I did **not shield**
    from buffets and spitting.

The **Lord** GOD is my help,
    therefore I am **not** disgraced;
I have set my face like flint,
    knowing that I shall not **be put to** shame.

Read these lines with more intensity.

blessed = BLES-uhd

Isaiah = Ī-ZAY-uh

Take your time in proclaiming this reading. Smile throughout. God has blessed Isaiah with many gifts. Let the assembly see and hear that Isaiah has a special relationship with God.

buffets = BUF-its (slaps)

---

interest in portraying Jesus in continuity with and fulfillment of Jewish tradition.

Along with thousands of other pilgrims, Jesus and his disciples had come to Jerusalem for the feast of Passover. He would be well aware that the enthusiasm of the crowds had the potential for violence, and knew of the looming presence of Rome's military might. Jesus could have come into the city quietly, but instead chose an entrance that is paradoxically both humble and majestic. His procession was not like that of the Romans on war-

horses, whose entry into conquered cities was a symbol of oppression and imperial power. In addition to the contrast between Jesus' humility and the arrogance of Rome, his meekness of riding on an ass fulfills a prophecy of Zechariah, presenting him as the king, God's anointed one (9:9).

As the crowds that gathered for Passover remembered the ancient slavery in Egypt, they hoped that God would again liberate them from their current warlords. The sight of Jesus arriving both in humility and majesty inspires them to treat him as

a king entering the city. He is a living sign of hope and promise. Using their own cloaks and branches and foliage from the roadside, they create a pathway for the one they honor as son of David. Their cry of "Hosanna" ("Save, I pray") is a word of both plea and praise, a liturgical acclamation from Psalm 118, one of the psalms recited at Passover. They acclaim Jesus as the descendant of King David, worthy of their homage. The wider response, particularly that of Roman authorities and Jewish leaders, is one of alarm. Such a dis-

For meditation and context:

RESPONSORIAL PSALM   Psalm 22:8–9, 17–18, 19–20, 23–24 (2a)

R. My God, my God, why have you abandoned me?

All who see me scoff at me;
    they mock me with parted lips, they wag
        their heads:
"He relied on the LORD; let him deliver him,
    let him rescue him, if he loves him."

Indeed, many dogs surround me,
    a pack of evildoers closes in upon me;
they have pierced my hands and my feet;
    I can count all my bones.

They divide my garments among them,
    and for my vesture they cast lots.
But you, O LORD, be not far from me;
    O my help, hasten to aid me.

I will proclaim your name to my brethren;
    in the midst of the assembly I will
        praise you:
"You who fear the LORD, praise him;
    all you descendants of Jacob, give glory
        to him;
    revere him, all you descendants of Israel!"

READING II   Philippians 2:6–11

Philippians = fih-LIP-ee-uhnz

Proclaim this reading with confidence. Let the assembly hear strength in your voice. Take your time and speak with clarity. Pay attention to the words in bold.

A reading from the Letter of Saint Paul to the Philippians

Christ Jesus, though **he was** in the **form** of God,
    did **not** regard equality with **God**
    something to be grasped.
Rather, he emptied himself,
    taking the form of a slave,
    coming in human **likeness**;
    and found human in **appearance**,
    he humbled himself,
    becoming obedient to the point of death,
    even death on a cross.
Because of this, **God greatly** exalted him
    and bestowed on him the name
    which is above every name,
    that at the name of Jesus
    every **knee** should bend,

Build intensity.

---

play of enthusiasm during Passover could ignite a fire among the people. The city is shaken, portending the earthquake that is about to shake the foundations. The cause of the coming earthquake is Jesus, humble king, descendant of David, and divinely anointed prophet.

READING I In the reading from Isaiah, the prophet is speaking in the first person as he describes his role as a prophet to whom God has given a tongue to speak and ears to hear. His description

here has a thematic link with three other poetic passages in Isaiah (42:1–4; 49:1–6, and 52:13—53:12), each of them contributing to a portrait of a servant called to fulfill a divinely ordained mission. In each of these prophecies, Isaiah may well be describing himself, or he may be depicting an ideal servant of God, reminiscent of Moses or David or Jeremiah. He may also be alluding to Israel as a whole, regularly called God's servant in Isaiah (e.g., 41:8; 43:10; 49:3). With the identity of the servant veiled and open to differing interpretations,

Christians have long seen Jesus as the fullest embodiment of Isaiah's faithful servant.

The poem today begins with God giving the servant a tongue, well-trained like that of a disciple, so he will know how to speak a word that will rouse the weary. In the original context of Isaiah, those who are weary may refer to the disheartened exiles in Babylon. Beyond the original context, God bestows the prophetic word to be given to anyone in need of physical and spiritual restoration. Every morning the Lord opens the servant's ear so he may hear the life-giving

Pause and say slowly: "Jesus Christ is Lord."

of those **in** heaven and on **earth** and under the earth,
and **every** tongue confess that
Jesus Christ **is** Lord,
to the glory **of God the** Father.

Iscariot = ih-SKAYR-ee-uht

The Passion of Our Lord is full of emotion. Take your time. Pause before different people speak. Rehearse for emotion in your voice. Always use good volume and eye contact.

Speak in an informative tone.

Read with clarity and purpose.

GOSPEL   Matthew 26:14—27:66

The Passion of our Lord Jesus Christ according to Matthew

One of the **Twelve**, who was called Judas Iscariot,
    went to the chief **priests** and said,
    "What are you willing to give me
    if I hand him over to you?"
They paid him thirty pieces of **silver**,
    and from that time on he looked for **an opportunity**
        to hand him over.

On the first day of the **Feast of Unleavened Bread**,
    the disciples **approached Jesus** and said,
    "Where do you want us to **prepare**
    for you to eat the Passover?"
He said,
    "Go into the city to a certain man and tell him,
    'The teacher says, "My **appointed time** draws **near**;
    in **your** house I shall **celebrate** the Passover with
        my **disciples**."'"
The disciples then **did** as Jesus had ordered,
    and prepared the Passover. ≫

Word afresh. The servant saying, "I have not rebelled, have not turned back," suggests that God's Word may be difficult for him to hear, and even more difficult to speak. While the intention of the Word is to give solace to the faint of heart, the immediate and harsh result for the prophet is beating, buffeting, and bruising. What makes the servant's task even more onerous is that the ones persecuting him seem to be the very ones he came to restore.

After such torment, the servant's declaration, "The Lord God is my help," sounds both like a martyr's statement of faith and an agonized cry for God's help. Though he seems disgraced in human eyes, the Lord God will not put him to shame. The declaration that he is "setting his face like flint" presents a dramatic visual contrast with his current battered appearance. The image is similar to Jeremiah's picturing himself as a pillar of iron, and a wall of brass (1:18), and to Ezekiel's self-image of being stubborn of brow, with face like diamond (3:9). Isaiah's own face, with plucked beard, buffeted, and covered in spittle, is still as sharp and firm as flint. God's prophets and servants, often rejected and mistreated by their own people, are analogous to the hardest of rocks and metals. They remain resolute in speaking the word that God has given them, for the Lord God is always their help, their shield, and their vindication.

READING II   This hymn from Philippians, like many other Christian hymns throughout the ages, was probably composed for liturgical celebrations. Whether Paul wrote the hymn himself or

Proclaim with calmness in your voice.

When it was **evening**,
   he **reclined** at table with the Twelve.
And while they were **eating**, he said,
   "Amen, I say to you, **one** of you will betray me."
Deeply distressed at this,
   they began to say to him one after another,
   "**Surely** it is not I, Lord?"
He said in reply,
   "He who has dipped his hand into the dish with me
   is the one who will **betray** me.
The Son of Man indeed **goes**, as it is written of him,
   but woe to that man by whom the **Son of Man** is betrayed.
It would be **better** for **that** man if he had **never** been born."
Then **Judas**, his **betrayer**, said in reply,
   "Surely it is not I, Rabbi?"
He answered, "**You** have said so."

Slowly proclaim Jesus' words.

While they were eating,
   Jesus **took** bread, said the **blessing**,
   broke it, and **giving** it to his disciples said,
   "Take **and** eat; **this is my** body."
Then he took a **cup**, gave **thanks**, and **gave** it to them, saying,
   "Drink from it, all of you,
   for this is **my** blood of the covenant,
   which will be shed on behalf of many
   for the forgiveness of sins.
I tell you, from **now** on I shall **not drink** this fruit of the vine
   until the day when I drink it **with you** new
   in the kingdom **of my Father**."

Pause.

Then, after singing a **hymn**,
   they went out to the **Mount of** Olives.

used one that was already known to the community, he used the song of Jesus' humility and emptying of himself as a model for his audience. They are to have the same attitude that is in Christ Jesus.

The first part of the hymn is about Christ's status and actions, and the second part is about God's response. Announced in this hymn, proclaimed in creeds, and pondered by theologians, the opening verse proclaims a great mystery: Christ Jesus is eternally equal with God, one with God in divine nature, essence, and power. Yet, not clinging to his divine form, he emptied himself, taking the form of a slave. The hymn is often entitled "The Kenosis Hymn" based on the Greek word that means "emptying." The word evokes an image of a vessel being poured out completely, drained of whatever filled it. While mysteriously always retaining his divinity, in emptying himself Christ came in human likeness, sharing fully in the human condition. After this profound emptying of himself in the Incarnation, Christ further humbled himself by his obedience that led to his death on the cross.

"Because of this" initiates the second part of the hymn. God reverses Christ's lowering of himself by greatly exalting him. From the lowest status, God raises him to the highest. Added to his name, Jesus, is the title Lord, a divine name that he shares with his Father, the Lord God. In the context of the letter to the Philippians, the hymn has a dual purpose. First, it is a deeply moving proclamation of Christ's eternal divinity, his Incarnation, death, and exaltation. The com-

Then Jesus said to them,
  "This night all of you will have your **faith** in **me** shaken,
  for it is written:
    I will strike the shepherd,
      and the sheep ***of the flock will be*** dispersed;
  but **after** I have been raised **up**,
  I shall go before you to **Galilee**."
Peter said to him in reply,
  "Though **all** may have their faith in you shaken,
  mine will never be."
Jesus said to him,
  "**Amen**, I say to you,
  this **very** night before the cock crows,
  you will deny me three times."
Peter said to him,
  "Even though I should have to die with you,
  I will not deny you."
And all the disciples spoke **likewise**.

Then Jesus came with them to a place called **Gethsemane**,
  and he said to his disciples,
  "Sit here while I go over there and pray."
He took along Peter and the two sons of Zebedee,
  and began to feel sorrow and distress.
Then he said to them,
  "My **soul** is **sorrowful** even to death.
  Remain here and keep watch with me."
He advanced a little and fell prostrate in prayer, saying,
  "My Father, if it is possible,
  let this cup pass from me;
  yet, **not** as I will, but as you will."
When he returned to his disciples he found them asleep. »

Strongly say Peter's words.

Keep up your energy.
Gethsemane = gehth-SEM-uh-nee

Zebedee = ZEB-uh-dee

prostrate = PROS-trayt (face down)
Proclaim Jesus' words as if you are praying.

munity is drawn into the mystery of Christ through song, prayer, and praise. Secondly, Christ's humbling of himself, his emptying and obedience is a pattern for all who follow him. The hymn concludes with a sign of believers' humble homage as they kneel before him and join in universal acclamation: Jesus Christ is Lord!

GOSPEL The passion narrative is the longest portion of each of the four canonical (official) Gospels. The accounts are filled with details, times, and

places, each one telling the story of Jesus with their own audiences in mind. As the evangelist Matthew narrates the events of Jesus' last days, he weaves in allusions and citations from the Hebrew Scriptures, often subtly. Writing for an audience made up primarily of Jews who believed in Jesus as their messiah, Matthew draws on their own heritage to show how Jesus fulfills it. Even Jesus being betrayed, his suffering and death, scandalous and distressing to his followers, had long been foretold. Jesus himself will explain how prophecies from

Judaism are brought to fulfillment in shocking, unexpected ways.

After Jesus' dramatic entrance into Jerusalem to the acclamation of the Passover crowds, he immediately went into the temple area. Seeing people engaged in buying and selling there, he overturned the tables of the money changers. He used their own Scriptures against them, quoting Isaiah: "My house shall be a house of prayer, but you have made it a den of thieves." Jesus' authoritative act, followed by his curing of the blind and lame, and the

Say this in frustration a second and third time.

He said to Peter,
　"So you could **not** keep **watch** with me for one hour?
Watch and pray that you may not undergo the **test**.
The **spirit** is willing, but the **flesh** is weak."
Withdrawing a **second** time, he prayed **again**,
　"My Father, if it is not possible that this cup pass
　　without my drinking it, your will be **done**!"
Then he returned once **more** and found them **asleep**,
　for they could not keep their eyes open.
He **left** them and withdrew again and prayed a **third** time,
　saying the **same** thing **again**.
Then he returned to his disciples and said to them,
　"Are you **still sleeping** and taking your rest?

Now say Jesus' words with acceptance in your voice.

Behold, the **hour is at** hand
　when the **Son of Man** is to be handed over to **sinners**.
Get up, let us **go**.
Look, my **betrayer** is at hand."

Be sure to read clearly with good volume.

While he was still speaking,
　Judas, one of the **Twelve**, arrived,
　accompanied by a large crowd, with **swords** and **clubs**,
　who had come from the chief priests and the elders
　　of the people.
His betrayer had arranged a sign with them, saying,
　"The man I shall kiss is the one; arrest him."
Immediately he went over to Jesus and said,
　"**Hail**, Rabbi!" and he **kissed** him.
Jesus answered him,
　"Friend, **do** what you have **come** for."
Then stepping forward they **laid** hands on Jesus and arrested him.
And **behold**, one of those who accompanied Jesus
　put his hand to his **sword**, **drew** it,
　and struck the high priest's servant, **cutting** off his **ear**.

children's acclamation of "Hosanna to the Son of David" made the chief priests and scribes indignant. When Jesus taught in the temple area, the Jewish leaders questioned, "By what authority are you doing these things?" They wanted to arrest him, but feared the crowds, particularly worrying that there would be a riot among the people gathered for the feast of Passover. Their solution was to arrest Jesus by stealth and put him to death.

The leaders in Jerusalem who were plotting to arrest Jesus surreptitiously found a coconspirator from among Jesus' closest friends, Judas, one of the twelve. When the twelve are listed in Matthew's Gospel, Judas is identified by his act of betrayal, "Judas Iscariot, who betrayed him" (10:4). It is Judas, not the chief priests, who takes the initiative in putting the plot into motion. Approaching the Jerusalem leaders, Judas asks them what they will give him to hand Jesus over to them. The Greek verb "to hand over" (*paradidomi*) also means "to betray." Thus, another ren-

dering of Judas' question would be, "How much will you give me to betray him?"

Even with the plot against him in the shadows, Jesus is totally in control of the situation, as he has been throughout Matthew's Gospel. He knows where he will celebrate the Passover with his disciples and directs them to prepare. Aware that his death is imminent, Jesus gathers them to share in an intimate and solemn farewell meal. Matthew's comment that Jesus reclined at table with the twelve does not exclude the likelihood that others of his dis-

Jesus is speaking in a tone of control with a firm purpose. Let the assembly hear that in your voice.

Then Jesus said to him,
 "**Put** your sword **back** into its sheath,
 for all who take the sword will perish by the sword.
Do you think that I **cannot** call upon my **Father**
 and he will **not** provide me at this moment
 with **more** than twelve **legions** of angels?
But then **how** would the Scriptures be fulfilled
 which say that it must come to pass in this **way**?"
At that hour **Jesus** said to the crowds,
 "Have you come out as against a robber,
 with swords and clubs to seize me?
Day after day I sat **teaching** in the temple area,
 yet you **did not** arrest me.
But all this has come to **pass**
 that the **writings** of the **prophets** may be fulfilled."
Then **all** the disciples left him and fled.

As you continue to read the Passion, keep your voice strong with good eye contact.

As you continue to read the Passion, keep your voice strong with good eye contact.

Those who had arrested Jesus **led** him away
 to **Caiaphas** the high priest,
 where the scribes and the elders were assembled.
Peter was following him at a distance
 as far as the high priest's courtyard,
 and going **inside** he sat down with the servants to see
 the outcome.
The chief priests and the entire Sanhedrin
 kept trying to obtain **false testimony** against Jesus
 in order to **put** him to death,
 but they found none,
 though many false witnesses came forward.
Finally two came forward who stated,
 "This man said, 'I can destroy the temple of God
 and within **three** days **rebuild** it.'" »

Caiaphas = KAY-uh-fuhs or KI-uh-fuhs

Proclaim this line in a hateful way.

ciples were also present. Having welcomed sinners and outcasts at other meals, why would Jesus exclude them on this occasion? Whoever was present at the meal, it was from this circle of his friends that one would betray him. Jesus sees and knows that one of them sharing from a common dish will violate the bond of friendship. The act of betrayal in this setting resonates with Psalm 41: "Even the friend who had my trust, who shared my table, has scorned me." Hearing Jesus' prediction, his distraught disciples ask Jesus, one by one,

"Is it I?" Each of them addresses Jesus as "Lord," a title born of faith, respect, and reverence. Only Judas addresses him as "Rabbi," as do others in the Gospel who have no faith. Jesus' response to Judas leaves no doubt that he is the betrayer.

Acting as their host at the meal, Jesus leads his friends in a ritual that includes elements common to Jewish festive meals: blessings and sharing of bread and wine. As he uses familiar words and gestures, Jesus gives new meaning to the meal, the ritual, and the community. He stretches the

significance from the past, to the present, and into the future. The ordinary bread and wine will become Jesus' own body and blood. The ancient covenant becomes a new covenant in Jesus' own blood. Only in Matthew's Gospel does Jesus say that the shedding of his blood, looking ahead to his death on the cross, will be for the forgiveness of sins. Giving his life for the sake of others, Jesus is like the suffering servant of Isaiah, who "shall take away the sins of many" (Isaiah 53:12). At this very meal are sinners, including the one who would hand

Say with great urgency.

Jesus remains calm in his response.

blasphemed = blas-FEEMD

The crowd is angry. Let the congregation hear that as you say the words *spat, struck, slapped.*

prophesy (verb) = PROF-uh-sī

Galilean - gal-ih-LEE-uhn

The assembly must hear fear in your voice and it must build as Peter continues to deny Jesus.

Nazorean = naz-uh-REE-uhn

The high priest rose and addressed him,
    "Have you **no answer**?
What are these men **testifying** against you?"
But Jesus was silent.
Then the high priest said to him,
    "I **order** you to **tell** us **under** oath **before the living God**
    whether you **are** the Christ, **the Son of God**."
Jesus said to him in reply,
    "**You** have said so.
But I tell you:
    From now on you will **see** the 'Son of Man
        seated at the **right** hand of the **Power**'
        and '**coming** on the clouds of heaven.'"
Then the high priest tore his robes and said,
    "He has blasphemed!
What further need have we of witnesses?
You have now **heard** the blasphemy;
    what is your **opinion**?"
They said in reply,
    "**He deserves to** die!"
Then they spat in his face and struck him,
    while some slapped him, saying,
    "Prophesy for us, **Christ**: who **is** it that **struck** you?"

Now Peter was sitting outside in the courtyard.
One of the maids came over to him and said,
    "You too were with **Jesus the Galilean**."
But he denied it in front of everyone, saying,
    "I do not know what you are talking about!"
As he went out to the gate, **another** girl saw him
    and said to those who were there,
    "This man was **with** Jesus the Nazorean."
Again he denied it with an **oath**,
    "I do **not know** the **man**!"

Jesus over, undoubtedly leaving his disciples feeling an uneasy mix of sorrow, gratitude, wondering, and fear. The meal concludes with the singing of a hymn, traditionally taken from the psalms, with the words expressing the great range of emotions on this occasion.

When they go from the meal to the Mount of Olives, Jesus again foretells what is about to happen. In using a prophecy from Zechariah, he continues to explain that everything is proceeding according to the Scriptures. Just as he had known of

Judas' betrayal, Jesus also knows that the faith of all his disciples will be shaken. As he foretells their response to the coming events, Jesus uses a word group frequent in Matthew's Gospel. Their faith shaken, they will stumble (*skandalizo*); they will trip on the stone (*skandalon*). Earlier in the Gospel, Jesus had told Peter he was a *skandalon*, or stumbling stone, when Peter tried to prevent Jesus from going to Jerusalem (16:23). Peter will again trip over the scandal of the cross. When Peter vehemently denies that

his faith will ever be shaken, Jesus foretells Peter's coming triple denial.

Peter's assurance that he will never fall away is followed shortly by his falling asleep instead of keeping watch with Jesus, who withdraws from his disciples three times to ask his Father to let the cup pass by. In the Old Testament, the cup is often a symbol that refers to an individual's or a nation's fate, particularly when it is harsh and intense. Jesus had previously used the cup image when he asked James and John if they could drink of the cup he was to

A little later the bystanders came over and said to Peter,
    "**Surely** you **too** are **one** of them;
    even your speech **gives** you away."
At that he began to curse and to swear,
    "I do not **know** the man."
And immediately a **cock crowed**.
Then Peter **remembered** the words that Jesus had spoken:
    "Before the cock **crows** you will deny me three times."
He went out and began to **weep bitterly**.

Pause.

There is a change of time and place; we must hear that in your voice. Pause before you begin. Proclaim with renewed energy.

Pilate = PI-luht

Slowly proclaim this line.

Read the chief priest's words in a nasty tone.

When it was morning,
    all the chief **priests** and the elders of the people
    took counsel **against** Jesus to put him to **death**.
They bound him, led him away,
    and handed him over to Pilate, the governor.

Then Judas, his betrayer, seeing that Jesus had
        been **condemned**,
    deeply regretted what he had done.
He **returned** the thirty pieces of silver
    to the chief priests and elders, saying,
    "I have sinned in betraying innocent blood."
They said,
    "**What** is that to **us**?
    Look to it yourself."
Flinging the money into the temple,
    he **departed** and **went off** and hanged himself.
The chief **priests** gathered up the money, but said,
    "It is **not lawful** to deposit this in the **temple** treasury,
    for it is the **price of** blood."
After consultation, they used it to **buy** the **potter's field**
    as a **burial** place for foreigners.
That is **why** that field **even** today is called the **Field of** Blood. **»**

drink, in effect asking if they were able to drink from the deep well of suffering. Though the depth of suffering lies before him, Jesus remains faithful to his Father. Having already taught his disciples to pray, "Thy will be done," Jesus now embodies that prayer as he obediently accepts the cup he is to drink. As soon as he finishes his prayer, Jesus rouses the sleeping disciples, telling them sharply, "My betrayer is at hand."

The scene of Judas arriving with a large crowd bearing swords and clubs is a striking reversal of the event just a few days before, when the crowds waved palm branches and acclaimed Jesus as Son of David. As he approaches Jesus, Judas again addresses him as "Rabbi," and kisses him in what was ordinarily a sign of respect and friendship. Jesus does not address Judas by name either, and Judas seems to vanish from the scene. His role in the betrayal is complete. Then the anonymous "they" lay hands on Jesus and arrest him, this first act of violence followed quickly by another. One of those with Jesus (identified in John's Gospel with Simon Peter) strikes the high priest's servant with his sword, cutting off his ear. Jesus remains calm and decisively rejects such violence, even though it is used against him. He takes the opportunity to teach all those present, focusing once more on Scripture being fulfilled. And Jesus' own prophecy to his disciples that "this night all of you will have your faith in me shaken" is being fulfilled as they leave him and flee.

Events then move quickly as the ones arresting Jesus lead him away to the high

Jeremiah = jayr-uh-MI-uh

Then was fulfilled what had been said through Jeremiah
      the prophet,
   And they took the **thirty** *pieces of silver,*
   the **value** *of a man with a price on his head,*
   a price set by some of the Israelites,
   and they **paid** *it out for the potter's* **field**
   just as the **Lord** *had commanded me.*

[Now **Jesus** stood before the governor, and he questioned him,
   "**Are** you the king of the Jews?"

Say this with an accusing tone.

Jesus said, "**You** say so."
And when he was **accused** by the chief priests and elders,
   he made **no answer**.
Then **Pilate** said to him,

Proclaim with more intensity.

   "Do you **not** hear how many things they are **testifying**
      against you?"
But he did **not** answer him **one word**,
   so that the governor was greatly amazed.

Use good volume with an informative tone.

Now on the occasion of the feast
   the governor was accustomed to **release** to the crowd
   one prisoner whom they **wished**.
And at that time they had a notorious prisoner called Barabbas.
So when they had assembled, **Pilate** said to them,

Barabbas = buh-RAB-uhs

Start proclaiming Pilate's words with arrogance as he asks whom he should release. Build the intensity of his words as he continues to question the crowds.

   "Which one do you want me to **release** to you,
      Barabbas, or **Jesus** called **Christ**?"
For he knew that it was out of envy
   that they had handed him over.
While he was still **seated** on the bench,
   his wife sent him a message,
   "Have nothing to do with that righteous man.
I **suffered** much in a **dream** today because of him."
The chief priests and the elders persuaded the crowds
   to ask for **Barabbas** but to destroy **Jesus**.
The governor said to them in reply,
   "**Which** of the two do you want me to release to you?"

priest, Caiaphas. The trial before Caiaphas can aptly be described as a mockery, a sham, a show trial, with the guilty verdict determined before a word is spoken. Details of the timeline, trials, and people involved vary in the four Gospels, not surprising because of the clandestine nighttime arrest, the rapidity of events, and the fluid nature of oral tradition. What is clear and consistent in all of the accounts is the determination of the Jerusalem leaders to find Jesus guilty. Standing before Caiaphas, Jesus is facing a judge who was a willing

collaborator with Rome, concerned more with not offending the emperor and his minions than with adhering to the Jewish law. Caiaphas would be well aware how Roman authorities would respond to rioting that could easily erupt with the large crowds of Passover pilgrims.

The charges against Jesus were that he threatened to destroy the temple and that he claimed to be the messiah. False witnesses and false testimony served purposes of Caiaphas and those who had brought Jesus to him. After first remaining silent

before his accusers, Jesus speaks the truth about his identity, leading to the charge of blasphemy. Jesus' acceptance of the title "the Christ, the Son of God" is not in fact blasphemy, but it is a claim that is politically explosive. As a leader hoped for and followed by crowds, Jesus would be regarded as a threat to Roman power. When Caiaphas tears his robes, he is appealing to the chief priests and Sanhedrin who would see him cooperating in their plot. Although he asks for their opinion, Caiaphas already knows their judgment, "He deserves to die!"

They answered, "Barabbas!"
Pilate said to them,
   "Then what shall I **do** with **Jesus** called **Christ**?"
They all said,
   "**Let him be** crucified!"
But he said,
   "**Why**? What **evil** has he done?"
They only **shouted** the **louder**,
   "Let him be crucified!"
When Pilate saw that he was **not** succeeding at all,
   but that a riot was breaking out instead,
   he took water and washed his hands in the sight of the crowd,
   saying, "I am innocent of this man's blood.
Look to it **yourselves**."
And the **whole** people said in reply,
   "His **blood** be **upon** us and upon our children."
Then he released **Barabbas** to them,
   but after he had **Jesus** scourged,
   he handed **him over** to be **crucified**.

Then the **soldiers** of the governor took Jesus
      inside the praetorium
   and **gathered** the whole cohort around him.
They stripped off his clothes
   and **threw** a scarlet **military cloak** about him.
Weaving a crown out of **thorns**, they **placed** it on his **head**,
   and a reed in his right hand.
And kneeling before him, they **mocked** him, saying,
   "Hail, King **of the Jews**!"
They spat upon him and took the reed
   and kept striking him on the **head**.
And when they had mocked him,
   they stripped him of the cloak,
   dressed him in his own clothes,
   and led him off to crucify **him**. »

Pause before you say, "I am innocent of this man's blood."

praetorium = prih-TOHR-ee-uhm

Say this line in a mocking tone as well as the words spat, striking, mocked, and stripped.

While Jesus is facing his accusers alone, Peter is outside in the courtyard. In an ironic scene, just after Jesus has been mocked as a prophet, the prophecies he had announced about Peter's denials are coming true. Each time he is questioned, Peter's denials grow stronger. He begins by saying simply that he doesn't know what the maid is talking about and ends by vehemently cursing and swearing, "I do not know the man." He matches the intensity of his denials with the intensity of his remorse, marked by bitter weeping. Judas'

remorse is another story. Unable to undo the betrayal by returning the money, he hangs himself, an episode recounted only in Matthew's Gospel. The hypocrisy of the indifferent chief priests in carefully adhering to the law is on full display whey they buy the potter's field with blood money.

Since the power to put someone to death was reserved to Rome, the Jewish leaders hand Jesus over to Pilate, the Roman prefect. Pilate's question of Jesus, "Are you the king of the Jews?" had political ramifications, again putting Jesus in conflict

and competition with the Roman emperor. Jesus' first succinct reply, followed by silence, subtly depicts him as God's servant described by Isaiah; Jesus is the righteous suffering victim who did not open his mouth (Isaiah 53:7). Even Pilate's amazement contributes to Jesus' portrait as God's servant: "So shall he startle many nations, because of him kings shall stand speechless" (Isaiah 52:15). While the Jewish authorities were intent on finding Jesus guilty, Pilate looks for a way out of condemning him. He hoped to release him in

Cyrenian = sī-REE-nee-uhn

As they were going out, they met a **Cyrenian** named Simon;
    this man they **pressed** into service
  to carry **his cross**.

Golgotha = GAWL-guh-thuh

gall = gawl

And when they came to a place called Golgotha
    —which means **Place of the** Skull—,
  they **gave** Jesus **wine** to drink mixed with **gall**.
But when he had **tasted** it, he refused to drink.
After they had **crucified** him,
    they divided his garments by casting **lots**;
  then they **sat** down and kept watch over him there.
And they placed **over** his head the written charge **against** him:

Pause.

  This **is** Jesus, **the** King **of the** Jews.
Two revolutionaries were crucified with him,
  one on his **right** and the other on his **left**.
Those passing by reviled him, shaking their heads and saying,

Proclaim the words of the passers-by with an abusive tone.

  "You who would **destroy** the temple and **rebuild** it in **three** days,
  save **yourself**, if you **are** the **Son of God**,
  and **come** down from the cross!"
Likewise the chief **priests** with the **scribes** and **elders** mocked
    him and said,

Say in a mocking tone.

  "He **saved others**; he cannot save **himself**.
So he is the **king** of Israel!
Let him come **down** from the cross now,
  and we will believe in him.
He trusted in **God**;
  let him **deliver him** now if he wants him.
For **he** said, '**I am the Son of God**.'"
The revolutionaries who were crucified with him
  also kept **abusing** him in the **same** way.

From noon onward, darkness came over the **whole** land
  until three in the afternoon.

Eli, Eli, lema sabachthani = ay-LEE, ay-LEE, luh-MAH sah-bahk-TAH-nee
Pause before you say this line. Proclaim slowly with good volume.

And about three o'clock Jesus cried out in a **loud voice**,
  "*Eli*, *Eli*, *lema sabachthani*?"
  which means, "**My** God, **my** God, why **have you** forsaken **me**?"

accord with the custom of freeing a prisoner on the feast of Passover, a practice known of only through the Gospel accounts. Then Matthew has a unique insertion about Pilate's wife with her dream about Jesus, whom she calls a righteous man. The scene has a thematic connection with Joseph, the husband of Mary, also called a righteous man to whom God revealed the divine plan through a dream. Unlike the self-righteous Jewish leaders, both Joseph and this Gentile woman are open to divine revelation coming unexpectedly through dreams. In contrast, the chief

priests and elders, determined to put Jesus to death, incite the crowds to shout for Jesus' crucifixion and to release the notorious Barabbas.

While Pilate distances himself from any guilt in handing Jesus over to be crucified, the people accept responsibility. Tragically, their cry "His blood be upon us and upon our children" has been a centuries-long excuse for hostility toward the Jewish people. Some have interpreted these words as making Jews of all generations guilty of deicide. Yet in the context of Matthew's Gospel, the destruction of the

temple in the year 70 was seen as the disaster unleashed on the children of those present in Jerusalem. They suffer the consequences of the acts of the leaders and those who followed them. No guilt passes on to future generations.

After scourging him, Pilate hands Jesus over to be crucified. Since that Greek word used frequently in the passion narrative (*paradidomi*) can mean either "betray" or "hand over," each time Jesus is handed over can be seen as another act of betrayal. Jesus is betrayed not only by Judas, but also by the chief priests, by the elders, by

Elijah = ee-LI-juh

Some of the bystanders who heard it said,
    "This one is calling for Elijah."
Immediately one of them ran to get a **sponge**;
    he soaked it in **wine**, and putting it on a **reed**,
    gave it to him to **drink**.
But the rest said,
    "Wait, let us see if **Elijah** comes to save him."
But Jesus **cried** out again in a loud voice,
    and gave up his spirit.

[Here all kneel and pause for a short time.]

Take your time with this section of the Passion. Speak clearly. Pay attention to the words in bold. Use good volume.

And **behold**, the **veil** of the **sanctuary**
    was **torn** in **two** from top to bottom.
The earth quaked, rocks were split, **tombs** were opened,
    and the **bodies** of many saints who had fallen asleep
        were raised.
And **coming** forth from their tombs **after** his **resurrection**,
    they **entered** the holy city and **appeared** to **many**.
The **centurion** and the men with him who were keeping watch
        over Jesus
    feared greatly when they saw the **earthquake**
    and all that was happening, and they said,
    "Truly, this **was** the **Son of** God!"]

centurion = sen-TOOR-ee-uhn

Pause before you say this line.

There were **many** women there, looking on from a distance,
    who had **followed Jesus** from Galilee, ministering to him.
Among them were **Mary** Magdalene and Mary the mother of
        James and Joseph,
    and the **mother** of the sons of **Zebedee**.

Magdalene = MAG-duh-luhn or MAG-duh-leen

Zebedee = ZEB-uh-dee

Proclaim with an informative tone.
Arimathea = ayr-ih-muh-THEE-uh

When it was evening,
    there came a rich man from Arimathea named Joseph,
    who was himself a disciple of **Jesus**.
He **went** to **Pilate** and **asked** for the body of Jesus;
    then Pilate **ordered** it to be handed over.
Taking **the body**, Joseph **wrapped** it in **clean linen**
    and laid it in his new **tomb** that he had hewn in the rock. »

hewn = hyoon

Caiaphas, and also by Pilate. Degradation after degradation, tortured and mocked as a king, Jesus is treated as an object of scorn, with his true identity hidden from view. Finally, burdened with the cross, Jesus is led away to the place of his crucifixion.

Throughout the scene of Jesus on the cross, multiple allusions to psalms and prophets contribute to Matthew's emphasis on Jesus as fulfillment of the Jewish Scriptures. Psalm 22 in particular can be heard in the background. It is the lament of an innocent, righteous person who had been treated harshly and unjustly. Casting lots for Jesus' clothing, the mocking of all who see him, the taunt that since he trusted God, let God deliver him, and even Jesus' own words from the cross are a tapestry woven from Psalm 22. Though barely able to breathe, Jesus' loud cry from Psalm 22 is one of agony but not despair. He knows the entirety of Psalm 22, with its hopeful ending that says to God that the divine deliverance will be proclaimed to a people yet unborn.

Jesus' agony on the cross continues for three hours in the heat of the midday sun. But Matthew notes that instead of the brightness of the sun, darkness came over the whole land, symbolic of the whole earth being in distress along with Jesus. Finally, with another loud cry, Jesus dies on the cross. His cry signaling his death seems to unleash a cataclysmic response from temple to tombs. The earthquake at Jesus' death, like other quakes in Matthew's Gospel (at the stilling of the storm and at the Resurrection of Jesus) are signs of revelation and divine power, felt in the depths of the earth. Matthew echoes the Hebrew prophets, who had also used cosmic upheaval and heavenly portents to reveal

Pharisees = FAYR-uh-seez

Read with a tone of urgency.

Then he **rolled** a huge **stone** across the entrance to the tomb
and departed.
But **Mary** Magdalene and the **other Mary**
remained sitting there, **facing** the tomb.

The next day, the one **following** the day of preparation,
the chief **priests** and the Pharisees
gathered before Pilate and said,
"Sir, we remember that this impostor while still alive said,
'After **three** days **I** will be raised **up**.'
Give orders, then, that the grave be secured until the third day,
lest his disciples come and steal him and say to the people,
'He has been **raised** from the **dead**.'
This last **imposture would be worse than the** first."
Pilate said to them,
"The guard is yours;
go, secure it as best you can."
So they went and **secured** the tomb
by **fixing** a seal to the **stone** and **setting** the **guard**.

[Shorter: Matthew 27:11–54 (see brackets)]

divine control and majesty. They are also signs of God's ultimate conquering of all evil. Jesus' entire passion, from betrayal to death, fulfills the Scriptures, greatly expanding their meaning. Even with all the connections to the Jewish tradition, the first to recognize Jesus' identity is neither one of the Jewish authorities, nor Jesus' own (absent) disciples. A Roman centurion proclaims him as Son of God. Matthew also notes that women who had followed Jesus, including Mary Magdalene, looked on from a distance. They did not flee the scene as had Jesus' other disciples.

In the evening, after Jesus' death, Joseph of Arimathea, a wealthy disciple, asked for the body of Jesus. After all the physical beating and torture of Jesus, the scene of Joseph taking the body of Jesus is filled with tenderness. According to Jewish custom, he wraps the body in clean linen, then lays it in his own tomb. Burying Jesus on the same day as his death may be another subtle fulfillment: "His body shall not remain all night upon the tree, but you shall bury him the same day" (Deuteronomy 21:23). The women's presence at the tomb provided by Joseph presents them as true

disciples who keep watch at Jesus' tomb. The same women who had seen Jesus die now see where he is buried. In the final scene, the fear and intrigue against Jesus continues as the chief priests arrange for the sealing of Jesus' tomb. As they remember Jesus' words, "After three days I will be raised up," they have ironically proclaimed the truth of Jesus' claim. Since Jesus remains a threat to them even in his death, guards remain stationed at the tomb. The stage is set for his Resurrection, the fulfillment of ancient promises and Jesus' own prophetic words. E.P.

HOLY THURSDAY: MASS OF THE LORD'S SUPPER

LECTIONARY #39

READING I   Exodus 12:1–8, 11–14

A reading from the Book of Exodus

The LORD said to **Moses** and **Aaron** in the land of Egypt,
    "This **month** shall stand at the **head** of your calendar;
    you shall reckon it the first month of the year.
Tell the **whole community** of Israel:
    On the **tenth** of this month every one of your **families**
    must procure for itself a lamb, **one** apiece for each household.
If a family is too small for a **whole** lamb,
    it shall join the nearest **household** in procuring one
    and shall share in the lamb
    in proportion to the number of persons who partake of it.
The lamb must be a **year-old** male and **without** blemish.
You may take it from either the sheep or the goats.
You shall keep it until the fourteenth **day** of this month,
    and **then**, with the **whole** assembly of Israel **present**,
    it shall be slaughtered during the **evening twilight**.
They shall take some of its blood
    and **apply** it to the **two** doorposts **and the** lintel
    of **every house** in which they partake of the **lamb**.
That **same night** they shall eat its roasted flesh
    with unleavened bread and **bitter** herbs. **»**

Exodus = EK-suh-duhs
Aaron = AYR-un
Moses = MOH-zis

Take your time in giving the Lord's instructions. Proclaim in a tone of authority. Be sure your words are clear as you read.

READING I   The Passover is so central to the identity of the Israelites and their relationship with God that they remember it in multiple ways. Throughout the Torah, brief statements of belief identify the Lord as the one who delivered them from slavery: "I, the Lord, am your God who brought you out of the land of Egypt to be your God" (Numbers 15:41; compare with Exodus 20:2, Deuteronomy 26:6–10). These creedal statements are often embedded in longer stories that recount how God set the people free. The story begins when "a new king, who knew nothing of Joseph, rose to power in Egypt" (Exodus 1:8) and quickly moves to the account of Moses' encounter with God who tells him, "I have witnessed the affliction of my people in Egypt and . . . have come down to rescue them from the power of the Egyptians" (Exodus 3:7, 8). The divine deliverance of Israel reaches a highpoint in the instructions God gives to Moses and Aaron recounted in today's reading. Along with creed and story, another way to forge community identity is through ritual celebrations that involve the whole community at set times, with prescribed actions and prayers. Creed, story, ritual: three essential ways to remember God's acts of deliverance of those enslaved in Egypt.

At the heart of the Passover story and ritual is the meal, described in detail. The time of year, the actions, and foods have significance for coming generations who will celebrate it as a perpetual institution. Ever after, the month of the Passover is to be the beginning of the liturgical year. In fact, the directions for the meal sound much like instructions for a liturgical celebration. People are to gather, prepare everything for

girt = belted

Pause before you proclaim this line.

"This is how you are to eat it:
   with your **loins** girt, sandals on your feet and your staff
      in hand,
   you shall eat like those who are in flight.
It is the Passover **of the LORD**.

Pause before you proclaim this line.

For on this same night **I** will go through Egypt,
   striking down every firstborn of the land, **both** man and beast,
   and **executing judgment** on all the **gods** of Egypt—I, **the** LORD!
But the **blood** will **mark** the houses where you are.
Seeing the blood, I will **pass** over **you**;
   thus, when I strike the land of **Egypt**,
   no destructive blow will come **upon** you.

"This day shall be a memorial **feast** for **you**,
   which **all** your **generations** shall celebrate
   with pilgrimage to the LORD, as a perpetual **institution**."

For meditation and context:

RESPONSORIAL PSALM   Psalm 116:12–13, 15–16bc, 17–18
(1 Corinthians 10:16)

R. Our blessing-cup is a communion with the Blood of Christ.

How shall I make a return to the LORD
   for all the good he has done for me?
The cup of salvation I will take up,
   and I will call upon the name of the LORD.

To you will I offer sacrifice of thanksgiving,
   and I will call upon the name of the LORD.
My vows to the LORD I will pay
   in the presence of all his people.

Precious in the eyes of the LORD
   is the death of his faithful ones.
I am your servant, the son of your handmaid;
   you have loosed my bonds.

---

the meal, eat and dress in a certain way, and keep the feast as a memorial celebration. All who gather for the meal are to share in the lamb procured ahead of time. It must have no blemish, since it is set aside as a sacrifice to God. Applying the blood of the lamb to the doorposts may be an adaptation of an ancient pastoral practice of spreading the blood of a lamb to ward off evil. Whatever the origin, the blood attains a new meaning on this night. The Lord will pass over any houses marked with the blood of the lamb, initiating the beginning of the Lord bringing them out of Egypt.

READING II Today's reading from 1 Corinthians is the oldest written account of the Last Supper. Although it is the oldest written account, dating from about twenty or so years after the actual event, Paul says that he received it, indicating that it was a tradition passed on to him orally and through the celebration of the Lord's Supper itself. In using the language of receiving and handing on, Paul is implying that he is faithful to a living tradition rooted in Jesus' own actions on the night he was betrayed. It was important for the Corinthians to be reminded anew of

Jesus' words and actions because, as Paul had just chastised them, their own gatherings "are doing more harm than good" (11:17). The divisions in the community are evident when "one goes hungry while another gets drunk" (11:22). Instead of sharing in the Lord's Supper, each one is eating his own supper, making the meal a sign of division rather than communion. Their individualistic, selfish behavior is, in effect, another instance of betrayal of Jesus.

   The meal that Jesus shared with his disciples was, in contrast, one of intimacy. Jesus begins in a manner typical of a Jewish

Corinthians = kohr-IN-thee-uhnz

This is a beautiful passage from St. Paul. Proclaim with good volume and eye contact. Pause before you say Jesus' words, proclaiming with tenderness in your tone.

READING II   1 Corinthians 11:23–26

A reading from the first Letter of Saint Paul to the Corinthians

Brothers and sisters:
I received from the **Lord** what I **also** handed on to you,
    that the **Lord** Jesus, on the night he was handed over,
    took bread, and, after he had given **thanks**,
    broke it and said, "This is **my body** that is **for you**.
Do this in remembrance of me."
In the same way also the **cup**, after supper, saying,
    "This **cup** is the new **covenant** in my **blood**.
Do this, as **often** as you **drink** it, in remembrance of me."
For as often as you eat this bread and drink the cup,
    you **proclaim** the **death** of the **Lord** until he comes.

This Gospel is a learning moment for the disciples. Before the washing of the feet begins, proclaim using an informative tone.

Iscariot = ih-SKAYR-ee-uht

GOSPEL   John 13:1–15

A reading from the holy Gospel according to John

Before the feast of Passover, Jesus **knew** that his **hour** had **come**
    to pass from **this** world to the Father.
He loved his own in the world and he loved them to the end.
The **devil** had already **induced** Judas, son of **Simon the** Iscariot,
        to hand him **over**.
So, during **supper**,
    fully aware that the Father had put everything into his power
    and that he had come from **God** and was **returning to God**,
    he **rose** from supper and took **off** his outer garments.
He took a **towel** and **tied** it around his waist.
Then he **poured** water into a basin
    and began to wash the disciples' **feet**
    and **dry** them with the **towel** around his waist. »

meal. His thanksgiving draws the participants together before God. When Jesus gives his body "for you," "you" includes more than the first disciples gathered in Jerusalem, but embraces all who gather in remembrance of him. Both bread and cup are a participation in the very body and blood of Christ, in his very life. Sharing in Christ's own body makes the community "though many . . . one body" (10:17). Jesus binds the community through a new covenant in his blood. His language is reminiscent of that of the prophet Jeremiah (31:31), thereby fulfilling the ancient promise.

The wording in Paul's account is close to that in Luke's Gospel. Only Luke and Paul include the command to "do this in remembrance of me." The verb form for "do in remembrance" means to keep on doing this, not do it as a one-time action, but as one that is repeated. Like the Passover, Jesus' supper is a new memorial; "doing in remembrance" means that Jesus' self-gift is present at each celebration of the Lord's Supper.

| GOSPEL | The hour of Jesus has been long anticipated in John's Gospel. Now that the hour has come, John |

finally makes clear what the hour means: passing from this world to the Father. John says that Jesus was aware "that he had come from God and was returning to God." It is the hour of Jesus' own Passover, from this world to the Father, from death to life. As he gathers with his disciples for a final supper, Jesus prepares them for the coming hour. All that he will do is a sign of his loving them "to the end" (*eis telos*). As the evangelist has done many times throughout his Gospel, he uses a phrase with a double meaning. *Eis telos* can have a temporal meaning, meaning that Jesus loves

During the conversation between Jesus and Simon Peter, use emotion in your voice as well as facial expression. Pause before you say their words.

He came to Simon **Peter**, who said to him,
    "Master, are you going to **wash my feet**?"
Jesus answered and said to him,
    "What **I** am **doing**, you do **not understand** now,
    but you will understand **later**."
Peter said to him, "You will never wash my feet."
Jesus answered him,
    "Unless I wash you, you will have **no inheritance** with me."
Simon Peter said to him,
    "**Master**, then **not** only my **feet**, but my hands and head
        as well."
Jesus said to him,
    "Whoever has **bathed** has **no need except** to have his
        feet washed, for he is **clean all** over;
    so you are clean, but **not all**."
For he knew who would **betray** him;
    for this **reason**, he said, "**Not** all of you are clean."

A slight pause is necessary for emphasis. Then slowly proclaim Jesus' words.

So when he had **washed** their feet
    and put his garments back on and **reclined** at table again,
    he said to them, "**Do** you realize what **I** have done for **you**?
You call me '**teacher**' and '**master**,' and rightly so, for indeed I **am**.
If I, therefore, the master and teacher, have **washed** your feet,
    you ought to wash **one** another's feet.
I have **given** you a **model** to follow,
    so that as **I** have **done** for you, you **should** also **do**."

his own until the very last moment. It also means "to the uttermost"; Jesus loved to the greatest degree possible.

The scene according to John is very different from the synoptic accounts, where the meal seems to be a Passover celebration. In John, it occurs before the Passover. Even more distinctive is the washing of the feet, whereas the other Gospel accounts include Jesus' institution of the Eucharist. The action of foot washing is rich in symbolism. In the cultural context, the expression "with unwashed feet" meant that someone was without sufficient preparation. Thus Jesus' washing of his disciples' feet is a means of preparing them for his coming hour. In the washing, we see another symbol: Jesus takes on the role of a servant. With a towel around his waist, he appears as a typical household slave, acting freely, motivated by love. Peter's resistance to Jesus' action is understandable; Jesus is his "Master" (*kyrios*), not a slave. Washing the feet of guests was also an act of hospitality, an expected sign of respect. Jesus is offering hospitality to all, even as he is about to be rejected—a development highlighted by the presence of Judas. In the brief account of the last supper in Corinthians, Jesus told his followers to "do this in remembrance of me." In a similar way, he now tells his disciples that his washing of their feet is a model for them: "As I have done for you, you should also do." E.P.

GOOD FRIDAY: CELEBRATION OF THE LORD'S PASSION

LECTIONARY #40

READING I   Isaiah 52:13—53:12

Isaiah = Ī-ZAY-uh

Proclaim with high energy.

A reading from the Book of the Prophet Isaiah

See, my **servant** shall prosper,
    he shall be **raised** high and **greatly exalted**.
Even as many were amazed at him—
    so marred was his look **beyond** human semblance
    and his appearance beyond that of the sons of man—
so shall he startle many nations,
    because of him **kings** shall stand speechless;
for those who have **not** been told shall **see**,
    those who have **not** heard shall ponder it.

You are asking two questions. Pause after each one.

Proclaim with emotion in your voice and in your facial expression. Take your time.

Who would believe what **we have heard**?
    To whom has the arm of the LORD been revealed?
He grew up like a sapling before him,
    like a shoot from the **parched earth**;
there was in him **no** stately bearing to make us **look** at him,
    nor appearance that would attract us to him.
He was spurned and **avoided** by people,
    a man of suffering, **accustomed** to **infirmity**,
one of those from whom people hide their faces,
    spurned, and we held him in no esteem. »

READING I | On Palm Sunday we heard the third of the poems from Isaiah commonly referred to as "servant songs," prophecies that describe an unidentified servant of God. Though righteous, the servant suffers and remains faithful no matter how harshly he is treated. Today's reading is the fourth and final of these "servant songs." In the opening and closing parts of the poem, we hear the voice of God, both times speaking of "my servant." The repeated designation emphasizes the personal and abiding relationship between the servant and God.

The opening Hebrew word of the prophecy is *hinneh*, "behold," or "see," a term that urges everyone to give careful attention to what follows. "See, my servant shall prosper." This is God's own servant who will ultimately flourish and be greatly exalted even though his appearance suggests just the opposite. Such a startling paradox will require careful attention and leave people speechless. God's concluding words expand the initial portrait of one marred in appearance, adding to the enigma. The very suffering of the servant will be a source of justification and pardon for others. Such an interpretation of anguish runs counter to the commonly held notion that suffering was the result of personal sinfulness. Yet it is the sin, injustice, and wickedness of others that is inflicted on God's servant; it is their guilt, not his own, that he bears—another paradox to be pondered.

God's words frame those of the community that relate what has been revealed to them. While the initial words of God

Let your voice build as you tell the intensity of his suffering.

Yet it was our infirmities that he bore,
    our sufferings that he **endured**,
while we thought of him as stricken,
    as one smitten by God and **afflicted**.
But **he** was pierced for our offenses,
    crushed for our **sins**;

Say slowly "makes us whole" and "the guilt of us all."

upon him was the **chastisement** that **makes** us **whole**,
    by his **stripes** we were healed.
We had all gone astray like **sheep**,
    each following his own way;
but the LORD laid upon him
    the **guilt** of us all.

Clearly pronounce each word ending. Emphasize the words in bold.

Though he was harshly treated, he **submitted**
    and **opened** not his **mouth**;
like a lamb **led** to the **slaughter**
    or a sheep before the **shearers**,
    he was silent and opened **not** his mouth.
Oppressed and condemned, he was taken **away**,
    and who would have **thought** any **more** of his destiny?
When he was cut **off** from the land of the **living**,
    and smitten for the **sin** of his people,
a grave was assigned him among the **wicked**
    and a burial place with **evildoers**,
though he had done **no** wrong
    nor spoken any **falsehood**.
But the LORD was **pleased**
    to **crush** him in infirmity.

If he **gives** his life as an **offering** for **sin**,
    he shall **see** his **descendants** in a **long life**,
    and the **will** of the LORD shall be accomplished
        through him.

referred only briefly to the marred appearance of his servant, the community develops the portrait in detail. The people begin with questions that express their own grappling with their experience of this mysterious servant, using first person plural pronouns. They admit that we held him in no esteem and thought of him as stricken. It is incomprehensible that he bore our infirmities, endured our sufferings. Coupled with the servant's physical suffering is his total rejection by the people for whom he

suffered. Yet, he never retaliated, submitting like a lamb led to the slaughter.

There is nothing in the servant songs that made the servant's identity clear, nor was it obvious if the servant referred to an individual or stood for a whole group, such as the Jewish people in exile. Only in light of Christ's redemptive suffering, his surrendering of himself to death for the sake of others, has the identity of the unnamed servant been able to shine forth with clarity. Jesus is God's servant, the one who took upon him-

self the guilt of us all, taking away our sins, and winning pardon for our offenses.

READING II   Jesus is a great high priest and Son of God! In the reading from Hebrews, this twofold proclamation not only offers insights into Jesus' identity but is also the basis for steadfast faith in him. The author of Hebrews exhorts us to hold fast to our confession, probably referring to baptismal faith and commitment.

A central theme in Hebrews is Jesus' role as high priest, first described as "a

What wonderful news! Proclaim with a tone of gratefulness.

Because of his **affliction**
    he shall **see** the **light** in **fullness** of days;
through his **suffering**, my servant shall justify many,
    and their guilt he shall **bear**.
Therefore I will give **him** his portion among the **great**,
    and he shall **divide** the **spoils** with the mighty,
because he **surrendered** himself to death
    and was counted **among** the **wicked**;
and he shall **take away** the **sins** of many,
    and **win pardon** for their **offenses**.

For meditation and context:

RESPONSORIAL PSALM   Psalm 31:2, 6, 12–13, 15–16, 17, 25 (Luke 23:46)

R. Father, into your hands I commend my spirit.

In you, O LORD, I take refuge;
  let me never be put to shame.
In your justice rescue me.
Into your hands I commend my spirit;
  you will redeem me, O LORD,
    O faithful God.

For all my foes I am an object of reproach,
  a laughingstock to my neighbors,
    and a dread to my friends;
  they who see me abroad flee from me.
I am forgotten like the unremembered dead;
  I am like a dish that is broken.

But my trust is in you, O LORD;
  I say, "You are my God.
In your hands is my destiny; rescue me
  from the clutches of my enemies
    and my persecutors."

Let your face shine upon your servant;
  save me in your kindness.
Take courage and be stouthearted,
  all you who hope in the LORD.

READING II   Hebrews 4:14–16; 5:7–9

A reading from the Letter to the Hebrews

Brothers and sisters:
Since we have a great high priest who has passed through
    the heavens,
    Jesus, **the Son of God**,
    let us **hold** fast to our **confession**. »

This Scripture reading is all good news. Proclaim with clarity and reverence.

merciful and faithful high priest" (2:17), two qualities that characterize Jesus' priestly ministry. The portrait of Jesus as high priest in Hebrews draws on the Jewish tradition, where the high priest was regarded as the mediator between God and the people. On the Day of Atonement, the high priest would pass through the veil of the temple to enter the holy of holies, the very presence of God. There, he would sprinkle the blood of a sacrificial animal as expiation for sin. The designation "great high priest" presents Jesus as one greatly exalted, even

more than the Jewish high priest who only passed through the curtain of the temple, while Jesus passed into the heavenly presence of God. Not the blood of a sacrificial animal, but the pouring out of his own blood was the means of mercy. Though high priest is a lofty title, ordinarily suggesting a distance from those who are sinful and weak, Hebrews emphasizes that Jesus the high priest is intimately connected with us. He sympathizes with our weakness, having similarly been tested in every way.

His high priesthood is ever exercised in mercy and grace.

The second part of the reading (heard also on the Fifth Sunday of Lent) brings together Jesus' divine sonship and his humanity, the "days when [he] was in the flesh." Like the designation "high priest," that of "Son" is an exalted title. Yet Jesus' sonship is exercised in lowliness, in suffering, and obedience. As Son, he shares with us our human condition, remaining faithful even as he cries out to God in his agony. Our response to Jesus, the Son of God, is to

For we do **not** have a high priest
   who is **unable** to **sympathize** with our **weaknesses**,
   but one who has **similarly** been **tested** in **every way**,
   yet without sin.
So let us **confidently** approach the throne of grace
   to receive mercy and to **find** grace for timely **help**.

In the days when **Christ** was in the flesh,
   he offered prayers and supplications with loud **cries** and **tears**
   to the **one** who was able to save him from death,
   and he was **heard** because of his reverence.
Son though he was, he learned obedience from what he suffered;
   and when he was made **perfect**,
   he became the **source** of **eternal** salvation for **all** who obey him.

GOSPEL   John 18:1—19:42

The Passion of our Lord Jesus Christ according to John

Jesus went out with his disciples across the **Kidron** valley
   to where there was a garden,
   into which he and his disciples **entered**.
Judas his **betrayer** also knew the place,
   because Jesus had **often** met there with his disciples.
So Judas got a band of **soldiers** and **guards**
   from the chief **priests** and the **Pharisees**
   and **went there** with **lanterns**, **torches**, and **weapons**.
Jesus, **knowing** everything that was going to **happen** to him,
   went out and said to them, "Whom are you looking for?"
They answered him, "**Jesus** the **Nazorean**."
He said to them, "I AM."
Judas his betrayer was also with them.
When he said to them, "**I AM**,"
   they turned away and fell to the ground.

Kidron = KID-ruhn
Proclaim with a loud voice in an informative tone. High energy is needed throughout.

Pharisees = FAYR-uh-seez
Always pause before you read Jesus' words.

Nazorean = naz-uh-REE-uhn

live in similar lowliness, obedience, and reliance on God.

GOSPEL Each of the Gospel accounts has a long passion narrative that tells of Jesus' betrayal, mock trial, suffering, and death. While it is clearly the same story, the portraits of Jesus are somewhat different in each version, developed along the same lines that the four evangelists already began to sketch in the earlier parts of their accounts. For example, in Luke's Gospel, Jesus began his ministry by announcing his release to captives and liberty to prisoners; from the cross, he offers release and liberty in the form of forgiveness to a thief crucified with him, and even asks for mercy on those who crucified him. In John's Gospel, the narrative we hear on this Good Friday, Jesus knows everything that is about to happen, displaying the same knowledge that was his throughout the Gospel. His portrait displays a king, majestically lifted up on the cross, just as he had told Nicodemus early in the Gospel: "So must the Son of Man be lifted up" (3:14). As we listen to John's account, we will hear and see Jesus moving deliberately and serenely to fulfill what he knows must happen. All of Jesus' words and actions throughout the passion account flow from his having loved his own, and loving them to the end (13:1). Beginning with the betrayal in the garden and concluding with his handing over the spirit from the cross, Jesus shows compassion and infinite love for those who are his disciples.

Our reading begins with Jesus and his disciples going to a garden, a place familiar

So he **again** asked them,
    "Whom are you looking for?"
They said, "**Jesus** the **Nazorean**."
Jesus answered,
    "**I** told you that I AM.
So **if** you are looking for me, let these men go."
This was to fulfill what he had said,
    "I have **not** lost any of those you gave me."
Then **Simon** Peter, who had a **sword**, drew **it**,
    struck the high priest's slave, and cut off his right **ear**.
The slave's name was **Malchus**.
Jesus said to Peter,
    "**Put** your **sword** into its **scabbard**.
Shall I **not** drink the cup that the **Father gave** me?"

So the band of soldiers, the tribune, and the Jewish guards
        seized Jesus,
    bound him, and **brought** him to Annas first.
He was the father-in-law of **Caiaphas**,
    who was high priest that year.
It was **Caiaphas** who had **counseled** the **Jews**
    that it was better that one man should **die rather** than
        the **people**.

Simon Peter and another disciple **followed** Jesus.
Now the **other** disciple was **known** to the high priest,
    and he **entered** the courtyard of the high priest **with** Jesus.
But Peter stood at the gate outside.
So the other **disciple**, the **acquaintance** of the high priest,
    went out and **spoke** to the **gatekeeper** and brought Peter in.
Then the maid who was the **gatekeeper** said to Peter,
    "You are not one of this man's **disciples**, **are** you?"
He said, "I am not." »

Malchus = MAL-kuhs

scabbard = SCA-b*rd

Continue to articulate as you read.

Annas = AN-uhs
Caiaphas = KĪ-uh fuhs

Use expression in your voice especially as the gatekeeper asks Peter a question and Peter answers her.

to Judas as well. As he has done throughout his Gospel, the evangelist uses symbolism and paradox in the passion narrative. His symbolic universe is rich and multifaceted, able to embrace diverse imagery throughout the narrative: Jesus will be portrayed as king, priest, the Lamb of sacrifice, and the righteous sufferer, opening the account to a wide variety of interpretations and insights.

John has already used darkness and night as symbolic of ignorance and evil, and does so in the garden scene as well. Jesus, the light of the world, simply entered the garden with his disciples, but Judas and those who will arrest Jesus need lanterns and torches since they are walking in the darkness. Jesus meets them calmly, already knowing all that will happen. Unlike the garden scene in the synoptic Gospels, Jesus is not crying out in agony, since this is the hour for which he came (12:27). His apparently simple answer identifies himself as the one they are seeking, "I AM," as he has done so often throughout the Gospel. Yet as the "I AM," Jesus is intimately identified with the great "I AM" of the Torah, the name by which God identified himself to Moses (Exodus 3:14). The reaction of falling to the ground highlights the power of the name in the face of enemies. Judas and company have come prepared for violence, carrying weapons along with their lanterns. When Simon Peter meets violence with violence, Jesus uses the moment to again teach the necessity of drinking of the cup that the Father gave him. His disciples must share in his suffering. With no sign of resis-

Now the **slaves** and the **guards** were standing around
    a charcoal **fire**
  that they had made, because it was cold,
  and were warming themselves.
Peter was **also** standing there keeping **warm**.

The high priest **questioned** Jesus
  about his **disciples** and about his doctrine.
Jesus answered him,
  "I have spoken publicly to the world.
I have always taught in a synagogue
  or in the temple **area** where **all** the Jews gather,
  and in secret I have said nothing. **Why** ask me?
Ask those who heard me what I said to them.
They know what I said."
When he had said this,
  one of the temple guards standing there struck Jesus and said,
  "Is this the way you **answer** the high priest?"
Jesus answered him,
  "If I have spoken **wrongly**, **testify** to the **wrong**;
  but if I have spoken rightly, **why** do you strike me?"
Then Annas sent him **bound** to **Caiaphas** the high priest.

Now Simon **Peter** was standing there keeping warm.
And they said to him,
  "**You** are **not** one of his disciples, **are** you?"
He denied it and said,
  "I am **not**."
One of the **slaves** of the high priest,
  a relative of the **one** whose ear Peter had cut off, said,
  "**Didn't** I see you in the garden **with** him?"
Again Peter denied it.
And immediately the **cock** crowed.

Then they brought Jesus **from** Caiaphas to the **praetorium**.
It was morning.

As Jesus is being questioned, his responses are given directly and in a calm manner.

praetorium = prih-TOHR-ee-uhm

It is morning. Keep up the energy in your voice.

tance on his part, Jesus is seized, bound, and brought to trial.

While Jesus is brought before Annas, Simon Peter and another disciple cautiously enter the courtyard. This is the second appearance of Peter in the account, having just cut off the ear of the high priest's slave. Peter's first denial is that he is not one of "this man's" disciples, putting a distance between himself and the group of Jesus' followers. While Jesus had readily acknowledged his identity in the garden, Peter denies who he is. Ironically, Peter's

denial that he is a disciple appears to be true as he distances himself from Jesus and his companions. He is standing with the slaves and guards, warming himself by the fire, seeming to belong more to that group than to Jesus.

Between Peter's first denial and the second, the narrative again focuses on Jesus, appearing in sharp contrast to Peter. Annas, his interrogator, asks Jesus about two things: his disciples, and his doctrine. Jesus' answers are straightforward and fearless. Jesus tells Annas that he has spoken

publicly (*parresia*), a term often used to describe prophetic speech, including both frankness and boldness. His teaching has not been in secret, as those who have heard him can testify. Jesus seems to be saying that Annas should ask his disciples about him and his teaching. Peter, warming himself along with Jesus' opponents, has failed even to admit being one of Jesus' disciples. Before the scene switches again to the fearful Peter, we see Jesus facing his accusers with prophetic assurance. Then he is led, bound, to Caiaphas the high priest.

And they themselves **did** not enter the praetorium,
    in order **not** to be **defiled** so that they **could** eat the **Passover**.
So Pilate came out **to them** and said,
    "What **charge** do you bring against this man?"
They answered and said to him,
    "If he were **not** a **criminal**,
    we would not have handed him **over** to you."
At this, Pilate said to them,
    "**Take** him **yourselves**, and **judge** him according to your law."
The **Jews** answered him,
    "**We** do **not** have the **right** to execute anyone,"
    in order that the word of Jesus might be fulfilled
    that he said indicating the **kind** of death he would **die**.
So Pilate went back into the praetorium
    and summoned **Jesus** and said to him,
    "Are you the **King** of the **Jews**?"
Jesus answered,
    "Do you say this on your own
    or have others told you about me?"
Pilate answered,
    "I am **not** a **Jew**, am I?
Your **own nation** and the **chief priests** handed **you** over to **me**.
What have you done?"
Jesus answered,
    "**My** kingdom does **not** belong to **this** world.
If my kingdom did belong to this world,
    my attendants would be fighting
    to keep me from being handed over to the Jews.
But as it **is**, my kingdom is **not** here."
So Pilate said to him,
    "Then you are a king?"
Jesus answered,
    "**You** say I am a king.
For this I was born and for **this** I came into the world,
    to testify to the truth. »

In this exchange, Jesus is teaching even as he humbly answers Pilate. As you proclaim, let us hear arrogance in Pilate's questions. Rehearse for strong eye contact.

The contrast between Jesus and Peter continues, with two more denials. Even the mention of the garden, where Peter had cut off the ear of Malchus, brings another denial. This is Peter's trial, where his guilt is heard in the crowing of the cock, bringing to fulfillment Jesus' prophecy: "The cock will not crow before you deny me three times" (13:38). The evangelist creates another irony: even as Jesus had been questioned as a false prophet and messianic pretender, he is shown to be a true prophet.

The Jewish leaders now hand Jesus over to the Roman authority, the governor Pilate. Only Rome would have power to condemn anyone to death, the outcome hoped for by the Jewish authorities. There is dynamic movement in the trial before Pilate, with scene changes alternating between inside and outside the praetorium, Pilate's headquarters. While Pilate hurries back and forth, from one setting to another, Jesus continues to be unafraid; Pilate's scurrying back and forth from Jesus inside the praetorium to the priests and

crowds outside exhibits his growing fear. His question to Jesus, "Are you the King of the Jews?" initiates a thematic emphasis that will continue through the rest of the passion narrative. In delving into the mystery of Jesus' kingship, the Fourth Gospel combines history and theology, paradox and irony.

From a historical perspective, Pilate's question to Jesus is a political one. Anyone claiming kingship would be regarded as a threat to Rome, guilty of insurrection or attempting to seize power. Pilate's fear was

Everyone who **belongs** to the truth listens to my voice."
Pilate said to him, "What is **truth**?"

When he had said this,
    he **again** went out to the Jews and said to them,
    "I find **no guilt** in him.
But **you** have a **custom** that I **release one** prisoner to you
        at **Passover**.
Do you want me to **release** to you the King **of the Jews?**"
They cried out **again**,
    "Not this one but **Barabbas**!"
Now Barabbas was a revolutionary.

Then Pilate took Jesus and had him scourged.
And the soldiers wove a **crown** out of **thorns** and placed it
    on his head,
    and **clothed** him in a **purple** cloak,
    and they came to him and said,
    "Hail, King of the Jews!"
And they struck him **repeatedly**.
Once **more** Pilate went out and said to them,
    "**Look**, I am bringing him **out** to you,
    so that you may **know** that I find **no** guilt in **him**."
So Jesus came out,
    wearing the crown of **thorns** and the purple **cloak**.
And he said to them, "**Behold**, the man!"
When the chief priests and the guards saw him they **cried** out,
    "**Crucify** him, crucify **him**!"
Pilate said to them,
    "**Take** him yourselves and crucify him.
I find **no guilt** in him."
The Jews answered,
    "We have a law, and according to **that** law he ought to die,
    because he **made himself** the **Son** of God."

Say this line with intensity.
Barabbas = buh-RAB-uhs

scourged = skerjd

Say Pilate's words in a calm tone.

Proclaim angrily.

likely complicated. He was fearful of alienating Caiaphas, with whom he collaborated, since Caiaphas was a reliable supporter of Pilate, useful in keeping the Jewish populace under control. Pilate wouldn't want to alienate such a powerful ally. He was also fearful of the crowds from all over the empire, greatly increased in size because of the Passover feast. Going against their wishes could well lead to the kind of chaos that Pilate wanted desperately to avoid. And then there is Jesus. For Pilate, Jesus could be the kind of subversive so feared by Rome. Is he in fact claiming to be a king? Pilate is not interested in Jesus' teaching, but in the political consequences, the threat that he poses to Pilate's power, and ultimately to that of Rome. His movement from one place to another reflects well the uncertainty and fear that must have motivated his actions.

While Pilate's question on whether Jesus is a king is based on political and practical concerns, Jesus' answer moves outside of such earthly concerns. His kingdom is not of this world. Unlike the kings and kingdoms with which Plate is familiar, Jesus' kingship is in another realm. His mission is to testify to the truth, a concept totally lost on Pilate. "What is truth?" is a question that sounds more dismissive than probing. Pilate is interested in getting the case resolved before the situation gets out of control. Though he finds no guilt in Jesus, the fearful Pilate leaves the decision to others. His question, in which he refers to Jesus as "king of the Jews," is another case of irony: unrecognized by Pilate, Caiaphas, the soldiers, or crowds, Jesus is indeed a

Now when Pilate heard this statement,
   he became even **more afraid**,
   and went back into the praetorium and said to Jesus,
   "**Where** are you **from**?"
Jesus did not **answer** him.
So Pilate said to him,
   "Do you **not speak** to **me**?
Do you **not** know that I have **power** to release you
   and I have **power** to crucify you?"
Jesus answered him,
   "You would have no power **over** me
   if it had **not** been given to **you** from **above**.
For this reason the **one** who handed me over to you
   has the greater sin."
Consequently, Pilate **tried** to release him;
   but the **Jews cried** out,
   "**If** you release him, you are **not** a Friend **of** Caesar.
Everyone who makes himself a **king opposes** Caesar."

When Pilate heard these words he brought Jesus out
   and **seated** him on the **judge's** bench
   in the place called Stone Pavement, in Hebrew, Gabbatha.
It was preparation day for **Passover**, and it was about noon.
And he said to the Jews,
   "**Behold**, your **king**!"
They **cried** out,
   "**Take him** away, take him **away**! **Crucify** him!"
Pilate said to them,
   "Shall I crucify your **king**?"
The chief priests answered,
   "We have no king but Caesar."
Then he handed him over to them to be **crucified**.

So they **took** Jesus, and, carrying the cross **himself**,
   he went **out** to what is called the **Place of the** Skull,
   in Hebrew, Golgotha. »

Let the assembly hear Pilate's frustration in your voice.

Jesus is firm in his answer.

Gabbatha = GAB-uh-thuh

Proclaim Pilate's words with authority.

Keep energy up. Timing is important. Pause before you read the dialogue. Read with vocal expression.

Golgotha = GAWL-guh-thuh

king. The trappings of kingship, including a crown of thorns on his head and purple clothing, continue the ironic portrait of Jesus as king. In their mockery, they have correctly identified Jesus, who will make his way to the cross still wearing the signs of kingship.

Twice Pilate presents Jesus to the crowd, first saying, "Behold the man," and later "Behold your king." This first time, Pilate seems to be calling attention to Jesus' humanity, weak and humiliated. The second time, identifying Jesus as "your

king," Pilate has again, ironically, correctly identified Jesus, although the volatile crowd rejects the title. Spurred on by the chief priests, the people react by attacking Pilate at his weakest point: his fear of Rome. They accuse him of being no friend of Caesar, and that their only king is Caesar, a jarring admission at the holy time of Passover. The combination of fear of the crowds and fear of Rome overcomes Pilate's fear of Jesus. No longer vacillating, Pilate hands him over to be crucified.

Unlike the synoptic Gospels, in which Simon of Cyrene is forced to help Jesus carry his cross, in John's Gospel he carries the cross himself. Paradoxically, he is acting as the one in control, even majestic, as he is led to his Crucifixion. Ancient sources attest to the horror of death by crucifixion. The Jewish author Josephus called it "the most miserable of all deaths," and Cicero described it as "the cruelest, most terrible punishment." The evangelist omits all the shock of crucifixion, focusing instead on Jesus' identity and final words. Pilate's

There they **crucified** him, and with him **two others**,
    one on either side, with **Jesus** in the middle.
Pilate also had an **inscription** written and put on the cross.
It read,
    "Jesus **the** Nazorean, **the** King **of th**e Jews."
Now many of the Jews read this inscription,
    because the place where Jesus was crucified was near the **city**;
    and it was written in **Hebrew, Latin, and Greek**.
So the **chief priests** of the Jews said to Pilate,
    "**Do** not write 'The King of the Jews,'
    but that he said, 'I am the King of the Jews.'"
Pilate answered,
    "What **I** have **written**, **I** have written."

When the **soldiers** had crucified Jesus,
    they took his clothes and divided them into four shares,
    a share for **each** soldier.
They **also** took his tunic, but the tunic was **seamless**,
    woven in **one** piece from the top **down**.
So they said to one another,
    "Let's not tear it, but **cast** lots for it to see whose it will be,"
    in order that the passage of Scripture might be **fulfilled**
        that says:
        They divided **my garments among the**m,
            and for my vesture they cast lots.
This is what the soldiers did.
Standing by the **cross** of Jesus were his **mother**
    and his mother's sister, **Mary** the wife of Clopas,
    and **Mary of Magdala**.
When Jesus **saw** his **mother** and the disciple there whom
        he loved
    he said to his **mother**, "**Woman**, behold, your **son**."
Then he said to the disciple,
    "Behold, your **mother**."
And from **that hour** the disciple **took** her into his home.

Take your time. Maintain strong eye contact.

Magdala = MAG-duh-luh

inscription, "Jesus the Nazorean, the King of the Jews," correctly identifies Jesus, but is angrily objected to by the chief priests. In an act in which he finally opposes the Jewish leadership, Pilate remains steadfast, stating for all to see who Jesus is, even on the cross. The inscription in Hebrew, Greek, and Latin proclaims him as king for the whole world.

The Jewish crowd, so adamant in forcing Jesus' crucifixion, is no longer mentioned, for the Roman soldiers are now overseeing his death. Their dividing of Jesus' garments and casting lots for his

seamless tunic seem an odd interruption to the narrative. Such details must be included for symbolic value. In addition to the scriptural fulfillment noted by the evangelist are other possible meanings. Not tearing the garment may symbolize the unity of Jesus and his Father, a unity not broken by Jesus' death; some patristic authors interpreted the untorn tunic as symbolic of the unity of Jesus' followers. Others have seen the seamless tunic as an allusion to the garment of the high priest, thereby presenting Jesus as both king and high priest.

Those standing by the cross, according to John, include Jesus' mother, other women, and the disciple whom Jesus loved. Only in John are the mother and Beloved Disciple mentioned. The mother of Jesus first appeared at the wedding feast at Cana, when Jesus addressed her as "woman." Again, he speaks to her as "woman," an unusual way for a son to address his mother, immediately suggesting a symbolic meaning. In addition to being a real historical person, the mother of Jesus, the "woman" brings to mind another woman mentioned in the book of

hyssop = HIS-uhp

After this, aware that everything was **now** finished,
in order that the Scripture might be fulfilled,
Jesus said, "**I thirst**."
There was a vessel filled with common **wine**.
So they put a sponge soaked in wine on a sprig of hyssop
and put it up to his mouth.
When Jesus had taken the wine, he said,
"**It is** finished."
And bowing his **head**, he handed **over** the spirit.

[Here all kneel and pause for a short time.]

Emphasize the words in bold. Keep up your
volume. Keep the narrative moving.

Now since it was **preparation** day,
in order that the bodies might **not** remain
on the cross on the sabbath,
for the sabbath day of that week was a solemn one,
the **Jews** asked Pilate that their legs be broken
and that they be **taken down**.
So the soldiers came and broke the legs of the first
and then of the other one who was crucified with **Jesus**.
But when they came to Jesus and saw that he was already dead,
they did not break his legs,
but one soldier **thrust** his **lance** into his **side**,
and **immediately blood** and **water** flowed out.
An **eyewitness** has **testified**, and his testimony **is** true;
he **knows** that he is speaking the truth,
so that you also may come to believe.
For **this** happened so that the Scripture passage might be **fulfilled**:
Not a bone of it will be broken.
And again **another** passage says:
They will look upon him whom they have pierced.

Arimathea = ayr-ih-muh-THEE-uh

Articulation is crucial. Proclaim each syllable
and word ending for a better understanding
of the reading.

After **this**, Joseph **of** Arimathea,
secretly a disciple of Jesus for fear of the Jews,
asked Pilate if he could remove the body of Jesus. **»**

Revelation. In both places the woman is a representative of the Church. Standing faithfully at the cross, the woman and the Beloved Disciple—those who remain faithful to Jesus—are to "behold" each other, signifying a new relationship in which the family of Jesus will continue beyond his death. As we look at these two figures, both real and symbolic, we can meditate on their continuing significance for believers.

Jesus has two additional words from the cross: "I thirst" and "It is finished." In response to Jesus' cry of thirst, they offer him a sponge of wine on a sprig of hyssop.

The evangelist is likely suggesting the hyssop used for sprinkling the blood of the paschal lamb (Exodus 12:22). First proclaimed as "Lamb of God" by John the Baptist (1:29), Jesus is the lamb of sacrifice on the cross. His thirsting, according to John, fulfills the Scripture. Though he doesn't cite the passage, a likely candidate is Psalm 69:4: "I am weary with crying out; my throat is parched."

Jesus' final word, "It is finished," connects his death with the introduction to the passion account: having "loved his own, . . . he loved them to the end" (13:1).

We can hear his final word addressed to his Father, with whom he is always united, to those who stand at the cross, and to all who hear the Gospel. Jesus' death exhibits the totality of his love for his own. His kingship, his offering of himself as lamb of sacrifice, and his priestly mission are brought to completion at his death. Having been handed over in betrayal and arrest, Jesus now hands over his spirit, his final gift from the cross.

After Jesus' death, John's symbolism continues. Jesus' unbroken legs are evocative of the paschal lamb, for the lamb must

Nicodemus = nik-uh-DEE-muhs

myrrh = mer

aloes = AL-ohz

And Pilate **permitted** it.
So he came and **took** his body.
Nicodemus, the one who had **first** come to him at **night**,
    also came bringing a mixture of myrrh and aloes
        weighing about one **hundred** pounds.
They **took** the **body** of Jesus
    and **bound it** with burial cloths **along** with the **spices**,
        according to the Jewish burial custom.
Now in the **place** where he had been crucified there was a garden,
    and in the garden a **new** tomb, in which **no** one had **yet**
        been buried.
So they **laid** Jesus there because of the Jewish preparation day;
    for the tomb was close by.

TO KEEP IN MIND

Always pause at the end of the reading, before you proclaim the closing dialogue ("The Word of the Lord" or "The Gospel of the Lord").

---

be unblemished and perfect. In addition, the image of the righteous sufferer may be implied: "Many are the troubles of the righteous, but the LORD delivers him from them all. He watches over all his bones; not one of them shall be broken" (Psalm 34:20–21). Blood and water reflect more than the historical reality of Jesus' death on the cross, suggesting further symbolism. The water flowing from Jesus' side brings to mind Jesus' own words when he offered life-giving water to the Samaritan woman (4:14), as well as his promise of fulfilling the Scripture that says "Rivers of living water will flow from within him" (7:38). Blood as well has symbolic value, particularly related to the blood of the paschal lamb that delivers the Hebrews from the final plague in Egypt. Associated with birth, the blood and water flowing from the side may also point to new birth offered through the Eucharist and Baptism, now flowing from Jesus to the believing community.

The passion account began in a garden, and concludes in another garden. The first was a garden of betrayal, and the final one, of burial. There, Jesus is buried with honor and attentiveness by two secret disciples. The disciples who were with Jesus throughout his ministry, the Twelve, were sadly absent in his passion. They are also absent at his burial. Joseph of Arimathea and Nicodemus come forth to claim his body, tending it with spices and burial cloths. The burial is extravagant, one appropriate for a king, with a hundred pounds of myrrh and aloes. Final mention of the tomb sets the stage for finding it empty on the first day of the week. E.P.

HOLY SATURDAY: EASTER VIGIL

LECTIONARY #41

READING I   Genesis 1:1—2:2

A reading from the Book of Genesis

[**In** the **beginning**, when God created the heavens and the earth,]
　　the earth was a **formless wasteland**, and darkness covered
　　　　the abyss,
　　while a mighty wind **swept** over the waters.

Then God **said**,
　　"**Let there be** light," and there was light.
God saw how good the light was.
God then **separated** the **light** from the **darkness**.
God called the light "day," and the darkness he called "night."
Thus evening came, and **morning followed**—the first day.

Then God **said**,
　　"Let there be a dome in the middle of the waters,
　　　to **separate** one body of water from the other."
And so it happened:
　　God made the dome,
　　and it separated the water **above** the dome from the water
　　　below it.
God called the dome "**the sky**."
Evening came, and **morning** followed—the second day.

Then God **said**,
　　"Let the **water** under the sky be gathered into a **single** basin,
　　　so that the **dry** land may appear." ≫

Genesis = JEN-uh-sihs

The beautiful story of Creation! Proclaim with authority. Do not rush. Use strong eye contact as you proclaim. Articulate every word so that no word is lost. Rehearse this reading often for a polished presentation.

abyss = uh-BIS

Read with renewed energy each time you say "Then God said."

There are options for readings today. Ask your parish staff which ones will be used.

READING I **Genesis 1:1—2.2.** The readings of the Easter Vigil move from the poetic account of creation to the testing of Abraham, to Israel's deliverance from Egypt, and to beautiful hope-filled prophetic promises. The readings immerse us in the great moments in the story of salvation. After these dramatic traditions from the Old Testament, the New Testament readings culminate in the Gospel, long prepared for and wondrously fulfilled in Jesus' Passover from death to life. The readings that begin with creation conclude with the new creation manifest in Jesus' Resurrection.

The first reading is rhythmically ordered around six days of creation and a final day of divine rest. Like other ancient creation accounts, this one is not a scientific or historical treatise. It is a sacred text, an expression of the faith of Israel that announces the sovereignty and uniqueness of God. In contrast with the myths of other cultures, there is no cosmic battle, no pantheon of competing gods, no evil. The distinctiveness of the first chapter of Genesis is the power of the one God who has made all of creation—both time and space—and has made it good. The account is designed so that every generation can learn of a God who accomplishes everything simply by divine speech, is infinitely creative and powerful, and brings about only what is good. For their part, people are to recognize their duty of reverence to this God,

Read with renewed energy each time you say "Then God said."

And so it happened:
    the water under the sky was **gathered** into its basin,
    and the dry **land appeared**.
God called the dry land "**the** earth,"
    and the basin of the water he called "**the** sea."
God saw how good it was.
Then God **said**,
    "Let the earth bring **forth vegetation**:
    every kind of **plant** that bears seed
    and every kind of fruit **tree** on earth
    that bears fruit with its seed in it."
And so it happened:
    the earth **brought forth** every kind of plant that bears **seed**
    and every kind of **fruit** tree on earth
    that bears fruit with its **seed** in it.
God saw how good it was.
Evening came, and morning **followed**—the third day.

Then God **said**:
    "Let there be lights in the dome of the sky,
    to separate **day** from **night**.
Let them mark the **fixed times**, the **days** and the **years**,
    and serve as luminaries in the dome of the sky,
    to shed light upon the earth."
And so it happened:
    God made the two great lights,
    the **greater** one to **govern** the day,
    and the **lesser** one to govern the night;
    and he made the stars.
God **set** them in the **dome** of the sky,
    to shed light upon the earth,
    to **govern** the **day** and the **night**,
    and to **separate** the **light** from the **darkness**.
God saw how good it was.
Evening came, and **morning** followed—the fourth day.

their responsibility of stewardship over creation, the dignity that God has given to them, and their sharing in God's own rest on the seventh day. This poetic opening chapter of the Old Testament enhances the atmosphere of wonder and awe, so fitting for the Easter Vigil.

    The structure of the story contributes to the image of a God who orders creation according to a plan, establishing everything in harmony. Each day begins with God speaking: "Then God said," followed by God's command, accomplished immedi-ately. God says only "Let there be light," and there was light! For each element of creation, God sees that it is good, and then gives a name to the newly created reality, beginning with the names "day" and "night." Then, almost as a musical antiphon, God's creative act is concluded, "Evening came, and morning followed—the first day." The pattern creates a peaceful rhythm.

    Along with other biblical texts that reflect on creation (for example, Proverbs 8 and Psalms 33 and 104), Genesis 1 explains that God is the cause of all of the rhythms and diversity of life that we see and experience: night and day, rain water and sea water, plants and animals, sun and moon, and humanity itself. God's actions on the first five days create a world of time and space filled with God's own goodness. On the sixth day God creates male and female in the divine image and gives to them both blessing and responsibility. Thus, before the entry of sin and hostility into the world, God entrusts to humanity the task of keeping the world in the divinely established harmony.

Read with renewed energy each time you say "Then God said."

Then God **said**,
"Let the water **teem** with an **abundance** of **living creatures**,
and on the earth let birds fly beneath the dome of the sky."
And so it happened:
God created the **great** sea **monsters**
and **all** kinds of **swimming** creatures with which the
water **teems**,
and all kinds of winged **birds**.
God saw how good it was, and God blessed them, saying,
"**Be fertile**, **multiply**, and fill the water of the seas;
and let the birds multiply on the earth."
Evening came, and **morning** followed—the fifth day.

Then God **said**,
"Let the earth bring **forth** all kinds of **living creatures**:
cattle, **creeping** things, and wild **animals** of all **kinds**."
And so it happened:
God made **all** kinds of wild animals, all kinds of cattle,
and all kinds of creeping things of the earth.
God saw how good it was.

Then [God **said**:
"Let us make man in **our image**, after our **likeness**.
Let them have dominion over the fish of the sea,
the birds of the air, and the cattle,
and over all the wild animals
and all the creatures that crawl on the ground."
God **created** man in **his** image;
in the image of **God** he **created** him;
male and female he created them.
God **blessed** them, saying:
"Be fertile and **multiply**;
fill the earth and **subdue** it.
Have **dominion over** the fish of the sea, the birds of the air,
and **all** the living things that move on the earth." »

TO KEEP IN MIND
Repetition of the same word or phrase over the course of a reading emphasizes a point. Make each instance distinct, and build your intensity with each repetition.

Then God rests, creating rest itself on the seventh day. Since men and women are created in God's image, the seventh day is to be a day of rest (*menuha*) for them as well. On the Sabbath, humanity is to share in God's own peace, serenity, and tranquility. Creation itself, both time and space, is ordered to this day of rest. So important is this day that the creation account concludes with God blessing the day (a verse unfortunately not included in the lectionary): "God blessed the seventh day and made it holy" (Genesis 2:3). This final blessing is the culmination of the creation account.

READING II **Genesis 22:1–18.** Omitted from the readings on this night are a few other episodes in the history of salvation. After the creation account, characterized by harmony and goodness, the next chapters of Genesis present a world increasingly filled with sin and estrangement from God. Though created in God's image and likeness, men and women did not reflect God's own goodness. In this context of alienation, God steps into the story. The LORD speaks to a seventy-five-year-old childless man named Abram: "I will make of you a great nation, and I will bless you" (12:2). This call initiates the saga of Abram, whose name God will change to Abraham, "father of a multitude." He is to be the means of God extending the divine blessing: "All the families of the earth shall find blessing in you" (12:3). This promise appears with no strings attached; God does not ask Abram to perform specific acts or rituals, but simply to trust in the

God **also** said:
    "**See**, I **give** you every seed-bearing plant all over the **earth**
        and **every tree** that has seed-bearing fruit on it to be **your food**;
        and to all the animals of the land, all the birds of the air,
        and all the living creatures that crawl on the ground,
    I **give** all the **green** plants for **food**."
And **so** it **happened**.
God **looked** at **everything** he had made, and he found it
        very good.]
Evening came, and **morning** followed—the sixth day.

Thus the heavens and the earth and all their array
        were completed.
Since on the **seventh** day God was **finished**
    with the work he had been doing,
        he rested on the seventh day from **all** the **work** he
            had undertaken.

[Shorter: Genesis 1:1, 26–31a (see brackets)]

For meditation and context:

RESPONSORIAL PSALM   Psalm 104:1–2, 5–6, 10, 12, 13–14, 24, 35 (30)

R. **Lord, send out your Spirit, and renew the face of the earth.**

Bless the LORD, O my soul!
    O LORD, my God, you are great indeed!
You are clothed with majesty and glory,
    robed in light as with a cloak.

You fixed the earth upon its foundation,
    not to be moved forever;
with the ocean, as with a garment, you
        covered it;
    above the mountains the waters stood.

You send forth springs into the watercourses
    that wind among the mountains.
Beside them the birds of heaven dwell;
    from among the branches they send forth
        their song.

You water the mountains from your palace;
    the earth is replete with the fruit
        of your works.
You raise grass for the cattle,
    and vegetation for man's use,
producing bread from the earth.

How manifold are your works, O LORD!
    In wisdom you have wrought them all—
the earth is full of your creatures.
    Bless the LORD, O my soul!

Or:

promise. Trust will be needed, since Abram and his wife, Sarai, continue to wait for the promised descendant. When God again comes to Abram in a vision, Abram moans, "What good will your gifts be, if I keep on being childless?" (15:2). Expanding on the original promise, God makes a covenant with Abram, announcing that his descendants will be as numerous as the stars. Trusting in the promise, Abram puts his faith in God, who does fulfill the promise, giving a son, Isaac, to Abram and Sarai in their old age.

In the second reading for the Easter Vigil, God puts Abraham to the test. Throughout the Abraham cycle, he faces numerous tests, with this account, regarded in the Jewish tradition as the tenth and final test of Abraham's faith. Having waited so long to bring about the promise of a descendant, now God commands Abraham to take his beloved son and sacrifice him as a burnt offering. Abraham's response sounds almost wooden as he rises early, saddles a donkey, and even cuts wood for

the sacrifice, careful actions performed with a kind of numbness and shock.

We hear nothing of Isaac's reaction to his father's actions, until, having the altar of sacrifice prepared, he asks, "Father, . . . where is the sheep for the holocaust?" Abraham sorrowfully tells him. "God himself will provide (*elohim yir'e*) the sheep for the holocaust." The God who had provided a son to the elderly couple will, somehow, again provide. When they reach their destination, Abraham continues his numbed actions: he builds an altar, lays the wood,

For meditation and context:

RESPONSORIAL PSALM   Psalm 33:4–5, 6–7, 12–13, 20, and 22 (5b)

R. The earth is full of the goodness of the Lord.

Upright is the word of the LORD,
  and all his works are trustworthy.
He loves justice and right;
  of the kindness of the LORD the earth
    is full.
By the word of the LORD the heavens
    were made;
  by the breath of his mouth all their host.
He gathers the waters of the sea as in a flask;
  in cellars he confines the deep.

Blessed the nation whose God is the LORD,
  the people he has chosen for his
    own inheritance.
From heaven the LORD looks down;
  he sees all mankind.

Our soul waits for the LORD,
  who is our help and our shield.
May your kindness, O LORD, be upon us
  who have put our hope in you.

READING II   Genesis 22:1–18

A reading from the Book of Genesis

Genesis = JEN-uh-sihs

Proclaim with a strong voice and good eye contact. Pause before you say God's words.

Moriah = moh-RĪ-uh

[**God** put Abraham to the **test**.
He called to him, "**Abraham**!"
"**Here** I am," he replied.
Then God said:
  "Take your son **Isaac**, your only one, whom you love,
    and go to the land of **Moriah**.
There you shall offer **him up** as a holocaust
  on a height that I will point out to you."]
Early the next morning Abraham saddled his donkey,
  took with him his **son Isaac** and two of his servants as well,
    and with the **wood** that he had cut for the holocaust,
  set **out** for the place of which God had told him.

On the third day Abraham **got** sight of the place from afar.
Then he said to his servants:
  "Both of you **stay here** with the donkey,
    while the **boy** and I **go on** over **yonder**.
We will **worship** and then come back to you." »

binds his son, lays him on the altar, and takes a knife to kill his son. Anyone hearing the story must feel the same horror at his actions. An angel intervenes, stopping the sacrifice at the last moment, and pointing out a ram in a nearby thicket. The angel tells Abraham that he has shown his fear of God and his total obedience. He has passed the test. Then Abraham names the place for God's providence: *Yahweh-yir'eh*, which means "the Lord will provide." The term, *yir'e* can be translated either "provide" or "see"; the two meanings together suggest

that whatever God sees, God will watch over providently. Abraham affirmed his trust that God would see and provide even before the divine intervention. Faith in divine providence, particularly in the face of the inexplicable or seemingly impossible, is one of the theological teachings of the story. Not only has God provided the animal of sacrifice, but God provides an abundant blessing in renewing the promise that Abraham will have numerous offspring and that all nations of the earth will find blessing because of his obedience.

This is a difficult story to hear and to understand. Many attempts have arisen to mitigate the incomprehensible command of God that Abraham sacrifice his own son. Although the biblical account focuses on Abraham rather than Isaac, many rabbinic commentators regard Isaac as an adult, a willing participant in the sacrifice. He thereby became a prototype of a martyr in Judaism, and an image of Christ in Christianity. In one paraphrase of the story, an Aramaic version, Isaac himself asks his father to bind him securely so that

Thereupon Abraham took the wood for the holocaust
    and **laid** it on his son **Isaac's** shoulders,
    while he himself carried the **fire** and the **knife**.
As the two walked on **together**, Isaac spoke to his father
    Abraham:
    "**Father!**" Isaac said.
"**Yes**, son," he replied.
Isaac continued, "Here are the **fire** and the **wood**,
    but where is the sheep for the holocaust?"
"**Son**," Abraham answered,
    "God himself will provide the sheep for the holocaust."
Then the two continued going forward.

[When they came to the place of which God had told him,
    Abraham built an **altar** there and arranged the **wood** on it.]
Next he **tied** up his son Isaac,
    and **put** him on **top** of the wood on the altar.
[Then he **reached out** and **took** the **knife** to slaughter his son.
But the LORD's messenger **called** to him from heaven,
    "Abraham, Abraham!"
"**Here** I am," he answered.
"Do not lay your hand on the boy," said the messenger.
"Do **not** do the least thing to him.
I **know now** how devoted you are to **God**,
    since you did **not** withhold **from** me your own beloved son."
As Abraham looked **about**,
    he **spied** a **ram** caught by its horns in the thicket.
So he went and took the ram
    and offered it up as a **holocaust** in **place** of his son.]
Abraham named the site Yahweh-yireh;
    hence people now say, "On the mountain the LORD will **see**."

Keep your energy up. Keep the dialogue between the messenger and Abraham direct and clear.

Yahweh-yireh = YAH-way-YEER-ay

he not kick and make the sacrifice unworthy. Other interpretations also present Isaac as willing victim, ready to participate in whatever God asks.

READING III **Exodus 14:15—15:1.** The third reading of the Easter Vigil is central to the traditions of both Jews and Christians. The account of the passing through the waters of the sea is rich in literary skill and forceful symbols, told both in prose and poetry. It is yet one more manifestation of the Lord's power over Egypt,

particularly over the obstinate Pharaoh who refused to let the people go. Even after the Pharaoh had finally released the enslaved people following the tenth plague, he changed his mind and pursued them with an army, with horses, chariots, and charioteers. While the people were encamped by the sea and they saw the Egyptians on the march in pursuit, they immediately complained to Moses, "Were there no burial places in Egypt that you brought us to die in the wilderness?" (14:11). In response, Moses assures the

people, "The LORD will fight for you" (14:14). This is the point where our reading begins, when the Lord commands Moses to stretch his hand over the sea to divide it. In the creation account heard in the first reading, God had similarly separated the waters, gathering them into one place so that dry land appeared. Now Moses' action at God's command also makes dry land appear from the separated water. Repetition of "divided waters" and "dry land" emphasizes the connection with Genesis. Moreover, as at the narrative of creation, the Lord has

The Lord is pleased with Abraham. Let the assembly hear happiness in your voice. Smile.

[Again the LORD's messenger **called** to Abraham from heaven
    and said:
"I swear by myself, declares the LORD,
that because you acted as you **did**
in **not withholding** from me your **beloved** son,
I will **bless you abundantly**
and make your **descendants** as **countless**
as the stars of the sky and the sands of the seashore;
your descendants shall take possession
of the gates of their enemies,
and in your descendants **all** the nations of the earth shall
    find **blessing**—
all this because you obeyed my command."]

[Shorter: Genesis 22:1–2, 9a, 10–13, 15–18 (see brackets)]

For meditation and context:

RESPONSORIAL PSALM   Psalm 16:5, 8, 9–10, 11 (1)

R. You are my inheritance, O Lord.

O LORD, my allotted portion and my cup,
    you it is who hold fast my lot.
I set the LORD ever before me;
    with him at my right hand I shall not
        be disturbed.

Therefore my heart is glad and my
        soul rejoices,
    my body, too, abides in confidence;
because you will not abandon my soul to
        the netherworld,
    nor will you suffer your faithful one to
        undergo corruption.

You will show me the path to life,
    fullness of joys in your presence,
    the delights at your right hand forever.

TO KEEP IN MIND
As you prepare your proclamation, make choices about what emotions need to be expressed. Some choices are evident from the text, but some are harder to discern. Understanding the context of the Scripture passage will help you decide.

power over all the elements of nature: darkness, light, and over the winds and waters. The passing through the waters of the sea is portrayed as a new creation!

The presence and power of God dominate the event. An angel of God and a pillar of cloud are images associated with theophanies (appearances of God to humankind) in the biblical tradition. In addition to such well known symbols, we hear over and over of the Lord's actions and presence. The Lord drove the sea back; the Lord in the pillar of fire and cloud

looked down. The Egyptians retreated when they saw that the Lord was fighting with the Israelites against them. Then as the water moves back into place, the Egyptians are thrown into the midst of the sea. In these ways, the Lord saved Israel, and they saw the great work the Lord had done. Each time we hear "the LORD," the Hebrew text uses the sacred name "Yahweh." This is the God revealed to Moses on Mount Horeb, who promised to rescue the suffering people from the hands of the Egyptians. Now that promise is being

fulfilled, with no doubt about who is accomplishing the wonder.

Although the dramatic tale of the Egyptian pursuit results in the drowning of the Egyptians in the sea, the greatest result is God's glory. This glory is the LORD's weighty magnificence, observable in the works of creation, new creation, and redemption, and in all of the divine acts of deliverance and compassion. God also displays glory in the conquering of evil and destruction of injustice. God's glory means that the God of Moses is more powerful

READING III   Exodus 14:15—15:1

A reading from the Book of Exodus

Exodus = EK-suh-duhs

Proclaim the Lord's words with urgency and firmness.

The LORD said to Moses, "Why are you crying out to me?
Tell the Israelites to **go** forward.
And **you**, **lift up** your **staff** and, with hand outstretched
over the sea,
split the sea in two,
that the Israelites may **pass through** it on **dry** land.
But **I** will make the **Egyptians** so obstinate
that they will **go** in after them.
Then I will receive glory through Pharaoh and **all** his **army**,
his chariots and charioteers.
The Egyptians shall know that I **am the** Lord,
when I **receive glory** through Pharaoh
and his chariots and charioteers."

Read with an informative tone.

The angel of God, who had been leading Israel's camp,
now moved and went around behind them.
The column of **cloud also**, leaving the **front**,
took up its place **behind** them,
so that it came between the camp of the **Egyptians**
and that of **Israel**.
But the cloud **now** became **dark**, and **thus** the night passed
without the rival camps coming **any** closer together all
night long.

As you continue to proclaim the story of Moses and the sea, let the assembly hear more energy and urgency in your voice.

Then Moses **stretched** out his hand over the **sea**,
and the LORD swept the sea
with a strong east **wind throughout** the night
and so **turned** it into dry land.
When the water was thus divided,
the Israelites **marched** into the **midst** of the sea on **dry** land,
with the water like a wall to their right and to their left.

---

than Pharaoh and the gods of Egypt, powerful over nature and over intractable evil. When God shows forth glory, even the Egyptians will know that the Lord is God. When God saved the people, they feared him, and they believed in the Lord and his servant Moses. The joy and celebration of the whole people follows the story, both in the book of Exodus and in this liturgy. The responsorial psalm is the poetic complement to the narrative in which the Lord accomplishes the wondrous passage through the sea, showing forth majestic glory.

READING IV   **Isaiah 54:5–14.** When the people of Israel were in exile in Babylon, the words of divinely inspired prophets gave them hope that God had not abandoned them. Today's fourth reading comes near the end of the exile in the sixth century BC, in a part of the book of Isaiah usually referred to as Second Isaiah. Whoever the author was, he continued the tradition that was begun by Isaiah of Jerusalem long before the exile. Faced with the apparently powerful gods of Babylon, particularly Marduk, the exiles needed a deeper understanding and relationship with their God. The prophet thus gives them a rich and personal collection of images for God: Lord, God of hosts, your maker, your husband, the Holy One of Israel, your Redeemer. The guiding image in this passage is God as husband, and Israel, as well as Jerusalem itself, as the wife. In the verses just before today's reading, Isaiah offered astounding words of hope:

The Egyptians followed in pursuit;
>   all Pharaoh's horses and chariots and charioteers went
>   after them
>   **right** into the midst of the sea.
In the night watch just before **dawn**
>   the LORD **cast through** the column of the fiery cloud
>   upon the Egyptian force a glance that threw it into a panic;
>   and he **so clogged** their chariot wheels
>   that they could **hardly** drive.
With that the Egyptians sounded the **retreat** before Israel,
>   because the LORD was fighting **for** them against the Egyptians.

Then the LORD told Moses, "Stretch out your hand over the sea,
>   that the water may flow back upon the **Egyptians**,
>   upon their **chariots** and their **charioteers**."
So Moses stretched out his hand over the sea,
>   and at **dawn** the sea flowed **back** to its **normal** depth.
The Egyptians were **fleeing** head on **toward** the sea,
>   when the LORD hurled them into its midst.
As the water flowed **back**,
>   it covered the chariots and the charioteers of Pharaoh's
>   whole army
>   which had **followed** the Israelites into the **sea**.
Not a **single one** of them escaped.
But the Israelites had **marched** on **dry** land
>   **through** the **midst** of the sea,
>   with the water like a wall to their right and to their left.
Thus the LORD saved Israel on **that** day
>   from the **power** of the Egyptians. »

Build the intensity as you read about the fate of the Egyptians.

Pause before you say this line.

Proclaim as one sentence—no break.

"Enlarge the space for your tent, spread out your tent cloths unsparingly" (54:2). The prophet was telling Israel, portrayed as the once abandoned wife, that she will again have a tent to live in, and she will even need to enlarge it for her numerous offspring. Once shamed because of sin, she was like a wife forsaken and grieved, cast off like the wife of a man's youth. We can well iMagine the collective shame felt by the people, who regarded their exile as punishment for their betrayal. Their idolatry in particular was akin to adultery, blatant unfaithfulness to the covenant they had with their God.

Because of Israel's faithlessness, God abandoned her in wrath, but only for a moment. In contrast to the brief punishment, God's compassion will be everlasting, his steadfast love will never depart, and his covenant of peace will not be removed. Divine compassion (*rehem*) appears three times in this passage, emphasized as an abiding characteristic of God toward Israel. Rooted in the word *raham*, "womb," it signifies a deep, inti-mate, unshakable feeling, like the love of a mother for the child in the womb. Along with *rehem* is another repeated divine quality, *hesed*, love that is everlasting and steadfast, often associated with God's covenant fidelity. *Hesed* is love that is manifest in action.

Finally, the prophetic promise presents to the people still in exile a vision of a renewed city. The prophecy has an immediacy about it; this isn't a vision of some far-distant future, but reveals something that God is about to do. Their exile will soon

When Israel saw the Egyptians lying dead on the seashore
  and **beheld** the **great power** that the LORD
  had shown **against** the Egyptians,
  they feared the LORD and believed in him and in his
    servant Moses.

Then Moses and the Israelites sang this song to the LORD:
  I will sing to the LORD, for he is **gloriously** triumphant;
  horse and **chariot** he has cast into the sea.

Pause before you read the song. Smile.

For meditation and context:

RESPONSORIAL PSALM   Exodus 15:1–2, 3–4, 5–6, 17–18 (1b)

R. Let us sing to the Lord; he has covered himself in glory.

I will sing to the LORD, for he is
    gloriously triumphant;
  horse and chariot he has cast into the sea.
My strength and my courage is the LORD,
  and he has been my savior.
He is my God, I praise him;
  the God of my father, I extol him.

The LORD is a warrior,
  LORD is his name!
Pharaoh's chariots and army he hurled into
    the sea;
  the elite of his officers were submerged
    in the Red Sea.

The flood waters covered them,
  they sank into the depths like a stone.
Your right hand, O LORD, magnificent
    in power,
  your right hand, O LORD, has shattered
    the enemy.

You brought in the people you redeemed
  and planted them on the mountain of
    your inheritance—
the place where you made your seat,
  O LORD,
  the sanctuary, LORD, which your
    hands established.
The LORD shall reign forever and ever.

Tiberius = tĭ-BEER-ee-uhs; Caesar = SEE-zer
Judea = joo-DEE-uh
Ituraea = ih-too-REE-ah
Trachonitis = trak-uh-NĪ-tis
Lysanias = lĭ-SAY-nee-uhs
Annas = AN-uhs
Caiaphas = KĪ-uh-fuhs
Zechariah = zek-uh-RĪ-uh

READING IV   Isaiah 54:5–14

A reading from the Book of the Prophet Isaiah

The One who has **become** your **husband is** your **Maker**;
  his **name** is the LORD **of hosts**;
  your redeemer is the **Holy One of** Israel,
    called **God** of all the earth.

Isaiah =Ī-ZAY-uh

Proclaim with good volume and eye contact. Speak with authority.

end. No longer in ruins, Jerusalem will shine with precious stones from the foundations to the pinnacles, with jewels embedded in the walls and on the gates. It is almost as if Jerusalem itself is a bride bedecked with myriad treasures that a loving bridegroom can bestow. All of the oppression, fear, and terror of the present will be transformed. In newly re-created Zion, the Lord himself will teach the children, and all will once again experience God's bountiful prosperity.

READING V   **Isaiah 55:1–11.** Like the fourth reading, from Isaiah 54, the reading from Isaiah 55 is a prophecy of hope and fulfillment. While Isaiah 54 promises a renewed Jerusalem to the exiles in Babylon, the assurances in the next chapter are more expansive, directed to "everyone who thirsts." The wide-open invitation to come and receive water and bread without cost is applicable to all individuals and nations, and in every historical circumstance. It resonates with the invitation of Wisdom to be guests at her feast:

"Come, eat of my food, and drink of the wine I have mixed" (Proverbs 9:5). The biblical writers develop the imagery of food and drink with multivalent possibilities. Some rabbinic commentators interpreted water as a metaphor for Torah, and in the Wisdom tradition, bread and water together symbolize wise teaching: "She will feed him with the bread of learning, and give him the water of understanding to drink" (Sirach 15:3). Thirsting for water is also a metaphor for people yearning for a relationship with God: "Those who drink of me will thirst for

Say in a tone of tenderness.

The Lord **calls** you **back**,
     like a wife forsaken and grieved in spirit,
     a wife **married** in youth and then **cast** off,
     says your God.
For a brief moment I abandoned you,
     but with great **tenderness** I **will** take you back.
In an **outburst of** wrath, for a moment
     I hid my face **from** you;
but with **enduring** love I take pity on you,
     says the Lord, your **redeemer**.

Noah = NOH-uh

This is for **me** like the days of **Noah**,
     when I swore that the **waters** of **Noah**
     should never again deluge the earth;
so I have sworn **not** to be angry with you,
     or to rebuke you.
Though the mountains leave their place
     and the hills be **shaken**,

Slowly proclaim this line.

my love **shall** never **leave you**
     nor my covenant of **peace** be shaken,
     says the Lord, who has mercy on you.
O afflicted one, storm-battered and unconsoled,
     I **lay** your pavements in carnelians,
     and **your** foundations in sapphires;

carnelians = kahr-NEEL-yuhnz (red semiprecious stones)

I will **make** your battlements of **rubies**,
     your gates of **carbuncles**,
     and **all** your **walls** of precious **stones**.

carbuncles = KAHR-bung-k*lz (bright red gems)

What wonderful news! Proclaim in a tone of gratefulness and joy.

All **your** children shall be taught by the Lord,
     and **great** shall be the peace of your children.
In justice shall you be **established**,
     far from the **fear** of **oppression**,
     where **destruction cannot** come **near** you.

---

more" (Sirach 24:21). Isaiah doesn't limit his food and drink imagery to the basic necessities of life, but presents a picture of a banquet where people will delight in rich food. The banquet imagery highlights God's abundant care for Israel and evokes the hope of a new age of fulfillment. Isaiah of Jerusalem created a beautiful scene that is a background for today's reading: "On this mountain the Lord of hosts will provide for all peoples a feast of rich food and choice wines" (Isaiah 25:6).

Isaiah's prophecy makes a universal appeal to respond to the divine invitation: come, eat, listen, delight, seek, forsake evil, return to the Lord. Such apparently ordinary human acts bring people into God's presence to receive the promised rich fare. The divine bounty includes life, an everlasting covenant, and steadfast love, *hesed*. The promise of *hesed* goes beyond David and his descendants, and even beyond the Jewish people to embrace the nations. Isaiah declares that the nations unknown to the exiles will run to them because God

"has glorified you." The wording of the promise brings the future glory into the present. What God has promised is so certain that it is as if already accomplished.

The invitation continues: "seek the Lord," used elsewhere to exhort people to the sanctuary, often understood as the Jerusalem Temple. In this prophecy, Isaiah tells everyone to find the Lord whenever and wherever God may be present. Those who respond to this gentle invitation, who turn away from evil ways and even unrighteous thoughts, will know God's mercy. The

For meditation and context:

RESPONSORIAL PSALM   Psalm 30:2, 4, 5–6, 11–12, 13 (2a)

R. I will praise you, Lord, for you have rescued me.

I will extol you, O LORD, for you drew
   me clear
    and did not let my enemies rejoice over me.
O LORD, you brought me up from
   the netherworld;
   you preserved me from among those
    going down into the pit.

Sing praise to the LORD, you his faithful ones,
   and give thanks to his holy name.
For his anger lasts but a moment;
   a lifetime, his good will.
At nightfall, weeping enters in,
   but with the dawn, rejoicing.

Hear, O LORD, and have pity on me;
   O LORD, be my helper.
You changed my mourning into dancing;
   O LORD, my God, forever will I give
    you thanks.

READING V   Isaiah 55:1–11

A reading from the Book of the Prophet Isaiah

Thus says the LORD:
All you who are **thirsty**,
   come to the **water**!
You who have **no money**,
   come, receive **grain** and eat;
come, without paying and without **cost**,
   drink wine and **milk**!
Why spend your money for what is **not bread**,
   your wages for what **fails** to satisfy?
Heed **me**, and you shall eat well,
   you shall delight in **rich** fare.
Come to me heedfully,
   listen, that you may **have** life.
I will renew with you the everlasting covenant,
   the **benefits** assured to David.

Proclaim with high energy this great news from the Lord. Pay attention to the words in bold.

reading concludes with another water image: the rain and snow that come down from heaven soak into the earth, bringing about seed and bread. So too is God's Word. It soaks down deeply into the human spirit, and accomplishes God's purpose.

Isaiah's promise of life-giving waters, bread freely given, and a rich banquet is particularly appropriate at the Easter Vigil. The waters of Baptism, the bountiful proclamation of God's Word, and the Eucharistic feast provide a banquet far richer than any envisioned by Isaiah. This night everyone is invited: come, eat, listen, and delight in the Lord's rich fare.

READING VI **Baruch 3:9–15, 32—4:4.** The sixth Easter Vigil reading, a poem from Baruch, is a beautiful hymn that praises Wisdom, not as an abstract reality but as a personified and relational entity. Although ascribed to Baruch, a scribe of the prophet Jeremiah, the hymn to Wisdom (along with the rest of the book) was perhaps written long after the life of Jeremiah and the Babylonian exile. Yet the reality of the exile remained a forceful example of the consequences of disobedience and the necessity of repentance. The whole book can be read as a perennial exhortation to see God's Law as the source of life and well-being. Just before today's hymn to Wisdom is a prayer of supplication (2:11—3:8) that is a helpful theological context for understanding the hymn. In the prayer, the people with "anguished soul, the dismayed spirit" (3:1) call out to God to save them, and to again show mercy on them, even though their

As I made him a witness to the peoples,
  a **leader** and commander of **nations**,
so shall **you** summon a nation you **knew** not,
  and nations that knew you not shall run to you,
because of the Lord, your God,
  the Holy One of Israel, who has glorified you.

Say in a gentle tone.

Seek the Lord while he may be found,
  call him while he is near.
Let the scoundrel forsake his way,
  and the wicked man his thoughts;
let him turn to the Lord for mercy;
  to our God, who is generous **in forgiving**.
For my thoughts are **not** your thoughts,
  nor are your ways my ways, says the Lord.
As high as the heavens are **above** the **earth**,
  so **high** are my ways **above** your ways
  and **my thoughts above** your thoughts.

The Lord's words are firm. Let the assembly hear his words clearly.

For just as **from** the heavens
  the **rain** and **snow** come down
and do **not return** there
  till they have watered the earth,
  making it **fertile** and **fruitful**,
giving seed to the **one** who sows
  and **bread** to the one who **eats**,
so shall my word **be**
  that goes **forth** from my mouth;
my **word** shall **not** return to me **void**,
  but shall do my will,
  achieving the end for which I **sent** it.

sins are many. They are impious, and have violated all God's statutes; they did not heed the voice of the Lord. Although the exile is their rightful punishment, they remind God that they are God's own people, and the Lord is able to turn them back from their "stiff-necked stubbornness and from their evil deeds" (2:33). The prayer, in which Israel admitted its disobedience, opens the possibility of restoration if they turn away from their sinful deeds and are obedient to God's commandments.

After this plea to God, Baruch addresses the people: "Hear, O Israel, the commandments of life: listen, and know prudence!" The essential way to learn Wisdom is through the "commandments of life," the very law that Israel had disobeyed. Prayer and hymn each emphasize the necessity of adherence to God's statutes if the people are to live. The Mosaic Law, equated with Wisdom, gives life in all its dimensions, both individually and collectively. But Israel has forsaken the fountain of Wisdom, bringing about their exile in the land of their enemies, and they have grown old in a foreign country. Now if they are to learn anew the depth and richness of God's Wisdom, they must listen and walk in the way of God through adherence to God's commandments.

Throughout the hymn, as elsewhere in Wisdom writings, Wisdom is personified as a woman with quasi-divine qualities. Those who find her will find strength and understanding, and will discern where there is life, light, and peace. In this text, as well as elsewhere in Wisdom literature

For meditation and context:

RESPONSORIAL PSALM   Isaiah 12:2–3, 4, 5–6 (3)

R. You will draw water joyfully from the springs of salvation.

God indeed is my savior;
  I am confident and unafraid.
My strength and my courage is the LORD,
  and he has been my savior.
With joy you will draw water
  at the fountain of salvation.

Give thanks to the LORD, acclaim his name;
  among the nations make known his deeds,
  proclaim how exalted is his name.

Sing praise to the LORD for his
  glorious achievement;
  let this be known throughout all the earth.
Shout with exultation, O city of Zion,
  for great in your midst
  is the Holy One of Israel!

READING VI   Baruch 3:9–15, 32—4:4

Baruch = buh-ROOK

Wake up, Israel! Proclaim with urgency. Take your time. Articulate every word. Rehearse for strong volume and eye contact.

A reading from the Book of the Prophet Baruch

Hear, O Israel, the **commandments** of **life**:
  listen, and **know** prudence!
How is it, Israel,
  that **you** are in the land of your foes,
  grown **old** in a foreign land,
defiled with the **dead**,
  accounted **with those** destined for the netherworld?
You have **forsaken** the **fountain of** wisdom!
  Had you **walked** in the way **of God**,
  you would have **dwelt** in **enduring** peace.
Learn where prudence is,
  where strength, where understanding;
that you may **know** also
  where are **length** of days, and life,
  where light of the eyes, and peace.
Who has found the **place** of **wisdom**,
  who has **entered** into her **treasuries**?

(for example Proverbs 8:22–31 and Wisdom 8:1), Wisdom was present at creation; she was present as well in the history of God's people. The Lord gave her to Jacob and to Israel, and ultimately Wisdom lived with humanity.

Having begun the poem with an exhortation to hear the commandments, Baruch continues, "She [Wisdom] is the book of the precepts of God, the law that endures forever." Though the figure of Wisdom is mysterious, she will be found in the Law. This understanding of Wisdom should lead the

exiles to obey the ancient commandments that they had so often abandoned. Holding fast to Wisdom is equivalent to obeying the commandments. Holding fast to Wisdom, to the Law itself, will give life. Forsaking Wisdom, forsaking the commandments, will result in death. The hymn concludes with a hope-filled invitation to turn toward Wisdom and walk in her shining light. Embracing Wisdom by keeping the commandments is not a burden, but a means of life, light, glory, and happiness.

READING VII   **Ezekiel 36:16–17a, 18–28.** Like the Easter Vigil readings from Isaiah and Baruch, the setting for the reading from the prophet Ezekiel is the exile in Babylon. With language reminiscent of that of the other prophets, Ezekiel begins by delineating the sins of the people that led to their exile. They defiled their own land with their deeds, their conduct was unclean, they shed blood on the land, and they polluted it with idols. The verbs describing their actions create a sharp sense of putrid contamination; we can visu-

The One who knows **all** things **knows her**;
    he has **probed** her by his knowledge—
the **One** who **established** the earth for all time,
    and filled it with four-footed beasts;
he who **dismisses** the **light**, and it departs,
    calls it, and it obeys him trembling;
before whom the stars at their posts
    shine and rejoice;
when he calls them, they **answer**, "Here **we are!**"
    shining with **joy** for their **Maker**.
Such **is our** God;

Say this line slowly and smile.

    no other is to be **compared** to him:
he has traced out the **whole way** of understanding,
    and has **given** her to Jacob, his servant,
    to **Israel**, his beloved son.

Since then she has appeared on earth,
    and moved among people.
She is the **book** of the **precepts of** God,
    the law that **endures** forever;
all who cling to her will live,
    but those will die who **forsake** her.
Turn, **O** Jacob, and **receive** her:
    walk by her light toward splendor.
Give not your glory to **another**,
    your privileges to an alien **race**.
Blessed are **we**, **O** Israel;
    for **what** pleases God is known **to us!**

Proclaim with energy.

she = wisdom

blessed = BLES-uhd

alize and even smell death throughout the land. God's response is severe: "I scattered them among the nations, dispersing them over foreign lands."

In all of their sinful, death-dealing actions, Israel did more than pollute the land. They profaned God's holy name. For Ezekiel, this is the most serious of sins, clearly indicated by his use of the word "profane" (*halal*) five times in this passage. Something profane is the polar opposite of what is holy; to make profane is to cheapen what is esteemed, to violate what is per-

fect, to demean what is exalted, to be impious before One who should be worshipped. And Israel profaned what is most esteemed, perfect, and exalted: God's holy name. In the biblical idiom, a name (*shem*) refers to the identity, the reputation, the presence, the true reality of who a person is. God's name is holy (*qadosh*), meaning that the identity of God is One set apart from what is commonplace; God's holy name is splendid and majestic, to be recognized with reverence and awe.

In the face of Israel's profaning God's holy name, God tells the prophet, "Not for your sakes do I act, house of Israel, but for the sake of my holy name." The multiple actions that God does for Israel are therefore first and foremost so that the holiness of God's name will be known, not only in Israel, but also among the nations. The Lord will display his radiant holiness before their very eyes. For God's sinful people, along with the foreign nations, to know the name of God implies more than recognizing or understanding God; knowing God's name

For meditation and context:

RESPONSORIAL PSALM   Psalm 19:8, 9, 10, 11 (John 6:68c)

R. Lord, you have the words of everlasting life.

The law of the LORD is perfect,
  refreshing the soul;
the decree of the LORD is trustworthy,
  giving wisdom to the simple.

The fear of the LORD is pure,
  enduring forever;
the ordinances of the LORD are true,
  all of them just.

The precepts of the LORD are right,
  rejoicing the heart;
the command of the LORD is clear,
  enlightening the eye.

They are more precious than gold,
  than a heap of purest gold;
sweeter also than syrup
  or honey from the comb.

READING VII   Ezekiel 36:16–17a, 18–28

Ezekiel = ee-ZEE-kee-uhl

A reading from the Book of the Prophet Ezekiel

The **word** of the LORD **came** to me, saying:
  Son of man, when the house of Israel **lived** in their **land**,
  they defiled it by their **conduct and deeds**.
Therefore I **poured** out my **fury** upon them
  because of the **blood** that they **poured** out on the ground,
  and because they **defiled** it with idols.
I scattered them among the nations,
  dispersing them over **foreign** lands;
  according to their conduct and deeds I judged **them**.
But when they came among the nations **wherever** they came,
  they served to profane my **holy name**,
  because it was said of them: "**These** are the people **of the** LORD,
  yet they **had to** leave their land."
So I have relented because of my holy name
  which the house of Israel **profaned**
  among the nations where they came.
Therefore say to the house of **Israel**: **Thus** says the **Lord** GOD:
  Not for your sakes do **I act**, house of **Israel**,
  but for the sake of **my holy** name,
  which you **profaned among** the nations to which you came.

Proclaim this reading with authority. Use good volume and eye contact. Rehearse for expression in your voice. Do not rush the words. Pause for emphasis.

Before you begin, pause and say with energy.

means to have an intimate relationship with God, expressed in fidelity, obedience, and reverent worship.

The divine actions that transform the profanation of God's holy name will at the same time transform Israel itself. The first actions in Ezekiel's prophecy were about God's punishment in scattering and dispersing the people through the countries. Now the prophecy moves stunningly from emphasis on the sin of Israel to the wondrous, healing, and transforming actions that God will perform. The repetition of God's promise "I will" is grounds for hope among the exiled people. I will take you, I will gather you, I will bring you, I will sprinkle clean water upon you. The first actions assure the exiles that they will be brought back to their land, and that the sprinkling action of God will cleanse both land and people. Instead of pollution and death, there will be new life. Then God will create the people anew. I will give you a new heart and a new spirit, God's own spirit placed within them. The final words of God's promise, "You shall be my people and I will be your God" signify a restoration of the covenant made with Israel's ancestors. They will once again, by the power of God's holy name, be God's own people, and the Lord will be their God.

EPISTLE   **Romans 6:3–11.** After the last of the readings from the Old Testament, the altar candles are lit, bells are rung, and the Gloria is sung. Such expressions of joy signal that the story of God's work of salvation has reached a new and joyous phase. The two

I will **prove** the holiness of my great name, profaned among
    the nations,
  in whose midst **you** have profaned it.
Thus the nations shall know that **I am the** Lord, says the
    Lord **God**,
  when in **their** sight I **prove** my **holiness through** you.
For I will take **you** away from among the nations,
  gather you from **all** the foreign lands,
  and **bring you** back to your own land.
I will **sprinkle** clean water upon you
  to cleanse you from all your **impurities**,
  and from **all** your idols **I** will cleanse you.
I will **give** you a **new** heart and **place** a new spirit **within** you,
  taking **from** your bodies your stony hearts
  and **giving** you natural hearts.
I will **put my spirit within** you and **make** you **live** by
    my statutes,
  careful to **observe** my **decrees**.
You shall live in the land I gave your fathers;
  you shall be **my people**, and I **will be your** God.

Proclaim with joy all the things God will do for us.

Say this last line slowly.

For meditation and context:

RESPONSORIAL PSALM   Psalm 42:3, 5; 43:3, 4 (2)   **When baptism is celebrated.**

R. Like a deer that longs for running streams, my soul longs for you, my God.

Athirst is my soul for God, the living God.
  When shall I go and behold the face
    of God?

I went with the throng
  and led them in procession to the house
    of God,
amid loud cries of joy and thanksgiving,
  with the multitude keeping festival.

Send forth your light and your fidelity;
  they shall lead me on
and bring me to your holy mountain,
  to your dwelling-place.

Then will I go in to the altar of God,
  the God of my gladness and joy;
then will I give you thanks upon the harp,
  O God, my God!

Or:

New Testament readings, first from Paul's Letter to the Romans and then from the Gospel, tell of the astonishing fulfillment of God's ancient promises. It is the inauguration of a new age.

The reading from Paul begins with a question (actually a series of questions, with three others preceding our reading). He uses questions not so much to elicit or develop an intellectual understanding, but to help his audience get involved in the story of salvation. Using the personal pronouns "you" and "we," Paul connects himself to the community, for all have been baptized into Christ, and baptized into his death. In using forms of the word "baptize" (*baptizo*), Paul refers to the ritual experience of Baptism, and he is likely also using the word *baptizo* in its most basic meaning: to be immersed, submerged, or plunged into. Jesus used *baptizo* with this meaning when he, like Paul, asked a question of his disciples: "Can you drink the cup that that I drink or be baptized with the baptism with which I am baptized?" (Mark 10:38). Both Jesus and Paul are asking about being immersed into the very death of Jesus.

Paul explains that believers are plunged into Christ's death, and also into every dimension of his life. This reality is so new that Paul develops a new vocabulary to describe it. Throughout the passage, he coins a series of compound verbs with the prefix *syn-*, meaning "together," or as a prefix "co-." He says literally that we have been co-crucified, co-buried, and that we co-grow with Christ. If we have died with Christ, we will co-live with him.

For meditation and context:

RESPONSORIAL PSALM   Isaiah 12:2–3, 4bcd, 5–6 (3)

When baptism is not celebrated.

R. You will draw water joyfully from the springs of salvation.

God indeed is my savior;
  I am confident and unafraid.
My strength and my courage is the LORD,
  and he has been my savior.
With joy you will draw water
  at the fountain of salvation.

Give thanks to the LORD, acclaim his name;
  among the nations make known his deeds,
  proclaim how exalted is his name.

Sing praise to the LORD for his glorious
    achievement;
  let this be known throughout all the earth.
Shout with exultation, O city of Zion,
  for great in your midst
  is the Holy One of Israel!

Or:

For meditation and context:

RESPONSORIAL PSALM   Psalm 51:12–13, 14–15, 18–19 (12a)

When baptism is not celebrated.

R. Create a clean heart in me, O God.

A clean heart create for me, O God,
  and a steadfast spirit renew within me.
Cast me not out from your presence,
  and your Holy Spirit take not from me.

Give me back the joy of your salvation,
  and a willing spirit sustain in me.
I will teach transgressors your ways,
  and sinners shall return to you.

For you are not pleased with sacrifices;
  should I offer a holocaust, you would not
    accept it.
My sacrifice, O God, is a contrite spirit;
  a heart contrite and humbled, O God, you
    will not spurn.

EPISTLE   Romans 6:3–11

A reading from the Letter of Saint Paul to the Romans

Brothers and sisters:

Proclaim this letter from St. Paul with energy.

Are you unaware that we who were baptized into Christ Jesus
    were baptized **into his** death?
We were **indeed buried with** him **through** baptism into **death**,
    so that, just as Christ was **raised** from the dead
    by the glory of the **Father**,
    we too might live in **newness** of **life**.

Paul's opening questions are the catalyst for him to develop an explanation of what the believers have already experienced by Baptism—both the ritual and the continued immersion into Christ's life—and how they should live accordingly. The intimate participation of believers who are plunged into Christ, as explained by Paul, has practical implications. The last verse of the reading begins with the word "consequently," a term that Paul often uses when he moves from theological teaching to exhortation. He tells the community members how they are to live in light of their belief. In the verses following our reading, Paul develops the "consequently," telling the believers in Rome how they are to co-live in Christ, not as a burden, but as an expression of their intimate relationship with the risen Christ.

The readings from the Old Testament can be heard and interpreted anew in light of the mystery of Christ as proclaimed by Paul. In Christ there is a new creation, new freedom from enslavement, new release from exile. The transformation proclaimed by Israel's prophets is even greater than they could have hoped for, for the transformation entails a "newness of life" in Christ. Ezekiel's prophecy of a new heart and a new spirit, and the promise "You will be my people and I will be your God" find extraordinary, uniMaginable fulfillment through the profound intimacy of life with Christ.

GOSPEL   **Matthew 28:1–10.** The setting for the Gospel is "after the sabbath, as the first day of the week was dawning." The day of Sabbath rest is

Keep building your energy.

For if we have **grown** into **union with him** through a death
   like his,
we shall **also** be united with him in the resurrection.
We know that our old self was crucified with him,
   so that our sinful body might be **done** away with,
   that we might **no** longer be in slavery to sin.
For a **dead** person has been absolved from sin.
If, then, we have died with Christ,
   we **believe** that we shall also live with him.
We **know** that **Christ**, raised from the dead, **dies no** more;
   death no longer has **power** over him.
As to **his death**, he died to sin once **and for** all;
   as to his **life**, he lives for **God**.
Consequently, you too must think of yourselves as being dead
   to sin
   and living **for** God **in Christ Jesus**.

This line is important. Pause before you proclaim it. Use good eye contact.

For meditation and context:

RESPONSORIAL PSALM   Psalm 118:1–2, 16–17, 22–23

R. Alleluia, alleluia, alleluia.

Give thanks to the LORD, for he is good,
   for his mercy endures forever.
Let the house of Israel say,
   "His mercy endures forever."

The right hand of the LORD has struck
      with power;
   the right hand of the LORD is exalted.
I shall not die, but live,
   and declare the works of the LORD.

The stone which the builders rejected
   has become the cornerstone.
By the LORD has this been done;
   it is wonderful in our eyes.

---

over, and a new day has begun, bringing with it a totally unexpected and wondrous newness. It is the "first day" of a new creation. Three women who had also witnessed the death of Jesus brought spices to anoint him at the tomb where he had been buried by Joseph of Arimathea. Shortly before his death, another woman had anointed Jesus' body in preparation for his burial, and now these three women plan to anoint it after burial. The three are named, unlike so many anonymous men and women: Mary Magdalene; Mary, the mother of James; and Salome. They were among the women who had ministered to Jesus in Galilee, and their desire to anoint him was to be a final ministry to him. Wondering who would roll away the large stone from the tomb entrance, the women see instead that the stone had already been rolled back. On entering the tomb, to their amazement, they see a young man clothed in white. We can well understand their astonishment, noted by Mark with a strong verb (*exethambethesan*), portraying them as completely amazed, utterly over-whelmed. More than simple surprise at the presence of the young man, theirs is a typical reaction in the face of the divine. The mysterious young man is a heavenly messenger, announcing to them that Jesus has been raised. His use of the passive verb "has been raised," is a biblical idiom to indicate that that action has been accomplished by God. Although Jesus appeared to be abandoned by God at the crucifixion, God has not abandoned his Son. Always present and powerful, God has transformed Jesus' death into life.

GOSPEL   Matthew 28:1–10

A reading from the holy Gospel according to Matthew

Proclaim in an informative tone using good volume.

After the **sabbath**, as the **first** day of the week was dawning,
    Mary Magdalene and the other **Mary came** to see the **tomb**.
And behold, there was a **great earthquake**;
    for an angel of the Lord **descended** from **heaven**,
    approached, **rolled** back the **stone**, and **sat** upon it.
His **appearance** was like lightning
    and his **clothing** was **white** as snow.
The guards were shaken with **fear** of him
    and **became** like dead men.
Then the angel said to the **women** in reply,
    "**Do not be** afraid!

Say Mary's words urgently.

I **know** that you are **seeking Jesus** the crucified.
He is **not here**, for he has been raised just as he **said**.
Come and see the place where he **lay**.
Then go quickly and **tell** his **disciples**,
    'He has been raised from the **dead**,

Galilee = GAL-ih-lee

    and he is going **before** you to Galilee;
    there you will see **him**.'
    Behold, I have told you."
Then they went **away quickly** from the tomb,
    fearful yet overjoyed,
    and ran to **announce** this to his disciples.
And behold, Jesus **met** them on **their way** and greeted them.
They approached, **embraced** his **feet**, and did him homage.
Then **Jesus** said to them, "Do not be **afraid**.

Pause before you say the last line.

Go tell my **brothers** to go to Galilee,
    and **there** they will see **me**."

Having told the women that Jesus is not here, the messenger adds that "he is going before you to Galilee." The place where Jesus had begun his ministry is the place where he will again meet the disciples whom he had called in Galilee. These closest disciples had not only deserted Jesus in his suffering, but their leader, Peter, had three times denied him. The messenger is assuring his disciples, through the women, that Jesus has not forsaken them, even mentioning Peter specifically. Jesus had predicted their fall and their scattering, and promised them that he would go before them into Galilee. Now, as the risen Messiah, he will fulfill that promise. No longer scattered in fear and discouragement, his disciples will meet Jesus, as utterly amazed as the women at the tomb.

In this Easter Vigil Gospel, we see the empty tomb, but not the appearance of the risen Jesus. On Easter Sunday, the first day of the new creation, we will encounter him, far from the empty tomb, alive among us. E.P.

EASTER SUNDAY OF THE RESURRECTION OF THE LORD

LECTIONARY #42

READING I   Acts of the Apostles 10:34a, 37–43

A reading from the Acts of the Apostles

Peter proceeded to **speak** and said:
   "You **know** what has **happened all** over **Judea**,
   beginning in Galilee **after** the **baptism**
   that **John** preached,
   how God **anointed Jesus** of **Nazareth**
   with the **Holy** Spirit and power.
He went about doing good
   and healing all those **oppressed** by the devil,
   for God was with **him**.
We are **witnesses** of **all** that he **did**
   both in the **country** of the **Jews** and in **Jerusalem**.
They put him to death by hanging him on a tree.
This man God raised on the third day and granted
      that he be visible,
   not to all the people, but **to** us,
   the witnesses chosen by God in advance,
   who ate and drank with him after he rose from the dead.
He **commissioned us** to preach to the people
   and testify that **he** is the **one** appointed by God
   as **judge** of the **living** and the **dead**.
To him all the **prophets bear** witness,
   that **everyone** who **believes** in him
   will **receive** forgiveness of **sins through** his **name**."

Begin proclaiming in an informative tone as Peter reviews Jesus' life and good works.
Judea = joo-DEE-uh

Start to build intensity.

We are called to action. Good eye contact and high energy are needed as you proclaim the ending.

There are options for readings today. Ask your parish staff which ones will be used.

READING I   Beginning with today's Easter Sunday liturgy, the first reading every day of the Easter season is taken from the Acts of the Apostles. The book begins in Jerusalem where the risen Jesus gives his disciples a commission and a promise before he ascends into heaven. He promises his followers that when they receive the Holy Spirit they are to be his witnesses beginning in Jerusalem and extending to the ends of the earth. After they wait faithfully in prayer, the Holy Spirit does indeed empower Jesus' once-fearful apostles so that they proclaim him, first to Jews and then to Gentiles.

Although the majority of the Gentile mission as recounted in Acts is undertaken by Paul, in today's reading we hear a speech given by Peter in the house of the Gentile centurion Cornelius. Peter opens his speech with an important statement that is unfortunately omitted from the lectionary. He tells his Gentile audience, "In truth, I see that God shows no partiality. Rather, in every nation whoever fears him and acts uprightly is acceptable to him." Before Peter made his journey to Cornelius' house, he had a vision that led him to the realization "that I should not call any person profane or unclean." Prior to his vision, Peter would neither enter the house of a

For meditation and context:

RESPONSORIAL PSALM　Psalm 118:1–2, 16–17, 22–23 (24)

R. This is the day the Lord has made; let us rejoice and be glad.
or
R. Alleluia.

Give thanks to the LORD, for he is good,
　　for his mercy endures forever.
Let the house of Israel say,
　　"His mercy endures forever."

"The right hand of the LORD has struck
　　with power;
　　the right hand of the LORD is exalted.
I shall not die, but live,
　　and declare the works of the LORD.

The stone which the builders rejected
　　has become the cornerstone.
By the LORD has this been done;
　　it is wonderful in our eyes.

Colossians = kuh-LOSH-uhnz

READING II　Colossians 3:1–4

A reading from the Letter of Saint Paul to the Colossians

Brothers and sisters:
If then **you** were **raised with Christ, seek** what is above,
　　where Christ is seated at the **right** hand of God.
Think of what is above, **not** of what is on earth.
For you have died, and your **life** is **hidden with** Christ **in** God.
When Christ your life appears,
　　then **you too** will appear with him in **glory.**

Or:

Take your time. Proclaim clearly with good eye contact. Proclaim with gratefulness.

Gentile, nor eat with them, considering Gentiles unclean.

The proclamation that Peter gives to his Gentile audience, like that given to Jews, culminates in the death and Resurrection of Jesus. The preaching of John the Baptist and Jesus' own ministry had each prepared the way for Jesus' death and Resurrection: the Paschal Mystery. Fulfilling the mission that Jesus gave to his disciples, Peter is a witness to Jesus and all that he did, culminating in his death and Resurrection. Hearing

the core creed of the Paschal Mystery announced to Gentiles on Easter Sunday is a reminder that the good news of the Resurrection is for all people. Peter's perspective is like Paul's: "There is neither Jew nor Greek, slave or free, male or female, for you are all one in Christ Jesus" (Galatians 3:28). Peter concludes his speech by affirming that everyone who believes in the Lord will receive forgiveness of sins. Good news to remember on this greatest of feasts.

READING II **Colossians.** Christ's Resurrection from the dead is the beginning, the foretaste, the pattern, and the source of new life for those who have been immersed into him at Baptism. In this baptismal catechesis to the Colossians, Paul explains that everyone who has been baptized into Christ has died with him, and has been raised with him. Their union with Christ has already begun to transform them, even as they await future transformation when Christ appears,

READING II   1 Corinthians 5:6b–8

Proclaim this reading with high energy.

A reading from the first Letter of Saint Paul to the Corinthians

Brothers and sisters:
Do you not know that a **little** yeast **leavens** all the dough?
Clear out the old yeast,
    so that **you** may **become** a fresh batch of dough,
    inasmuch as you are unleavened.
For our **paschal lamb, Christ, has been sacrificed**.
Therefore, let us celebrate the feast,
    not with the **old** yeast, the yeast of **malice and wickedness**,
    but with the unleavened **bread** of **sincerity and truth**.

SEQUENCE   Victimae paschali laudes

For meditation and context:

Sequences originated as extensions of the sung Alleluia before the proclamation of the gospel, although they precede the Alleluia now. The Easter Sequence is an ancient liturgical hymn that praises Christ, the Paschal victim, for his victory over death. Mary Magdalene recounts her experience at Christ's tomb, proclaiming, "Christ my hope is arisen."

Christians, to the Paschal Victim
    Offer your thankful praises!
A Lamb the sheep redeems;
    Christ, who only is sinless,
    Reconciles sinners to the Father.
Death and life have contended in that
        combat stupendous:
    The Prince of life, who died, reigns
    immortal.

Speak, Mary, declaring
    What you saw, wayfaring.
"The tomb of Christ, who is living,
    The glory of Jesus' resurrection;
Bright angels attesting,
    The shroud and napkin resting.
Yes, Christ my hope is arisen;
    to Galilee he goes before you."
Christ indeed from death is risen, our new
        life obtaining.
    Have mercy, victor King, ever reigning!
    Amen. Alleluia.

signifying his coming again in glory. So new and intimate is believers' union with Christ that Paul develops new terminology to express this great mystery. Developing his own original words, he says here (and elsewhere, e.g., at Romans 6:2–11) that believers have co-died, and have been co-raised with Christ.

Because Christ has been raised, has ascended into heaven, and is no longer physically present on earth, believers must seek what is above, where Christ is seated at God's right hand. The image of the Lord Christ seated at the right hand of the Lord God is an allusion to Psalm 110:1, a psalm cited or implied some twenty-five times in the New Testament: "The Lord says to my lord, 'Sit at my right hand until I make your enemies your footstool.'" Seeking and thinking of what is above involves more than engaging in quiet meditation of Christ at God's right hand. Seeking and thinking implies a continuous, intense focus on Christ that includes a sustained union with him, and imitating his way of life. In the verses immediately following today's reading, Paul specifies the kind of life that seeking and thinking of what is above entails: "Put to death, therefore, the parts of you that are earthly," followed by a list of specific actions that are to be "put to death."

1 Corinthians. Passover is the Jewish feast that celebrates God freeing the enslaved Hebrews from their bondage in Egypt. In the Gospels, Jesus' crucifixion

GOSPEL John 20:1–9

A reading from the holy Gospel according to John

On the first day of the week,
    Mary of Magdala came to the tomb **early** in the **morning,**
    while it was **still dark,**
    and saw the stone removed from the tomb.
So she ran and went to **Simon** Peter
    and to the other disciple whom Jesus loved, and told them,
    "They have taken the **Lord** from the **tomb,**
    and we **don't know** where they put him."
So Peter and the other disciple went **out** and **came** to the tomb.
They both ran, but the other disciple ran faster than Peter
    and **arrived** at the tomb first;
    he bent down and **saw** the **burial** cloths there, but did **not go in.**
When Simon **Peter** arrived **after** him,
    he went **into** the tomb and saw the **burial** cloths **there,**
    and the cloth that had **covered** his **head,**
    not with the burial cloths but rolled up in a separate place.
Then the other disciple also went in,
    the **one** who had arrived at the tomb first,
    and he saw and believed.
For they did **not yet understand** the Scripture
    that he had to rise from the **dead.**

Proclaim in an informative tone using good volume.

Magdala = MAG-duh-luh

Say Mary's words urgently.

Calmly read to the end of the Gospel.

Pause before you say the last line.

takes place in the context of this feast, and his passing over from death to life is seen as a new Passover. Jesus himself is the perfect paschal lamb of sacrifice, an image that Paul shares with other New Testament writers (e.g., John 1:29; 1 Peter 1:19). For the communities to whom Paul wrote, Passover is a powerful reminder of Christ's sacrifice for them, and of their participation in his death and Resurrection through Baptism.

In today's reading, Paul uses the symbolism of the combined feast of Passover and Unleavened Bread as a means of moral exhortation. The unleavened bread shared at family tables at Passover is the leading symbol that he employs. At the feast, old yeast is thrown out, since it is seen as a source of contamination for the dough. So serious was having no leaven in the house for a full seven days that anyone who ate leavened food was to be cut off from the community (Exodus 12:19).

Drawing on the yeast symbolism, Paul compares the prideful boasting of some in the Corinthian community to being "puffed up" by yeast. Some of them not only tolerated immoral behavior, but even boasted about it. He asks them rhetorically, "Do you not know that a little yeast leavens all the dough?" He implies that boasting and immoral behavior contaminate the community just as much as yeast contaminates the entire batch of dough. Therefore the old yeast of malice and wickedness, including

AFTERNOON GOSPEL   Luke 24:13–35

A reading from the holy Gospel according to Luke

That very day, the first day of the week,
  two of **Jesus'** disciples were going
  to a village seven miles from Jerusalem called **Emmaus**,
  and they were conversing about all the things that
    had occurred.
And it happened that while they were conversing and debating,
  Jesus himself drew near and **walked with them**,
  but their eyes were prevented from recognizing him.
He asked them,
  "What are you **discussing** as you walk along?"
They **stopped**, looking **downcast**.
One of them, named Cleopas, said to him in reply,
  "Are you the **only** visitor to Jerusalem
  who does **not know** of the things
  that have taken **place** there in these days?"
And he replied to them, "What sort of things?"
They said to him,
  "The things that happened to Jesus **the** Nazarene,
  who was a **prophet mighty** in deed and word
  before God and **all** the people,
  how our chief priests and rulers both handed him over
  to a sentence of death and crucified him.
But we were hoping that he would be the **one** to **redeem** Israel;
  and **besides all this**,
  it is **now** the **third** day since this took place.
Some **women** from our group, however, have astounded us:
  they were at the **tomb early** in the morning
  and did **not** find his **body**;
  they came back and reported
  that they had indeed seen a vision **of angels**
  who **announced** that he was alive. »

You are setting the stage for the conversation that is about to happen between Jesus and his disciples. Proclaim with an informative tone.

Emmaus = eh-MAY-uhs

Pause and use expression in your voice.

Cleopas = KLEE-oh-puhs
Help the assembly visualize their exchange by using expression in your voice.

Nazarene - NAZ-uh-reen

---

boasting about immorality, must be removed, so that the community itself will become unleavened bread of sincerity and truth. This is the right way to celebrate the feast and to be united with Christ, the Passover lamb.

GOSPEL **John.** Jesus' crucifixion and death occur in the context of the great Jewish feast of Passover. Now, as John the evangelist narrates the account of Jesus' rising from the dead, the Passover with all its crowds and rituals is no longer mentioned. It is now "the first day of the week," signaling a new stage in the story. In the early morning of that first day, it is still dark. In John's Gospel, darkness symbolizes a variety of unenlightened human experiences and emotions: sin, betrayal, doubt, sadness, fear, ignorance. The darkness of sadness and confusion in this scene is on the verge of becoming daylight for Mary of Magdala, Simon Peter, and the disciple whom Jesus loved.

In this predawn darkness, Mary Magdalene, who had stood by the cross with the other women and the beloved disciple, comes to the tomb. John narrates Mary's actions in the present tense, giving the episode an energetic and urgent feeling: Mary *comes* to the tomb; she *sees* the stone removed; she *runs* to Peter and the other disciple; she *tells* them bluntly that they have taken the Lord from the tomb, and we don't know where he is. Her understanding is still in the darkness. Having

Jesus is frustrated. Let us hear that in your reading of his words.

"Then some of those with us **went** to the tomb
    and found things just as the women had described,
    but **him** they did **not** see."
And he said to them, "Oh, how foolish you are!
How slow of heart to believe **all** that the **prophets** spoke!
Was it **not necessary** that the **Christ** should suffer these things
    and **enter** into his glory?"
Then beginning with **Moses** and all the prophets,
    he interpreted to them what referred to him
    in **all** the Scriptures.
As they approached the village to which they were going,
    he gave the impression that he was going on **farther**.
But they **urged** him, "Stay **with us**,
    for it is nearly evening and the day is almost over."
So he went in to stay with them.
And it happened that, while he was with them at **table**,
    he **took bread**, said the blessing,
    broke it, and **gave** it to them.

Speak with a renewed energy and excitement.

With that their eyes were opened and they recognized him,
    but he vanished from their sight.
Then they said to each other,
    "Were not our hearts burning within us
    while he spoke to us on the way and **opened** the Scriptures
        to us?"
So they **set out** at once and **returned** to Jerusalem
    where they found gathered **together**
    the eleven and those with them who were saying,
    "The Lord has truly been **raised** and has **appeared** to **Simon**!"
Then the **two recounted**
    what had taken place on the way
    and how he was **made** known to them in the breaking **of** bread.

TO KEEP IN MIND
Use inflection (the high or low pitch of your voice) to convey attitude and feeling. High pitch expresses intensity and excitement; low pitch expresses sadness, contrition, or solemnity.

---

come to Jesus' garden tomb to mourn or to anoint his body, Mary was shocked at what she saw. Her words to the two disciples clearly show that she had no expectation that Jesus would be risen from the dead. Like many Jews of the day, most notably the Pharisees, Mary probably looked for the resurrection of the dead only on the last day.

Simon Peter and the beloved disciple, like Mary of Magdala, also played a part in the account of Jesus' passion and death.

Peter is remembered for his denial and abandonment of Jesus, and the other disciple for being a faithful witness at Jesus' death. Peter's rehabilitation begins at this early morning darkness. Both disciples run immediately to the tomb, exhibiting the same urgency as Mary. Although it is common to refer to the "empty tomb" because Jesus' body is not there, the tomb is not entirely empty. They see the burial cloths in which Jesus had been wrapped. These garments of death have been left behind

because death has no dominion over the risen Jesus. Unlike Lazarus, Jesus will not die again. For the beloved disciples, seeing the tomb and the burial cloths was enough; "He saw and believed." He believes, even though the evangelist adds that they did not yet understand. Their darkness of sadness and not comprehending will gradually be transformed to joy and understanding so great that they will proclaim it abroad. Then others will also come to believe.

SECOND SUNDAY OF EASTER (DIVINE MERCY SUNDAY)

LECTIONARY #43

READING I   Acts of the Apostles 2:42–47

A reading from the Acts of the Apostles

They devoted themselves
    to the **teaching** of the apostles **and** to the **communal life**,
    to the **breaking** of bread and to the **prayers**.
Awe came upon **everyone**,
    and many wonders **and** signs were done **through** the apostles.
All who believed were together and had **all** things in common;
    they would sell their property and possessions
    and divide them among all according to **each one's** need.
Every **day** they devoted themselves
    to meeting together in the temple area
    and to **breaking** bread in their homes.
They ate their meals with exultation and sincerity **of heart**,
    praising God and **enjoying** favor with **all** the people.
And **every** day the **Lord** added to their number those who were
      being saved.

You are proclaiming what life was like for the early Christians. Put expression in your voice. Rehearse for strong eye contact and project your voice.

Pause, smile, and slowly say the last line.

READING I   After Jesus' Ascension, his followers were locked in the upper room, prayerfully awaiting the Spirit Jesus had promised. Appearing as tongues of fire, the Spirit rests on each of them. Then they speak in other tongues, thereby beginning the mission that Jesus had given them. The Spirit poured out on the community at Pentecost remains the abiding gift of God for the Church. By the power of the Spirit, the believers are faithful to four essential characteristics of the church described in today's reading.

Fidelity to the first element, the teaching of the apostles, involves both the reception of the apostles' teaching, and passing on what has been received. Peter gives the first apostolic teaching on Pentecost. In his address, he proclaims the death and Resurrection of Jesus, a proclamation that is reiterated in all the speeches in Acts of the Apostles. Besides teaching through the Word, the apostles also teach through signs and wonders, and by witnessing to Jesus through their whole way of life. Remaining faithful to the teaching of the apostles means that all believers also

teach by announcing the good news in word and deed.

The next three elements, the communal life, the breaking of the bread, and the prayers, are closely linked. Communal life (*koinonia*) entails communion with God and with one another. One way of expressing this communion is to hold all things in common, and dividing possessions according to need. Another way of expressing communion is by participating in the breaking of the bread, the evangelist's way of referring to the Eucharist. As Jews who believed in Jesus, the believers in Jerusalem continue

157

Proclaim with energy.

RESPONSORIAL PSALM   Psalm 118:2–4, 13–15, 22–24 (1)

R. Give thanks to the Lord for he is good, his love is everlasting.
or
R. Alleluia.

Let the house of Israel say,
  "His mercy endures forever."
Let the house of Aaron say,
  "His mercy endures forever."
Let those who fear the LORD say,
  "His mercy endures forever."

I was hard pressed and was falling,
  but the LORD helped me.
My strength and my courage is the LORD,
  and he has been my savior.
The joyful shout of victory
  in the tents of the just.

The stone which the builders rejected
  has become the cornerstone.
By the LORD has this been done;
  it is wonderful in our eyes.
This is the day the LORD has made;
  let us be glad and rejoice in it.

READING II   1 Peter 1:3–9

Blessed = BLES-uhd

Proclaim with high energy. There is much to celebrate! Let the assembly hear happiness in your reading.

A reading from the first Letter of Saint Peter

Blessed be the **God and Father** of our **Lord Jesus Christ**,
  who in his **great mercy gave** us a new **birth** to a **living** hope
  through the resurrection of Jesus Christ **from** the dead,
  to an **inheritance** that is imperishable, undefiled, and unfading,
  kept in heaven **for you**
  who by the power of God are **safeguarded** through faith,
  to a **salvation** that is **ready** to be **revealed** in the **final** time.
In this you rejoice, although **now** for a **little** while
  you may have to suffer through various **trials**,
  so that the genuineness of your **faith**,
  more **precious** than gold that is **perishable even though**
    tested by **fire**,
  may **prove** to be for praise, glory, **and** honor
  at the **revelation** of Jesus **Christ**.
Although you have **not seen** him you love him;
  even though you do **not** see him now yet believe in him,
  you rejoice with an **indescribable** and glorious joy,
  as you **attain** the goal of your faith, the salvation **of your** souls.

Pause before you proclaim this last sentence with tenderness.

---

to meet in the temple area, and also to celebrate the Lord's Supper in their homes. Prayer, the fourth essential characteristic, further expresses communion with God and God's people. Praise of God in both temple and home, and prayers of the community members in threatening or fearful circumstances (e.g., 4:29; 12:12) reinforce the communion experienced at the breaking of the bread.

 READING II | The second reading opens with a proclamation of praise, "Blessed be the God and Father of

our Lord Jesus Christ." The word "Blessed" (*eulogetos*) echoes Zechariah's Benedictus (Luke 1:68), hymns in the Pauline tradition (2 Corinthians 1:3; Ephesians 1:3), and the eighteen blessings of Jewish synagogue liturgy. Although all of these divine praises have an enduring and universal meaning, Peter addresses his audience personally: God's mercy is for us; you have reason for hope. Everything that follows the opening proclamation motivates people to give praise to God, who has shown abundant mercy. Peter (or someone writing in his name) develops the reasons for praising God

in a long, complicated explanation that stretches from the past, into the present, and includes a well-founded hope in the future. Christ's Resurrection is a past reality with enduring consequences in the present, and has given us hope in the future imperishable inheritance and salvation.

There is a tangible tension between the present reality of trials and being tested by fire on earth and the awaited inheritance in heaven. Peter explains that the suffering now is only for a short time, while the future goal in heaven is imperishable and unfading. Jesus' Resurrection

GOSPEL John 20:19–31

A reading from the holy Gospel according to John

On the **evening** of that first day of the week,
>   when the **doors** were locked, where the disciples were,
>   for fear of the Jews,
>   **Jesus came** and stood in their midst
>   and said to them, "Peace **be with you.**"

When he had said this, he **showed** them his hands and his side.
The disciples rejoiced when they **saw** the Lord.
Jesus said to them **again**, "**Peace** be with you.
As the **Father** has **sent me**, so I **send** you."
And when he had said this, he breathed on them and said
>   to them,
>   "Receive **the Holy** Spirit.

Whose **sins** you forgive **are** forgiven them,
>   and whose sins you retain **are** retained."

Thomas, called Didymus, one of the **Twelve**,
>   was **not with** them when Jesus came.
So the **other** disciples said to him, "**We have** seen **the** Lord."
But he said to them,
>   "Unless I see the mark of the **nails** in his hands
>   and **put** my **finger** into the nailmarks
>   and **put** my **hand** into his side, I will **not believe.**" **»**

Proclaim with authority and clarity.

Say Jesus' words with firmness and purpose.

Didymus = DID-uh-muhs

---

from the dead, a sign of God's mercy, draws believers into the mystery of death and resurrection. Jesus' Resurrection required suffering and death, those who have new birth in him must also expect to experience suffering as they look forward in hope to resurrection.

Peter reminds his audience that although you do not see him, you love him, believe in him, and rejoice. By stating as a fact that they love, believe, and rejoice, Peter is actually encouraging them to live in this way. Their love, faith, and joy in Christ express a deep and continuing rela-

tionship with him and give God praise, honor, and glory.

GOSPEL When Simon Peter and the disciple whom Jesus loved had seen only Jesus' burial cloths in the tomb, they returned home where they remained with the other disciples behind locked doors for fear of the Jews. In today's Gospel, it is evening of the first day of the week when Jesus stands in their midst. His presence, unrestrained by the locked doors, is sudden and mysterious. He begins with a traditional greeting of peace, with

his peace transforming their fear into joy. To assure the gathered community of his identity, Jesus shows them his hands and side. The wound in his side is also a visual link between the risen Jesus with Jesus on the cross, when blood and water flowed from his side. With a second "Peace be with you," Jesus gives his disciples a mission based on his own mission from his Father. Along with peace, Jesus gives his followers the Holy Spirit, God's life-giving and permanent presence. By breathing the Holy Spirit on them, Jesus inaugurates a new creation, comparable to God giving the

Proclaim in a gentle tone, "Put your finger here and see my hands, and bring your hand and put it into my side. . . ."

Blessed = BLES-uhd.

Proclaim with renewed energy.

Now a week **later** his disciples were again inside
     and Thomas was **with** them.
Jesus came, although the doors were **locked**,
     and **stood** in their **midst** and said, "**Peace** be with you."
Then he said to **Thomas**, "**Put** your **finger** here and **see** my **hands**,
     and bring your **hand** and **put** it into my **side**,
     and do **not** be **un**believing, but **believe**."
Thomas answered and said to him, "**My** Lord **and my** God!"
Jesus said to him, "Have you **come** to **believe** because you have
     seen **me?**
Blessed are those who have not seen and have **believed**."

Now, Jesus did **many other signs** in the **presence** of his **disciples**
     that are **not** written in this book.
But **these are written** that **you** may come **to** believe
     that Jesus **is the** Christ, **the Son of** God,
     and that **through** this belief you may **have** life in his name.

breath of life into humanity (Genesis 2:7). Empowered by the Spirit, his followers will continue Jesus' mission of forgiveness, going into the world, no longer fearful behind locked doors.

Before Jesus appears to his disciples again on the following first day of the week, Thomas, absent from Jesus' Easter appearance, does not believe the other disciples. He puts specific conditions for believing; he must be able to touch Jesus' wounds, even thrusting his hand into Jesus' side. Although Thomas is the only disciple whose lack of belief is noted, the fact that the oth-

ers remain behind locked doors indicates they have not yet gone into the world where Jesus sent them. They say the words, "We have seen the Lord," but have not yet acted on what they profess.

When Jesus once more stands in their midst, after extending peace to all, he speaks only to Thomas. The first part of Jesus' command to him sounds brusque, based on Thomas' own condition for believing. The second part expresses the underlying purpose: Thomas should move from unbelieving to believing, with both verbs signifying an ongoing relationship, one of

doubt and distance, the other of fidelity and intimacy. Thomas responds immediately with an exuberant proclamation of faith: "My Lord and my God!" Jesus then asks Thomas a gentle question, "Have you come to believe because you have seen me?" Continuing with a beatitude for all who have believed without seeing, Jesus looks ahead to later generations who can neither see nor touch him. E.P.

THIRD SUNDAY OF EASTER

LECTIONARY #46

READING I   Acts of the Apostles 2:14, 22–33

A reading from the Acts of the Apostles

Proclaim Peter's words with much forcefulness and vigor. Use good contact and volume. Peter's love for Christ is evident through this speech to the crowd.

Nazorean = naz-uh-REE-uhn

Pause before you begin. Read with gentleness in your voice.

Then Peter stood **up** with the Eleven,
  raised his voice, and proclaimed:
  "You who are Jews, indeed all of you staying in Jerusalem.
Let this be **known** to you, and listen to my words.
You who are **Israelites**, hear these words.
Jesus **the** Nazorean was a man **commended** to you by **God**
  with **mighty deeds**, **wonders**, and **signs**,
  which God worked through him in your **midst**,
    as you yourselves know.
This man, delivered up by the set plan and **foreknowledge** of God,
  you killed, using lawless men to **crucify** him.
But God **raised** him up, **releasing** him from the **throes** of death,
  because it was impossible for him to be held by it.
For David says of him:
  *I saw the Lord ever **before** me,*
    *with him at my right hand I shall **not** be **disturbed**.*
  ***Therefore** my heart has been glad and my tongue has exulted;*
    *my flesh, too, will dwell in **hope**,*
  *because you will **not** abandon my soul to the netherworld,*
    *nor will you suffer your holy one to see **corruption**.*
  *You have made **known** to me the **paths** of **life**;*
    *you will **fill me** with **joy** in your presence.* »

READING I On the day of Pentecost, after the outpouring of the Holy Spirit, Peter proclaims the good news to the awestruck crowd. Because he is Spirit-filled, everything that Peter says has prophetic power, as did the words of the prophets of old. Today's reading from the Acts of the Apostles is a portion of Peter's discourse on that day, the first of many in Acts, and message to the situation of his audience. Since they have just heard those who received the Spirit speaking in other tongues, Peter tells them that this very event was spoken of by the prophet Joel. Beginning with Peter's Pentecost discourse, each of the speeches interprets the Old Testament to develop the message, makes reference to those who are witnesses, and calls the audience to repentance. At the heart of the speeches is the proclamation of Jesus' death and Resurrection, the *kerygma*, that is, the foundation of Christian faith. The portion of Peter's speech that we hear today develops the *kerygma* in light of the Jewish Scriptures.

As he develops the account of Jesus, Peter reinforces the connection with his audience, telling them that Jesus did signs and wonders "in your midst, as you yourselves know." Their own tradition had prepared the way for Jesus; even his being delivered up and put to death was according to God's plan and foreknowledge. According to Peter, Jesus' death and Resurrection opens up a new way of understanding the Bible, particularly the words of the psalms. In Psalm 16, attributed to King David, David had said that God would not abandon him to the netherworld nor let God's holy one see corruption, two ways of referring to death. But King David had

Proclaim with energy.

"My brothers, one can confidently say to you
    about the patriarch David that he died and was buried,
    and his **tomb** is in **our** midst **to this day**.
But since he was a prophet and knew that God had sworn an
        oath to him
    that he would set **one** of his **descendants** upon **his** throne,
    he foresaw and spoke of the resurrection of the Christ,
    that **neither** was he **abandoned** to the netherworld
    nor did his flesh see **corruption**.

Pause before you begin to end the reading.

God raised this Jesus;
    of this we are **all witnesses**.
Exalted at the right hand of God,
    he received the promise of the **Holy** Spirit from the Father
    and poured him forth, as you see **and** hear."

For meditation and context:

RESPONSORIAL PSALM   Psalm 16:1–2, 5, 7–8, 9–10, 11 (11a)

R. **Lord, you will show us the path of life.**
or
R. **Alleluia.**

Keep me, O God, for in you I take refuge;
    I say to the LORD, "My Lord are you."
O LORD, my allotted portion and my cup,
    you it is who hold fast my lot.

I bless the LORD who counsels me;
    even in the night my heart exhorts me.
I set the LORD ever before me;
    with him at my right hand I shall not
        be disturbed.

Therefore my heart is glad and my
        soul rejoices,
    my body, too, abides in confidence;
because you will not abandon my soul
        to the netherworld,
    nor will you suffer your faithful one to
        undergo corruption.

You will show me the path to life,
    abounding joy in your presence,
    the delights at your right hand forever.

---

certainly died, as Peter reminds his audience, for "his tomb is in our midst to this day." Therefore David, who spoke as a prophet, must have been referring to someone else: the descendant promised by God. David had spoken prophetically of Jesus' Resurrection that fulfilled God's oath to David.

Though Peter's interpretation may seem a stretch to modern ears, he used a well-established and accepted Jewish method of interpretation called *midrash* that creatively develops the original meaning of a text to make it relevant and useful

to a later generation. Peter, addressing a Jewish audience, has used a Jewish method of making their own Scriptures, Jesus' death and Resurrection, and their present experience of the outpouring of the Spirit more understandable to them. From the beginning to the end of his speech, Peter draws his audience into the events, for they too have seen and heard signs of what God has done by raising Jesus from the dead.

READING II   The First Letter of Peter, attributed to "an apostle of

Jesus Christ," appears to be a pastoral letter sent to many churches around the Mediterranean, similar to an encyclical meant for the whole Church. He addresses his audience during the time of their sojourning, or their exile (*paroikia*), using a word that implies believers are living in a foreign country. Their true home is the realm toward which they are making their journey. In writing to them as *you* plural, Peter creates an image of them traveling together as companions on the road. On this journey, they face persecution and suffering, as did Jesus himself. Through their

READING II 1 Peter 1:17–21

A reading from the first Letter of Saint Peter

Beloved:
If you invoke as Father him who **judges impartially**
  according to each one's **works**,
    conduct yourselves with reverence during the time
      of your **sojourning**,
    realizing that you were ransomed from your **futile** conduct,
    handed on by your ancestors,
    not with perishable things like silver or gold
    but with the **precious blood** of Christ
    as of a **spotless** unblemished lamb.

He was **known** before the foundation of the world
  but **revealed** in the final time for you,
  who **through** him believe in **God**
  who raised him from the dead and gave him glory,
  so that **your faith** and **hope** are **in** God.

Peter is continually teaching us about God and his son. Take your time when reading this letter from Peter. Speak with authority.

sojourning = SOH-jern-ing

See how God loves us! Proclaim with joy.

TO KEEP IN MIND
Pause to break up separate thoughts, set apart significant statements, or indicate major shifts. Never pause in the middle of a single thought. Your primary guide for pauses is punctuation.

suffering, even during this stay in exile, they already share in Christ's glory (see 1:6–7; 4:13); their faith in his death and Resurrection and hope of future glory sustain them.

In today's reading, Peter exhorts his audience to show reverence toward the Father who is the impartial judge. Such reverence is not an artificial piety or adherence to ritual, but signifies an enduring sense of awe at God's majesty and sovereignty. Reverence elicits obedience, humility, and fidelity. It flows from the realization of what God has already done through the

sacrificial blood of Christ. Even more than the blood of the Passover lamb that saved the enslaved Hebrews, the blood of Christ has ransomed believers from the futile way of life and patterns of behavior of the past.

According to Peter, we are living in "the final time" because Jesus' death and Resurrection has inaugurated the last stage of history. This was God's plan all along, even from the world's foundation, but is only revealed in this final time. Until the messiah comes again in glory, believers abide in faith and hope as they continue their journey together.

GOSPEL Today's Gospel (also the Gospel for Easter afternoon) opens with two dejected disciples leaving the community in Jerusalem, and closes with the two of them, rejoicing, back in Jerusalem. Between this opening and closing is the story of their encounter with Jesus, unrecognized, and his walking with them. On the road, he explains the Scriptures to them, and in the evening shares in the breaking of the bread when they finally recognize them. All of this happens on the first day of the week, the very day that the women had discovered Jesus'

GOSPEL   Luke 24:13–35

A reading from the holy Gospel according to Luke

That very day, the first day of the week,
    two of **Jesus'** disciples were going
    to a village seven miles from Jerusalem called **Emmaus**,
    and they were conversing about all the things that
        had occurred.
And it happened that while they were conversing and debating,
    Jesus himself drew near and **walked with** them,
    but their eyes were **prevented** from **recognizing** him.
He asked them,
    "What are you **discussing** as you walk along?"
They **stopped**, looking **downcast**.
One of them, named Cleopas, said to him in reply,
    "Are you the **only** visitor to Jerusalem
    who does **not know** of the things
    that have taken **place** there in these days?"
And he replied to them, "What sort of things?"
They said to him,
    "The things that happened to Jesus **the** Nazarene,
    who was a **prophet mighty** in deed and word
    before God and **all** the people,
    how our chief priests and rulers **both** handed him over
    to a sentence of death and crucified him.
But we were **hoping** that **he** would be the **one** to **redeem** Israel;
    and **besides all this**,
    it is **now** the **third** day since this took place.
Some **women** from our group, however, have astounded us:
    they were at the **tomb early** in the morning
    and did **not** find his **body**;
    they came back and reported
    that they had indeed seen a vision **of angels**
    who **announced** that he was alive.

You are setting the stage for the conversation that is about to happen between Jesus and his disciples. Proclaim with an informative tone.

Emmaus = eh-MAY-uhs

Pause and use expression in your voice.

Cleopas = KLEE-oh-puhs
Help the assembly visualize their exchange by using expression in your voice.

Nazarene = NAZ-uh-reen

empty tomb. On one level, the story is about the experience of Jesus' disciples after his death and Resurrection; on another level, it is the story of Jesus' disciples in later eras and circumstances who also meet him on their journey. Those who hear this account can see their own questions, actions, and emotions in those of the two Emmaus-bound disciples. And Jesus' words and deeds teach every generation about his identity and how he is present among them.

One of the themes of Luke's Gospel, evident in today's story, is the journey of Jesus and his disciples. Earlier in the Gospel, Jesus had made the journey to Jerusalem with his followers, both men and women. Now as he walks with these two, it becomes apparent that the risen Jesus is just as present to them as was the earthly Jesus to his disciples. Although the two on the road do not understand what they tell Jesus, they accurately recount his story and the hope that they once had. Their recital is reminiscent of that of Peter, who

correctly identified Jesus as the messiah, even though he did not understand. Peter, the two confused disciples, and present-day believers as well need Jesus to interpret the words of faith that they proclaim. After the disciples on the road review the story of Jesus, the risen Jesus himself teaches them in the same way he had taught Peter and the other disciples when they made the journey to Jerusalem. He listens to them, questions them, corrects misunderstanding, and uses the Scriptures to lead them to new knowledge. He explains

Jesus is frustrated. Let us hear that in your reading of his words.

Then some of those with us **went** to the tomb
    and found things just as the women had described,
        but **him** they did **not** see."
And he said to them, "Oh, how foolish you are!
How slow of heart to believe all that the **prophets** spoke!
Was it **not necessary** that the **Christ** should suffer these things
    and **enter** into his glory?"
Then beginning with **Moses** and all the prophets,
    he interpreted to them what referred to him
    in **all** the Scriptures.
As they approached the village to which they were going,
    he gave the impression that he was going on **farther**.
But they **urged** him, "Stay **with us**,
    for it is nearly evening and the day is almost over."
So he went in to stay with them.
And it happened that, while he was **with** them at **table**,
    he **took bread**, said the blessing,
    broke it, and gave it to them.
With that their eyes were opened and they recognized him,
    but he vanished from their sight.
Then they said to each other,
    "Were not our hearts burning within us
    while he spoke to us on the way and **opened** the Scriptures
        to us?"
So they **set out** at once and **returned** to Jerusalem
    where they found gathered **together**
    the eleven and those with them who were saying,
    "The Lord has truly been **raised** and has **appeared** to **Simon**!"
Then the **two recounted**
    what had taken place on the way
    and how he was **made** known to them in the breaking **of** bread.

Speak with a renewed energy and excitement.

how the entirety of the Jewish tradition pointed to him, and that his suffering was necessary for him to enter into his glory.

When it is nearly evening, they reach Emmaus and invite Jesus, still unrecognized, to stay with them. As they sit at table, Jesus' words and actions repeat what he had done at the last supper, and also anticipate what the Church will do in his name. By the time Luke's Gospel was written, believers were already celebrating the Lord's Supper in their homes (see Acts 4:46), where the Lord is again present with

them. At each of these extraordinary meals, the same actions are repeated: the taking of bread, saying the blessing, breaking the bread, and giving it to the gathered community. St. Augustine affirms the continuing significance: "When is the Lord made known? In this breaking of the bread. . . . In the sharing of bread, the Lord was made present" (Sermon 235).

The two parts of today's Gospel reflect the two parts of the Eucharistic celebration: Liturgy of the Word and Liturgy of the Eucharist. As the two disciples met Jesus in

both word and sacrament, so too does the Church. When the disciples finally recognized Jesus and remembered that their hearts were burning within them as he explained the Scriptures, they returned to the community in Jerusalem. Like these two disciples who told how Jesus was made known to them, now all who participate in the liturgy also go forth to bring the Good News to others. E.P.

FOURTH SUNDAY OF EASTER

LECTIONARY #49

READING I Acts of the Apostles 2:14a, 36–41

A reading from the Acts of the Apostles

Then Peter stood up with the Eleven,
 raised his voice, and proclaimed:
"Let the **whole** house of **Israel know** for **certain**
 that God has made both Lord **and** Christ,
 this Jesus whom you **crucified**."

Now when they **heard** this, they were cut to the **heart**,
 and they asked Peter and the other apostles,
 "What are we **to** do, my brothers?"
Peter said to them,
 "Repent **and be** baptized, **every one** of you,
 in the name of Jesus **Christ** for the forgiveness of your sins;
 and you will receive the gift of the Holy **Spirit**.
For the promise is made to you and to **your** children
 and to **all** those **far** off,
 whomever the Lord our God will **call**."
He **testified** with many other arguments, and was exhorting them,
 "Save **yourselves from this corrupt generation**."
Those who accepted his message were baptized,
 and about **three** thousand **persons** were added that day.

Proclaim Peter's words with authority and good volume.

Pause and read with energy. Take your time and be articulate with your words.

READING I Peter's speech on Pentecost, like all the speeches in the Acts of the Apostles, centers on Jesus being raised from the dead. At the conclusion of this first discourse, Peter announces that the crucified and risen Jesus is both Lord and Christ. As Lord, Jesus shares divine authority with the Lord God. As Christ, he is the long-awaited anointed descendant of David. After Peter's proclamation, the audience asking "What are we to do?" shows that Peter has imparted more than information, but has jolted the hearers to an active response. In telling them to repent, Peter calls for conversion of mind, heart, behavior, and relationships, as had Israel's prophets, John the Baptist, and Jesus himself, who had specifically instructed his followers "that repentance, for the forgiveness of sins, would be preached in his name to all the nations, beginning in Jerusalem" (Luke 24:47).

Baptism in the name of Jesus is a sign of repentance that brings about the forgiveness that Jesus announced and also imparts the gift of the Holy Spirit to each of the baptized. The apostolic mission that begins in Jerusalem will extend to the descendants of those baptized and even to *those far off*, implying inclusion of Gentiles. When Peter declares "save yourselves," the passive verb form does not imply that the believers' own actions will save them, but that they will be saved by God's action, as announced by Joel and cited by Peter (Acts 2:21).

The final verse in today's reading notes the numerical increase of believers that will continue as the Lord adds to their number through the power of the Word and gift of the Holy Spirit (2:47; 4:4; 5:14; 6:1, 7).

For meditation and context:

RESPONSORIAL PSALM   Psalm 23:1–3a, 3b–4, 5, 6 (1)

R. The Lord is my shepherd; there is nothing I shall want.
or
R. Alleluia.

The LORD is my shepherd; I shall not want.
  In verdant pastures he gives me repose;
beside restful waters he leads me;
  he refreshes my soul.

He guides me in right paths
  for his name's sake.
Even though I walk in the dark valley
  I fear no evil; for you are at my side,
with your rod and your staff
  that give me courage.

You spread the table before me
  in the sight of my foes;
you anoint my head with oil;
  my cup overflows.

Only goodness and kindness follow me
  all the days of my life;
and I shall dwell in the house of the LORD
  for years to come.

READING II   1 Peter 2:20b–25

A reading from the first Letter of Saint Peter

Beloved:
If you are **patient** when you suffer for doing what is **good**,
  this is a **grace** before God.
For to this you have been **called**,
  because Christ **also** suffered for **you**,
  leaving you an **example** that you should follow in his **footsteps**.
*He committed no **sin**, and no **deceit** was found in his mouth.*

When he was **insulted**, he returned **no** insult;
  when he **suffered**, he did not **threaten**;
  instead, he **handed** himself over to the one who judges **justly**.
He himself **bore** our sins in his **body** upon the **cross**,
  so that, **free** from sin, we might live for **righteousness**.
By his **wounds** you have been **healed**.
For you had gone **astray** like sheep,
  but you have now **returned** to the **shepherd** and **guardian** of
    your **souls**.

Peter is teaching us how to live—with Christ as an example. Speak with purpose and intent. Use eye contact to connect with the assembly.

Pause after the commas.

Proclaim this line slowly.

READING II   The first letter attributed to Peter is one of seven New Testament writings commonly designated as "catholic epistles" because they have a catholic, or universal, message. Much of the letter (1:3—4:11) appears to be baptismal catechesis, hymns, and preaching that combine teaching with exhortation, inspiration and encouragement for believers. What Peter (or one of his disciples) says to the baptized community of the first century is applicable to the baptized in every time and place. Christ is always the foundation

for belief and behavior, a model for how to live as well as being the source of salvation.

In today's reading, Peter uses a Christological hymn to connect believers' suffering "for doing what is good" with Christ's own suffering. As it portrays Christ's unjust suffering, the hymn alludes extensively to a poem of the prophet Isaiah that describes a suffering servant (Isaiah 53:4–12). Christ who suffered "for you" provides an example (*hypogrammos*), a term used in the first-century milieu for a pattern to be copied in writing or drawing. Those who are baptized should also follow in

Christ's footsteps, meaning that they must walk the path of suffering that he walked. Like Christ, they do not return insult for insult, or threaten those who cause them to suffer.

Example and pattern that Christ is, the self-giving suffering that he endured is much more than a model to follow. On the cross, he bore our sins in his own body so that we might be free from sin. By his wounds we are healed. Besides being a servant who saves, Christ is also a shepherd. As shepherd of the flock, he protects,

GOSPEL   John 10:1–10

A reading from the holy Gospel according to John

Proclaim with good volume and eye contact.

Jesus said:
   "**Amen**, **amen**, I say to you,
   whoever does **not** enter a sheepfold **through** the gate
   but **climbs over elsewhere** is a **thief** and a **robber**.
But whoever **enters through** the gate is the **shepherd** of the
      sheep.
The gatekeeper **opens it** for him, and the sheep **hear** his voice,
   as the shepherd calls his **own** sheep by name and **leads**
      them out.
When he has driven out **all** his own,
   he walks **ahead** of them, and the sheep **follow** him,
   because they **recognize** his voice.
But they will **not** follow a stranger;
   they will **run away** from him,
   because they do **not** recognize the voice of strangers."
Although Jesus used this figure of **speech**,
   the **Pharisees** did **not** realize what he was trying to tell them.

Pharisees = FAYR-uh-seez

Read with energy.

So Jesus said **again**, "Amen, amen, **I say to you**,
   I am the **gate** for the sheep.
All who came before me are **thieves and robbers**,
   but the sheep did **not** listen to them.
I am the gate.
Whoever enters **through me** will be **saved**,
   and will come **in** and go out and find pasture.
A **thief** comes only to **steal** and **slaughter** and **destroy**;
   I came so that **they** might have **life** and have it
      more abundantly."

---

guides, guards, and feeds those who follow in his footsteps.

GOSPEL Jesus' authoritative, emphatic "Amen, amen" introduces each of the two segments about shepherds in today's Gospel. Shepherding was so much a part of daily life in ancient Israel that the image was applied both to God and to Israel's leaders. The Lord God was described as the attentive shepherd caring for the flock (e.g., Psalms 23 and 100:3). Israel's leaders were described either as shepherds who justly led the flock

(Numbers 27:16–18), or as those who destroyed and scattered it (Jeremiah 23:103). In the scene Jesus describes, such Old Testament imagery provides the background for depicting shepherds and thieves, robbers and strangers. Only the authentic shepherd, recognized by the flock, calls the sheep by name, leads them, and walks ahead of them. Others cause fear and panic in the flock.

In the second segment, Jesus identifies himself as "the gate of the sheep." Using an "I am" statement, he presents himself as the way through which sheep

can enter safely into the protection of the sheepfold, and go out to pasture. In the wilderness, the shepherd would lie down at the opening or gate of the enclosure as a guardian for the flock. He "saves" whoever enters through him. On the cultural, physical level, saving the sheep implies rescuing them from danger, providing safety, and healing wounds. On a deeper level, typical of John's Gospel, Jesus, the gate for the sheep, brings the flock securely to eternal life, as he tells his audience, "I came that you might have life." E.P.

FIFTH SUNDAY OF EASTER

LECTIONARY #52

READING I Acts of the Apostles 6:1–7

A reading from the Acts of the Apostles

As the number of **disciples** continued to **grow**,
 the **Hellenists** complained **against** the Hebrews
 because their **widows**
 were being **neglected** in the daily **distribution**.
So the Twelve called together the **community** of the disciples
 and said,
 "It is **not** right for us to **neglect** the **word of God** to serve
 at table.
Brothers, **select** from among you **seven reputable** men,
 filled with the **Spirit and wisdom**,
 whom we shall **appoint** to this task,
 whereas we shall **devote** ourselves to **prayer**
 and to the **ministry of the word**."
The **proposal** was **acceptable** to the whole community,
 so they chose **Stephen**, a man **filled** with **faith** and the
 Holy Spirit,
 also **Philip**, **Prochorus**, **Nicanor**, **Timon**, **Parmenas**,
 and **Nicholas of Antioch**, a convert to Judaism.
They **presented** these men to the apostles
 who **prayed** and **laid hands** on them. ≫

Start to proclaim in an informative tone.

Hellenists = HEL-uh-nists = Greek-speaking Jewish Christians.

Pause before you begin the instructions of the apostles.

Keep your energy and volume up. Take your time with the names.

Prochorus = PRAH-kuh-ruhs
Nicanor = nī-KAY-nuhr
Timon = TĪ-muhn
Parmenas = PAHR-muh-nuhs
Antioch = AN-tee-ahk

READING I The first portraits of the Church in Acts of the Apostles present a community of one heart and mind. Besides their common belief in Jesus, the first believers in Jerusalem shared their Jewish heritage, the tradition of caring for those in need, and a common language. As the Church grew, its membership became more diverse, eventually comprising Samaritans and Gentiles, people who came from the Diaspora and spoke different languages. Today's reading describes the challenge to Church unity that arose in this context of widening diversity, specifi-

cally a conflict between Hebrews and Hellenists. *Hebrews* refers to Palestinian Jews who spoke Aramaic and comprised the earliest followers of Jesus, including the Twelve. *Hellenists* may refer either to Greek-speaking Gentile Christians or to Jews who spoke only Greek. Whoever was meant by the designation Hellenists, the different language along with differences in culture resulted in different treatment, exemplified in the neglect of the widows among the Hellenists.

Widows, as well as orphans and sojourners, receive special attention in the

Torah. Even more importantly, Jesus' compassion to such often-isolated people presented a pattern for the Church to follow. Neglect in the daily distribution for the Hellenist widows means that they did not receive the traditional help to the marginalized commanded in the Torah and exhibited by Jesus. Recognizing that fidelity to Jesus, the material needs of the widows, and the unity of the Church are all at stake, the Twelve call the assembly of the disciples together. Rather than making the decision alone, the Twelve have involved the broader community in solving the conflict.

The word of God continued to spread,
> and the number of the **disciples** in Jerusalem
> > **increased greatly**;
> even a **large** group of **priests** were becoming **obedient**
> > to the faith.

For meditation and context:

RESPONSORIAL PSALM   Psalm 33:1–2, 4–5, 18–19 (22)

R. Lord, let your mercy be on us, as we place our trust in you.
or
R. Alleluia.

Exult, you just, in the LORD;
> praise from the upright is fitting.
Give thanks to the LORD on the harp;
> with the ten-stringed lyre chant
> > his praises.

Upright is the word of the LORD,
> and all his works are trustworthy.
He loves justice and right;
> of the kindness of the LORD the earth is full.

See, the eyes of the LORD are upon those
> who fear him,
> upon those who hope for his kindness,
to deliver them from death
> and preserve them in spite of famine.

READING II   1 Peter 2:4–9

We are called to holiness from St. Peter. Be inviting in your tone as you read.

A reading from the first Letter of Saint Peter

Beloved:
Come to him, a living stone, **rejected** by human beings
> but **chosen** and **precious** in the sight of God,
> and, like living stones,
> let **yourselves** be built into a **spiritual** house
> to be a **holy** priesthood to offer **spiritual** sacrifices
> **acceptable** to God through Jesus Christ.
For it says in Scripture:
> Behold, *I am laying a* stone *in* **Zion**,
> *a* cornerstone, chosen *and* precious,
> *and whoever* **believes** *in it shall* **not** *be put to* shame.

Zion = Zī-uhn or Zī-ahn

They are to make the selection of seven men filled with the Holy Spirit and wisdom. The seven men chosen all bear Greek names, indicating that they were Hellenists, thereby extending the leadership and care of believers beyond its Hebrew origins. Appointed to fulfill the task of the daily distribution, they will go further than this one task. Two of them, Stephen and Philip, will share in the apostolic mission of preaching in fulfillment of Jesus' mandate. Stephen was even the first to bear witness by giving his life, following the example of Jesus. The conflict between the two groups thus resulted not in further division, but in the widening of service and extension of the Gospel.

READING II   Much of the imagery in the biblical tradition is based on readily observable objects that provide insight into unseen, spiritual realities. In today's reading from Peter's first letter, the author creatively uses stone imagery from psalms and prophets to develop his teaching about Christ and the Church. As he uses the stone motif, Peter gives the ancient texts and symbols new meaning. First, he develops the stone symbol from the writings of Isaiah, in which God lays a cornerstone in Zion. For Isaiah in the eighth century BC, "Zion" could refer to the city of Jerusalem as well as to its inhabitants. God has made both the city and its people, chosen and precious, the foundation stone standing secure against foreign enemies and corrupt leaders. Now, according to Peter, it is Christ himself who is the chosen and precious stone; even though rejected, Christ is a living and effective cornerstone. Peter exhorts the people united to Christ

Pause before you begin this line.

Therefore, its value is for **you** who have faith, but for those
   without faith:
   *The stone that the builders **rejected***
   has become *the* cornerstone,
and
   *a stone that will make people **stumble**,*
   *and a rock that will make them **fall**.*
They stumble by **disobeying** the word, as is their destiny.

Proclaim with conviction and passion.

You are "a **chosen** race, a **royal priesthood**,
   a **holy nation**, a people of **his** own,
   so that you may **announce** the praises" of him
   who called you **out** of darkness into his **wonderful light**.

GOSPEL   John 14:1–12

A reading from the holy Gospel according to John

Jesus said to his disciples:
   "**Do not let your hearts be troubled**.
You have faith **in** God; have faith **also in me**.
In my Father's house there are **many** dwelling places.
If there were **not**,
   would I have told you that I am going to **prepare** a place
      for you?
And **if I go** and prepare a place for you,
   I will **come back** again and **take you** to myself,
   so that **where** I am you **also** may be.
Where I am going **you know** the way."
Thomas said to him,
   "Master, we do **not** know where you are going;
   how can we know the way?"
Jesus said to him, "I am the **way** and the **truth** and the **life**.
No one comes to the Father **except through** me.
If you **know** me, then you will **also** know my Father. »

Proclaim Jesus' words in a gentle but firm tone.

Jesus is clear about how we know his Father. Let the assembly hear that in your tone.

also to become living stones for God to build into a spiritual house.

Continuing to draw on the stone metaphor, Peter uses Psalm 118 in which the rejected stone that becomes the cornerstone refers to the people of Israel. As in his interpretation of Isaiah, Peter gives new significance to the cornerstone, now understood to be Christ. With Christ as the cornerstone, the people are living stones who fulfill God's ancient promise, "You shall be to me a kingdom of priests and a holy nation" (Exodus 19:6). The entire people, chosen, priestly, and holy, belong to God.

As a priestly people they participate in Christ's unique priesthood. Together, as a temple of living stones, the holy people announce the praises of the God who has called them from darkness to light.

GOSPEL   At his last supper with his disciples, Jesus prepared them for his impending passion through a long and intimate farewell discourse. Typical of farewell addresses to family and friends, such as that of the patriarch Jacob, Jesus uses this final opportunity to teach, comfort, warn, and inspire his followers.

Throughout his discourse, he reminds them of his earlier instruction and promises, gives them guidance for their future, and draws them ever more deeply into relationship with him, with his Father, and with one another. Although they are understandably troubled, Jesus begins by advising them to move from troubled hearts to believing. The believing that Jesus desires in all his disciples is more than adherence to a creed or set of truths, but is characterized by personal trust and fidelity, the kind of believing Jesus always showed to his Father. Jesus is telling his troubled disciples to trust that,

Jesus explains again about his Father. Use strong eye contact and let the congregation hear impatience in your reading.

From now on you **do** know him and **have seen** him."
Philip said to him,
"Master, **show** us the Father, and that will be **enough** for us."
Jesus said to him, "Have I been with you for so long a time
and you still **do not know me**, Philip?
Whoever has **seen me** has **seen the Father.**
How can you say, '**Show** us the Father'?
Do you **not** believe that **I** am in the **Father** and the Father
is **in me**?
The words that I speak to you I do **not** speak on **my own**.
The Father who **dwells in me** is doing his works.
Believe me that **I** am in the Father and the **Father** is in me,
or else, believe because of the **works themselves**.
Amen, **amen**, I say to you,
whoever believes in **me** will do the **works** that **I do**,
and will do **greater** ones than these,
because I am **going** to the Father."

Proclaim in an authoritative tone.

even though he will leave, he is going to prepare a permanent dwelling for them, and will come back so they will be together. He is encouraging their fidelity in the face of coming trials.

Even before this speech, Jesus had answered questions and corrected misunderstanding among his followers. Now, he responds similarly to the confusion of Thomas and to the request of Philip, both of whom speak not only for themselves, but for the group: "*we* do not know . . . show *us* the Father." To Thomas' lament, "How can we know the way?"

Jesus answers with an "I am" statement, as he had often done before, each one conveying Jesus' identity in relationship with his disciples: I am the bread of life, light of the world, good shepherd. Here the threefold "I am" again speaks of his relationship with them. He is the way—the path, the means, the source, and the pattern—that leads to both truth and life. His disciples follow Jesus, "the way," so closely that the term becomes synonymous with the church (Acts 9:2).

Jesus is the way to the Father whom the disciples believe in, see, and know

through him. In response to Philip's asking to see the Father, Jesus reinforces his teaching about the close and abiding relationship he has with his Father. When Jesus again stresses believing, he includes those present with him as well as all those who will believe in him. They will also do the works that Jesus himself has been doing. E.P.

SIXTH SUNDAY OF EASTER

LECTIONARY #55

READING I   Acts of the Apostles 8:5–8, 14–17

A reading from the Acts of the Apostles

Proclaim in an informative tone as you read about the early stages of Christianity.

Samaria = suh-MAYR-ee-uh

Philip went down to the city of **Samaria**
    and **proclaimed** the Christ to them.
With **one** accord, the crowds **paid attention** to what was **said**
      by Philip
    when they **heard** it and **saw** the **signs** he was doing.
For **unclean** spirits, **crying out** in a loud voice,
    came out of many possessed people,
    and many **paralyzed or crippled** people were **cured**.
There was **great joy** in that city.

Build excitement in your voice as you proclaim the growth in numbers who were baptized.

Now when the apostles in **Jerusalem**
    heard that Samaria **had accepted** the word of God,
    they **sent** them **Peter and John**,
    who went down and **prayed for them**,
    that they might receive **the Holy Spirit**,
    for it had **not** yet fallen upon any of them;
      they had **only** been **baptized** in the name of the **Lord Jesus**.
Then they **laid hands** on them
    and they **received the Holy Spirit**.

READING I After Stephen was put to death, a severe persecution broke out, and all the followers of Jesus except the apostles scattered throughout Judea and Samaria. Among those scattered was Philip, one of the seven disciples chosen to assist in resolving the conflict between the Hebrew and Hellenist Christians. Neither the conflict nor the persecution destroyed the unity of the church and the spreading of the Gospel. When he leaves Jerusalem, Philip goes north to Samaria, a region of long animosity between Jews and Samaritans, where he proclaims

Jesus Christ. In spite of their many differences of belief and practice, both Jews and Samaritans hoped for an anointed one sent by God, as seen in the story of Jesus and the Samaritan woman when she asks the townspeople, "Could he possibly be the Messiah?" (John 4:29). Not only does Philip proclaim Jesus as the Christ, he also does signs, casting out unclean spirits and healing the lame, similar to the signs done both by Jesus and the apostles in Jerusalem. The ensuing joy of the Samaritans echoes that of others who also experience the power of the Gospel.

Peter and John, physical links with the Church in Jerusalem, are sent to Samaria where they pray that those baptized in Samaria would receive the Holy Spirit. Although elsewhere in the Acts of the Apostles, Baptism includes the gift of the Holy Spirit (e.g., 2:38; 11:16), the Samaritan baptism does not. It is not clear why there is this difference, but one reason may be the apostolic role of unifying distant communities with the Church in Jerusalem. When the apostles lay hands on the Samaritans, these new believers receive the Holy Spirit, the

RESPONSORIAL PSALM　Psalm 66:1–3, 4–5, 6–7, 16, 20 (1)

R. Let all the earth cry out to God with joy.
or
R. Alleluia.

Shout joyfully to God, all the earth,
　sing praise to the glory of his name;
　proclaim his glorious praise.
Say to God, "How tremendous are
　　your deeds!"

"Let all on earth worship and sing praise
　　to you,
　sing praise to your name!"
Come and see the works of God,
　his tremendous deeds among the children
　　of Adam.

He has changed the sea into dry land;
　through the river they passed on foot;
　therefore let us rejoice in him.
He rules by his might forever.

Hear now, all you who fear God,
　while I declare
　what he has done for me.
Blessed be God who refused me not
　my prayer or his kindness!

READING II　1 Peter 3:15–18

A reading from the first Letter of Saint Peter

Beloved:
Sanctify Christ as Lord in **your hearts.**
Always be ready to give an **explanation**
　to anyone who asks you for a **reason** for your **hope**,
　but do it with **gentleness and reverence**,
　keeping your **conscience** clear,
　so that, when you are **maligned**,
　those who **defame** your good conduct in Christ
　may **themselves** be put to **shame**.
For it is **better** to **suffer** for doing **good**,
　if that be the **will of God**, than for doing **evil**.
For Christ **also** suffered for sins once,
　the **righteous** for the sake of the **unrighteous**,
　that he might **lead** you to God.
Put to death in the **flesh**,
　he was **brought to life** in the **Spirit**.

St. Peter tells us how we are to act as followers of Christ. Proclaim slowly with clarity of purpose and with passion.

divine presence that brings believers everywhere into communion.

READING II　The communities to whom Peter writes "may have to suffer through various trials" (1 Peter 1:6) and "suffer because of righteousness" (3:14). While his audience may naturally react to having suffering unjustly inflicted on them with anger and vengeance, Peter advises a different response, centered on Christ. They are to "sanctify Christ as Lord." This means that they are to affirm Christ's holiness, recognizing that he is

both sublimely majestic, apart from all that is sinful, as well as personally involved in acts of compassion and justice. With Christ in their hearts, believers have a living, vibrant explanation of the hope they maintain, even if they are maligned and defamed. With Christ as the model for responding to suffering without retaliation, believers can offer their defense with clarity and conviction. If they treat persecutors with kindness, as did Christ, the persecutors themselves will put them to shame.

Peter had earlier told his audience that suffering is sometimes a consequence of

doing evil (2:20). In what sounds like a proverb, he now states that suffering for doing good, if it is God's will, is better than suffering for doing evil. As Peter had looked to Christ as the source for hope, he again turns to Christ, this time as the model for those who suffer for doing good. Christ's suffering and death, in accord with God's will, was the necessary path to resurrection. Christ, once put to death in the flesh is now alive in the spirit. He is the reason for their hope.

GOSPEL   John 14:15–21

A reading from the holy Gospel according to John

Jesus said to his disciples:
"If you **love** me, you will **keep** my commandments.
And I will **ask** the Father,
   and he will **give** you another **Advocate** to be **with you always**,
   the **Spirit of truth**, whom the world **cannot** accept,
   because it **neither sees** nor **knows** him.
But you **know** him, because he **remains** with you,
   and will be **in you**.
I will **not leave** you orphans; I will **come** to you.
In a little while the world will **no longer** see me,
   but **you** will see me, because **I live** and **you will live**.
On **that** day you **will realize** that **I** am **in** my Father
   and **you** are **in me** and **I in you**.
Whoever **has** my commandments and **observes** them
   is the **one who loves me**.
And whoever **loves** me will be **loved** by my **Father**,
   and **I** will **love him** and **reveal** myself to him."

This is a teaching moment: proclaim Jesus' words with clarity. Use strong volume and eye contact to connect with the assembly. Your pace is important: you want the congregation to listen and understand what Jesus is saying. Take your time.

GOSPEL In Jesus' last supper farewell address to his disciples, he prepared them for his coming passion and death; he also assured them of his future presence. He has a twofold focus in this section of his discourse: the love and obedience his disciples are to exhibit, and the promises Jesus gives them. The reading today is framed by his statements about the relationship between love and the observance of the commandments. He tells his disciples that they will keep his commandments "if you love me." He thus teaches that adherence to the commandments is based not on fear or legalism, but flows from love of Jesus. The fullest and surest way of keeping the commandments is to follow Jesus, imitating the way he shows love, for he has just told them, "I am the way."

As an abiding assistance for his disciples to live as he had exhorted them, Jesus will send them another Advocate, or counselor (*paracletos*). The term means someone who is called to another's aid, like a defense attorney who will stand beside the client. The Advocate also advises, mediates, intercedes, and comforts. Jesus promises to send "another" Advocate, for they have already had an Advocate, Jesus himself. The future Advocate that Jesus will send is the Holy Spirit, who will continue to stand beside them. Knowing that he is about to leave them, Jesus further promises that they will see him again. He may be speaking of his Resurrection appearances, his coming again on the last day, or to both manifestations. When his disciples see him again, they will realize the union Jesus has with his Father, as well as with them. E.P.

THE ASCENSION OF THE LORD

LECTIONARY #58

READING I   Acts of the Apostles 1:1–11

A reading from the Acts of the Apostles

In the **first** book, **Theophilus**,
    I **dealt** with **all** that Jesus **did** and **taught**
    until the **day** he was **taken up**,
    after **giving** instructions **through** the **Holy Spirit**
    to the **apostles** whom he **had chosen**.
He presented himself **alive** to them
    by **many** proofs after he had **suffered**,
    appearing to them during **forty days**
    and **speaking** about the kingdom of God.
While meeting with them,
    he **enjoined** them **not** to depart from Jerusalem,
    but to **wait** for "the promise of the Father
    about which you have heard me speak;
    for John **baptized** with water,
    but in a few days **you** will be baptized **with the Holy Spirit**."

When they had gathered **together** they **asked** him,
    "Lord, are you at **this time** going to restore the kingdom
        to Israel?"

Theophilus = thee-AWF-uh-luhs
Proclaim in an informative tone.

READING I   This reading forms a transition between Luke's two-part work, the Gospel, which deals with Jesus' life, death, and Resurrection, and the Acts of the Apostles, which shows how Jesus' work is carried on by those who believe in him, by the Church. Their mission is to bring the Lord to people and in places that he could not reach while in the flesh. Luke addresses his readers as Theophilus, a lofty title which means "friend of God" and reminds readers of the close relationship that God offers to them through Jesus.

Crucial to the continuation of Jesus' mission on earth is the apostle's conviction that he was truly raised from the dead. Hence the many proofs that he gave them for forty days after his Resurrection, forty being a symbolic number which represents the amount of time required to accomplish a divine project. During this time, Jesus focused his teaching on the Kingdom of God. That the apostles failed to grasp the spiritual nature of this kingdom is shown by their question about Jesus' restoration of Israel. He sidesteps the issue by telling them, basically, that no one can know, nor do they need to know the details of divine plans.

God's friends focus, rather, on their mission to be Jesus' witnesses, a task that entails more than simply passing on the facts of his life, death, and Resurrection. To become *credible* witnesses, they must re-pattern their lives on that of their risen Lord. And the changes involved in this conformation require the powerful aid of the Holy Spirit.

Luke insists that the same Spirit who led Jesus in the Gospel will orchestrate the work of his witnesses in Acts. For example,

Pause before Jesus speaks and proclaim in a clear and direct voice. Use good eye contact.

He answered them, "It is **not** for you to **know the times or seasons**
    that the Father has established **by** his own authority.
But you **will receive power** when the **Holy Spirit** comes upon you,
    and you **will be my witnesses** in Jerusalem,
      throughout **Judea** and **Samaria**,
    and to the **ends of the earth**."

Judea = joo-DEE-uh

When he had said this, as they were looking on,
    he was **lifted up**, and a **cloud** took him from their sight.
While they were looking **intently** at the sky as he was going,
    suddenly two men dressed in white garments **stood**
      beside them.

Calmly ask the question.

They said, "Men of **Galilee**,
    why are you standing there looking at the **sky?**
This Jesus who has been taken up from you into heaven
    will return in the **same** way as you have seen him going
      into heaven."

Galilee = GAL-ih-lee

For meditation and context:

RESPONSORIAL PSALM   Psalm 47:2–3, 6–7, 8–9 (6)

R. **God mounts his throne to shouts of joy: a blare of trumpets for the Lord.**
or
R. **Alleluia.**

All you peoples, clap your hands,
    shout to God with cries of gladness,
for the LORD, the Most High, the awesome,
    is the great king over all the earth.

God mounts his throne amid shouts of joy;
    the LORD, amid trumpet blasts.
Sing praise to God, sing praise;
    sing praise to our king, sing praise.

For king of all the earth is God;
    sing hymns of praise.
God reigns over the nations,
    God sits upon his holy throne.

---

the Spirit descends on Jesus when he is baptized by John (Luke 3:22), leads him into the desert for forty days to be tempted by the devil, and afterward to Galilee where he begins his public ministry (Luke 4:1, 14). And in Acts, it leads and works through the first generation of believers: Peter (Acts 4:8); Philip (Acts 8:29); Saul/Paul and Barnabas (Acts 13:2–4); Paul and Timothy (Acts 16); and others. And today, the same Spirit guides and works through all the baptized.

READING II Though the opening verses of this letter are addressed to the Ephesians, its content indicates that it was written for the universal Church. Our reading is, in Greek, a one-sentence prayer of Paul for "the saints," for believers past and present. Though Paul earlier praised their exemplary faith in the Lord and their love for each other, he now prays that the experience of God working in them may be deepened.

To this end, he asks that God give them a spirit of wisdom and revelation. Both terms deal with the discovery of the ever-present and always active God in the human realm. Wisdom, in the Old Testament writings, is drawn from the observation of and reflection on human and animal life and all creation. Under later Hellenistic influence, wisdom was identified with the all-pervasive and all-powerful spirit at work in creation. "Revelation" is the consequence of an unveiling, the drawing back of a curtain to disclose the subtle, often missed workings of the invisible God on earth. In short, the spirit of wisdom and revelation will give believers insight into how God is at work in their midst. Paul prays that as the minds of believers, "the eyes of their hearts," are opened and expanded by this

READING II   Ephesians 1:17–23

A reading from the Letter of Saint Paul to the Ephesians

Brothers and sisters:
May the **God of our Lord Jesus Christ**, the Father of glory,
    give you a **Spirit of wisdom and revelation**
    resulting in **knowledge** of him.
May the **eyes** of your hearts be **enlightened**,
    that you may **know** what is the **hope** that belongs to his call,
    what are the riches of glory
    in his **inheritance** among the **holy ones**,
    and what is the **surpassing greatness** of his power
    for us who believe,
    in accord with the exercise of his **great might**,
    which he worked **in Christ**,
    raising him from the dead
    and **seating** him at his **right** hand in the heavens,
    far above every principality, authority, power, and dominion,
    and **every** name that is named
    not only in this age but **also** in the one to come.
And he put **all** things **beneath** his feet
    and gave him **as head** over **all** things to the church,
    which is **his body**,
    the **fullness** of the one who **fills all things** in **every** way.

Proclaim St. Paul's words with enthusiasm and energy. Take your time and speak clearly.

Slowly say this line.

Connect with the assembly by using good eye contact.

knowledge they might also grasp the hope to which they are called and appreciate the bounty of what they already share with all believers in Christ.

The last five verses of Paul's prayer dwell on the unimaginable divine power that God wields for believers. It surpasses all physical and spiritual powers including ones that might be discovered or "named" in the future. It is the same power that raised Jesus from the dead and seated him at God's right hand. Paul uses language found in Psalm 110:1 to describe the risen Lord's new position as God's king: "Sit at

my right hand, while I make your enemies your footstool." This decree was read when an Israelite king ascended his throne and began his reign as God's messiah or "anointed one," a title which is translated in Greek as "christos." The image of Israel's enemies as the royal footstool reflects a custom from the biblical world wherein a king proclaims his dominance by ceremonially placing his foot on the neck of a vanquished prostrate enemy.

GOSPEL   Matthew places Jesus' last post-Resurrection appear-

ance on a mountain in Galilee. In this Gospel, insights into Jesus' divine nature and his access to the spiritual realm are revealed on mountains. He goes to pray to be with his Father, on a mountain (14:23). On a "very high" mountain, he resists the lure of temporal kingdoms offered by the devil (4:5–8). Like God giving divine teaching to Moses on Mount Sinai, Jesus teaches potential followers in the Sermon on Mount. His divinity shines through his human form when he is transfigured (Matthew 17:9). His prayer or conversation

GOSPEL   Matthew 28:16–20

A reading from the holy Gospel according to Matthew

The **eleven** disciples went to **Galilee**,
    to the mountain to which Jesus had **ordered** them.
When they **saw** him, they **worshiped**, **but** they **doubted**.
Then Jesus **approached** and said to them,
    "**All power** in heaven and on earth has been **given** to me.
Go, therefore, and **make disciples** of **all** nations,
    baptizing them in the name of the **Father**,
    and **of the Son**, and of the **Holy Spirit**,
    teaching them to **observe all** that I have commanded you.
And behold, **I am with you always**, until the end of the age."

Proclaim in an informative tone.

Pause before you read Jesus' words. Start to proclaim his words in a tone of gratefulness and then build energy in your voice as he speaks to the disciples.

with his Father during his agony takes place on the Mount of Olives in Jerusalem.

And yet, when the disciples see Jesus on this last mountain, they waver even as they worship him. That their familiar teacher has divine status strains their belief. They still have only a "little faith," only the tepid trust that allowed fear to overwhelm them during the storm on the Sea of Galilee and that could not keep Peter's eyes on Jesus as the wind raised waves beneath his feet.

In the Gospels, Jesus does not call disciples because they have absolute faith in him or their comprehension of his identity is flawless. He invites people whose faith wavers occasionally but whose knowledge of him grows as they spend time with him and learn more about him. The Greek word for disciple, "learner," conveys their status. Even though the eleven doubt when they see Jesus, they also worship him. And he sends them forth to make disciples of all nations.

Matthew concludes his Gospel with an astounding promise. It is signaled by the Greek word *idou*, "behold," which functions like a finger pointing to something unex-pected. Then, the Greek word order and grammar of the following statement, especially the addition of the unnecessary pronoun "I," underscore a twist that is often lost in translation. Jesus' last words to his disciples, to those who are described in the Gospel as being "with him," reads more literally "Behold! *I, with you*, I am always until the end of the age." E.N.

SEVENTH SUNDAY OF EASTER

LECTIONARY #59

READING I   Acts of the Apostles 1:12–14

A reading from the Acts of the Apostles

After Jesus had been taken up to heaven the **apostles**
   returned to Jerusalem
   from the mount called **Olivet**, which is near Jerusalem,
   a **sabbath** day's journey away.

When they **entered** the city
   they went to the **upper** room where they were **staying**,
   Peter and **John** and **James** and **Andrew**,
   Philip and **Thomas**, **Bartholomew** and **Matthew**,
   James son of **Alphaeus**, **Simon** the **Zealot**,
   and **Judas** son of **James**.
All these **devoted** themselves with **one accord to prayer**,
   together with some **women**,
   and **Mary the mother of Jesus**, and his brothers.

Proclaim in an informative tone using good eye contact and volume.

Olivet = OL-ih-vet

Bartholomew = bahr-THAHL-uh-myoo
Alphaeus = AL-fee-uhs
Zealot = ZEL-uht

READING I   After Jesus was taken from their sight, the eleven remaining apostles return to Jerusalem where, as Jesus commanded them in the previous verses, they wait to be baptized with the Holy Spirit. Luke's notation that their walk from the Mount of Olives to Jerusalem is a Sabbath's day journey (about a thousand yards) shows that they still see themselves as faithful Jews. His naming of the apostles forges a link with the Gospel; they are eyewitnesses who know Jesus personally and can also attest to his death and Resurrection.

Other people are with the eleven, among them women disciples who assisted Jesus during his public ministry, and perhaps also witnessed his death and Resurrection. Mary, Jesus' mother, is the only one named. All of those present in the upper room unite together in prayer as they await the baptism of the Holy Spirit.

READING II   Though there were early persecutions of Christians by Roman authorities, the sufferings described in this passage seem more likely to be ones imposed by the local Gentile pop-ulation on recent converts to Christianity. As the baptized readjust their views and priorities to those of Jesus and make the serious lifestyle changes that discipleship requires, they become targets of derision by their former neighbors and associates.

Peter reframes this victimization as a blessing. Persecution for belief in Christ and living an openly Christian life is a good thing! It is proof that the Spirit of God is resting upon them and that they are sharing Christ's suffering. For this they must rejoice. They must not be cowered by the normal human feelings of shame or disgrace that insults

For meditation and context:

RESPONSORIAL PSALM   Psalm 27:1, 4, 7–8 (13)

R. I believe that I shall see the good things of the Lord in the land of the living.
or
R. Alleluia.

The LORD is my light and my salvation;
   whom should I fear?
The LORD is my life's refuge;
   of whom should I be afraid?

One thing I ask of the LORD;
   this I seek:
to dwell in the house of the LORD
   all the days of my life,
that I may gaze on the loveliness
    of the LORD
   and contemplate his temple.

Hear, O LORD, the sound of my call;
   have pity on me, and answer me.
Of you my heart speaks; you my glance seeks.

READING II   1 Peter 4:13–16

A reading from the first Letter of Saint Peter

Beloved:
Rejoice to the extent that you **share** in the sufferings of Christ,
   so that when his glory is **revealed**
   you may **also** rejoice **exultantly**.
If you are **insulted** for the name of Christ, **blessed are you**,
   for the **Spirit** of glory and of **God rests** upon you.
But let **no** one among you be made to **suffer**
   as a murderer, a thief, an evildoer, or as an intriguer.
But whoever is made to suffer as a **Christian** should **not**
   be ashamed
   but **glorify God** because of the **name**.

Proclaim Peter's words with energy. Take your time and connect with the congregation by using strong eye contact and facial expression.

---

call forth. They must override these and display joy. This is what Christians do. This is one way they glorify God.

Peter cautions his readers not to suffer for the wrong things, like committing murder, stealing, doing evil, meddling in the business of others, and plotting plans to their detriment. Everyone suffers for something, so why not suffer with Christ?

GOSPEL In today's Gospel, we see Jesus at his last meal with "his own" shortly before his arrest. He has been speaking to them for three chapters (John 14–16) and has just announced that his "hour" is coming and that when it does they will abandon him. Though in some passages hour marks a time of day, here it indicates the sequence of events that constitute Jesus' return to the Father—his death or in John "his lifting up on the cross," his Resurrection, and his Ascension.

Jesus suddenly begins speaking with his Father, with whom he existed "in the beginning" and whom he trusts to be with him during his hour. There is something mystical about overhearing Jesus' part of their intimate conversation. Glory is a theme that runs through Jesus' prayer. He glorified the Father by witnessing to him and revealing him to the world during his public ministry. And now as his hour approaches, he asks that the Father glorify him.

To understand Jesus' request, we need to recognize that in John's Gospel, glory and glorification convey more than the fame and prestige that are bestowed on people for outstanding achievements. Glory denotes the manifestation of the invisible God powerfully at work on earth. Thus, when Jesus prays that the Father glorify him so that he can continue to glorify

GOSPEL   John 17:1–11a

A reading from the holy Gospel according to John

Pause before you begin to say Jesus' words.

Jesus **raised** his eyes to heaven and said,
   "**Father**, the hour **has come**.
Give glory to your **son**, so that your **son** may glorify **you**,
   just as you gave him **authority** over **all** people,
   so that your son may give **eternal life** to **all** you gave him.
Now this **is** eternal life,
   that they should **know you**, the **only true God**,
   and the one whom you sent, **Jesus Christ**.
I glorified you on earth
   by accomplishing the **work** that you gave me **to do**.
Now glorify **me**, Father, **with you**,
   with the glory that I had with you before the world began.

Proclaim Jesus' words as if he is praying to the Father. Articulate and take your time so the assembly will clearly understand what Jesus is saying. Use good volume and eye contact. You want to stay connected to the assembly. Use vocal and facial expression.

"I **revealed** your name to those whom you **gave** me **out**
      of the world.
They **belonged** to **you**, and you **gave** them to me,
   and they **have kept** your word.
Now they know that **everything** you **gave me** is from **you**,
   because the words you gave to me **I have given** to them,
   and they **accepted** them and **truly understood** that **I** came
      from **you**,
   and they have **believed** that **you** sent **me**.
I **pray** for them.

Pause before you say this line.

I do **not** pray for the world but for the **ones** you **have given** me,
   because they **are yours**, and **everything** of mine is **yours**
   and everything of **yours is mine**,
   and **I** have been **glorified** in them.

Slowly proclaim this last line.

And now I will **no longer** be in the world,
   but **they are** in the world, **while I am coming to you**."

---

the Father, he is asking not only that the Father be with him as he completes his mission but also that his divine status, his preexistence with God, and the intimate nature of his relationship with the Father become visible on earth.

In the second part of his prayer, Jesus' thoughts turn to his disciples. How moving that as he faces his passion he thinks of them (and us). They are the ones to whom he revealed the Father's "name," those he taught by word and deed all that he could about God. The surprising statement that the disciples belonged first to the Father,

who subsequently gave them to Jesus, illustrates the unique relationship that is offered to those who believe in him. We hear Jesus say that both he and his Father view us as members of their immediate family, as children with whom they wish to share their divine love for each other. They want us to be with them.

The last verses of the Gospel insist that the boundaries and separations that define most relationships are entirely lacking within the divine family. Disciples of every age have a home in the open, intimate love of Jesus and his Father. When we

reveal and extend this reality to others by laying down our life for them, Jesus continues to be glorified in us. For we show the world that God is self-sacrificing love, and give it a glimpse of eternal life. E.N.

PENTECOST SUNDAY: VIGIL

LECTIONARY #62

READING I   Genesis 11:1–9

A reading from the Book of Genesis

The **whole world** spoke the **same** language, using the **same** words.
While the people were **migrating** in the east,
    they came upon a **valley** in the land of **Shinar** and settled there.
They said to one another,
    "**Come**, let us **mold** bricks and harden them with **fire**."
They used **bricks** for stone, and **bitumen** for mortar.
Then they said, "Come, let us **build** ourselves a **city**
    and a **tower** with its top in the **sky**,
    and so make a **name** for **ourselves**;
    otherwise **we** shall be **scattered** all over the earth."

The Lord **came down** to see the city and the tower
    that the people had built.
Then the Lord said: "**If now**, while they are **one** people,
    all speaking the **same** language,
    they have started to do this,
    nothing will later **stop** them from doing **whatever**
        they presume to do.
Let us then **go down** there and **confuse** their language,
    so that **one will not understand** what another says."
Thus the Lord **scattered them** from there **all** over the earth,
    and they **stopped building** the city. »

Genesis = JEN-uh-sihs

Proclaim using an informative tone.

Shinar = SHĪ-nahr
bitumen = bih-TYOO-m*n

Pause before you start the Lord's words.
Speak in a firm and direct tone.

Transition to an informative tone.

READING I The narrative of the city and tower of Babel, like other stories in Genesis 1–11, draws on a universal experience to reveal something about the relationship between humankind and the Creator God. The author aims therefore, to write neither a scientific explanation nor the history of why people speak different languages and live in distinct clusters around the globe. Rather, he writes to illustrate the consequences of acting as if human intellect and free will give creatures divine prerogatives.

By modern standards, our story is very short. The plot moves quickly from verse 1, where all people live together and speak a common language, to verse 9, where they are scattered and can no longer understand each other. While able to communicate, they settle and decide to build a tower that they think will reach to the sky (God's realm), make them famous, and prevent their separation from each other. The author does not explain the people's dread of being dispersed. However, on one level, their anxiety reflects the cer-

tainty of people in biblical times that security and existence are possible only within a unified group. On another, it displays the Jews' fear for their survival as a people after they lost the land and were dispersed among other nations.

The people's goals echo those of Adam and Eve, who sought to be like God and to follow their own desires. Indeed, the tower builders are called "the people"—literally "the sons of Adam"—in 11:5, where God comes down to see their puny structure and scatters them. What they feared

Babel = BAB-*l

That is why it was called **Babel**,
    because **there** the LORD confused the **speech of all the world**.
It was from **that place** that he scattered them all over the earth.

For meditation and context:

RESPONSORIAL PSALM   Psalm 33:10–11, 12–13, 14–15

R. Blessed the people the Lord has chosen to be his own.

The LORD brings to nought the plans
    of nations;
    he foils the designs of peoples.
But the plan of the LORD stands forever;
    the design of his heart, through
    all generations.

Blessed the nation whose God is the LORD,
    the people he has chosen for his own
    inheritance.
From heaven the LORD looks down;
    he sees all mankind.

From his fixed throne he beholds
    all who dwell on the earth,
He who fashioned the heart of each,
    he who knows all their works.

READING II   Exodus 19:3–8a, 16–20b

Exodus = EK-suh-duhs

A reading from the Book of Exodus

Moses went **up** the mountain **to God**.
Then the LORD **called** to him and said,
    "**Thus** shall you say to the house of **Jacob**;
    tell the **Israelites**:
    You have **seen** for yourselves how I **treated** the **Egyptians**
    and how **I bore you up** on eagle wings
    and brought you here to **myself**.
Therefore, if you **hearken** to my voice and **keep** my covenant,
    you shall be **my special possession**,
    dearer to me than **all** other people,
    though all the earth is mine.
You shall be to **me** a kingdom of priests, **a holy nation**.
That is what you **must tell** the Israelites."
So Moses went and **summoned** the elders of the people.

Pause before you begin the Lord's words and
proclaim with authority his commands.

Transition to a tone of informing.

and planned to avoid by their project befalls them. So long after its expulsion from God's garden, humanity still has not grasped that only the Creator's plans will bring them security and fulfill their hopes.

READING II The opening verses of this passage remind Israel of what God did for them in the exodus. This archetypal rescue is sketched simply as how God treated the Egyptians and flew Israel away to the wilderness where they could begin their new life together. The

eagle or vulture wings symbolize transcendence over earthly events and are commonly associated in ancient Near Eastern iconography with kings or treaty lords.

In the wilderness, the Lord offers Israel the great gift of the covenant. This pact is not, as frequently viewed, a tedious set of arbitrary laws which must be followed to avoid the Lord's wrath and punishment. It is a set of divine teachings whose goal is to transform Israel into a people who mirrors God and divine ways to the world. If Israel is faithful to the covenant, they will become

God's special possession, a kingdom of priests, and a holy nation.

In the biblical world and in other Hebrew Scriptures, the term translated as a "special possession" often refers to a king's personal property. When applied to a person it indicates royal favor. This is the status that the Lord who is king of all the nations offers to Israel. The parallel phrases, "kingdom of priests" and " holy nation," indicate that fidelity will also make them "holy" (in Hebrew "different" or "other") like their Lord. They are to forsake the lifestyles and

Use good eye contact and volume. Keep up your energy.

When he **set** before them
  all that the LORD had **ordered** him to tell them,
  the people all **answered** together,
  "Everything the Lord has said, we will do."

On the morning of the **third** day
  there were peals of **thunder and lightning**,
  and a **heavy** cloud over the mountain,
  and a **very loud** trumpet blast,
  so that **all** the people in the camp **trembled**.
But Moses **led** the people **out** of the camp to **meet God**,
  and they stationed themselves at the **foot** of the mountain.
Mount Sinai was **all wrapped** in smoke,
  for the **Lord** came down **upon it** in fire.
The smoke **rose** from it as though from a furnace,
  and the whole mountain **trembled violently**.
The trumpet blast **grew** louder and louder, while **Moses**
    was speaking,
  and **God answering** him with thunder.

When the LORD came down to the top of Mount Sinai,
  he summoned Moses to the top of the mountain.

Sinai = SĪ-nī

Proclaim with vocal expression. Let the assembly hear the power of God in your voice: "wrapped in smoke," "in fire," "trembled violently," "thunder."

mores of those around them, and live rather as God's people in the world.

A full-blown theophany accompanies the giving of the covenant. We stand with the people at the foot of the volcanic-like mountain and experience the thunder, lightning, and clouds that reveal yet obscure God's presence. The din swells with repetitions of the Hebrew *qol* that can be translated both by "thunder" and "voice." The noise—the Lord's "voice / *qol*," the rumbling "thunder / *qol*," and twice the "voice / *qol* of the shofar," (the trumpet blast)—grows ever louder as the heavenly gift enters the earthly realm through Moses speaking and the Lord answering him with "thunder / *qol*."

READING III Ezekiel is prophesying to Israel during the lowest point in salvation history. After Israel has failed to keep the covenant for centuries, God has now exiled them to Babylon (early sixth century BC). They have lost all the tangible signs that they were God's people: the land, their king, and the temple in Jerusalem. Depressed and despairing, they conclude that their relationship with God is over. For these people, God gives a vision of unimaginable hope to the prophet and priest, Ezekiel.

The Lord's "hand" or power overtakes the prophet, and the Lord's Spirit sets him down in a place that a priest would never go, a valley full of unclean bones. And then the Spirit makes him walk "around and around," the Hebrew says, evoking a liturgical circumambulation. ■

For meditation and context:

RESPONSORIAL PSALM   Daniel 3:52, 53, 54, 55, 56

R. Glory and praise for ever!

"Blessed are you, O Lord, the God of
    our fathers,
    praiseworthy and exalted above
    all forever;
And blessed is your holy and glorious name,
    praiseworthy and exalted above all for
    all ages."

"Blessed are you in the temple of your
    holy glory,
    praiseworthy and glorious above
    all forever."

"Blessed are you on the throne of
    your Kingdom,
    praiseworthy and exalted above
    all forever."

"Blessed are you who look into the depths
    from your throne upon the cherubim,
    praiseworthy and exalted above
    all forever."

"Blessed are you in the firmament of heaven,
    praiseworthy and glorious forever."

Or:

For meditation and context:

RESPONSORIAL PSALM   Psalm 19:8, 9, 10, 11

R. Lord, you have the words of everlasting life.

The law of the LORD is perfect,
    refreshing the soul;
The decree of the LORD is trustworthy,
    giving wisdom to the simple.

The precepts of the LORD are right,
    rejoicing the heart;
The command of the LORD is clear,
    enlightening the eye.

The fear of the LORD is pure,
    enduring forever;
The ordinances of the LORD are true,
    all of them just.

They are more precious than gold,
    than a heap of purest gold;
Sweeter also than syrup
    or honey from the comb.

READING III   Ezekiel 37:1–14

A reading from the Book of the Prophet Ezekiel

Ezekiel = ee-ZEE-kee-uhl

Proclaim Ezekiel's words with clarity and in a tone of obedience to the Lord.

The **hand of the LORD** came **upon me**,
    and he **led** me out in the **spirit** of the LORD
    and **set me** in the **center** of the plain,
    which was now **filled** with bones.
He made me **walk** among the bones in **every** direction
    so that **I saw** how many they were on the surface of the plain.
How **dry** they were!

The ten repetition of "bones" in the passage emphasizes irreversible deadness. They are dry, very dry, disarticulated, and strewn upon the valley floor. (Shortly we hear that these bones are the House of Israel.) As the vision continues, God asks: "Can these bones come to life?" This is Israel's question after the exile: can they survive as a people now that their relationship with the Lord is over?

The Lord commands Ezekiel to prophesy over the desiccated bones and to impress the people with the importance of heeding the divine word. As Ezekiel prophesies and the Lord's words are fulfilled, an eerie, noisy scene unfolds: there is a thunderous rattling as bone clatters into bone seeking its proper mate, tendons appear, and skin crawls upward covering the skeletons. But these remain corpses. The Lord tells Ezekiel to prophesy again, and the Spirit coming into the skeletons transforms them into a vast army, literally, "a very, very great army."

The interpretation of the vision in 37:11–14 announces that when the Lord puts the Spirit in Israel, they will regain hope, enjoy unimaginable new life, and be settled by God on their land. In effect, this passage presents the covenant between Israel and God as unconditional. In other words, one thing that Israel learned when they lost everything was that the continuation of the divine-human relationship depends on divine, not human, fidelity.

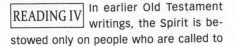 In earlier Old Testament writings, the Spirit is bestowed only on people who are called to

prophesy (verb) = PROF-uh-sī
Proclaim God's words with a tone of authority.

sinews = sin-yooz

As you read, build your energy and enthusiasm. Let the assembly hear emotion in your voice. It is all good news. Smile.

He asked me:
   Son of man, can these bones come to **life?**
I answered, "Lord God, you **alone** know that."
Then he said to me:
   Prophesy over these bones, and say to them:
   Dry bones, **hear** the word of the Lord!
Thus says the Lord God to these bones:
   See! I will **bring spirit** into you, that you may come to **life.**
I **will put** sinews upon you, make **flesh** grow over you,
   cover you with skin, and put **spirit** in you
   so that you may come **to life** and know that **I am the** Lord.
I, **Ezekiel, prophesied** as **I had been told,**
   and even as I was prophesying I **heard** a noise;
   it was a **rattling** as the bones came together, bone joining bone.
I **saw** the sinews and the **flesh** come upon them,
   and the skin **cover** them, but there was **no** spirit in them.
Then the Lord said to me:
   Prophesy to the **spirit,** prophesy, son of man,
   and **say** to the spirit: **Thus** says the **Lord** God:
   From the four winds **come, O spirit,**
   and **breathe** into **these slain** that they may **come to life.**
I prophesied as he told me, and the **spirit** came **into them;**
   they came **alive** and stood upright, a vast army.
Then he said to me:
   Son of man, these bones are the whole house of **Israel.**
They **have been** saying,
   "Our bones are dried up,
   our **hope is lost,** and we **are cut off."**
Therefore, prophesy and say to them: Thus says the Lord God:
   O my people, I will **open** your graves
   and have you **rise** from them,
   and **bring you back** to the land of **Israel.**
Then you **shall know** that **I am the** Lord,
   when I **open** your graves and have you **rise** from them,
   O my people! »

perform a special divine task, for example, kings and prophets. Joel makes the astonishing announcement that at some future time the Lord will pour out the Spirit on "all flesh." To emphasize the inclusiveness of those whom God will call, Joel names specifically the young, the old, and servants, those who were undervalued in the biblical world and would be the least likely to be chosen for important missions. Nevertheless, when the Lord pours out the Spirit, they too will prophesy. They will take up the tasks of seeing and communicating where God is acting in the human realm.

Joel associates the universal ability to prophesy with the long-expected "day of the Lord," the time when all the invisible divine attention to and working within human affairs through the ages will be recognized by all peoples and nations. This "day" is the Old Testament version of the Parousia, the return of the risen Christ at the end of time. Both testaments employ apocalyptic language—like Joel's wonders in the heavenly and earthly realm, the darkened sun, the bloodied moon—to convey the Lord's unrivaled power and reach.

Depending on its biblical context, this eschatological day will be either a day of judgment and doom for Israel or, as is the case here, a joyful day on which God will vindicate them. In either case, the Lord's coming inspires anxiety, awe, and terror. Only those who "call on the name of the Lord," that is, those who recognize God's sovereignty, will survive it.

I will put **my spirit in you** that you may **live**,
    and I will **settle** you upon your land;
    thus **you shall know** that I **am** the LORD.
I have promised, **and I will do it**, says the LORD.

For meditation and context:

RESPONSORIAL PSALM   Psalm 107:2–3, 4–5, 6–7, 8–9

R. Give thanks to the Lord; his love is everlasting.
    or R. Alleluia.

Let the redeemed of the LORD say,
    those whom he has redeemed from the
        hand of the foe
And gathered from the lands,
    from the east and the west, from the
        north and the south.
They went astray in the desert wilderness;
    the way to an inhabited city they did
        not find.
Hungry and thirsty,
    their life was wasting away within them.

They cried to the LORD in their distress;
    from their straits he rescued them.
And he led them by a direct way
    to reach an inhabited city.

Let them give thanks to the LORD for
        his mercy
    and his wondrous deeds to the children
        of men,
Because he satisfied the longing soul
    and filled the hungry soul with
        good things.

Or:

READING IV   Joel 3:1–5

Joel = JOH-*l

A reading from the Book of the Prophet Joel

Proclaim boldly with good volume. Read with clarity and energy.

prophesy (verb) = PROF-uh-sī

Thus says the LORD:
I will **pour out my spirit** upon all flesh.
Your sons and daughters shall **prophesy**,
    your **old men** shall dream **dreams**,
    your **young men** shall see **visions**;
even upon the servants and the handmaids,
    in those days, I will **pour** out **my spirit.**
And I will **work wonders** in the **heavens** and on the **earth**,
    blood, **fire**, and **columns** of smoke;
the **sun** will be turned to **darkness**,

EPISTLE   In Romans 8, Paul discusses how Christians are to live in the period between Christ's Resurrection and his Parousia or return to earth at the end of time. Many of the baptized are frustrated. Their expectation that the fullness of the redemption accomplished by Christ's Resurrection from the dead would be immediately apparent to all was not met. Life goes on around them seemingly unchanged. They ache for a deeper experience of their new life in Christ, just as we still do today.

Paul reminds his readers that they do not suffer alone. All creation, of which they are an inseparable part, is lamenting and groaning with them as it too longs for complete transformation and newness of life. For its sake as well as their own, Christians must sustain their hope. They must openly display their confidence that what will one day be visible to all is truly unfolding in the present moment. In other words, they are to live by a different vision of reality than those who set their hearts on and put their

hope in only what they can see, in earth-bound and transient matters.

The apostle also reminds Christians that the Spirit who dwells in them is the first fruit of redemption, a foretaste and pledge of what is to come. When their stamina to live in God's reality wanes, and they are so frustrated that they know not even how to pray or for what to pray, the Spirit asks God to give them what they need to accomplish the divine will in them.

and the **moon** to **blood**,
　at the **coming** of the day of the LORD,
　　the **great** and **terrible** day.
Then everyone shall be **rescued**
　who **calls** on the **name of the LORD**;
for on **Mount Zion** there shall be a **remnant**,
　as the LORD has said,
and in Jerusalem **survivors**
　whom the LORD **shall cail**.

Zion = Zī-uhn or Zī-ahn

For meditation and context:

RESPONSORIAL PSALM   Psalm 104:1–2a, 24, 35c, 27–28, 29bc–30 (30)

R. Lord, send out your Spirit, and renew the face of the earth.
or
R. Alleluia.

Bless the LORD, O my soul!
　O LORD, my God, you are great indeed!
You are clothed with majesty and glory,
　robed in light as with a cloak.

How manifold are your works, O LORD!
　In wisdom you have wrought them all—
the earth is full of your creatures;
　bless the LORD, O my soul! Alleluia.

Creatures all look to you
　to give them food in due time.
When you give it to them, they gather it;
　when you open your hand, they are filled
　　with good things.

If you take away their breath, they perish
　and return to their dust.
When you send forth your spirit,
　they are created,
and you renew the face of the earth.

EPISTLE   Romans 8:22–27

A reading from the Letter of Saint Paul to the Romans

Brothers and sisters:
We know that **all creation** is **groaning** in **labor** pains **even**
　　until now;
　and **not** only that, but we **ourselves**,
　who have the **firstfruits** of the Spirit,
　we **also** groan within ourselves
　　as we **wait** for **adoption**, the **redemption** of our bodies.
For **in hope** we were **saved**.

Pause before you begin. Proclaim with energy and compassion in your voice.

GOSPEL   The setting for today's Gospel is the Jewish Feast of Tabernacles, which celebrates and gives thanks for the late-summer harvest. During this eight-day feast, the people pray for the winter rains upon which future crops depend. These rains are unpredictable, unreliable, and come only between late September and April. The people's prayers are accompanied by a ritual wherein water is ceremonially brought from the Pool of Siloam, the reservoir for the "living" water that surges up from the Gihon spring below the temple mount, and poured on the altar of sacrifice in the temple.

It is during this feast, and probably in the temple where he was teaching earlier, that Jesus announces that anyone who is thirsty should come to him and drink. He is claiming that the age-old human longing to experience God, which is expressed, for example in Psalms 42–43 and 63, as thirsting, can be sated by belief in him. Quoting Scripture, he adds: "Rivers of living water will flow from within him who believes in me." Though this citation does not appear in our Bible, other scriptural passages illuminate its meaning. Among these is a prophecy about the restoration of Jerusalem after the Babylonian exile (Ezekiel 47:1–12). In a vision, the Lord shows Ezekiel water flowing out from the threshold of the temple and deepening as it runs eastward through the Wadi Kelt in the arid Judean wilderness until it becomes an impassible river. This river of flowing or living water brings life where none was previously possible. It even freshens the salt waters of the Dead Sea. In John 2:21, Jesus

After you ask this question, pause.

Good news! The Holy Spirit comes to help us! Be clear in proclaiming Paul's words. Let the assembly hear conviction in your tone.

Now hope that sees is **not** hope.
For **who** hopes for what one **sees**?
But if we hope for what we do **not see**, we wait **with endurance**.

In the same way, the **Spirit** too comes to the aid of our **weakness**;
for we do **not** know how to **pray** as we **ought**,
but the **Spirit** himself **intercedes** with **inexpressible groanings**.
And the **one** who **searches hearts**
knows what is the **intention** of the Spirit,
because he **intercedes** for the **holy ones**
according to **God's will**.

GOSPEL   John 7:37–39

A reading from the holy Gospel according to John

Proclaim John's Gospel with good volume and strong eye contact. Pause before and after you read Jesus's words.

On the **last and greatest** day of the **feast**,
Jesus **stood up** and exclaimed,
"Let anyone who **thirsts** come to **me and drink**.
As Scripture says:
Rivers of living water will flow from within him who believes in me."

He said this in reference to the **Spirit**
that those who came to **believe** in him were **to receive**.
There was, of course, **no Spirit yet**,
because Jesus had not yet been glorified.

taught that his body replaced the temple. Now he claims that living water, that is, the life-giving knowledge of God, flows out from him and brings unimaginable life to those who believe in him.

John's connection of life-giving water and the Spirit appears also in another postexilic prophecy. In Isaiah 44:3, the prophet announces that God will pour out water on the thirsty ground (Israel) and the Spirit on Israel's descendants, who eventually came to include the people whom Jesus addresses.

PENTECOST SUNDAY: DAY

LECTIONARY #63

READING I Acts of the Apostles 2:1–11

A reading from the Acts of the Apostles

Proclaim the first line with an informative tone.

When the time for Pentecost was **fulfilled**,
　　they were **all** in **one place together**.

Start to build intensity as you proclaim.
Take your time.

And **suddenly** there came from the sky
　　a **noise** like a strong driving wind,
　　and it **filled** the entire house in which they were.
Then there **appeared** to them tongues **as of fire**,
　　which **parted** and came **to rest** on **each one** of them.

This line is the highest point of the reading.
This is what we have waited and longed for!
Let the congregation hear gratefulness and
amazement in your voice.
Keep up your energy by using good volume
and eye contact.

And they were **all filled** with the **Holy Spirit**
　　and began to speak in **different tongues**,
　　as the Spirit **enabled** them **to proclaim**.

Now there were **devout Jews** from **every** nation under heaven
　　staying in Jerusalem.
At this sound, they **gathered** in a large crowd,
　　but they were **confused**
　　because each one heard them **speaking in his own language**.

Pause before you ask the questions.
Rehearse the names of all the different
countries.
Parthians = PAHR-thee-uhnz; Medes =meedz
Elamites = EE-luh-mīts
Mesopotamia = mes-uh-poh-TAY-mee-uh
Judea = joo-DEE-uh
Cappadocia = cap-uh-DOH-shee-uh
Pontus = PON-tuhs; Phrygia = FRIJ-ee-uh
Pamphylia = PAM-fil-ee-uh
Libya = LIB-ee-uh
Cyrene = sī-REE-nee

They were **astounded**, and in **amazement** they asked,
　　"Are not all these people who are speaking **Galileans**?
Then **how** does **each of us hear** them in his **native language**?
We are **Parthians**, **Medes**, and **Elamites**,
　　inhabitants of **Mesopotamia**, **Judea** and **Cappadocia**,
　　Pontus and **Asia**, **Phrygia** and **Pamphylia**,
　　Egypt and the districts of **Libya** near **Cyrene**,
　　as well as travelers from **Rome**,

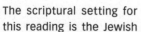

READING I The scriptural setting for this reading is the Jewish feast of Pentecost, so called because it was celebrated on the fiftieth day after Passover. It was one of three pilgrimage feasts that, if possible, Jews were to celebrate in Jerusalem. Jesus' disciples are in the city awaiting the baptism with the Holy Spirit.

Its sudden coming is manifested by noise and fire, typical biblical metaphors for the divine presence. The noise that fills the whole house is not exactly a violent rushing wind but is "like" such a wind. And tongues "as" of fire distribute themselves

and settle on each of the disciples. These analogies remind us that while the ever-mysterious and ineffable God truly acts on earth, human language limps when it tries to communicate this reality. On Pentecost, when the Spirit fills the disciples, it gives them new languages to preach about Jesus. Their discourse is not merely an account of their experiences with him. Their Spirit-filled words reveal the meaning of what God did through his life, death, and Resurrection.

The rest of the reading describes the effect of the disciples' preaching on "devout

Jews from every nation under heaven." Each person is bewildered and astonished as he hears Galileans speaking his native language. In this scene, we see the Spirit redressing the human situation that began at Babel (see Pentecost Vigil, Genesis 11:1–9). There God came down and thwarted the plan of "the sons of Adam"—the plan to reach and live in God's realm through their own efforts—by confusing their languages and scattering them over the earth. On Pentecost, God's Spirit comes down from heaven and restores communication among the nations, and the first thing they

Cretans = KREE-tuhnz; Arabs = AYR-uhbz

Say this line slowly.

both Jews and converts to **Judaism**, **Cretans** and **Arabs**,
yet we **hear** them **speaking** in **our own tongues**
of the **mighty** acts of God."

For meditation and context:

RESPONSORIAL PSALM   Psalm 104:1, 24, 29–30, 31, 34 (30)

R. Lord, send out your Spirit, and renew the face of the earth.
or
R. Alleluia.

Bless the LORD, O my soul!
  O LORD, my God, you are great indeed!
How manifold are your works, O LORD!
  the earth is full of your creatures.

If you take away their breath, they perish
  and return to their dust.
When you send forth your spirit,
   they are created,
  and you renew the face of the earth.

May the glory of the LORD endure forever;
  may the LORD be glad in his works!
Pleasing to him be my theme;
  I will be glad in the LORD.

READING II   1 Corinthians 12:3b–7, 12–13

Corinthians = kohr-IN-thee-uhnz

What a wonderful reading! It is a teaching moment for us. Take your time. To keep the attention of the congregation, rehearse for strong eye contact and expression in your voice. Read with clarity.

A reading from the first Letter of Saint Paul to the Corinthians

Brothers and sisters:
No one can say, "Jesus is Lord," **except** by the **Holy Spirit**.

There are **different** kinds of **spiritual** gifts but the **same** Spirit;
  there are different **forms of service** but the **same** Lord;
  there are different **workings** but the same **God**
  who produces **all** of them in **everyone**.
To **each** individual the **manifestation** of the Spirit
  is given for some **benefit**.

As a **body** is **one** though it has **many parts**,
  and **all** the parts of the body, **though many**, are **one** body,
  so also Christ.
For in **one Spirit** we were **all baptized** into **one body**,
  whether **Jews** or **Greeks**, **slaves** or **free persons**,
  and we were **all given** to drink of **one Spirit**.

Say this line slowly.

---

understand together is the disciples' inspired proclamation of the mighty deeds that God accomplished in Christ.

READING II In this section of his letter, Paul writes to the very divided Corinthian community about the Spirit who is at work in each of them. Indeed, it was the Spirit who led them to recognize Jesus' divinity and to acknowledge it openly by being baptized. The confession that "Jesus is Lord" may have been part of this early Christian rite.

One evidence of the Spirit's presence in the baptized is an individual charism —i.e., a gift, a kind of service, or an activity or "working." The variety of these charisms is unlimited, but the same God "produces," "activates," or "works" them together for the sake of all. Though it is difficult to translate into English, the Greek text highlights the energy that comes into play as the baptized develop and exercise their unique gifts, and God orchestrates their efforts for divine purposes.

Chief among these is the primary mission of every parish and of the Church at large to manifest the risen and living Christ in the world. Paul warns that internal divisions blur the image that a community projects. One source of disunity is that some consider their gift to be more important than those of others. Another is the persistent use of pre-Christian categories that sort and separate people, like national and ethnic labels, and universal status indicators. Worldly distinctions have no place among the baptized.

 GOSPEL When Jesus appears to his disciples, they are together

For meditation and context:

Sequences originated as extensions of the sung Alleluia before the proclamation of the gospel, although they precede the Alleluia now. The Pentecost Sequence is an ancient liturgical hymn praising the Holy Spirit. It is also called the Golden Sequence, and is the source of the hymn "Come, Holy Ghost."

SEQUENCE   Veni, Sancte Spiritus

Come, Holy Spirit, come!
And from your celestial home
   Shed a ray of light divine!
Come, Father of the poor!
Come, source of all our store!
   Come, within our bosoms shine.
You, of comforters the best;
You, the soul's most welcome guest;
   Sweet refreshment here below;
In our labor, rest most sweet;
Grateful coolness in the heat;
   Solace in the midst of woe.
O most blessed Light divine,
Shine within these hearts of yours,
   And our inmost being fill!

Where you are not, we have naught,
Nothing good in deed or thought,
   Nothing free from taint of ill.
Heal our wounds, our strength renew;
On our dryness pour your dew;
   Wash the stains of guilt away:
Bend the stubborn heart and will;
Melt the frozen, warm the chill;
   Guide the steps that go astray.
On the faithful, who adore
And confess you, evermore
   In your sevenfold gift descend;
Give them virtue's sure reward;
Give them your salvation, Lord;
   Give them joys that never end. Amen.
   Alleluia.

GOSPEL   John 20:19–23

A reading from the holy Gospel according to John

On the evening of that **first** day of the week,
   when the doors were **locked**, where the disciples were,
   for **fear** of the Jews,
   Jesus **came** and **stood** in their midst
   and said to them, "**Peace be with you**."
When he had **said** this, he **showed** them his **hands** and his **side**.
The disciples **rejoiced** when they **saw** the Lord.
Jesus said to them again, "Peace be with you.
As the **Father** has sent me, so **I** send you."
And when he had said this, he **breathed** on them and said to them,
   "**Receive the Holy Spirit**.
Whose sins **you forgive** are forgiven them,
   and whose sins **you retain** are retained."

Begin proclaiming in an informative tone.

Transition to a tone of calmness as you proclaim Jesus' words.

Proclaim with happiness. Smile.

Pause before you read "Receive the Holy Spirit." Let the congregation hear emotion in your voice.

behind locked doors for fear of what the religious authorities who plotted his crucifixion might now do to them. Unexpectedly, Jesus comes into the room and stands in their midst. His first words to them are "Peace be with you." While this was a common greeting in the biblical world, in John's Gospel it proffers the profound peace that the world cannot give. It drives away fear and works all things together for the good of all. This is the peace that God planned for creation in the beginning, that was disrupted by human failure to recognize the

Creator, and that is now restored by Jesus' Resurrection.

The shocked disciples do not grasp that it is truly Jesus who stands before them until they see the scars on his body. Their consequent joy is more than mere pleasure. They experience unimaginable elation they experience when they realize that the Lord triumphed over death as he had promised.

Jesus breathes the Holy Spirit on his disciples and sends them forth to continue the mission given him by his Father. While providing the scriptural basis for the later

Sacrament of Reconciliation, Jesus' command to forgive or retain sins entails more than the absolution of sins committed after Baptism. It should be understood in the context of his larger mission to take away the sins of the world, to reconcile all humanity with God and, for those who believe in him, to open the way to eternal life. E.N.

THE MOST HOLY TRINITY

LECTIONARY #164

READING I   Exodus 34:4b–6, 8–9

A reading from the Book of Exodus

Exodus = EK-suh-duhs
Sinai = SĪ-nī
Moses = MOH-zis
Proclaim with clarity and purpose.

Early in the morning **Moses** went up **Mount Sinai**
    as the LORD had **commanded** him,
    taking along the two stone **tablets**.

Having come down in a cloud, the LORD **stood** with Moses there
    and proclaimed his name, "LORD."
Thus the Lord passed before him and cried out,
    "The LORD, the LORD, a **merciful** and **gracious God**,
    slow to anger and rich in **kindness** and **fidelity**."
Moses **at once** bowed down to the ground in worship.
Then he said, "If I find **favor** with you, O LORD,
    do come along in our **company**.
This is indeed a stiff-necked people;
    yet **pardon** our wickedness and sins,
    and **receive us as your own**."

(margin notes:)

Pause before you say "Lord."

Proclaim the Lords' words with a gentle tone.

Moses responds with humility. Let the congregation hear that in your voice.

READING I Woven through today's reading are themes of covenant, fidelity, and the desire to see God. In the opening verse we see Moses carrying a second set of stone tablets back up Mount Sinai. He smashed the first one, upon which God had inscribed the covenant, when he saw the Israelites worshiping the golden calf. Ironically, their worry that something happened to Moses led them to ask Aaron to "make us a god who will go before us." The second set of stone tablets portends the future of the divine-human relationship.

Its endurance would always depend not on human fidelity but on God's intense desire to live with humankind.

The next verses describe the Lord's response to Moses' request to see the divine glory. The Lord explained to Moses that he would only see the Lord's back. In other words, he would perceive only the identifying markers of God's presence and action in the world. These are solemnly proclaimed as the Lord passes by Moses: "The Lord is a merciful and gracious God, slow to anger and rich in kindness and fidelity."

Translations necessarily limit the richness of the Hebrew terms used to describe the Lord. "Merciful" entails empathy and means more literally "compassionate." The Hebrew word for it is associated with a pregnant woman's womb and thus also evokes the tender concern of a mother for her child. "Gracious" also means to show favor to someone. "Slow to anger" is the biblical phrase for patience and long-suffering.

Most difficult to translate adequately is the last phrase, *rab hesed we'emeth. Rab*

For meditation and context:

RESPONSORIAL PSALM   Daniel 3:52, 53, 54, 55 (52b)

R. Glory and praise for ever!

Blessed are you, O Lord, the God
    of our fathers,
        praiseworthy and exalted above all forever;
and blessed is your holy and glorious name,
        praiseworthy and exalted above all for
        all ages.

Blessed are you in the temple of your
        holy glory,
        praiseworthy and glorious above
        all forever.

Blessed are you on the throne
    of your kingdom,
        praiseworthy and exalted above all forever.

Blessed are you who look into the depths
        from your throne upon the cherubim,
        praiseworthy and exalted above all forever.

Corinthians = kohr-IN-thee-uhnz

St. Paul is teaching us how to live as followers of Christ. Proclaim with high energy and excitement.

READING II   2 Corinthians 13:11–13

A reading from second Letter of Saint Paul to the Corinthians

Brothers and sisters, **rejoice**.
Mend your ways,
        encourage one another,
    agree with one another, **live in peace**,
    and the **God of love and peace will be with you**.
Greet one another with a **holy** kiss.
All the holy ones greet you.

The **grace** of the **Lord Jesus Christ**
    and the **love of God**
    and the **fellowship of the Holy Spirit** be with all of you.

---

denotes abundance. *Hesed* conveys the continuous outpouring of divine kindness, goodness, or steadfast love. *Emeth* is derived from *amen* and denotes firmness, constancy, loyalty, and truth. The combination of these expresses something like the abounding, incomparable, and unconditional love that God continually pours out on Israel and on all creation. Is it any wonder that Moses begs such a covenant Lord to forgive the people's infidelity and accompany them personally on the journey to the Promised Land?

READING II | In the closing of his second letter to the Corinthians, Paul addresses the fractured community as "brothers and sisters," reminding them that at Baptism they were reconciled to God and became siblings in the divine family. For these and the countless blessings they received in Christ, they are to rejoice. Paul uses the Greek present tense for this and the following exhortations, indicating that he expects not an isolated action but an ongoing response to them.

The exhortations summarize his earlier instructions to the Corinthian community. Basically, they need to be mending their ways or putting things in order so that their life conforms more closely to that of Christ. Paul's appeal that they agree with one another does not mean that they need to hold the same opinion on every topic, but that they should agree on matters that are vital to their functioning as the Body of Christ. Living together in peace, which works all things together for the good of all, is the issue that Paul singles out. He

Proclaim in a tone of authority. It is important that we understand what John is telling us. Take your time. Rehearse for good eye contact.

GOSPEL   John 3:16–18

A reading from the holy Gospel according to John

God so loved the world that he **gave** his only **Son**,
  so that everyone who **believes** in him might **not** perish
  but might have **eternal life**.
For God did not send his Son into the world to **condemn**
    the world,
  but that the world might be **saved** through him.
Whoever believes in him will **not** be condemned,
  but whoever does **not** believe has **already** been condemned,
  because he has not believed in the name of the **only Son**
    of God.

assures the baptized that as they put the common good above personal preferences they will experience God's own boundless love and peace. Finally, whenever they meet they are to exchange a holy kiss as a sign and reminder of their relationship with each other in Christ.

Paul's tripartite blessing provides a scriptural basis for the Church's later doctrine of the Trinity. His words trace the path of revelation from the human perspective: through Baptism, Christians receive the grace of the Lord Jesus, in whom the love of God was fully and finally manifested, and

from then on live in communion with the Spirit and with each other.

GOSPEL | The human desire to see the face of God was fulfilled by the Incarnation of the only-begotten Son. In Jesus, the tender compassion, the personal favor, the patience, and the unconditional love that Israel recognized as the signs of God's presence with them were manifested in human form.

But Jesus is more than an icon of God. He was sent to show how deeply God loves all creation. No one gauged the depth of

divine love until Jesus laid down his life, and God raised him up, opening the way to eternal life for all who believe in him.

Biblical believing, especially for John, entails not only an assent to what is revealed about Jesus in the Gospel. It also requires a personal commitment to him and participation in his mission to reveal God's love to the world. Those who so believe, those who are "born again of water and the Spirit" (John 3:5), already share in God's life. In such an outpouring of divine love, condemnation has no place. Those who do not believe in Jesus sentence themselves. E.N.

THE MOST HOLY BODY AND BLOOD OF CHRIST (CORPUS CHRISTI)

LECTIONARY #167

READING I   Deuteronomy 8:2–3, 14b–16a

A reading from the Book of Deuteronomy

Moses said to the people:
  "Remember how for **forty years** now the LORD, **your God**,
  has directed **all** your journeying in the desert,
  so as to **test** you by affliction
  and find out whether or **not** it was your intention
  to **keep his commandments.**
He therefore let you be **afflicted** with **hunger**,
  and then **fed** you with **manna**,
  a food **unknown** to you and your fathers,
  in order to show you that **not** by bread **alone** does one **live**,
  but by **every** word that comes forth from the **mouth**
    of the LORD.

"Do not **forget** the LORD, your God,
  who **brought** you out of the land of Egypt,
  that place of slavery;
  who **guided** you through the vast and terrible desert
  with its **saraph serpents** and scorpions,
  its **parched** and waterless ground;
  who brought forth **water** for you from the flinty rock
  and **fed** you in the desert with manna,
  a food unknown to your fathers."

Deuteronomy = doo-ter-AH-nuh-mee
Moses = MOH-zis.

Proclaim in a tone of firmness and authority. Pause before you begin Moses' words.

Take your time with Moses' words. Proclaim with clarity. Rehearse for strong eye contact.

Use vocal variety in the reading.

Proclaim with high energy.

saraph = SAYR-uhf (fiery)

READING I   The Pentateuch (the first five books of the Bible, also called Torah) describes the deliverance of Israel from Pharaoh and the Egyptians at the Red Sea as the birth of the people of God. And it presents the subsequent period of their wandering in the desert, the setting for today's reading, as the time during which God and Israel got to know each other. In our passage, the desert is described as a vast and dangerous wasteland. Poisonous snakes, snakes with a fiery stinging bite, and scorpions live there. The ground is parched and waterless. Through

this area that is hostile to human life, God leads Israel for forty years in order to test them by affliction and find out how committed to him they are.

The test in this passage has two parts: to let Israel experience hunger and then to feed them manna, a food unknown to them or their ancestors. One goal of the test seems to be to teach the people that while God continually supplies what they need, these divine provisions may come from places and in forms they do not expect. In this text, God reveals that manna—probably

the resin of a tamarisk tree or the secretion of an insect that is found on it—is edible.

The narratives of the Lord bringing water from a rock follows a similar pattern. The people thirst because there seems to be no water to drink. Then, divine instructions go forth from the Lord to Moses commanding him to strike a rock. In the Sinai wilderness, water and condensation seep down and collect in pockets within rock formations, and there remain concealed from human sight. As Moses obeys the Lord's command, the thin layer of rock covering

For meditation and context:

RESPONSORIAL PSALM   Psalm 147:12–13, 14–15, 19–20 (12)

R. Praise the Lord, Jerusalem.
or
R. Alleluia.

Glorify the LORD, O Jerusalem;
    praise your God, O Zion.
For he has strengthened the bars
        of your gates;
    he has blessed your children within you.

He has granted peace in your borders;
    with the best of wheat he fills you.
He sends forth his command to the earth;
    swiftly runs his word!

He has proclaimed his word to Jacob,
    his statutes and his ordinances to Israel.
He has not done thus for any other nation;
    his ordinances he has not made known
        to them. Alleluia.

READING II   1 Corinthians 10:16–17

Corinthians = kohr-IN-thee-uhnz

Proclaim this beautiful reading with a tone of gentleness and gratefulness.

A reading from the first Letter of Saint Paul to the Corinthians

Brothers and sisters:
The **cup** of blessing that we bless,
    is it **not** a participation in the **blood of Christ**?
The **bread** that we break,
    is it **not** a participation in the **body of Christ?**
Because the loaf of bread is **one**,
    we, though many, are **one body**,
    for we **all** partake of the **one loaf**.

---

the hidden pool shatters and water flows out for the people to drink.

The last two verses of today's reading follow Deuteronomy 8:4–13 (which are ommitted), wherein Moses addresses the people after they became prosperous in the land. He warns them not to exalt themselves, forgetting that their affluence is a divine blessing. It is not the product of their own abilities and efforts. Our passage picks up as Moses commands Israel (and their descendants including us) to "remember," to "not forget" all the things that God did for them. The Hebrew word for remember

denotes not only mental recall but more particularly a dynamic response to what is remembered. Put simply, to remember but do nothing is to forget. The proofs that Israel remembers the Lord's providential care in the wilderness are trust and obedience.

READING II The two verses of this reading belong to a larger section that warns the Corinthians against idolatry. It seems that they have not yet grasped that Baptism is a life-altering event, and that previous routines might not be compatible with their new life in Christ.

Some of them, for example, continue to join friends and associates for meals that are part of non-Christian liturgies. They apparently justify this custom by asserting that they neither believe in nor worship the gods celebrated in these rites. Paul informs them that what they view as a social event, he sees as idolatry.

He uses the term *koinonia*, variously translated as "participation," "fellowship," "sharing," or "communion," to explain why. In the Hellenistic (Greek) mystery religions of the area, the eating of a ritual meal was believed to effect *koinonia* with the god

For meditation and context:

Sequences originated as extensions of the sung Alleluia before the proclamation of the gospel, although they precede the Alleluia now. This sequence was composed around 1264 by St. Thomas Aquinas. At one point in history, many feasts had sequences, but only four remain: the sequences for Easter (*Victimae paschali laudes*), Pentecost (*Veni Sancte Spiritus*), the Feast of the Body and Blood of Christ (Corpus Christi) (*Lauda, Sion Salvatorem*), and the Feast of Our Lady of Sorrows (*Stabat Mater dolorosa*).

SEQUENCE   Lauda, Sion, Salvatorem

Laud, O Zion, your salvation,
Laud with hymns of exultation,
    Christ, your king and shepherd true:

Bring him all the praise you know,
He is more than you bestow.
    Never can you reach his due.

Special theme for glad thanksgiving
Is the quick'ning and the living
    Bread today before you set:

From his hands of old partaken,
As we know, by faith unshaken,
    Where the Twelve at supper met.

Full and clear ring out your chanting,
Joy nor sweetest grace be wanting,
    From your heart let praises burst:

For today the feast is holden,
When the institution olden
    Of that supper was rehearsed.

Here the new law's new oblation,
By the new king's revelation,
    Ends the form of ancient rite:

Now the new the old effaces,
Truth away the shadow chases,
    Light dispels the gloom of night.

What he did at supper seated,
Christ ordained to be repeated,
    His memorial ne'er to cease:

And his rule for guidance taking,
Bread and wine we hallow, making
    Thus our sacrifice of peace.

This the truth each Christian learns,
Bread into his flesh he turns,
    To his precious blood the wine:

Sight has fail'd, nor thought conceives,
But a dauntless faith believes,
    Resting on a pow'r divine.

Here beneath these signs are hidden
Priceless things to sense forbidden;
    Signs, not things are all we see:

Blood is poured and flesh is broken,
Yet in either wondrous token
    Christ entire we know to be.

Whoso of this food partakes,
Does not rend the Lord nor breaks;
    Christ is whole to all that taste:

Thousands are, as one, receivers,
One, as thousands of believers,
    Eats of him who cannot waste.

Bad and good the feast are sharing,
Of what divers dooms preparing,
    Endless death, or endless life.

Life to these, to those damnation,
See how like participation
    Is with unlike issues rife.

When the sacrament is broken,
Doubt not, but believe 'tis spoken,
    That each sever'd outward token
        doth the very whole contain.

Nought the precious gift divides,
Breaking but the sign betides
    Jesus still the same abides,
        still unbroken does remain.

[Shorter form begins here.]
Lo! the angel's food is given
To the pilgrim who has striven;
    See the children's bread from heaven,
        which on dogs may not be spent.

Truth the ancient types fulfilling,
Isaac bound, a victim willing,
    Paschal lamb, its lifeblood spilling,
        manna to the fathers sent.

Very bread, good shepherd, tend us,
Jesu, of your love befriend us,
    You refresh us, you defend us,
    Your eternal goodness send us
In the land of life to see.

You who all things can and know,
Who on earth such food bestow,
    Grant us with your saints, though lowest,
    Where the heav'nly feast you show,
Fellow heirs and guests to be. Amen. Alleluia.

being worshipped. In our reading, Paul asks questions that should compel the Corinthians to reexamine their understanding of the unique communion, the *koinonia*, they have with Christ and with each other in the Eucharistic meal. They need to avoid all behaviors that do not reinforce this bond of unity.

GOSPEL   The evangelist tells us at the end of this passage that Jesus is teaching in the Capernaum synagogue (John 6:59), the place where Jews assemble to praise God and to study Scripture. There they search their sacred writings to discover how God, who acted in the lives of their ancestors, is also present and acting in their midst.

In this setting, Jesus reapplies the accounts about God's providential feeding of the Israelites in the wilderness to himself. Repetitions of *living* and *life* help us follow his teaching. He is the living bread that came down from heaven, the Word who was (living) with God in the beginning, the Word who became flesh and lived a human life. His claim that whoever eats "this bread" will live forever is too much, how-ever, for his Jewish audience. The law forbade them to eat human flesh, and animal meat had to be drained of its blood before being consumed.

They quarrel and question how a man—because that's how they see Jesus—can give his flesh to them to eat. He is like the manna that was there in the wilderness but previously unknown to Israel and so not recognized as food. He is like the water hidden beneath a layer of rock until God brings it forth for the people to drink.

GOSPEL   John 6:51–58

A reading from the holy Gospel according to John

Pause before you read Jesus' words. Proclaim with a tone of firmness and clarity.

Jesus said to the **Jewish** crowds:
"I am the living bread that came down from heaven;
whoever eats this bread will **live forever**;
and the **bread** that **I** will give
is **my flesh** for the life of the world."

The **Jews** quarreled among themselves, saying,
"How can this man give us his **flesh** to eat?"
Jesus said to them,

Rehearse for a strong delivery: volume, pace, eye contact, and expression in your voice.

"Amen, **amen**, I say to you,
unless you **eat** the flesh of the **Son of Man** and **drink his blood**,
you do **not** have life **within you**.
Whoever eats my flesh and **drinks** my blood
has **eternal** life,
and I will **raise** him on the **last** day.
For my **flesh** is **true** food,
and my **blood** is true drink.
Whoever **eats** my flesh and **drinks** my blood
remains **in me** and **I in him**.
Just as the living Father sent me

Pause.

and **I** have life **because** of the Father,
so **also** the one who feeds on me
will have life **because** of me.
This is the bread that came down from heaven.
Unlike your ancestors who **ate** and **still died**,
whoever **eats** this bread will **live forever**."

Jesus is trying to make them understand that his flesh is true food and his blood true drink. He alone can provide the nourishment they need to sustain the life that he is offering them. He wants to be so clear about this that he states his bold claim twice: those who do not participate in the Eucharistic meal will not have life within them; and, those who do eat his flesh and drink his blood will have eternal life. And Jesus will raise them up to live with him forever.

But Jesus cannot wait that long. Already he abides in those who partake of his body and blood and they abide in him. At long last, in him humanity can see how closely God has desired to live with them since creation. The Jewish Scriptures trace the path of his drawing ever nearer. During Israel's wandering in the desert, the Lord dwelled with them in the tent of meeting, a portable sanctuary that was set up outside the camp. Later, the ark containing the covenant tablets travelled with them on their journey to the land. Eventually, the ark was moved into the temple built by Solomon in Jerusalem, and people went there to be with God. Then the Son of God, the Word became flesh and made his dwelling among us, and eventually within us. E.N.

TWELFTH SUNDAY IN ORDINARY TIME

LECTIONARY #94

READING I   Jeremiah 20:10–13

Jeremiah = jer-uh-MĪ-uh

Proclaim Jeremiah's words with high energy. He is anxious. Let the congregation hear that anxiety in your voice.

Transition to a tone of confidence as Jeremiah speaks about the Lord.

Proclaim in a tone of rejoicing.

A reading from the Book of the Prophet Jeremiah

Jeremiah said:
   "I **hear** the whisperings of many:
   '**Terror** on every side!
   Denounce! let us denounce him!'
All those who **were** my friends
   are on the watch for **any misstep** of mine.
'Perhaps he will be **trapped**; then we can **prevail**,
   and take our **vengeance** on him.'
But the LORD is with me, like a mighty champion:
   my persecutors will **stumble**, they will **not** triumph.
In their failure they will be put to **utter** shame,
   to lasting, **unforgettable** confusion.
O LORD of hosts, you who **test** the just,
   who **probe** mind and heart,
let me witness the vengeance you take on them,
   for to you I have **entrusted** my cause.
Sing to the LORD,
   praise the LORD,
for he has **rescued** the life of the **poor**
   from the **power** of the **wicked**!"

READING I   This lament of the prophet Jeremiah follows a clash with the priest Pashur over the prophet's recurring announcement that Jerusalem and Judah will fall to the Babylonians. His preaching angers the religious leaders and on this occasion Pashur puts Jeremiah in the stocks overnight. When released, the intrepid prophet repeats the condemnation of Judah, adding that Pashur himself will die in exile (Jeremiah 20:1–6).

But after his bold public confrontation, Jeremiah turns privately to God and laments his miserable life. He feels painfully ineffective and wants to quit. His detractors chant his own words to mock him. "Terror on every side" is the phrase he uses to describe the coming devastation (Jeremiah 6:25; 46:5; 49:29). And he has just told Pashur that the Lord renames *him* "Terror on every side," indicating the priest's part in the fall of Jerusalem.

At the heart of Jeremiah's struggle is the seeming superiority of earthly power over divine power. In the three verses preceding today's reading, he complains that the Lord worked on him in his mother's womb and later, knowing him so well, tricked him into accepting his prophetic call. When fidelity to his mission provoked constant derision and suffering, he decided to stop speaking for the Lord. But then the divine Word was like a fire burning within him that wore him out. He could not overpower it. Now, as his former friends decide to vanquish him, his past experiences of the Lord's overpowering him from without and from within convince him to trust that his Champion is more powerful than they are.

Jeremiah's prayer changes suddenly but only momentarily from lament to praise. (In Jeremiah 20:14–18 he wishes he

For meditation and context:

RESPONSORIAL PSALM   Psalm 69:8–10, 14, 17, 33–35 (14c)

R. Lord, in your great love, answer me.

For your sake I bear insult,
    and shame covers my face.
I have become an outcast to my brothers,
    a stranger to my children,
because zeal for your house consumes me,
    and the insults of those who blaspheme
        you fall upon me.

I pray to you, O Lord,
    for the time of your favor, O God!
In your great kindness answer me
    with your constant help.
Answer me, O Lord, for bounteous is
    your kindness;
    in your great mercy turn toward me.

"See, you lowly ones, and be glad;
    you who seek God, may your
        hearts revive!
For the Lord hears the poor,
    and his own who are in bonds he
        spurns not.
Let the heavens and the earth praise him,
    the seas and whatever moves in them!"

READING II   Romans 5:12–15

A reading from the Letter of Saint Paul to the Romans

This is a teaching moment for St. Paul. You want the congregation to understand what St. Paul is trying to get across. Articulate the words. Take your time.

Brothers and sisters:
Through one man **sin** entered the world,
    and through sin, **death**,
    and thus death came to **all** men, inasmuch as **all** sinned —
    for up to the time of the law, sin was in the world,
    though sin is **not** accounted when there is **no** law.

Pause.

But **death** reigned from **Adam to Moses**,
    even over those who did not sin
    after the pattern of the trespass of **Adam**,
    who is the type of the one who was to come.

Say this line with firmness.
End by proclaiming in a tone of thankfulness.

But the gift is **not** like the **transgression**.
For if by the transgression of the one the many died,
    how much **more** did the **grace** of **God**
    and the gracious **gift** of the one man **Jesus Christ**
    overflow for the many.

had died in his mother's womb.) A few commentators conjecture that the switch to praise was prompted by a reassuring word from the Lord, or a priest, or a cultic minister. But there is no evidence for such an intervention in the text. Like pray-ers of all ages who bring their troubles to the Lord, Jeremiah believes that the Lord is listening. Despite his continual suffering, he chooses to spend the rest of his life announcing the Word of the Lord.

READING II Paul preaches that from Adam until the coming of

Christ, humanity lived in a world ruled over by sin and death. This situation is the consequence of Adam's disobedience to God's command and of the sins of all humanity. In today's reading, "sin" and "death" are personified. Sin, referring to more than individual sins, is a cosmic power that works to lure people away from God. Likewise, death is more than physical death, which separates body and soul, or spiritual death, which separates one from God for all eternity. Personified "death" is a universal force that works to persuade humans that life is not a divinely bestowed gift, but rather a

hopeless existence filled with worry that ends in nothingness.

Paul's main point is that God's gracious gift of Christ is an extravagant response to Adam's offense and its consequences. Jesus did more than free people from the reign of sin and death and make it possible for them to enjoy a full rich life on earth. He acquitted them of their sins before God and offered to those who believe in him divine companionship and favor on earth, through death, and for all eternity.

GOSPEL Matthew 10:26–33

A reading from the holy Gospel according to Matthew

Jesus said to the Twelve:
  "**Fear no one.**
Nothing is concealed that will **not** be revealed,
  nor secret that will **not** be known.
What I say to you in the darkness, **speak** in the **light**;
  what you hear whispered, **proclaim** on the housetops.
And do **not** be afraid of those who kill the body
    but **cannot** kill the soul;
  rather, be **afraid** of the one who can **destroy**
    both **soul** and **body** in **Gehenna**.
Are not two sparrows sold for a small coin?
Yet **not** one of them **falls** to the ground
    without your **Father's knowledge**.
Even **all** the hairs of your head are counted.
So do **not be afraid; you** are worth **more** than many sparrows.
Everyone who acknowledges me before others
    I will acknowledge before my **heavenly Father**.
But whoever **denies** me before others,
    I will **deny** before my heavenly Father."

Proclaim with clarity and firmness. Use good volume and do not rush Jesus' words.

Gehenna = geh-HEN-nah

Proclaim in a gentle tone.

GOSPEL Jesus sends his disciples, including all the baptized, on a dangerous mission. He told them in the verses preceding this Gospel that they must expect to be hated, persecuted, flogged, and handed over to civil powers. In other words, his disciples should not expect their days to be filled always with safe comfortable routines and the constant welcome and admiration of others.

The command to "fear no one" is addressed in Scripture to people chosen, like Jesus' disciples, to perform specific tasks for God in the world. Jesus uses the issue of fear to impress upon them the magnitude of his project and what is at stake for those called to work for it. He teaches that fear of those who can inflict bodily harm and even death, while rational and understandable, is not a Christian fear. His disciples need to retrain themselves to fear God, who can consign them to eternal hell or to eternal life. He quickly adds that the Father, however, is not a cold, distant project manager. He is onsite moment by moment, noting all that happens to them. He has counted every single one of their hairs.

Jesus wraps up his teaching on what to fear by having the disciples imagine that moment when each of them will stand on his or her own before the Father and hear him say either, "This one is my faithful disciple," or "This one is not mine." What Jesus will say about us depends on how faithful we are daily to the unique mission for which God formed us in the womb. E.N.

THIRTEENTH SUNDAY IN ORDINARY TIME

LECTIONARY #97

READING I 2 Kings 4:8–11, 14–16a

Elisha = ee-LĪ-shuh
Shunem = SHOO-nuhm

You are reading a story to the congregation. Use expression in your voice so that we can visualize Elisha and Gehazi. Take your time. Rehearse for strong eye contact and articulation.

A reading from the second Book of Kings

One day **Elisha** came to **Shunem**,
    where there was a woman of influence, who urged him to
        dine with her.
Afterward, whenever he passed by, he used to stop there to dine.
So she said to her husband, "I know that **Elisha** is a **holy** man of
    God.
Since he visits us often, let us arrange a little room on the roof
    and furnish it for him with a bed, table, chair, and lamp,
        so that when he comes to us he can stay there."
Sometime later **Elisha** arrived and stayed in the room overnight.

Gehazi = geh-HAY-zĪ

Later **Elisha** asked, "Can something be **done** for her?"
His servant **Gehazi** answered, "Yes!
    She has no **son**, and her husband is getting **on** in years."
Elisha said, "**Call** her."
When the woman had been called and **stood** at the door,
    Elisha promised, "This time next year
    you will be fondling a baby **son**."

READING I Travelling in the biblical world was a dangerous undertaking. Water was not as available as in the modern world, and in many places the rights to it were owned by a clan or tribe who could decide not to share it. Since inns for food and lodging were sparse, sojourners depended on the hospitality of people they met along their way. Stories from this world often claim that hosts entertain gods unaware and are generously repaid.

In this reading, a wealthy and influential woman from Shunem offers Elisha a meal when he passes by on the Lord's business. After hosting the prophet several times, she sees that he is "a holy man of God," and prepares a place for him to lodge when in the area. The reward for her hospitality is Elisha's announcement that within a year she will be holding the divine gift of a son.

READING II Romans 6:1–11 presents Paul's main teaching on Baptism. In today's reading he expresses his frustration that many Christians do not seem to realize that Baptism is a life-changing event. They spend their time and energy pursuing their interests and working on their projects, as they did before they were baptized. Paul asks if they (and we) are unaware that they were "co-buried" with Christ into his suffering and death. At that time, they died to their former life so that they could share on earth in his resurrected life and enjoy the fullness of it for all eternity.

Paul wants them to understand that in Baptism they took on a new identity. They are no longer, for example, Mary or John but Mary-in-Christ and John-in-Christ. As

For meditation and context:

RESPONSORIAL PSALM   Psalm 89:2–3, 16–17, 18–19 (2a)

R. Forever I will sing the goodness of the Lord.

The promises of the LORD I will
    sing forever,
  through all generations my mouth shall
    proclaim your faithfulness.
For you have said, "My kindness is
    established forever";
  in heaven you have confirmed your
    faithfulness.

Blessed the people who know the
    joyful shout;
  in the light of your countenance,
    O LORD, they walk.
At your name they rejoice all the day,
  and through your justice they are exalted.

You are the splendor of their strength,
  and by your favor our horn is exalted.
For to the LORD belongs our shield,
  and to the Holy One of Israel, our king.

READING II   Romans 6:3–4, 8–11

A reading from the Letter of Saint Paul to the Romans

St. Paul asks a very important question. Answer in a tone of conviction.

Brothers and sisters:
Are you **unaware** that we who were **baptized** into **Christ Jesus**
    were baptized into his **death**?
We were **indeed** buried with him through baptism into **death**,
    so that, just as **Christ** was raised from the dead
    by the glory of the **Father**,
    we too might **live** in **newness of life.**

Proclaim with energy and passion. Build the energy until the end of the reading.

If, then, we have **died** with **Christ,**
    we **believe** that we shall **also live** with him.
We know that Christ, raised from the dead, **dies** no more;
    death no longer has **power** over him.
As to his death, he **died** to sin once and for all;
    as to his life, he l**ives for God**.
Consequently, **you too** must think of yourselves as **dead** to sin
    and **living** for **God** in **Christ Jesus**.

---

they die to their old habits and adopt the will and ways of the Risen Lord, they are transformed into him. The early Church writers boldly describe this experience as becoming other Christs in the world.

As the baptized grow in union with Christ, sin becomes less attractive to them. They notice that its consequences dampen or extinguish the profound joy and peace that begin to fill their days. They miss the experience of Christ's own energy flowing through them as they give their all to doing God's work. They are learning what it means to die to sin and live for God.

GOSPEL   During his public ministry Jesus of Nazareth could reach a limited number of people, so he chose disciples not only to teach others about him but also to bring him to them. The first sayings in today's Gospel set out what people must do to be worthy of this privilege.

First, they must love him, that is, act more loyally to him than to family members. This would be a deal-breaker for most people in the biblical world, where one's family is the primary source of help and security when misfortunes arise. Jesus

commands his disciples to forego this traditional means of support, and trust that no matter what happens, he and the Father will take care of them.

Disciples must also take up their cross and travel into the unknown with Jesus. In the preceding verses, Jesus outlines their mission. They must preach the Gospel by word and deed, give freely what was freely given to them, and endure the sufferings that following Jesus into dangerous places brings (Matthew 10:5–32). Discipleship requires energy and effort. It is not a hobby that people pick up when it is convenient or

Pause before you begin.

Speak Jesus' words with a tone of authority and purpose. He tells us how to be disciples. Take your time.

GOSPEL   Matthew 10:37–42

A reading from the holy Gospel according to Matthew

Jesus said to his apostles:
 "Whoever **loves** father or mother **more** than me is **not** worthy
  of me,
 and whoever loves son or daughter **more** than me is **not** worthy of me;
 and whoever does **not take up** his cross
 and **follow** after me is **not** worthy of me.
Whoever **finds** his life will **lose** it,
 and whoever **loses** his life for **my sake** will **find it**.

"Whoever **receives** you receives **me**,
 and whoever **receives** me receives the one who **sent** me.
Whoever receives a **prophet** because he is a prophet
 will receive a prophet's reward,
 and whoever receives a **righteous man**
 because he is a righteous man
 will receive a righteous man's **reward.**
And whoever **gives only** a **cup** of cold water
 to one of these **little** ones to drink
 because the little one is a **disciple**—
 amen, **I** say to you, he will surely **not** lose his reward."

Put expression in your voice and use eye contact.

TO KEEP IN MIND
Repetition of the same word or phrase over the course of a reading emphasizes a point. Make each instance distinct, and build your intensity with each repetition.

when they are in the right mood. It is a passion that leads to the discovery of a life that the faithful could never imagine.

The last sayings in the Gospel reveal how this new life materializes in the interaction of disciples and those who provide for their needs. Six repetitions of "receive" or "welcome" in verses 40–41 trace the process. Those who welcome a disciple welcome Jesus. Matthew emphasizes this point, a version of Jesus' teaching that what people do to others they do to him. It will be the standard used to separate the "sheep," whom Jesus will welcome into his

kingdom, from the "goats," who will go off to eternal punishment at the last judgment (25:31–46).

In today's Gospel Jesus adds that those who welcome him also welcome the Father, who will reward them. For example, if the welcomed disciples are prophets (imagine hosting someone like John the Baptist) or righteous, the Father gives their host a prophet's or a righteous person's reward. Jesus solemnly declares that whoever offers a minimum of hospitality, a cup of cold water, to his disciples "can never lose" the Father's reward. The smallest

considerate gesture to a little one earns eternal compensation.

Jesus' examples reveal that disciples on mission become channels of divine blessings to those who provide for their needs. After their meeting, both parties remain connected in Christ and are woven together into the life of the divine family, the family that protects them and provides for all their needs. E.N.

FOURTEENTH SUNDAY IN ORDINARY TIME

LECTIONARY #100

READING I Zechariah 9:9–10

A reading from the Book of the Prophet Zechariah

Thus says the LORD:
Rejoice heartily, O daughter **Zion**,
    shout for joy, O daughter **Jerusalem**!
See, your king shall come to you;
    a **just savior** is he,
meek, and riding on an ass,
    on a colt, the foal of an ass.
He shall **banish** the chariot from **Ephraim**,
    and the horse from **Jerusalem**;
the warrior's bow shall be **banished**,
    and he shall **proclaim peace** to the nations.
His dominion shall be from **sea to sea**,
    and from the **River** to the **ends of the earth**.

Zechariah = zek-uh-RĪ-uh

Great news! Proclaim with high energy throughout the reading.

Zion = ZĪ-uhn or ZĪ-ahn

Ephraim = EE-fray-im; EF-r*m

READING I The Promised Land was an international battleground throughout most of biblical history. The great civilizations that occupied Egypt and Mesopotamia envied its strategic position on the bridge of land that connected them. From the eighth to the fourth centuries BC alone, the Egyptians to the south, the Assyrians and Babylonians to the northeast in Mesopotamia, and the Persians from the Far East sought to control Israel. Then Alexander the Great came from the northwest, conquered the Persians, and established the Greek empire. To this battered world, Zechariah makes the astonishing announcement that the Lord is sending a savior who will bring justice and peace to all its inhabitants.

This king will arrive seated on a donkey, less as a sign of his humility than as a signal of his opposition to war. Rulers frequently rode donkeys as they travelled through their realms on business, and soldiers rode them into skirmishes in hilly terrain. But horses, which were more easily controlled, were the animals preferred for large battles. The Lord's king will banish these steeds, chariots, and bows—the main weapons of biblical warfare—from his kingdom.

Zechariah commands Jerusalem, also called Zion, to "shout for joy" because this king will take the option of war off the table. In Old Testament texts, the shouts that the prophet calls for are often war cries that announce the beginning of a battle or celebrate a victory. They erupt in jubilation that an attack on someone else's homeland begins. Or they burst forth from the victors who lost fewer of their loved ones than—in God's view—their brothers and sister did. In this passage, these shouts

207

For meditation and context:

RESPONSORIAL PSALM   Psalm 145:1–2, 8–9, 10–11, 13–14 (1)

R. I will praise your name for ever, my king and my God.
or
R. Alleluia.

I will extol you, O my God and King,
  and I will bless your name for ever
    and ever.
Every day will I bless you,
  and I will praise your name for ever
    and ever.

The LORD is gracious and merciful,
  slow to anger and of great kindness.
The LORD is good to all
  and compassionate toward all his works.

Let all your works give you thanks, O LORD,
  and let your faithful ones bless you.
Let them discourse of the glory of
    your kingdom
  and speak of your might.

The LORD is faithful in all his words
  and holy in all his works.
The LORD lifts up all who are falling
  and raises up all who are bowed down.

READING II   Romans 8:9, 11–13

A reading from the Letter of Saint Paul to the Romans

Proclaim with passion and conviction.

Brothers and sisters:
You are **not** in the flesh;
  on the contrary, you **are** in the **spirit**,
  if only the **Spirit of God** dwells in **you**.
Whoever does **not** have the **Spirit of Christ** does **not** belong
    to him.
If the **Spirit** of the one who raised **Jesus** from the dead **dwells**
    in you,
  the one who raised **Christ** from the dead
  will give **life** to your **mortal** bodies also,
  through his **Spirit** that **dwells in you**.

Read with energy and good eye contact.

Consequently, brothers and sisters,
  we are **not debtors** to the flesh,
  to live according to the flesh.
For if you live according to the flesh, you will **die**,
  but if by the **Spirit** you put to **death the deeds** of the body,
  you will **live**.

---

celebrate the coming savior who will remove the reason for war, injustice.

READING II   The focus of these winding verses is the mystery of the mutual indwelling of the Spirit in the baptized and the baptized in the Spirit. Christians will fully understand and experience this reality only when Christ returns. Meanwhile, they must remember that the Spirit living within them is the one who resurrected Jesus from the dead. They must cultivate the conviction that this powerful Spirit is always active, follow its lead, and

find its tracks in the details that fill their hours and become their life.

Competing with this divine Spirit for their attention and having the advantage because it is familiar to them is the "flesh." In the letter to the Romans, "flesh" (Greek *sarx*) denotes the fragile human body that comes from the earth and returns to it. Those who live "according to the flesh" allow temporal realities to determine their choices and fix their destiny. Because they ignore the Spirit, they cannot resist the body's natural desires, and so follow its path of least resistance. Their thoughts are

earthbound, narrow, and shabby; their life a vain shadow of what it could be if they lived "according to the Spirit."

GOSPEL   In the preceding passage, Jesus reproaches Capernaum, the home base for his ministry in Galilee, and nearby towns because their inhabitants do not heed his teachings, even after they see his mighty deeds. Now he contrasts others who reject him—the wise and religiously learned who are probably the Scribes and Pharisees—to the "little ones." For Matthew, these are Jesus' disci-

GOSPEL   Matthew 11:25–30

A reading from the holy Gospel according to Matthew

At that time **Jesus** exclaimed:
    "I give **praise** to you, **Father, Lord** of heaven and earth,
    for although you have hidden these things
    from the wise and the learned
    you have revealed them to **little ones**.
Yes, **Father**, such has been your **gracious will**.
All things have been handed over to **me** by my **Father**.
No one knows the **Son** except the **Father**,
    and **no** one knows the Father **except** the **Son**
    and anyone to whom the Son wishes to reveal him.

"**Come** to me, all you who labor and are burdened,
    and I will give you **rest**.
Take my **yoke** upon you and **learn** from me,
    for I am **meek** and **humble** of heart;
    and you will find **rest** for yourselves.
For my yoke is **easy**, and my burden **light**."

Proclaim as if Jesus is praying to the Father.

Proclaim in a tone of comfort and humility.

ples who commit their life totally to him. He bursts into praise that they are the ones his Father welcomes into the divine family.

He invites these Jewish Christians to come to him, take up his yoke, and find rest with him. Their burdens are most likely the 613 rules taught by the Pharisees, who do not lift a finger to help people carry them out (Matthew 23:4). In contrast, Jesus' yoke, his teachings, are simple and straightforward, and he accompanies his disciples as they put them into practice.

With Jesus working beside them, living his way is not only "easy" but also, based on the Greek, "useful," "worthy," "good," or "pleasant." Jesus himself is "gentle," or "unassuming" and "considerate." He is not self-absorbed but focuses on the needs of others. The phrase "humble of heart" conveys that he is not a leader who makes his superior position—indeed his divinity—felt by his coworkers. Unlike an aloof boss who piles work on his subordinates, Jesus notices when his disciples become weary and eases their load.

Like the savior whose coming Zechariah announced, Jesus does not spread his kingdom by conquering others. He quietly works alongside those who belong to him and his Father in every generation, humbly and tirelessly providing for their needs as they strive to bring divine justice and peace into a world inclined to war. To this we are called. Let us rejoice greatly. E.N.

FIFTEENTH SUNDAY IN ORDINARY TIME

LECTIONARY #103

READING I   Isaiah 55:10–11

Isaiah = Ī-ZAY-uh

Proclaim in a tone of gratefulness for the Lords' word.

A reading from the Book of the Prophet Isaiah

Thus says the LORD:
Just as from the heavens
    the rain and snow come down
and do not return there
    till they have **watered** the earth,
    making it **fertile** and **fruitful**,
giving **seed** to the one who **sows**
    and **bread** to the one who **eats**,
so shall my word be
    that goes forth from my mouth;
my word shall **not** return to me **void**,
    but shall do **my will**,
    achieving the end for which **I** sent it.

Transition to a tone of firmness.

TO KEEP IN MIND
Pay attention to the pace of your reading. Varying the pace gives listeners clues to the meaning of the text. The most common problem for proclaimers new to the ministry is going too fast to be understood.

READING I Israel became convinced of the effectiveness of the "Word of the Lord" when prophetic announcements of the fall of their northern and southern kingdoms were fulfilled. Some of these prophecies came from First Isaiah, who worked in Jerusalem in the eighth century BC and whose preaching is collected in Isaiah 1–39. Today's reading is from the prophet called Second Isaiah who worked in Babylon in the sixth century BC

and whose oracles are found in Isaiah 40–55. Second Isaiah applies the preaching of his predecessor to this later situation and adds his own Spirit-given insights, among them the unfailing power and effectiveness of the "Word of the Lord."

The Hebrew for "word," *dabar*, denotes not only a spoken word but also in certain contexts "a thing, an event, or an affair." In Israel's early traditions, the Lord's word referred primarily to the cov-

enant commandments. But for the prophets it conveys the Lord's all-powerful and dynamic presence in history.

Second Isaiah's metaphor of the rain and snow aptly conveys this invisible divine activity to his listeners. Yearly they watch in wonder as the snow melts, the rains come, and the parched desert wilderness around them bursts into bloom. They marvel as the dried-up earth of their fields brings forth food and seed to sustain their

For meditation and context:

RESPONSORIAL PSALM   Psalm 65:10, 11, 12–13, 14 (Luke 8:8)

R. The seed that falls on good ground will yield a fruitful harvest.

You have visited the land and watered it;
   greatly have you enriched it.
God's watercourses are filled;
   you have prepared the grain.

Thus have you prepared the land: drenching
   its furrows,
   breaking up its clods,
softening it with showers,
   blessing its yield.

You have crowned the year with your bounty,
   and your paths overflow with a
      rich harvest;
the untilled meadows overflow with it,
   and rejoicing clothes the hills.

The fields are garmented with flocks
   and the valleys blanketed with grain.
   They shout and sing for joy.

READING II   Romans 8:18–23

A reading from the Letter of Saint Paul to the Romans

Brothers and sisters:
I consider that the sufferings of this present time are as **nothing**
   compared with the **glory** to be revealed for us.
For creation awaits with **eager expectation**
   the **revelation** of the children of **God;**
   for **creation** was made subject to **futility,**
   not of its own accord but because of the **one** who subjected it,
   in **hope** that creation itself
   would be **set free** from slavery to corruption
   and share in the **glorious freedom** of the children of **God.**
We know that **all** creation is groaning in labor pains **even**
      until now;
   and not only that, but **we ourselves,**
   who have the firstfruits of the **Spirit,**
   we **also** groan within ourselves
   as we **wait** for adoption, the **redemption** of our bodies.

Pause before you begin and then speak with clarity and passion.

Proclaim with energy and continue to build energy as you read "and share in the glorious freedom of the children of God."

Transition to a tone of informing.

families for another year. The prophet assures listeners of every age that, no matter how arid and hopeless their situation appears to be, God is at work in it, bringing to fulfillment divine plans for their (and all creation's) present well-being and eternal glory.

READING II   In this reading, Paul seems to be working with the maxim, "misery loves company." He tells the baptized that they are not the only ones who are suffering from the limitations and distresses of life. All creation, which in this passage denotes everything that God made except people, is suffering with them.

The foundation of Paul's thought is the Old Testament conviction that the existence and destiny of creation and humankind are bound together. For example, in Genesis 1, God creates people in his image and gives them responsibility for what happens to the earth. In Genesis 3, the earth is cursed because of the first couple's sin. Today in Romans, Paul preaches that, because of Adam's sin (and all human sin), the earth was made subject to "futility," which in Greek also denotes a useless or meaningless existence. Paul further describes creation's lot as being in "slavery to corruption"; it is disintegrating and is powerless to change its situation.

GOSPEL   Matthew 13:1–23

A reading from the holy Gospel according to Matthew

Proclaim in an informative tone. You are setting the stage for the parable.

[On that day, **Jesus** went out of the house and sat down by the sea.
Such large crowds gathered around him
    that he got into a **boat** and sat down,
    and the whole crowd stood along the shore.
And he spoke to them at length in **parables**, saying:
    "A sower went out to sow.

Pause before you begin. In the reading of the parable, use vocal variety and good eye contact. Timing is key. You are telling a story. Help the congregation visualize the sower.

And as he sowed, some seed fell on the **path**,
    and birds came and ate it up.
Some fell on **rocky ground**, where it had **little** soil.
It sprang up at once because the soil was not deep,
    and when the sun rose it was **scorched**, and it **withered** for
        lack of roots.
Some seed fell among **thorns**, and the thorns grew up and
        choked it.
But some seed fell on **rich soil**, and **produced fruit**,
    a hundred or sixty or thirtyfold.
Whoever has ears ought to hear."]

Jesus explains. Take your time with his answer. Proclaim with a tone of clarity and purpose.

The disciples approached him and said,
    "Why do you speak to them in parables?"
He said to them in reply,

Transition to a conversational tone.

    "Because **knowledge** of the mysteries of the kingdom of
        heaven
    has been granted to **you**, but to them it has **not** been granted.
To anyone who has, **more** will be **given** and he will grow rich;
    from anyone who has **not,** even what he has will be
        taken away. »

Since creation's hope is the sons and daughters of God, it awaits their unveiling with eager expectation. For Paul, these are the baptized who enjoy on earth the freedom that comes from sharing life with Christ, and who are destined to fullness of life in the divine family forever.

What sustains God's children and gives them hope are the first fruits of the Spirit, which they received in Baptism. These are the pledge and foretaste of eter-

nal life. And yet, Christians groan because these "graced moments" leave them restless and increasingly dissatisfied with beauty and pleasures that fade. They long to be set free from life in the flesh. As the Nicene Creed puts it, they "look forward to the resurrection of the dead and the life of the world to come."

GOSPEL | The Gospel unfolds in three parts: the telling of the par-

able of the sower (Matthew 13:1–9); an explanation of why Jesus teaches in parables (13:10–17); and the interpretation of the parable (13:18–23). Key to understanding this passage is the significance of "bearing fruit" in Matthew's Gospel; namely, fruit is what one brings to the final judgment as evidence that he or she is Jesus' disciple.

The parable begins with an enthusiastic and prodigal farmer who sows on all

Pause before you read the words in italics.

This is why I speak to them in parables, because
  **they look but do not see, and hear but do not listen
    or understand.**
Isaiah's prophecy is fulfilled in them, which says:
  You shall indeed hear but not understand,
    you shall indeed look but never see.
  Gross is *the heart of this people,*
    they will **hardly** *hear with their ears,*
    they have **closed** *their eyes,*
    lest they see with their eyes
    and hear with their ears
  and understand with their hearts and be converted,
    and I **heal** *them.*

Proclaim in a firm tone.
Blessed = BLES-uhd

"But **blessed** are your eyes, because they **see**,
  and your **ears**, because they **hear**.
Amen, I say to you, many **prophets** and **righteous** people
  longed to see what you see but did not see it,
  and to hear what you hear but did not hear it.

Jesus further explains the parable. Keep up the energy in your voice. Look at the congregation. Help them to stay involved with what Jesus is teaching.

"Hear then the parable of the sower.
The seed sown on the **path** is the one
  who **hears** the word of the kingdom without **understanding it**,
  and the **evil** one comes and steals away
  what was sown in his heart.
The seed sown on **rocky ground**
  is the one who **hears** the word and receives it at once **with joy**.
But he has **no root** and lasts only for a time.

types of terrain or soil. Seventy-five percent of what he scatters produces nothing, but the yield of the rest is extraordinary. The word *sperma*, "seed," does not appear in the Greek text, but is conveyed by "some" (of what the sower sowed) and "that which" (was sowed). This lack of specificity about what is sown sparks the interest of the attentive listener.

Such elements of ambiguity are typical of Jesus' parables. They make it easy for their listeners, whose situations and experiences are unique, to apply the parables to their life. For this reason, parables should not be summed up in a one-size-fits-all message which, as the biblical scholar John R. Donahue puts it, "reduces the Good News to good advice." The parable of the sower intends to disturb all who hear it and challenges them to discern which description of "those who hear the word" best describes their life as Jesus' disciple.

In Matthew 13:10–17, the evangelist explains to his Jewish Christian community why Jesus switches to teaching in parables. He does so when his contemporaries reject him because their hearts are "gross" or "fat." Since in Hebrew, the heart often denotes the mind, a "fat heart" is a mind that is impermeable, resistant, or sluggish; those who reject Jesus are those who are too lazy to ponder and try to understand his teachings. They are like their ancestors

When some tribulation or persecution comes because of the word,
    he immediately **falls away.**
The seed sown among **thorns** is the one who **hears** the word,
    but then worldly **anxiety** and the lure of riches **choke** the word
    and it bears **no fruit.**
But the seed sown on **rich soil**
    is the one who **hears** the word and **understands it,**
    who **indeed bears** fruit and yields a hundred or sixty
        or thirtyfold."

[Shorter: Matthew 13:1–9 (see brackets)]

THE 4 STEPS OF *LECTIO DIVINA* OR PRAYERFUL READING

1. *Lectio:* Read a Scripture passage aloud slowly. Notice what phrase captures your attention and be attentive to its meaning. Silent pause.

2. *Meditatio:* Read the passage aloud slowly again, reflecting on the passage, allowing God to speak to you through it. Silent pause.

3. *Oratio:* Read it aloud slowly a third time, allowing it to be your prayer or response to God's gift of insight to you. Silent pause.

4. *Contemplatio:* Read it aloud slowly a fourth time, now resting in God's word.

---

who rejected the preaching of Isaiah in the eighth century BC, the people of Judah who doubted that the Lord was in their midst and became lackadaisical about keeping the covenant. Now, the failure of their descendants to accept that God is present and acting in Jesus once again fulfills Isaiah's prophecy.

In contrast to these unbelievers are people who accept Jesus and commit their life to him. They are "blessed" because they are beginning to understand "the mysteries of the kingdom of heaven" and to realize the opportunity that Jesus offers them. They yearn to learn more about God's kingdom. They want to contribute to its unfolding manifestation on earth.

In the interpretation of the parable (Matthew 13:18–23), "what is sown" in its telling is finally specified as the people who hear "the word of the kingdom" preached. Of all these, only those who take the time and make the effort to understand Jesus' teachings and live by them bear fruit—but the amount they bear is beyond their wildest imagining. There is no greater fulfillment nor nobler calling than living and working for the Lord's concerns—the privilege of the baptized in every age. E.N.

SIXTEENTH SUNDAY IN ORDINARY TIME

LECTIONARY #106

READING I   Wisdom 12:13, 16–19

A reading from the Book of Wisdom

There is **no** god besides **you** who have the care of **all**,
　that you need show you have **not unjustly** condemned.
For your might is the **source of justice**;
　your mastery over **all** things makes you **lenient** to all.
For you show your **might** when the perfection of your power
　is **disbelieved**;
　and in those who know you, you **rebuke temerity**.
But though you are **master** of might, you judge with **clemency**,
　and with much **lenience** you **govern** us;
　for power, whenever you will, **attends** you.
And you **taught** your people, by these deeds,
　that those who are **just** must be **kind**;
and you **gave** your children good ground for **hope**
　that you would permit **repentance** for their sins.

What a good and gracious God we have! Proclaim with a tone of authority and kindness. Take your time with this reading. It is powerful. Use strong eye contact.

temerity = tuh-MER-uh-tee (audacity)

clemency = KLEM-*n-see

READING I   The book of Wisdom was probably written between 30 BC and AD 14, making it the latest work in the Old Testament. Today's reading affirms Israel's hard-learned belief that their God is the almighty and only God. Every type of human power, any physical or mental means that people use to influence and control others, pales before divine might. Wisdom describes it as perfect or complete and always at God's disposal. Given its magnitude, God wields it ever so delicately, especially when it comes to dealing with fragile human beings.

Divine restraint is something that people must learn to imitate, for they are inclined to give full reign to the power that they possess. They must take care not to become like the unjust who say: "Let us oppress the righteous poor; let us neither spare the widow nor revere the aged. . . . [L]et our strength be our norm of righteousness; for weakness proves itself useless" (Wisdom 2:11). In other words, the unjust are bullies who do whatever they wish to others simply because they can.

If omnipotence were the norm for divine justice, humans could not survive.

The verses preceding today's reading describe how God's gracious tolerance allows people room for repentance (Wisdom 11:26—12:1). When Israel was about to enter the Promised Land, God could have wiped out all the evildoers among its inhabitants so that it "might receive a worthy colony of God's servants" (12:7). But instead, God who is a "lover of souls," gives them "space for repentance"; that is, time to learn divine ways and to imitate them. This passage also illustrates the assertion made in today's reading that divine power is the source of divine justice.

For meditation and context:

RESPONSIAL PSALM   Psalm 86:5–6, 9–10, 15–16 (5a)

R. Lord, you are good and forgiving.

You, O Lord, are good and forgiving,
   abounding in kindness to all who call
     upon you.
Hearken, O Lord, to my prayer
   and attend to the sound of my pleading.

All the nations you have made shall come
   and worship you, O Lord,
   and glorify your name.
For you are great, and you do
    wondrous deeds;
   you alone are God.

You, O Lord, are a God merciful
   and gracious,
slow to anger, abounding in kindness
   and fidelity.
Turn toward me, and have pity on me;
   give your strength to your servant.

READING II   Romans 8:26–27

A reading from the Letter of Saint Paul to the Romans

Brothers and sisters:
The **Spirit** comes to the **aid** of our **weakness**;
   for we do **not** know how to **pray** as we ought,
   but the **Spirit** himself **intercedes** with inexpressible groanings.
And the one who searches hearts
   knows what is the **intention of the Spirit,**
   because he **intercedes** for the holy ones
   according to **God's will.**

Proclaim in a tone of gratefulness for the Holy Spirit.

TO KEEP IN MIND
Be careful not to swallow words by mumbling. Articulate carefully, especially at the end of lines.

God displays his strength to those who deny it in order to frighten them into changing their ways. And he abides no insolence from those who acknowledge it but act as if they were beyond its reach. Every manifestation of divine strength is the hand of God gently drawing people closer to him.

Though "master of might," God is a sympathetic and lenient judge. The people of Israel discover this from the way God treats them. That God is "merciful, gracious, and slow to anger" becomes part of its creed. By the end of the first century BC, the ideal Jew is the just person. Wisdom adds that those who are just must also be "kind," in Greek, *philanthrōpos,* which means literally "one who loves people."

READING II   This reading describes the mystery of the divine activity (grace) that goes on within the baptized whose life is joined to Christ and thus to all Christians. Because God doesn't hand out blueprints that detail their lifelong-missions, and because God and divine ways are completely different or "other" (the basic meaning of "holy") from humans and their ways, Christians do not know what to pray for. And so, on a level beyond sensory experience and beneath consciousness, the Spirit whom God did hand out at Baptism intercedes for them "according to God's will" with its own inexpressible groanings, and God, "the one who searches hearts," understands the Spirit's intention.

In effect, Christians are like small children whose divine family dialogs continually about what they need to grow in holiness and how to prepare them for the next phase of their missions. The results of these consultations are the people, events, and seemingly empty spaces that fill the

GOSPEL   Matthew 13:24–43

A reading from the holy Gospel according to Matthew

[**Jesus** proposed another **parable** to the crowds, saying:
"**The kingdom of heaven** may be likened to a man
   who **sowed good seed** in his field.
While everyone was **asleep** his **enemy** came
   and sowed **weeds** all through the wheat, and then went off.
When the crop grew and bore **fruit**, the weeds **appeared** as **well**.
The slaves of the householder came to him and said,
   'Master, did you **not** sow good seed in your field?
Where have the weeds come from?'
He answered, 'An **enemy** has done this.'
His slaves said to him,
   'Do you want us to go and pull them up?'
He replied, 'No, if you pull up the weeds
   you might **uproot** the wheat along with them.
Let them grow **together** until harvest;
   then at harvest time I will say to the harvesters,
   "First collect the **weeds** and tie them in bundles for **burning**;
   but gather the **wheat** into my barn."'"]

He proposed **another** parable to them.
"The kingdom of heaven is like a **mustard seed**
   that a person took and sowed in a field.
It is the **smallest** of all the seeds,
   yet when full-grown it is the **largest** of plants.
It becomes a large bush,
   and the 'birds of the sky come and dwell in its branches.'"

He spoke to them another parable.
"The kingdom of heaven is like **yeast**
   that a woman took and mixed with three measures
    of wheat flour
   until the whole batch was **leavened**."

Pause before you begin Jesus' words.

During the conversation between the master and the servants, use vocal variety to help the congregation visualize the parable. Do not rush. Articulate each syllable and word ending.

Pause before you begin reading the next parable. Keep up your energy.

children's days. Everything that happens to the baptized has a holy and loving purpose that is known to God alone. They need only trust that the Spirit is always at work, accomplishing God's will for them.

GOSPEL The parable of the weeds and the wheat and its interpretation enclose two short parables about the hidden nature of the kingdom of heaven. Each unit compares the kingdom to all that happens as the parable unfolds, not only to a man who sowed, or to a mustard seed, or the to yeast. All three parables

focus on the concerns of disciples who live in the time between Jesus' Ascension and his final coming. In each one, Jesus reveals to them what has been "hidden from the foundation of the world."

In the first parable, the kingdom of heaven is like a man who sowed good seed in his field and his enemy came while everyone was sleeping, sowed weeds in it, and then went away. Since the initial growth of both plants was indistinguishable, no one realized this treachery. As soon as the servants identify the weeds, they think they should pull them out. But

the master knows that the roots of all the plants are intertwined and this would destroy the entire crop. He will let weeds and wheat grow together and separate them himself at the harvest. The servants are to do *nothing* about them.

In the interpretation of the parable, the Son of Man (Jesus' self-designation in this Gospel) sows good seed—the children of the kingdom—in the world. The enemy is the evil one, the devil who sows evildoers. The servants identify the evil being done and want to destroy the sinner, but Jesus, like God in the first reading, is *philanthropōs*.

Transition to an informative tone.

All these things **Jesus** spoke to the crowds in **parables**.
He spoke to them **only** in parables,
    to **fulfill** what had been said through the prophet:
        I will open my mouth in parables,
            I will announce what has lain hidden from
            the foundation of the world.

Then, dismissing the crowds, he went into the house.
His disciples approached him and said,
    "Explain to us the parable of the weeds in the field."

Jesus explains and teaches the parable of the weeds. Proclaim in a tone of clarity and firmness.

He said in reply, "He who sows good seed is the **Son of Man**,
    the field is the **world**, the **good seed** the **children**
        of the kingdom.
The weeds are the children of the **evil** one,
    and the **enemy** who sows them is the **devil**.
The harvest is the **end** of the age, and the harvesters are **angels**.
Just as weeds are collected and burned up with fire,
    so will it be at the **end** of the age.

Build your energy to the end of the reading.

The **Son of Man** will send his **angels**,
    and they will **collect** out of his kingdom
    all who cause others to **sin** and all **evildoers**.
They will **throw** them into the fiery furnace,
    where there will be **wailing** and **grinding** of teeth.
Then the **righteous** will **shine** like the sun
    in the kingdom of their **Father.**
Whoever has ears ought to **hear**."

[Shorter: Matthew 13:24–30 (see brackets)]

He loves people and gives them time and space to change their ways and follow him.

Nevertheless, he will sort people at the end of time. Those who persisted in their evil ways and caused others to sin will be sentenced to "wailing and grinding of teeth," that is, to eternal mourning and anxiety. But the children of the kingdom "will shine out like the sun." Their resurrected bodies will be transfigured, as was Jesus' human body that day on a mountain in Galilee when his face "shown like the sun" and his disciples glimpsed his divinity (Matthew 17:2).

The parables of the mustard seed and the yeast picture the small beginning of the kingdom of heaven and its invisible unstoppable growth into a realm beyond imagining. The large bush or tree and the huge batch of bread represent the kingdom at the end of days. Larger than the Church, it pervades the entire cosmos and extends beyond it. Its magnitude is inconceivable because it is a divine, not a human, venture.

The kingdom that Jesus inaugurated by his death and Resurrection belongs to the One who searches human hearts and the Spirit of the risen Christ. They manage it. They are at work in every generation, hidden within Jesus' disciples. What a privilege to be called to live in and work with the Triune God. E.N.

SEVENTEENTH SUNDAY IN ORDINARY TIME

LECTIONARY #109

READING I   1 Kings 3:5, 7–12

A reading from the first Book of Kings

The **LORD** appeared to **Solomon** in a dream at night.
God said, "**Ask** something of me and I will **give** it to you."
Solomon answered:
 "O **LORD**, **my God**, you have made **me**, your servant, king
  to succeed my father **David**;
 but I am a **mere** youth, **not** knowing at **all** how to act.
I serve you in the midst of the people whom you have **chosen**,
 a people so **vast** that it cannot be **numbered** or **counted**.
Give your servant, therefore, an **understanding heart**
 to **judge** your people and to **distinguish** right from wrong.
For **who** is able to govern this **vast** people of yours?"

The **LORD** was pleased that **Solomon** made this request.
So **God** said to him:
 "Because you have asked for this—
 not for a **long** life for yourself,
 nor for riches,
 nor for the life of your enemies,
 but for **understanding** so that you may know what is **right**—
 I do as you requested.
I give you a heart so **wise and understanding**
 that there has **never** been anyone like you up to now,
 and **after** you there will come **no one** to equal you."

Solomon = SOL-uh-muhn

Proclaim Gods' words with a kind tone in your voice.

Read Solomon's words with an expression of humbleness in your voice.

Take your time with Gods' words. Let the congregation hear how pleased God is.

Pause, then proclaim with tenderness.

READING I This reading unfolds in three parts: the Lord commands Solomon to ask for something, Solomon asks, and the Lord comments on his request. The Lord's command and the sevenfold repetition of "ask" (several of which are omitted in the translations of verse 11) focus the passage on the question: what, in God's view, should a just leader or person who exercises power over others seek?

Solomon, who recently ascended the throne of David, describes himself as "a mere youth." The Hebrew word for youth or child, *na'ar*, denotes in this context a young adult who lacks experience in a job. Solomon is new to leadership. He does not yet know "how to act," a translation of the idiom "how to go out and come in." And so, he asks for a "listening heart." This is a mind that attends closely to people and appreciates the complexity of their situation in order to discern right from wrong within it. The Lord is pleased that Solomon did not ask for what many in his position would be tempted to request: a long reign, wealth, and the permanent removal of his enemies.

READING II "Those who love God" is a designation for the people of Israel in the Old Testament (for example, Exodus 20:6; Deuteronomy 6:5; Psalm 97:10). In this passage, Paul reapplies it to their descendants and to all who believe that Jesus is God's Son. He wants to impress the baptized with the wonder that since the beginning of time God worked all things together for their advantage and continues to do so in their present circumstances.

From eternity, God knew each of them (and us) intimately and predestined them to play unique, intertwined roles in his plan

For meditation and context:

RESPONSORIAL PSALM   Psalm 119:57, 72, 76–77, 127–128, 129–130 (97a)

R. Lord, I love your commands.

I have said, O LORD, that my part
    is to keep your words.
The law of your mouth is to me more precious
    than thousands of gold and silver pieces.

Let your kindness comfort me
    according to your promise to
        your servants.
Let your compassion come to me that
    I may live,
    for your law is my delight.

For I love your commands
    more than gold, however fine.
For in all your precepts I go forward;
    every false way I hate.

Wonderful are your decrees;
    therefore I observe them.
The revelation of your words sheds light,
    giving understanding to the simple.

READING II   Romans 8:28–30

A reading from the Letter of Saint Paul to the Romans

Brothers and sisters:
We know that **all** things work for **good** for those who **love God**,
    who are **called** according to his **purpose**.
For those he foreknew he also **predestined**
    to be conformed to the **image** of his **Son**,
    so that he might be the **firstborn**
    among many brothers and sisters.
And those he predestined he **also** called;
    and those he called he **also justified**;
    and those he justified he also **glorified**.

Proclaim St. Pauls' words with energy and conviction. Take your time.

TO KEEP IN MIND

Pause after you announce where the book of the Bible the reading is taken from at the beginning of the reading. Pause again after the reading, before you proclaim the concluding statement ("The Word of the Lord" or "The Gospel of the Lord").

for the salvation of the cosmos. By predestined, Paul does not intend a divine predetermination of the fate of individuals to heaven or hell. This interest came to the fore later, during Augustine's early fifth-century AD controversy with Pelagius. Paul is saying that the communal destiny of Christians is conformity to the image of the Son, who himself displays the image of God in which every human being is created (Genesis 1:26–27).

Christians recognize their call and discover their purpose when they hear the Gospel preached. When they are baptized,

they are justified—which for Paul means declared innocent before God—and they are also glorified. They will experience the fullness of this glorification with the risen Christ and all of his other brothers and sisters at the end of time.

GOSPEL | This Gospel sets out three parables about the kingdom of heaven and a simile for a scribe instructed in its ways. The first two parables, which describe surprising and life-changing happenings, provoke thought

about the incomparable value and desirability of the kingdom.

The first parable compares the kingdom to someone who by chance finds a treasure buried in a field. Since the Promised Land was a battleground for most of its history, and in times of war people often buried their valuables but were unable to retrieve them, these remained hidden until another stumbled upon them. In this parable, the finder simply must have the treasure and takes immediate steps to acquire it: he hides it, leaves, sells all, and buys the field. He does all these things out

GOSPEL   Matthew 13:44–52

A reading from the holy Gospel according to Matthew

[**Jesus** said to his disciples:
   "The kingdom of heaven is like a **treasure** buried in a field,
   which a person **finds** and **hides** again,
   and out of joy goes and **sells all** that he has and **buys** that field.
Again, the kingdom of heaven is like a **merchant**
      searching for fine pearls.
When he finds a pearl of **great price**,
   he goes and sells **all** that he has and **buys** it.]
Again, the kingdom of heaven is like a **net thrown into the sea**,
   which collects fish of every kind.
When it is **full** they haul it **ashore**
   and sit down to put what is **good** into buckets.
What is **bad** they throw away.
Thus it will be at the **end** of the age.
The **angels** will go out and separate the **wicked**
      from the **righteous**
   and throw them into the fiery furnace,
   where there will be **wailing** and **grinding** of teeth.

"Do you understand all these things?"
They answered, "Yes."
And he replied,
   "Then every scribe who has been **instructed** in the kingdom
      of heaven
   is like the **head of a household**
   who brings from his storeroom both the **new** and the **old**."

[Shorter: Matthew 13:44–46 (see brackets)]

Pause before you begin. Jesus teaches about the kingdom of heaven in three different ways. Proclaim these examples with high energy using good eye contact and vocal expression.

This is the second way.

This is the third way.

Pause before you say this line.

---

of joy as opposed, for example, to a grudging sense of duty.

In the second parable, while carrying on business as usual, the merchant finds an extraordinary pearl of great price. He wants it so passionately that he immediately sells "all," his business and his personal assets, and buys it.

In the third parable, the kingdom is like what happens to a net that is thrown into the sea and collects fish of every kind. The details of the scene elicit in its hearers a mounting sense of dread that they could end up among the wicked. Fishermen haul the net ashore, sit down, sort what is good into baskets, and throw away the bad. Then suddenly there are angels (a feature of apocalyptic writings that deal with the end of time) who go out and separate the wicked disciples from righteous ones and throw them into the fire where there will be eternal wailing and grinding of teeth.

Jesus' question, "Do you understand all these things?" reinforces a point made in the parable of the sower (Fifteenth Sunday), namely, that disciples must ponder and study his teachings until they see how to put them into practice. He portrays his followers as evangelized scribes and likens them to heads of households who bring from their storerooms (literally their "treasure," the same Greek word used for the treasure found above) both the new and the old to nourish God's people. For Matthew, the new refers to knowledge of Jesus' life and teachings. The old refers to the Scripture of his day—the *Torah*, prophets, and writings that bear witness to all that God did for Israel. E.N.

EIGHTEENTH SUNDAY IN ORDINARY TIME

Proclaim this wonderful reading with excitement! Smile as you proclaim! This is all good news from our loving God! Don't rush. We long to hear these comforting words!

LECTIONARY #112

READING I   Isaiah 55:1–3

A reading from the Book of the Prophet Isaiah

Thus says the LORD:
All you who are **thirsty**,
    come to the water!
You who have **no money**,
    come, **receive** grain and eat;
come, without paying and **without** cost,
    drink wine and milk!
Why spend your money for what is **not** bread;
    your **wages** for what **fails to satisfy**?
Heed me, and you **shall eat** well,
    you **shall delight** in rich fare.
Come to me heedfully,
    listen, that you may have **life**.
I will **renew** with you the **everlasting covenant**,
    the benefits assured to **David**.

TO KEEP IN MIND
You can't proclaim what you don't understand. Read the Scripture passage and its commentary in *Workbook*. Then read it from your Bible, including what comes before and after it so that you understand the context.

READING I   The prophet known as Second Isaiah (Isaiah 40–55) brings comfort to God's people toward the end of their exile in Babylon (mid-sixth century BC). He reaches out especially to those who believe that because they broke the Mosaic covenant, it is now annulled and companionship with the Lord is a thing of the past (Isaiah 41:17; 58:11).

In today's reading, the prophet invites these and all people to come to the feast that the Lord prepares for them. In biblical times, meals of water, wine, milk, and rich fare injected joy into people's routines. They were not the norm, as they can be today with supermarkets providing daily fare fit for kings. The plenty and variety of the Lord's feast are a metaphor for divinely revealed teachings which the people feast on when they put them into practice. In the Lord's words: "Heed me, and you shall eat well."

Though Israel was not faithful to the covenant and lost everything, the Lord did not terminate his relationship with them. One of the inspired insights of Second Isaiah is that the covenant is everlasting and unconditional. It is like the one made with Noah in Isaiah 54:9–10 where the Lord says, "My love shall never fall away from you nor my covenant of peace be shaken." Second Isaiah saw that the continuation of the divine-human relationship would always depend, not on human fidelity but on God's steadfast love and loyalty. The "everlasting covenant" restores the benefits of the covenant with David and extends them to all the people.

READING II   In this passage, Paul asks the question: "What will

222

For meditation and context:

RESPONSORIAL PSALM   Psalm 145:8–9, 15–16, 17–18 (16)

R. The hand of the Lord feeds us; he answers all our needs.

The LORD is gracious and merciful,
    slow to anger and of great kindness.
The LORD is good to all
    and compassionate toward all his works.

The eyes of all look hopefully to you,
    and you give them their food in due season;
you open your hand
    and satisfy the desire of every living thing.

The LORD is just in all his ways
    and holy in all his works.
The LORD is near to all who call upon him,
    to all who call upon him in truth.

READING II   Romans 8:35, 37–39

A reading from the Letter of Saint Paul to the Romans

Brothers and sisters:
What will **separate** us from the **love of Christ**?
Will anguish, or distress, or persecution, or famine,
    or nakedness, or peril, or the sword?
No, in all these things we **conquer overwhelmingly**
    through him who **loved** us.
For I am **convinced** that neither death, nor life,
    nor angels, nor principalities,
    nor present things, nor future things,
    nor powers, nor height, nor depth,
    nor any other creature will be able to **separate** us
    from the **love of God in Christ Jesus our Lord.**

Say this line slowly with compassion.

Pause before you read the next question and take your time with each word in the line.

Transition to a tone of firm conviction. It is important that you use good eye contact as you proclaim.

---

separate us from the love of Christ?" His short answer is "nothing," but he elaborates to provide time for this certainty to settle in his readers' consciousness. The first set of trials that he lists impact a person's physical existence. It seems like he is challenging the baptized to identify their biggest worry. And when they do so he says, "No, neither can that ever get between you and Christ."

The second list conveys Paul's personal conviction that neither can the unseen forces in the cosmos separate Christians from Christ. In this list Paul uses

merisms, figures of speech that pair opposites to convey a totality and include all the range of stages or things that fall between them. For example, "neither life nor death" comprises all that happens between these events. "Nor height nor depth," probably a kind of astronomical measurement during Paul's time, encompasses everything in the cosmos.

In the middle of these lists, Paul reminds Christians that in all sufferings they are triumphing gloriously. In Christ, they are conquering completely the forces that appear to be crushing them. They

must choose to believe that just as Jesus was conquering death as he hung naked and suffering on the cross, so are they in him. He is alive and nothing visible or invisible, known or that will be identified in the future, can separate them from God's love in him.

GOSPEL   In the passage preceding this Gospel, Matthew relates the death of John the Baptist, the great prophet and the first person to recognize Jesus. Forces beyond John's control lead to his abrupt demise. Herod, whose

---

GOSPEL   Matthew 14:13–21

A reading from the holy Gospel according to Matthew

When **Jesus** heard of the death of **John the Baptist**,
    he withdrew in a boat to a **deserted** place by himself.
The crowds **heard** of this and **followed** him on foot from
        their towns.
When he disembarked and saw the vast crowd,
    his heart **was moved** with pity for them, and he **cured**
        their sick.
When it was evening, the disciples approached him and said,
    "This is a deserted place and it is already late;
    dismiss the crowds so that they can go to the villages
    and buy food for themselves."
Jesus said to them, "There is **no need** for them to go away;
    give them some food **yourselves**."
But they said to him,
    "Five loaves and two fish are all we have here."
Then he said, "Bring them here to me,"
    and he ordered the crowds to **sit** down on the grass.
Taking the five loaves and the two fish, and looking up
        to heaven,
    he said the **blessing**, **broke** the loaves,
    and **gave** them to the disciples,
    who in turn gave them to the crowds.
They **all** ate and were **satisfied**,
    and they picked up the fragments left over—
    twelve wicker baskets full.
Those who ate were about five thousand men,
    not counting women and children.

Start proclaiming in an informative tone.

Read with more energy in your voice.

Use vocal expression as you read the conversation between Jesus and the disciples.

In a prayerful tone.

Transition to an informative tone.

---

lust is elicited by a young woman's provocative dance at his birthday feast, swears a rash oath that results in John's beheading in a filthy, obscure dungeon. What an ignoble end for one who so boldly fulfilled the mission that God gave him. Is it any wonder that when Jesus hears of it, he goes off alone to pray?

But the Sea of Galilee is so small that many notice where a boat carrying Jesus lands and bring their sick to him. He turns his thoughts from John to their suffering and, moved with compassion in the depths of his being, he heals them.

His empathy extends to their need for nourishment at the end of the day. When his disciples suggest that Jesus send the crowds off to find food, he tells them, "give them some food yourselves." He means, it seems, the loaves and fish that they brought for their evening meal. They bring these to Jesus who takes them, looks up to heaven, blesses them, and breaks the bread. His actions, which are repeated in the account of his last meal with the disciples, probably reflect a rubric from the Eucharistic meal that Matthew's community celebrated.

Jesus' simple supper that nourishes roughly ten thousand people stands in stark contrast to Herod's feast that ended with the death of John. The superabundance of food and Matthew's portrayal of Jesus taking care of others through his disciples present Jesus as the Lord, who in earlier times provided food for those in need through Moses, Elijah, and Elisha. In other words, the evangelist shows that Jesus is divine. E.N.

NINETEENTH SUNDAY IN ORDINARY TIME

LECTIONARY #115

READING I   1 Kings 19:9a, 11–13a

A reading from the first Book of Kings

At the mountain of **God**, **Horeb**,
   Elijah came to a cave where he took shelter.
Then the LORD said to him,
   "**Go outside** and stand on the mountain before the LORD;
   the LORD will be passing by."
A strong and heavy **wind** was rending the mountains
   and **crushing** rocks before the LORD—
   but the LORD was not in the wind.
After the wind there was an **earthquake**—
   but the LORD was not in the earthquake.
After the earthquake there was **fire**—
   but the LORD was not in the fire.
After the fire there was a **tiny whispering sound.**
When he heard this,
   Elijah hid his face in his cloak
   and **went and stood** at the entrance of the cave.

(margin notes)

Horeb = HOHR-eb
Elijah = ee-LĪ-juh
Proclaim with good volume and eye contact.

Pause before you read the Lord's words. Use an informative tone in your voice.

Keep up the energy in your voice as you proclaim about the wind, earthquake, and fire.

Pause and say this line slowly.

TO KEEP IN MIND
Pay attention to the pace of your reading. Varying the pace gives listeners clues to the meaning of the text. The most common problem for proclaimers new to the ministry is going too fast to be understood.

READING I Preceding this passage, Elijah fled from Queen Jezebel, who swore to kill him after he killed her four hundred prophets of Baal (1 Kings 18:21—19:9). He escapes her grasp but feels that he is failing his prophetic mission and says to the Lord, "Enough. Take my life." Instead, the Lord sends an angel to strengthen him for a forty-day and forty-night walk to Mount Horeb (called Mount Sinai in some traditions). Now, having taken shelter there in a cave he is waiting for the Lord to show himself as promised.

Suddenly a wind so strong that it splits the mountains and crushes rocks sweeps past. Then an earthquake occurs, followed by fire. The Lord is in none of these typical displays of divine majesty. This time his presence is subtle and, for Elijah, more awesome. When he realizes that the Almighty comes to him in a tiny whispering sound, he draws his mantle over his face.

READING II Paul expresses his deep sorrow that for the most part his people, literally in Greek, his "brothers" according to the flesh, did not accept Jesus as the Messiah. His choice of the term *brothers*, which he normally reserves for his new kin in Christ, reveals the depths of his anguish.

He does not call his people "Jews," which was the ethnic designation used by foreigners, but "Israelites" to recall their privileged position in salvation history. They are the people whom the Lord chose for his own, the "son" brought out of bondage from Egypt. They saw the "Glory of the Lord," i.e., the manifestation of his presence and power, at the Red Sea, and again when the Lord provided food for them in

For meditation and context:

RESPONSORIAL PSALM   Psalm 85:9, 10, 11–12, 13–14 (8)

R. Lord, let us see your kindness, and grant us your salvation.

I will hear what God proclaims;
  the LORD—for he proclaims peace.
Near indeed is his salvation to those who
    fear him,
  glory dwelling in our land.

Kindness and truth shall meet;
  justice and peace shall kiss.
Truth shall spring out of the earth,
  and justice shall look down from heaven.

The LORD himself will give his benefits;
  our land shall yield its increase.
Justice shall walk before him,
  and prepare the way of his steps.

READING II   Romans 9:1–5

A reading from the Letter of Saint Paul to the Romans

Proclaim Paul's words with a tone of sincerity and truth. Take your time.

Brothers and sisters:
I speak the truth in **Christ**, I do not lie;
  my **conscience joins** with the **Holy Spirit** in bearing
    me witness
  that I have great **sorrow** and constant **anguish** in my heart.
For I could wish that **I** myself were **accursed** and cut off
    from Christ
  for the sake of my own people,
  my kindred according to the flesh.
They are **Israelites**;

Say this line boldly.

Start slowly and continue to build the intensity in your voice until you end with ". . . is the Christ."

  theirs the adoption, the glory, the covenants,
  the **giving** of the law, the **worship**, and the **promises**;
  theirs the patriarchs, and from them,
  according to the flesh, is the **Christ**,

Proclaim with humble gratitude.

  who is over **all**, **God blessed forever. Amen.**

---

the wilderness. Later the Lord's Glory took up residence in the temple in Jerusalem. When the Babylonians destroyed that city, Ezekiel's chariot visions revealed that the Glory left Jerusalem to be with Israel in exile, and then fifty years later it led them back through another wilderness back to the land where it again settled in the temple (Ezekiel 1; 43:1–7a).

With the Mosaic covenant came the gift of the Law, whose goal was to transform the Israelites into a people who manifests God to the world. In other words, they were to be a theophany. The divine plan

was that in them, the Gentiles would see God and come to worship in Jerusalem. Through other covenants that the Lord made with Israel, they discovered that divine love is unconditional. For Paul, the last and clearest sign of God's favor is the Messiah, the Christ, who through the Israelites came into the cosmos.

Paul will conclude that all these privileges are still in force for Israel. But he also teaches that those who believe in Christ can manifest God's glory in new and powerful ways.

GOSPEL In the evening, after feeding the crowds, Jesus made his disciples get in a boat and set sail for the other side of the lake. While he returns to the prayer and solitude that he sought before this miracle, they struggle far into the night, trying to reach land. They are battling a contrary wind when they see Jesus walking toward them on the sea. Thinking that he is "a ghost," they cry out in terror.

In this theophany, God is manifested not in the strong wind, but in Jesus. The evangelist discloses his divinity by portraying him saying and doing things that God

GOSPEL   Matthew 14:22–33

A reading from the holy Gospel according to Matthew

Proclaim with good volume and with an
informative tone.

After he had fed the people, **Jesus** made the disciples get
    into a boat
  and precede him to the other side,
  while he dismissed the crowds.
After doing so, **he** went up on the mountain by **himself** to **pray**.
When it was **evening** he was there **alone**.
Meanwhile the boat, already a few miles offshore,
  was being **tossed** about by the waves, for the **wind** was
    against it.
During the fourth watch of the night,
  he came toward them **walking** on the sea.

Keep up the energy in your voice as you read
the story.

When the disciples saw him walking on the sea they
  were **terrified**.
"It is a ghost, " they said, and they cried out in **fear**.
At once **Jesus** spoke to them, "**Take courage**, it is **I**; do not
  be **afraid**."

Read Jesus' words with expression so that
the congregation can easily visualize Peter's
moment of doubt.

Peter said to him in reply,
  "**Lord**, if it **is** you, command me to **come** to you on the water."
He said, "**Come**."
Peter got out of the boat and **began** to walk on the water
  toward Jesus.
But when he saw how **strong** the wind was he became
  frightened;
  and, beginning to **sink**, he cried out, "**Lord, save me!**"
Immediately **Jesus** stretched out his hand and caught Peter,
  and said to him, "O you of little faith, why did you **doubt**?"
After they got **into** the boat, the wind **died** down.
Those who were in the boat did him homage, saying,
  "**Truly**, you are the **Son of God**."

Pause.

does in the Old Testament. First, he tells the disciples to take courage and not to become afraid. His "it is I" or "I am" is spoken by the Lord, for example, in Second Isaiah when he promises Israel to be with them in exile and on the journey back to the land (Isaiah 43:10, 13; 46:4; 48:12; 52:6). Also, like the Creator in Job 9:8 and Psalm 77:20, Jesus makes his way upon the waves of the sea.

In response to Jesus' invitation, Peter steps down from the boat and walks on the waves—until he turns his attention from Jesus to the strength of the wind. It fright-ens him, and he begins to sink. Like the sailors who cry out in distress to the Lord in Psalm 107:23–32, Peter cries out to Jesus. His scream also echoes those of the psalmist in Psalm 69:2, "Save me, God, for the waters have reached my neck," and in Psalm 144:7, "Reach out your hand from on high; deliver me from the many waters." At Peter's cry, Jesus "stretched out his hand" and caught him, another stroke of Matthew's brush that depicts him as God (see also Matthew 12:13).

Holding on to Peter, Jesus asks "You of little faith, why did you doubt?" He asks us the same question. Why do we give up on projects that his Spirit inspires us to take on, projects whose goal is to manifest him in the milieu that we occupy? Why do we begin to "sink"? Do we fear the people we might encounter if we follow through? Or the disruptive forces that our actions could bring into our cherished routines? Do we truly believe that Jesus, the Son of God, is with us? E.N.

THE ASSUMPTION OF THE BLESSED VIRGIN MARY: VIGIL

LECTIONARY #621

READING I 1 Chronicles 15:3–4, 15–16; 16:1–2

A reading from the first Book of Chronicles

David assembled **all** Israel in Jerusalem to **bring** the **ark**
of the LORD
to the place that he had prepared for it.
David also **called** together the sons of **Aaron** and the **Levites**.

The **Levites** bore the **ark of God** on their shoulders with poles,
as **Moses** had ordained according to the word of the LORD.

David commanded the chiefs of the **Levites**
to **appoint** their kinsmen as **chanters**,
to play on musical instruments, harps, lyres, and cymbals,
to make a loud sound of **rejoicing**.

They brought in the ark of **God** and set it within the tent
which **David** had pitched for it.
Then they offered up **burnt offerings** and **peace offerings** to **God**.
When **David** had finished offering up the burnt offerings and
peace offerings,
he **blessed** the people in the name of the LORD.

Chronicles = KRAH-nih-k*ls

Project your voice throughout this reading.
Take your time using good eye contact.
Articulate each word.

Aaron = AYR-uhn
Levites = LEE-vīts

Smile as you proclaim. This is a time of
rejoicing.

Lyres = līrz
cymbals = SIM-buhlz

Proclaim with a tone of reverence.

TO KEEP IN MIND
Read the Scripture passage and its
commentary in Workbook. Then
read it from your Bible, including
what comes before and after it, so
that you understand the context.

READING I In the Old Testament, the
ark of the covenant is the
sacred object that reminds the Israelites of
God's faithful presence with their ancestors. It accompanied the people on their
journey through the wilderness and parted
the waters of the Jordan River so that they
could enter the Promised Land. It goes with
them into the battle for Jericho and the
Lord gives that city into their hands.

When David makes Jerusalem his capital, he decides to move the ark there. His
first attempt comes to a halt when one of
his men touches the ark to steady it

because the oxcart bearing it is tipping.
That man died on the spot, and David was
so frightened of the Lord that he left the
ark nearby in the hill country of Judah
(2 Samuel 6:1–10).

Today's reading recounts its final
transferal in joyful procession to Jerusalem.
All the attention to liturgical detail displays
reverence for the ark as the symbol of
God's fidelity to Israel. The Levites carry it
as Moses instructed, and provide the musical accompaniment and chanting. Once the
ark is in the tent, where it will remain until

Solomon builds the temple, David offers
sacrifices and blesses the people.

READING II Paul stresses in 1 Corinthians 15 that Jesus' Resurrection from the dead is the basis of
Christians' hope for their own resurrection
to eternal life. His hearers seem dubious.
They can't picture a resurrected life, and
Paul can't describe it in detail. He does
insist that a physical body, "flesh and
blood," cannot inherit the kingdom of God.
It will be changed after death, "in the blink
of an eye," into a glorified imperishable

For meditation and context:

RESPONSORIAL PSALM   Psalm 132:6–7, 9–10, 13–14 (8)

R. Lord, go up to the place of your rest, you and the ark of your holiness.

Behold, we heard of it in Ephrathah;
    we found it in the fields of Jaar.
Let us enter into his dwelling,
    let us worship at his footstool.

May your priests be clothed with justice;
    let your faithful ones shout merrily for joy.
For the sake of David your servant,
    reject not the plea of your anointed.

For the Lord has chosen Zion;
    he prefers her for his dwelling.
"Zion is my resting place forever;
    in her will I dwell, for I prefer her."

READING II   1 Corinthians 15:54b–57

A reading from the first Letter of Saint Paul to the Corinthians

Brothers and sisters:
When that which is **mortal** clothes itself with **immortality**,
    then the word that is written shall come about:

> *Death is swallowed up in victory.*
> *Where, O death, is your victory?*
> *Where, O death, is your sting?*

The sting of death is **sin**,
    and the **power** of sin is the **law**.
But **thanks** be to **God** who gives us the **victory**
    through our **Lord Jesus Christ**.

Corinthians = kohr-IN-thee-uhnz

Proclaim St. Paul's letter with conviction and purpose. Speak with good volume, don't rush.

Pause.

Use good eye contact.

---

body. Earlier, he compared this transformation of the mortal, corruptible body to a seed buried in the earth that grows into the specific plant that God destines it to be.

Paul did not meet Jesus during his earthly ministry. He knew only the risen Christ who spoke with him that day on the road to Damascus. Before this meeting, he refused to entertain the possibility that Jesus was raised from the dead. After it, he is convinced not only that Christ lives "out there somewhere" but that Christ lives in him. Filled with this conviction, he taunts death, "Where, O death, is your victory?"

Death seemed to conquer Jesus when he died on the cross and was laid in the tomb. But, as John J. Kilgallen, sj, writes, death is only victorious if it "really keeps one dead." He asks, "What kind of a victory is it if, after one dies, one returns to life?"

Paul, certain that death did not keep Jesus dead, continues his taunt, "Where, O death, is your sting?" In his letters, the sting of death is sin that infects people. It is like a debilitating poison that flows into the body from the bite of an insect or scorpion. Sin easily weakens people who fear death, but it

is far less effective in those who believe that Christ conquered this age-old human foe.

GOSPEL One day while Jesus is teaching, a woman in the crowd cries out and declares his mother blessed. Jesus uses the woman's tribute as an opportunity to repeat one of his key teachings about life in the Kingdom of God, namely, that disciples who hear and live by the Word of God are blessed. The Greek word used in both blessings, *makarios*, recognizes those who live in a state of righteousness before God and who experience

GOSPEL   Luke 11:27–28

A reading from the holy Gospel according to Luke

While **Jesus** was speaking,
  a woman from the crowd called out and said to him,
  "Blessed is the womb that carried you
  and the breasts at which you nursed."
He replied,
  "**Rather**, **blessed** are those
  who **hear** the word of **God** and **observe it**."

Blessed = BLES-uhd

Pause and then proclaim the woman's statement with energy.

Say this line to the congregation.

the profound happiness that comes from sharing in divine life.

For Luke, both blessings apply to Mary. The one spoken by the woman in the crowd echoes Elizabeth's inspired greeting to Mary in Luke 1:42: "Most blessed are you among women and blessed is the fruit of your womb." The one spoken by Jesus about those who hear and keep the Word of God are applied to Mary in two other passages. In Luke 1:38, she calls herself the servant of the Lord and then utters her famous *fiat*: "May it be done to me according to your word." And in Luke 1:45,

Elizabeth praises Mary's faith in God saying, "Blessed are you who believed that what was spoken to you by the Lord would be fulfilled."

Behind Mary's fiat is her belief that God is trustworthy and capable of bringing divine promises to fulfillment. She is so confident that, without understanding what could be involved in being the mother of the Son of God, and without being given a detailed plan to follow, she submits to God's will for her. For Luke, she is the first of Jesus' disciples and the model for all who follow him in every age.

She is also the first to enjoy life in the world to come. Today the Church celebrates that after the completion of her mission on earth, God assumed her body and soul into heavenly glory. Her assumption gives hope to all who imitate her faith and her *fiat*, saying, "May it happen to me as God wills, this day and for all eternity." E.N.

THE ASSUMPTION OF THE BLESSED VIRGIN MARY: DAY

Rehearse this reading for timing, volume, and eye contact. You can make this a powerful story.

Take your time while proclaiming. Use both facial and vocal expression. This will help the assembly visualize the woman, her son, and the dragon.

LECTIONARY #622

READING I   Revelation 11:19a; 12:1–6a, 10ab

A reading from the Book of Revelation

God's temple in heaven was **opened**,
    and the **ark** of his covenant could be **seen** in the temple.

A **great sign** appeared in the sky, a **woman** clothed with the sun,
    with the **moon** under her feet,
    and on her head a **crown** of twelve **stars**.
She was **with child** and wailed aloud in pain as she **labored** to
        give birth.
Then **another** sign appeared in the sky;
    it was a huge **red dragon**, with **seven** heads and **ten** horns,
    and on its heads were **seven** diadems.
Its tail swept away a third of the **stars** in the sky
    and **hurled** them down to the earth.
Then the dragon **stood** before the woman about to give birth,
    to **devour** her child when she gave birth.
She gave birth to a **son**, a **male** child,
    destined to rule **all** the nations with an iron **rod**.
Her child was **caught up to God** and his **throne**.
The woman herself **fled** into the desert
    where she had a place prepared by **God**. »

TO KEEP IN MIND
As you prepare your proclamation, make choices about what emotions need to be expressed. Some choices are evident from the text, but some are harder to discern. Understanding the context of the Scripture passage will help you decide.

READING I   The first verse of this reading concludes the account of the seventh trumpet, whose blowing announces that the kingdom of the world now belongs to God and to his Messiah, or in Greek, his Christ (Revelation 11:15–19). A series of cosmic phenomena—flashes of lightning, heavenly noises, thunder, an earthquake, and huge hail—mark the opening of God's temple in heaven and a glimpse of the ark of the covenant.

Chapter 12 begins a new cycle of visions, the first of which is the encounter between the woman and the dragon in the sky. This scene condenses the preceding millennia of salvation history and focuses on its turning point, the death and Resurrection of God's Christ. Since symbols can have multiple meanings even within the same biblical passage, those of the woman and the dragon allow for various interpretations.

For the writer of Revelation, the woman with the moon under her feet, clothed with the sun and wearing a crown of twelve stars probably represents the people of Israel from whom the Messiah came. The sun, moon, and stars appear earlier in salvation history in Joseph's dream in Genesis 37:9–11. There his father Jacob / Israel, who is presented as the father of the twelve tribes of Israel, interprets the sun as himself, the moon as Joseph's mother, and the stars as Joseph's brothers. Also, other Old Testament passages metaphorically describe the people of Israel as a woman about to give birth (Isaiah 26:17; 66:7–8). In the Catholic tradition, the woman clothed with the sun is identified with the Israelite Mary who bore the Messiah.

As the woman labors to give birth, the second sign, a huge red dragon with seven

Then I heard a **loud** voice in heaven say:
> "**Now** have **salvation and power** come,
>   and the Kingdom of our **God**
>   and the **authority** of his **Anointed One**."

Pause and say with a tone of authority.

For meditation and context:

RESPONSORIAL PSALM   Psalm 45:10, 11, 12, 16 (10bc)

R. The queen stands at your right hand, arrayed in gold.

The queen takes her place at your right hand
    in gold of Ophir.

Hear, O daughter, and see; turn your ear,
    forget your people and your father's house.

So shall the king desire your beauty;
    for he is your lord.

They are borne in with gladness and joy;
    they enter the palace of the king.

READING II   1 Corinthians 15:20–27

Corinthians = kohr-IN-thee-uhnz

A reading from the first Letter of Saint Paul to the Corinthians

Proclaim St. Paul's letter with energy and enthusiasm.

Brothers and sisters:
Christ has been raised from the dead,
    the firstfruits of those who have fallen asleep.
For since **death** came **through** man,
    the **resurrection** of the dead came **also** through man.
For just as in **Adam** all die,
    so too in **Christ** shall **all** be brought to **life**,
    but each one in proper order:
Christ the firstfruits;

Pause before you read the order. Use good eye contact.

    then, at his coming, those **who belong** to Christ;
    then comes the **end**,
    when he hands over the **Kingdom to his God and Father,**
    when he has **destroyed** every **sovereignty**
    and every **authority and power**.
For he must **reign** until he has put all his enemies **under his feet**.

Take your time proclaiming the last sentence.

The **last** enemy to be **destroyed** is **death**,
    for "he subjected everything under his feet."

---

crowned heads and ten horns appears in the sky. In the book of Revelation, red is the color of death in Revelation and here underscores the dragon's intent to kill the child. Its seven crowns probably represent the power of the Roman Empire during the times of Jesus and of the author of Revelation. In several biblical passages, monsters like the dragon represent cosmic chaos or powers that work against the Creator (see for example Psalm 74:13–14 and Isaiah 27:1). In this vision, the dragon represents the forces of evil that try to disrupt God's plan by preventing the

Incarnation of the Son. Though its powerful snaky tail sweeps a third of the stars from heaven to earth, the dragon fails to capture the child. Symbolically, the child is Jesus—not being born in Bethlehem but rather "being born," being "caught up to God and his throne," when he dies on the cross.

After giving birth, the woman flees into the wilderness where God prepared a place for her. At this point in the vision and in the Catholic tradition, she represents Christians who are under attack by the dragon who was thrown down to earth, where it exercises limited power—its death

throes—until Jesus returns at the end of time (Revelation 12:7–18). In the last verse, voices in heaven celebrate Christ's irreversible victory, assuring Christians that their salvation is secured, and the reign of God has begun.

READING II   Like the first reading, this one also focuses on the place of Jesus' death and Resurrection in God's plan for the salvation of the cosmos. Paul lays out its certain order. Jesus is the first fruits and the baptized, those "who belong to Christ," are the rest of the crop.

GOSPEL   Luke 1:39–56

As you proclaim the story of Mary and Elizabeth, use good eye contact and volume.

Judah = JOO-duh
Zechariah = zek-uh-RĪ-uh

Blessed = BLES-uhd
blessed = BLESD

Pause before you begin. Read Elizabeth's words with a tone of humbleness and gratefulness.

A reading from the holy Gospel according to Luke

Mary set out
    and traveled to the hill country in haste
    to a town of **Judah**,
    where she entered the house of **Zechariah**
    and greeted **Elizabeth**.
When Elizabeth heard Mary's greeting,
    the infant **leaped** in her womb,
    and Elizabeth, filled with the **Holy Spirit**,
    cried out in a loud voice and said,
    "**Blessed** are you among women,
    and blessed is the fruit of your womb.
And how does this happen to me,
    that the mother of my **Lord** should **come** to me?
For at the moment the sound of your greeting reached my ears,
    the infant in my womb leaped for **joy**.
Blessed are you who **believed**
    that what was spoken to you by the **Lord**
    would be fulfilled."

They will be raised from the dead when he comes back to earth, the event that is called in Greek the "Parousia" and that is often referred to as the "Second Coming." Upon his return, Christ will destroy all the powers and dominions who continued to challenge his victory, and then he will hand everything over to the Father.

GOSPEL After hearing of Elizabeth's pregnancy from the angel Gabriel, Mary hastens to go and help her. When Elizabeth hears her greeting, the child John leaps in her womb. Here the evangelist employs a "child in the womb" type scene, a literary technique used to foreshadow the roles or place of people in salvation history. For example, the fighting of Esau and Jacob in Rachel's womb depicts the hostile relationship that develops between the nations they represent, Edom and Israel respectively. And the Lord forms Jeremiah in the womb to be the fearless prophet who would announce the destruction of Jerusalem and Judah by the Babylonians. John's leaping in Mary's womb reveals that he will be the prophet who, filled with the Holy Spirit, first recognizes Jesus and points him out to others (Luke 1:15).

Elizabeth too is filled with the Spirit and cries out in a loud voice, blessing Mary and her child. The Greek for "blessed," *eulogemene*, expresses thanks to God for gifts given and promises kept. Elizabeth's words echo those of Deuteronomy 28:2, 4, which promise the blessing of fruit of the womb to those who obey the Lord. A different Greek word, *makaria*, which appears in the beatitudes, conveys Elizabeth's last blessing: "Blessed are you who believed . . . ." *Makaria* recognizes a

And **Mary** said:

"My soul proclaims the **greatness** of the **Lord;**
  my spirit **rejoices** in **God my Savior**
  for he has with favor on his lowly servant.
From this day **all** generations will call me **blessed:**
  the **Almighty** has done **great** things for me
  and **holy** is his **Name.**
  He has **mercy** on those who **fear** him
  in every generation.
He has shown the **strength** of his arm,
  and has **scattered** the **proud** in their **conceit.**
He has cast down the **mighty** from their thrones,
  and has **lifted up** the **lowly.**
He has **filled** the **hungry** with good things,
  and the **rich** he has sent away **empty.**
He has come to the **help** of his servant **Israel**
  for he has remembered his promise of **mercy,**
  the promise he made to our fathers,
  to **Abraham** and his children **for ever.**"

Mary remained with her about three months
  and then returned to her home.

Proclaim Mary's words with energy, using a tone of rejoicing. Focus on what Mary is telling us about God. This is important. Articulate. Take your time proclaiming.

Pause.

---

state of righteousness before God that is accompanied by the profound happiness that comes from sharing in divine life. Mary experiences this joy because she believes the Lord's word to her.

Her canticle celebrates not only the great work that God is beginning within her, but how God works throughout salvation history within people in every age who fear or recognize his sovereignty. The phrase "holy is his Name" conveys the uniqueness and unpredictability of divine methods, which usually reverse human expectations.

The examples given illustrate how differently God sees and deals with the proud and the lowly than the world does. He casts down the self-important, arrogant, and apparently mighty from their thrones, shattering their illusions of power. The rich, who are content with the passing pleasures that accumulated wealth can provide, he sends away empty. In contrast, God lifts the lowly and pours out on them divine gifts which are more precious and lasting than anything humans can attain for themselves.

Finally, the canticle presents the conception of Jesus in Mary's womb as God's remembering the ancient promise made to Abraham that he would come to the help of Israel. In the OT, the Hebrew word used frequently for "help" denotes the kind of assistance that only God can give. The canticle interprets this help as the Son who will come into the world through Mary, a lowly, faithful woman. E.N.

TWENTIETH SUNDAY IN ORDINARY TIME

LECTIONARY #118

READING I   Isaiah 56:1, 6–7

A reading from the Book of the Prophet Isaiah

Thus says the LORD:
Observe what is **right**, do what is **just**;
    for my **salvation** is about to **come**,
    my **justice**, about to be **revealed**.

The **foreigners** who join themselves to the LORD,
    ministering to him,
loving the name of the LORD,
    and becoming his **servants**—
all who keep the **sabbath** free from profanation
    and hold to **my covenant**,
them **I** will **bring** to my holy mountain
    and make **joyful** in my house of prayer;
their burnt offerings and sacrifices
    will be **acceptable** on my altar,
for **my house** shall be **called**
    a **house of prayer** for **all** peoples.

Isaiah = ī-ZAY-uh

Pause, then proclaim with a tone of authority.

Articulate the words and take your time.

profanation = prah-fuh-NAY-shuhn

READING I   In each of today's readings, outsiders play a role in the revelation of both God's love for all peoples and his desire to live in relationship with them. This reading is from chapters 56–66 of the Isaiah scroll, a collection of oracles addressed to the Israelites after they return to the land from exile in Babylon. Since conquerors mixed subjugated peoples to ensure control and discourage rebellion, God's people find themselves living closely with foreigners. When some of these ask to join their religion, the prophet welcomes them, a decision that actualizes the teach-ing of his predecessor, First Isaiah, that the Lord reigns over all nations.

Those who would be God's people must shape their life by the covenant. They must act justly, i.e., they must always do the right thing and so prepare them-selves for the justice or deliverance of the Lord that will soon be revealed. They must minister to the Lord, a phrase that usually denotes liturgical service or worship. The requirement to keep the Sabbath free from profanation is more specific than the pre-ceding ones. This practice of living differ-ently on the seventh day arose during the exile when, having lost their land and living among non-Jews, Israel also began to lose their unique identity as God's people.

The seven repetitions of "my" sprin-kled through this passage highlight what the Lord provides for those who serve him. This bounty includes my salvation, my jus-tice, my covenant, my holy mountain, my house of prayer (twice), and my altar. "My holy mountain" is Jerusalem and "my house" is the temple there. The Lord's mountain is holy or different from other places because on it all races find a home. Likewise, the temple is "a house of prayer

For meditation and context:

RESPONSORIAL PSALM   Psalm 67:2–3, 5, 6, 8 (4)

R. O God, let all the nations praise you!

May God have pity on us and bless us;
   may he let his face shine upon us.
So may your way be known upon earth;
   among all nations, your salvation.

May the nations be glad and exult
   because you rule the peoples in equity;
   the nations on the earth you guide.

May the peoples praise you, O God;
   may all the peoples praise you!
May God bless us,
   and may all the ends of the earth fear him!

READING II   Romans 11:13–15, 29–32

A reading from the Letter of Saint Paul to the Romans

Proclaim St. Pauls' words with a tone of compassion.

Brothers and sisters:
I am speaking to **you Gentiles**.
Inasmuch as **I** am the **apostle** to the **Gentiles**,
   I **glory** in my ministry in order to make my race **jealous**
   and thus **save** some of them.
For if their **rejection** is the **reconciliation** of the world,
   what will their **acceptance** be but **life** from the **dead?**

irrevocable = ir-REV-uh-kuh-b*l
Keep up the energy of St. Paul's words by using good volume and eye contact.

For the **gifts** and **the call of God** are **irrevocable**.
Just as you once **disobeyed God**
   but have now **received mercy** because of their disobedience,
   so they have **now** disobeyed in order that,
   by virtue of the **mercy** shown to you,
   they too may **now** receive mercy.
For **God** delivered **all** to disobedience,
   that he might have **mercy** upon **all**.

Pause before you say this last line and then proclaim slowly.

---

for all peoples," a joyful dwelling where believers celebrate and deepen the relationship they have with the Lord and with each other.

READING II Paul writes to Gentile Christians who live roughly five hundred years after the Jews and Gentiles addressed in the first reading. In this section of his letter he explains that, since Israel rejected God's messiah or Christ, the promises made to them are extended to all. Paul suggests that God

reaches out to the Gentiles to make Israel jealous in the hope of bringing them back.

All the promises that God made to the Jews remain in effect because divine charisms and grace are "irrevocable." The Greek, which can also be translated as "not to be regretted," conveys that, unlike humans, God does not rue granting favors when their recipients do not appreciate such benevolence and continue to go their own way. On the contrary, the disobedience of Gentiles and Jews provides occasions for God to reveal the infinite range and inclusiveness of divine mercy.

GOSPEL In this Gospel, another Gentile, a Canaanite woman whose daughter is tormented by a demon, comes looking for Jesus. The tag "Canaanite" evokes the people who inhabited the land when Israel came on the scene and also raises the issue of the place of Gentile converts in Matthew's mostly Jewish Christian community. The woman's thrice-repeated address of Jesus as "Lord" demonstrates her faith in him. The words of her initial plea, "Have pity or mercy on me, Lord" (in Greek ""eleēson, Kyrie") echo in the penitential rite of the Mass.

Tyre= tīr
Sidon = SĪ-duhn
Canaanite = KAY-nuh-nīt

In proclaiming the story of Jesus and the Canaanite woman, use good eye contact and vocal expression.

Timing is important. Pause before you read the parts of dialogue between Jesus and the disciples and Jesus and the woman.

Pause before proclaiming the last line.

GOSPEL   Matthew 15:21–28

A reading from the holy Gospel according to Matthew

At that time, **Jesus** withdrew to the region of **Tyre** and **Sidon**.
And behold, a **Canaanite** woman of that district came
    and called out,
  "Have pity on me, **Lord**, Son of David!
My daughter is **tormented** by a demon."
But **Jesus** did not say a word in answer to her.
Jesus' disciples came and asked him,
  "Send her away, for she keeps calling out after us."
He said in reply,
  "I was sent only to the lost sheep of the house of **Israel**."
But the woman came and did **Jesus** homage, saying,
    "**Lord, help me.**"
He said in reply,
  "It is **not** right to take the food of the **children**
  and **throw** it to the dogs."
She said, "**Please**, **Lord,** for even the dogs eat the scraps
  that fall from the table of their masters."
Then **Jesus** said to her in reply,
  "**O** woman, **great** is your **faith!**
Let it be done for you as you wish."
And the woman's daughter was **healed** from that hour.

Neither Jesus nor the disciples welcome the woman, perhaps reflecting the hesitation of Matthew's community to accept Gentiles. Initially, Jesus says nothing to her. As she keeps calling out to him, the disciples ask if they should send her away. Jesus replies that he is sent only to the lost sheep of Israel. Given the rest of the passage, it seems that he is not sure what to do and is "thinking out loud." Earlier in Matthew 10, when he sent out the first disciples, he sent them only to the lost sheep of Israel and told them not to enter pagan territory—like Tyre and Sidon, where we find him in this Gospel! The Gentile mother's faith in Jesus seems to raise questions in his mind about the extent of his mission.

On her own mission, the woman moves closer and does him homage, saying, "Lord (*Kyrie*), help me." Jesus seems uneasy about spending his time and energy on this outsider. But finally, the woman's challenge to him that even dogs eat scraps from table of their lords (Greek *kyrioi*), sways Jesus. Her unwavering faith moves him to do *her* will. His accession to her pleas, "Let it be done for you as *you* wish," echoes both the clause "your will be done" that he gives in the Our Father (Matthew 6:10) and his own prayer to the Father the night before his passion in the garden of Gethsemane (Matthew 26:42). Earlier he addressed the same words to the Gentile centurion who asked him to heal his servant (Matthew 8:13). In both miracles, the faith of outsiders moves Jesus to include them in his mission. E.N.

AUGUST 23, 2020

TWENTY-FIRST SUNDAY IN ORDINARY TIME

LECTIONARY #121

READING I   Isaiah 22:19–23

A reading from the Book of the Prophet Isaiah

Thus says the LORD to **Shebna**, master of the palace:
"**I** will **thrust** you from your office
　　and pull you **down** from your station.
On that day **I** will summon my servant
　　Eliakim, son of **Hilkiah;**
I will **clothe** him with your robe,
　　and **gird** him with your **sash,**
　　and **give** over to him your **authority.**
He shall be a **father** to the inhabitants of **Jerusalem,**
　　and to the house of **Judah.**
I will place the key of the **House of David** on **Eliakim's**
　　shoulder;
　　when he **opens,** no one shall **shut,**
　　when he **shuts,** no one shall **open.**
I will fix him like a peg in a sure spot,
　　to be a place of **honor** for his family."

Isaiah = Ī-ZAY-uh
Shebna = SHEB-nah

Pause before you begin and proclaim in a clear, authoritative voice.

Eliakim = ee-LĪ-uh-kim
Hilkiah = hil-KĪ-uh
Proclaim with a clear focus and purpose.

Articulate the words and use good volume. Take your time.

READING I In the first part of this unit of the Book of Isaiah, 22:15–18, the Lord sends Isaiah to Shebna, the self-important master of the palace. It seems that when the prophet finds him, he is admiring the fancy inscribed tomb that he had carved for himself. Isaiah tells him there that the Lord is removing him from his position and placing the key of the House of David on the shoulder of Eliakim. As the chief steward of the royal household, Eliakim will control access to its stores and treasures. His task is to attend to the needs of all the inhabitants of the realm like a father. The Lord's plan is to fix Eliakim like a peg in a sure or secure spot.

However, in the two verses following this reading, a later writer notes that Eliakim falls out of favor with the Lord (Isaiah 22:24–25). The metaphorical peg gives way, scholars suggest, because it was weighed down by Eliakim's abuse of his position and the favoring of his own household and friends.

READING II This short hymn expresses Paul's awe at how much "more" God is than the human mind can imagine. Divine riches, wisdom, and knowledge are infinite. And divine ways, though often baffling, always work everything together for the good of all. Paul's questions invite reflection on two common misperceptions about God and divine methods.

The first is to think that one knows what is in God's "mind." Israel's sages insist that anyone who thinks that they do is a fool. People can never figure out exactly what God is doing or grasp the novel approach that he is taking to their situation. Humans see only what their small slice of life shows them, and even this they do not

238

For meditation and context:

RESPONSORIAL PSALM   Psalm 138:1–2, 2–3, 6, 8 (8bc)

R. Lord, your love is eternal; do not forsake the work of your hands.

I will give thanks to you, O Lord, with all
    my heart,
  for you have heard the words of my mouth;
in the presence of the angels I will sing
    your praise;
  I will worship at your holy temple.

I will give thanks to your name,
    because of your kindness and your truth:
when I called, you answered me;
  you built up strength within me.

The Lord is exalted, yet the lowly he sees,
  and the proud he knows from afar.
Your kindness, O Lord, endures forever;
  forsake not the work of your hands.

READING II   Romans 11:33–36

What a beautiful letter from St. Paul praising God! The reading is short but powerful. Take your time. Put expression in the words you are proclaiming.

inscrutable = in-SKROO-tuh-b*l (unknowable)

A reading from the Letter of Saint Paul to the Romans

Oh, the **depth** of the riches and wisdom and knowledge of **God!**
How **inscrutable** are his judgments and how **unsearchable**
    his ways!
  *For **who** has known the mind of the Lord*
    *or **who** has been his counselor?*
  *Or **who** has given the Lord **anything***
    *that he may be **repaid?***
For **from** him and **through** him and **for** him are **all** things.
To him be glory forever. **Amen.**

TO KEEP IN MIND

As you prepare your proclamation, make choices about what emotions need to be expressed. Some choices are evident from the text, but some are harder to discern. Understanding the context of the Scripture passage will help you decide.

---

comprehend fully. Having only limited knowledge, they should not presume to give God advice—a piece of their mind perhaps as the psalmists frequently do, their hopes expressed in prayer certainly, but guidance on the best thing to do for all in a given set of circumstances, never.

Paul also corrects the common assumption that because people "do the Lord a favor," like make a difficult choice or decision, lay down their life to perform a charitable act, offer a costly sacrifice, etc., the Lord "owes" them. Baptism does not set up a quid pro quo relationship with the

Lord. All things come from God and through him and exist for him. Paul urges believers to contemplate God's all-encompassing presence and attention, and to seize the opportunities that the gift of a human life gives them to participate with all creation in giving glory to God.

GOSPEL | God's most awesome and inscrutable venture is the Incarnation of the Son. No human would have advised God to come in the flesh. People expect their God to be blatantly supernatural, to put on continuous displays

of omnipotence. In contrast, Jesus is obviously human, and his divinity flashes out only briefly in his miracles. He no doubt has habits like every person that irritated some people. He gets tired and on occasion impatient. He becomes frustrated by the constant challenges to his authority and teachings from the Pharisees and religious leaders who seek to discredit him. He is tempted like everyone, though he does not sin.

Jesus simply looks too human to be God's Son. He does remind some people of "the man of God," Elijah, a prophet who

GOSPEL   Matthew 16:13–20

A reading from the holy Gospel according to Matthew

Jesus went into the region of **Caesarea Philippi** and
    he asked his disciples,
    "**Who** do people say that the **Son of Man is**?"
They replied, "Some say **John the Baptist**, others **Elijah**,
    still others **Jeremiah** or one of the prophets."
He said to them, "But who do **you** say that I am?"
Simon Peter said in reply,
    "You are the **Christ**, the **Son** of the living **God**."
Jesus said to him in reply,
    "Blessed are you, **Simon** son of **Jonah**.
For flesh and blood has not revealed this to you, but my
        heavenly **Father**.
And so **I** say to you, you are **Peter**,
    and upon this rock **I** will **build** my church,
    and the gates of the netherworld shall **not prevail** against it.
I will give you the **keys** to the kingdom of **heaven**.
Whatever you **bind** on earth shall be **bound** in heaven;
    and whatever you **loose** on earth shall be **loosed** in heaven."
Then he strictly ordered his disciples
    to tell no one that he was the **Christ**.

Caesarea Philippi = sez-uh-REE-uh fih-LIP-ī

Proclaim with good volume.

Pause before you ask the question.

Proclaim in a tone of friendship as you say this line.

Transition to a tone of authority.

also worked miracles and raised a widow's son from the dead. And like other prophets he calls for conversion and teaches with a creative clarity that engages the crowds. For these, he is an inspired teacher or a holy man who has a close relationship to God, but not divine.

Peter did not figure out on his own that Jesus is the Son of God. This insight, one of Paul's "riches," is given him by the Father. Peter needs this knowledge to be the rock on which Jesus will build his Church and to carry out the formidable tasks that Jesus entrusts to him.

The first is to lead God's offensive against evil in the world. Jesus assures Peter that the gates of Hades—i.e., the underworld or realm of death—will not prevail or stand up against the onslaught of the Church. Peter must trust unswervingly that Jesus wins the battle with death and evil once and for all when he dies on the cross and is raised to eternal life. This will motivate him to courageously and tirelessly lead the baptized into battle against evil in all its forms.

Secondly, Jesus gives Peter the keys of the kingdom, the sign of his authority over

God's household and of his position as steward of its resources. These are all the baptized and the unique charisms that God gives to each of them to carry out their mission for the kingdom. The pairing of keys in today's readings provokes thought about the tremendous responsibility that comes with this oversight of God's people.
E.N.

TWENTY-SECOND SUNDAY IN ORDINARY TIME

LECTIONARY #124

READING I   Jeremiah 20:7–9

Jeremiah = jayr-uh-MĪ-uh

Jeremiah is discouraged in spreading the word of God. Let the congregation hear that in your voice as you proclaim.

Express emotions of frustration and anger as you read.

Pause before you say this last line. Transition to a tone of acceptance of God's will.

A reading from the Book of the Prophet Jeremiah

You **duped** me, **O Lord,** and I **let** myself be **duped**;
  you were too strong for me, and you **triumphed**.
All the day I am an object of **laughter**;
  everyone **mocks** me.

Whenever I speak, I must **cry out,**
  violence and **outrage** is my message;
the word of the **Lord** has **brough**t me
  derision and **reproach** all the day.

I say to myself, I will **not** mention him,
  I will **speak** in his name **no more**.
But then it becomes like **fire** burning in my **heart**,
  imprisoned in my bones;
I grow **weary** holding it in, I **cannot** endure it.

READING I │ This reading is part of Jeremiah's well-known complaint that fidelity to his vocation to prophesy for the Lord makes him miserable. The king and priests reject his pleas for conversion and declare unpatriotic his announcements of the coming fall of Judah to the Babylonians. Their attitude filters down to the people who mock Jeremiah continually. Looking back, he is convinced that the Lord seduced or lured or tricked him into taking up his thankless task. The Lord God naturally overpowered him since he is only a human being. As he

sees it, he didn't stand a chance of living a different life.

He longs to be given easy and pleasing messages to prophesy, but the Lord compels him to announce "violence" and "destruction." The Hebrew word for violence denotes the calculated abuse, often physical, that the powerful inflict on those who are weaker, less knowledgeable, or poorer than they are, simply because they can. Jeremiah declares that if these bullies persist in their behavior, their homes and land will be destroyed. And they hate him for it.

Now he has had enough. He decides to abandon his call, to not mention the Lord again. But then he senses a fire burning in his heart and mind, a blaze imprisoned within him. He wears himself out trying to hold it in; he cannot overpower it. And so once again, as he will for the rest of his life, he accepts the suffering that his call entails and submits to the Lord's will for him.

READING II │ Paul urges the baptized to offer their bodies as a "living sacrifice," an oxymoron since what is sacrificed is first killed. For Christians, this

241

For meditation and context:

TO KEEP IN MIND
The Responsorial Psalm "has great liturgical and pastoral importance, since it fosters meditation on the Word of God," the General Instruction on the Roman Missal says. Pray it as you prepare.

A short but inspirational passage from St. Paul. Proclaim with focus, purpose, and compassion.

RESPONSORIAL PSALM   Psalm 63:2, 3–4, 5–6, 8–9 (2b)

R. My soul is thirsting for you, O Lord my God.

O God, you are my God whom I seek;
    for you my flesh pines and my soul thirsts
    like the earth, parched, lifeless and
        without water.

Thus have I gazed toward you in
        the sanctuary
    to see your power and your glory,
for your kindness is a greater good than life;
    my lips shall glorify you.

Thus will I bless you while I live;
    lifting up my hands, I will call upon
        your name.
As with the riches of a banquet shall my soul
        be satisfied,
    and with exultant lips my mouth shall
        praise you.

You are my help,
    and in the shadow of your wings I shout
        for joy.
My soul clings fast to you;
    your right hand upholds me.

READING II   Romans 12:1–2

A reading from the Letter of Saint Paul to the Romans

I urge you, brothers and sisters, by the mercies of God,
    to **offer** your bodies as a **living sacrifice,**
    holy and pleasing to **God,** your spiritual worship.
Do not conform yourselves to this age
    but be **transformed** by the renewal of your mind,
    that you may **discern** what is the **will of God,**
    what is **good** and **pleasing** and **perfect.**

unusual sacrificial ritual begins at Baptism and is carried on through the rest of their earthly life. They are metaphorically being put to death each day as they sacrifice their desires and preferences so that Christ can use them for his purposes. Their circumstances and the events that impact them daily fan the flames that will eventually consume the offering.

Such extreme commitment to Christ is too difficult for most people to sustain on their own. And so, Paul reminds the baptized that *together* they offer a single sacrifice. Together, they can more radically and

effectively resist the pressures that society puts on them to conform themselves to its values, customs, and views instead of those of Christ. Together, they can act with more boldness and courage than one person can alone. Paul implores them to make a conscious continuous effort to stay with each other in the flames. As they do so they will see more clearly what God's will for them is and what is intrinsically good and dependable, pleasing, and perfect—the only things worth pursuing. And when the sacrificial ritual is ended, they will go in peace to live together with God forever.

GOSPEL In the first part of the Gospel, Jesus reveals the Father's will for him. And in the last, he teaches that the lives of his disciples must follow the same pattern. In between these sections, Peter rebukes Jesus saying that God forbid he should suffer so and die. He can't accept that God could will such a future for his Son.

Jesus' response exposes Peter's compassion as a temptation from Satan to reject the Father's plan; he was born to be killed. Peter's concern triggers Jesus' teaching that his disciples must not be preoccupied with

GOSPEL   Matthew 16:21–27

A reading from the holy Gospel according to Matthew

Proclaim with good volume and articulation.

Jesus began to show his disciples
    that he must go to **Jerusalem** and **suffer** greatly
    from the elders, the chief priests, and the scribes,
    and be **killed** and on the third day be **raised**.
Then **Peter** took **Jesus** aside and began to rebuke him,

Pause before you say this line.

    "**God** forbid, **Lord!** No such thing shall **ever** happen to you."

Proclaim Jesus' words in a tone of utter frustration.

He turned and said to **Peter**,
    "Get behind me, Satan! You are an **obstacle** to me.
You are thinking not as **God** does, but as **human beings** do."

Pause before you begin and transition to a calmer tone as you read with a firm belief in purpose.

Then **Jesus** said to his disciples,
    "Whoever wishes to come **after** me must **deny** himself,
    take up his cross, and **follow me**.
For whoever wishes to **save** his life **will lose** it,
    but whoever **loses** his life for **my** sake **will find** it.
What **profit** would there be for one to **gain** the whole **world**
    and **forfeit his life**?
Or what can one **give** in exchange for his **life?**

Say this line slowly and look at your congregation.

For the **Son of Man** will come with his angels in his
    Father's glory,
    and then he will **repay** all according to his **conduct**."

---

their physical existence. Three verbs—deny, save, and lose—elaborate the paradox that to save one's life one must lose it.

    Jesus begins, "Whoever wishes to come after me must deny himself, take up his cross, and follow me." Other translations of "deny" (Greek *aparneomai*) illustrate what Jesus means. To deny oneself can denote to disown, or refuse to acknowledge, or reject oneself so that, for example, one can attend to others. It can also mean to disagree with, or rebut, or challenge one's own views.

    Jesus continues: "Whoever wishes to save his life will lose it, but whoever loses his life for my sake will find it." "To save" (Greek *sozo*) can denote many natural concerns: to keep one's body safe and whole, to preserve it from dangers and deprivations, to liberate it, to rescue it, or to heal it from disease. And "to lose" (Greek *apollumi*) one's life can also be translated as destroy, ruin, or kill one's life.

    If we string together these possible meanings we hear Jesus saying something like this: "Whoever focuses on keeping his (used inclusively) life whole and healthy, on

staying free to do as he pleases, on being safe, and on striving for personal satisfaction will in fact destroy, ruin, or kill his kingdom life. But the one who destroys, ruins, or kills his life *for Jesus' sake* will find his kingdom life, i.e., the meaningful existence on earth that God intends for him." E.N.

TWENTY-THIRD SUNDAY IN ORDINARY TIME

Ezekiel = ee-ZEE-kee-uhl

Pause before you begin proclaiming Jesus' words. Use good volume and articulation.

Proclaim in a tone of firmness and conviction.

Proclaim with hopefulness in your voice.

TO KEEP IN MIND
Use inflection (the high or low pitch of your voice) to convey attitude and feeling. High pitch expresses intensity and excitement; low pitch expresses sadness, contrition, or solemnity.

LECTIONARY #127

READING I   Ezekiel 33:7–9

A reading from the Book of the Prophet Ezekiel

Thus says the LORD:
    You, son of man, I have **appointed** watchman for the house
        of **Israel;**
    when you **hear** me say anything, you shall **warn** them for me.
If **I** tell the wicked, "**O** wicked one, you shall **surely** die,"
    and you **do not** speak out to **dissuade** the wicked from his way,
    the wicked shall die for his **guilt,**
    but **I** will hold **you** responsible for his death.
But if you **warn** the wicked,
    trying to **turn** him from his way,
    and he **refuses** to turn from his way,
    he shall **die** for his guilt,
    but you shall **save** yourself.

READING I   The prophet Ezekiel envisions himself as a watchman for the house of Israel. In the biblical world, this sentinel stands on the wall and blows his trumpet to warn the people of approaching danger, especially in times of war. Ezekiel's original mission is to warn God's people that unless they turn back from their evil ways, the Babylonians will destroy their land. The people did not listen, lost their country, and are now in exile in Babylon. In this passage, Ezekiel repeats the warning, giving the people hope that though they broke the covenant, in and through it their relationship with the Lord can continue. To enjoy this privilege, however, they must change.

This passage is, however, mainly about Ezekiel's responsibility to carry out his prophetic mission to persuade disinterested people that if they do not change, they are in danger of being cut off from the Lord. If the Lord's "watchman" does not warn the recalcitrant of their peril, or if out of laziness he merely repeats the commandments to them, the Lord will hold him responsible for their deaths. His calling obliges him to communicate the Lord's will in ways that engage people's interest and sway them to alter radically the direction that their life is taking. The prophet's own salvation depends on the effort he makes.

READING II   Paul's opening command reads literally, "To no one, nothing owe except to love one another." For him, loving is not an activity that Christians perform in addition to keeping rules or the "law." It is an incalculable debt that believers owe to God for the love that he bestows on them through Christ. Because Christ died for all people, the bap-

244

For meditation and context:

RESPONSORIAL PSALM   Psalm 95:1–2, 6–7, 8–9 (8)

R. If today you hear his voice, harden not your hearts.

Come, let us sing joyfully to the LORD;
  let us acclaim the rock of our salvation.
Let us come into his presence
    with thanksgiving;
  let us joyfully sing psalms to him.

Come, let us bow down in worship;
  let us kneel before the LORD who made us.
For he is our God,
  and we are the people he shepherds,
    the flock he guides.

Oh, that today you would hear his voice:
  "Harden not your hearts as at Meribah,
    as in the day of Massah in the desert,
where your fathers tempted me;
  they tested me though they had seen
    my works."

READING II   Romans 13:8–10

A reading from the Letter of Saint Paul to the Romans

Brothers and sisters:
Owe nothing to anyone, except to **love** one another;
  for the one who **loves** another has **fulfilled** the law.
The commandments, "You shall **not** commit adultery;
    you shall **not** kill; you shall **not** steal; you shall **not** covet,"
  and whatever other commandment there may be,
  are summed up in this saying, namely,
    "You shall love your neighbor as yourself."
Love does **no** evil to the neighbor;
  hence, **love** is the **fulfillment** of the law.

Proclaim slowly with good volume and expression in your voice.

Pause before you say this line. Use as much eye contact as possible.

---

tized must not only love "one another." They must also love "another" or literally in the Greek, "the other." These last are people outside their group, those who are different and not congenial to them.

Christian love entails positive action toward everyone. It is more than not committing adultery, not killing, not stealing, and not coveting. All the commandments are summed up by the charge given in Leviticus 19:18, "You shall love your neighbor as yourself." In Leviticus, neighbors are other Jews, but Paul expands its meaning to include every person that one interacts

with face-to-face or from a distance, as for example by mail or in cyberspace.

In this passage, Christians are recognized by their habit of treating other people the same way that they treat themselves. Not to love even-handedly and prodigally indicates that they do not yet comprehend the love that God bestows on them through Christ.

GOSPEL   A given of the human condition is that people will offend each other. But whenever this happens in a Christian community, its mem-

bers must make a serious effort to reconcile the parties involved. To this end, Matthew's community sets up a procedure. The first step is a one-on-one meeting that is initiated by the person who is sinned against. (Due to the emphasis in this passage on individual responsibility for faults and for starting the process of reconciliation, "he" is used inclusively.)

If the sinner does not listen, the one offended arranges to meet with him a second time and takes along one or two members of the community. It is unclear whether these companions bear witnesses

GOSPEL   Matthew 18:15–20

A reading from the holy Gospel according to Matthew

Jesus said to his disciples:
   "If your brother **sins** against you,
   go and **tell** him his fault between you and him **alone**.
If he **listens** to you, you have **won** over your brother.
If he does **not** listen,
   take one or two **others** along **with** you,
   so that 'every fact may be established
   on the testimony of two or three **witnesses**.'
If he **refuses** to listen to them, **tell** the church.
If he refuses to listen **even** to the church,
   then **treat** him as you would a **Gentile** or a tax collector.
Amen, **I** say to you,
   whatever you **bind** on earth shall be **bound** in heaven,
   and whatever you **loose** on earth shall be **loosed** in heaven.
Again, amen, I say to you,
   if two of you **agree** on earth
   about anything for which they are to pray,
   it shall be **granted** to them by my heavenly **Father**.
For where **two** or **three** are **gathered together** in my **name**,
   there am **I** in the **midst** of them."

Pause before you begin Jesus' words.

Proclaim with renewed energy and intensity.

Pause and look at the assembly as you proclaim this last line.

---

to the facts of the sin as required by Deuteronomy 19:15 or to the fact that the one sinned against reached out and discussed the matter with the sinner.

If the sinner still refuses to listen, the matter goes to the church, probably meaning the local community. If he does not listen to the church, he is to be "treated like a Gentile or a tax collector." Though some posit that this treatment refers to excommunication, other texts in Matthew present Gentiles and tax collectors as people whom Jesus seeks out—like the lost sheep in the passage immediately preceding this one.

The procedure for reconciliation seems straightforward, but every step requires courage and a desire for unity.

After all the attention to the process of repairing a rift between two disciples, the Gospel shows why reconciliation is crucial to the Church's mission. In short, actions taken by parishes, which accord between even a few of their members, unite earth and heaven. First, whatever is bound or loosed by the community on earth is also considered bound or loosed in heaven. These functions, given earlier to Peter, are in this passage exercised in a complementary way also by the local Church. Second, if on earth only two members agree to pray for the same thing, the Father in heaven is hearing and grants their request. Third, where only a few come together in Christ's name on earth, Christ who is risen and seated at God's right hand is present with them. E.N.

TWENTY-FOURTH SUNDAY IN ORDINARY TIME

LECTIONARY #130

READING I   Sirach 27:30—28:7

A reading from the Book of Sirach

Sirach = SEER-ak

Proclaim Sirach's words using good volume. Read slowly, using good eye contact.

> Wrath and anger are **hateful** things,
>   yet the **sinner** hugs them **tight**.
> The vengeful will **suffer** the LORD's **vengeance**,
>   for **he remembers** their sins in detail.

Transition to a tone of compassion.

> **Forgive** your neighbor's injustice;
>   then when you **pray**, your own sins will be **forgiven**.

Pause, then say the next lines with more energy and intensity in your voice.

> Could anyone nourish **anger** against another
>   and expect **healing** from the LORD?
> Could anyone **refuse mercy** to another like himself,
>   can he **seek pardon** for his own sins?
> If one who is but flesh **cherishes wrath**,
>   who will **forgive** his sins?

Take your time proclaiming the ending of the reading. Use good eye contact.

> **Remember** your last days, set **enmity** aside;
>   remember **death and decay**, and **cease** from sin!
> Think of the commandments, **hate** not your neighbor;
>   **remember** the Most High's covenant, and **overlook** faults.

READING I   Sirach reflects on how difficult it is for mere mortals to forgive others even as they ask the Lord to forgive them. He observes that people are inclined to "hug tight" or "cherish" wrath and anger. They seem to enjoy holding grudges and keeping the memory of offenses against them alive. And so, Sirach warns them that if they do not grant mercy to others they will suffer the Lord's vengeance. This is especially undesirable since the Lord sees all the harmful ripple effects that a single sin sets off, and he will punish the sinner accordingly. Human vengeance, by comparison, is unimpressive.

To further persuade his hearers to show mercy, Sirach urges them to "remember" their last days on earth. Biblical remembering, always more than a cognitive operation, entails action. Those who want a happy death must do more than think about being merciful. They must immediately set aside all hostility, stop obsessing about vengeance, and ignore the faults of others.

READING II   In the preceding verses, Paul addresses the problem of Christians judging other Christians. The apparent need of some to criticize people, and perhaps to see themselves as better Christians than others, is dividing the community.

To break the baptized of this habit, Paul draws their attention to the essential truth that unites them, namely, that Christ died and came back to life so that each of them could live and die in him. A baptized person is never alone. He or she is born to live in and for the Lord. This call unites all

For meditation and context:

RESPONSORIAL PSALM   Psalm 103:1–2, 3–4, 9–10, 11–12 (8)

R. The Lord is kind and merciful, slow to anger, and rich in compassion.

Bless the Lord, O my soul;
   and all my being, bless his holy name.
Bless the Lord, O my soul,
   and forget not all his benefits.

He pardons all your iniquities,
   heals all your ills.
He redeems your life from destruction,
   he crowns you with kindness and
   compassion.

He will not always chide,
   nor does he keep his wrath forever.
Not according to our sins does he deal
   with us,
   nor does he requite us according
   to our crimes.

For as the heavens are high above the earth,
   so surpassing is his kindness toward
   those who fear him.
As far as the east is from the west,
   so far has he put our transgressions
   from us.

READING II   Romans 14:7–9

A reading from the Letter of Saint Paul to the Romans

Brothers and sisters:
None of us **lives** for oneself, and no one **dies** for oneself.
For if we **live**, we **live** for the **Lord**,
   and if we **die**, we **die** for the **Lord**;
   so then, whether we live or die, **we are the Lord's**.
For this is why **Christ** died and came to **life**,
   that he might be **Lord** of **both** the dead and the living.

St. Paul delivers a beautiful message in just a few sentences. Take your time and use as much eye contact as possible.

GOSPEL   Matthew 18:21–35

A reading from the holy Gospel according to Matthew

Peter approached **Jesus** and asked him,
   "**Lord**, if my brother sins **against** me,
   how **often** must I **forgive**?
     As many as seven times?"

Pause before you read Peter's question.

---

believers. Until they draw their final breath, their "occupation" is to live with Christ in whatever situation they find themselves. Paul will go on to remind readers, however, that all will stand alone before the judgment seat of God and give an account of how they spent their time on earth.

| GOSPEL | In chapter 18, Matthew sets out Jesus' teachings on life in a Christian community. Most of his discourse elaborates the statement from the Our Father, "forgive us our trespasses as we forgive those who trespass against

us." Today's Gospel draws attention to the emotions that either facilitate or impede one's forgiveness of another.

Peter's question, "Lord (Greek *Kyrios*), how often must I forgive?" conveys the weariness and frustration felt by people who forgive others repeatedly. When can they stop? When will God be satisfied? Jesus replies, "Never. Don't keep track. Decide to forgive always." It is important to note that Jesus is not saying that people may harm others with impunity. Or that personal forgiveness of perpetrators frees them from paying the social consequences

of their crimes. His concern is what goes on between believers in the kingdom, which he compares to the exchanges that take place between a king (the master or *kyrios*) and his debtors.

The first servant ran up an unpayable debt and the *kyrios* simply rules that he must pay the proscribed consequences. Case closed—until the servant importunes the *kyrios* and promises the impossible: that he will make amends for the damage that he did. The *kyrios* is moved with compassion in the depths of his being (in Greek *splagchnistheis*) for the servant who grov-

As you proclaim the parable use vocal and facial expression, strong eye contact, and pause for emphasis before the servants speak.

Jesus answered, "**I** say to you, **not** seven times
    but **seventy-seven** times.
That is why the **kingdom of heaven** may be likened to a **king**
   who decided to **settle accounts** with his servants.
When he began the accounting,
   a **debtor** was brought before him who **owed** him
     a **huge** amount.
Since he had no way of paying it back,
   his master **ordered** him to be **sold**,
    along with his wife, his children, and all his property,
    in payment of the debt.
At that, the servant fell down, did him homage, and said,
    '**Be patient with me, and I will pay you back in full.'**
Moved with **compassion** the master of that servant
   let him go and **forgave** him the loan.
When that servant had left, he found one of his fellow servants
   who owed him a much **smaller** amount.
He seized him and started to choke him, demanding,
    '**Pay back what you owe.'**
Falling to his knees, his fellow servant begged him,
    '**Be patient with me, and I will pay you back.'**
But he **refused**.
Instead, he had the fellow servant put in **prison**
   until he paid back the debt.
Now when his fellow servants saw what had happened,
   they were deeply **disturbed**, and went to their master
   and reported the whole affair.

Transition your tone to anger as you read the master's response to his servants.

His master summoned him and said to him, '**You wicked** servant!
I forgave you your **entire** debt because you begged me to.
Should you not have had pity on your fellow servant,
   as I had pity on you?'
Then in **anger** his master handed him over to the **torturers**
   until he should pay back the **whole** debt.

Pause and say in a calm tone.

So will my heavenly **Father** do to you,
   unless each of you **forgives** your brother from your **heart**."

---

els before him. He ignores the fact that the man got himself into this miserable mess and his insistence that he can fix it. He focuses only on the servant's anguish and sets him free.

Instead of rejoicing in his undeserved reprieve, the servant goes looking for a fellow servant who owes him a pittance. He grabs and chokes the offender and demands payment of all that he owes. Though his fellow debtor speaks the same words to him that he spoke to the *kyrios*, the servant is not moved with compassion. Why doesn't he forgive? A literal translation

of the Greek is, "He was not wanting to." His emotions take over and blind him to the other debtor's misery. He inflicts pain, though it cannot repair the damage done.

When the other community members see this, they are *greatly* disturbed. The unforgiving servant's lack of compassion and harsh treatment of his fellow servant disrupt the community's life. In Jesus' view, one disciple who harbors a grudge against another is a disaster that requires immediate attention.

Now the *kyrios* is angry. He calls the unforgiving servant "wicked" or "evil"

because he did not show mercy (Greek *eleison*) as he was shown mercy. The choice of adjective puts holding a grudge and seeking revenge on the same level of evil as "malicious intentions, murder, adultery, fornication, theft, false witness, and slander" (Matthew 15:19). In case his disciples still do not realize the danger they put themselves in when they withhold mercy, the *kyrios* adds endless torture to the unforgiving servant's sentence. E.N.

TWENTY-FIFTH SUNDAY IN ORDINARY TIME

LECTIONARY #133

READING I   Isaiah 55:6–9

Isaiah = Ī-ZAY-uh

Proclaim with good volume and with a sense of urgency.

A reading from the Book of the Prophet Isaiah

Say this line slowly with good eye contact.

> **Seek** the LORD while he may be **found**,
>   **call** him while he is near.
> Let the **scoundrel** forsake his way,
>   and the **wicked** his thoughts;
> let him **turn to the LORD** for **mercy**;
>   to our **God**, who is **generous** in **forgiving**.
> For **my** thoughts are **not** your thoughts,
>   nor are **your** ways **my** ways, says the LORD.
> As high as the heavens are above the earth,
>   so high are **my** ways **above** your ways
>   and **my** thoughts **above** your thoughts.

READING I | This reading is from the section of Isaiah known as "the little book of consolation" (Isaiah 40—55). The prophecies in it are primarily oracles, not of judgment, but of salvation. They are the first writings to use the term "glad tidings" or "good news" which through the Greek becomes "gospel."

The best news is that though the Lord punished Israel for its centuries of infidelity by the loss of their land and their exile to Babylon, he loves them too much to sever the covenant relationship with them. In fact, he follows them into exile and returns with them to the land. There the prophet urges them to "seek the Lord" once again in the Jerusalem temple.

Those who seek the Lord in this passage abandon their current "way" or "path" (Hebrew, *derek*). Specifically, the wicked must stop concocting intricate schemes (Hebrew *machsheboth*) and manipulating situations to serve their own ends and start working for the good of all.

The Lord, who is compassionate and eager to forgive, may still be found. But the prophet suggests that this may not always be the case. To persuade his hearers to change their course, he reminds them that the Lord's "thoughts" (*machsheboth*) and ways (*derakim*) are superior to and more intricate than theirs. In short, the Lord will always out-scheme them.

READING II | Paul writes from prison, where the possibility of being put to death sparks the reflections in today's reading. The omitted part of the first verse supplies the context for what follows. In it Paul expresses his unshakeable trust in Christ. He is convinced that he will never be shamed by what happens to him

For meditation and context:

RESPONSORIAL PSALM Psalm 145:2–3, 8–9, 17–18 (18a)

R. The Lord is near to all who call upon him.

Every day will I bless you,
    and I will praise your name forever
        and ever.
Great is the LORD and highly to be praised;
    his greatness is unsearchable.

The LORD is gracious and merciful,
    slow to anger and of great kindness.
The LORD is good to all
    and compassionate toward all his works.

The LORD is just in all his ways
    and holy in all his works.
The LORD is near to all who call upon him,
    to all who call upon him in truth.

READING II   Philippians 1:20c–24, 27a

A reading from the Letter of Saint Paul to the Philippians

Philippians = fih-LIP-ee-uhnz

Brothers and sisters:
Christ will be **magnified** in my body, whether by **life** or by **death**.
For to me **life** is Christ, and **death** is **gain**.
If I go on living in the flesh,
    that means **fruitful** labor for me.
And I **do not** know which I shall choose.
I am caught between the two.
I **long** to depart this life and be with **Christ**,
    for that is far better.
Yet that I remain in the flesh
    is **more** necessary for **your benefit**.

Using good eye contact, proclaim, with focused intent, St. Paul's teaching about life and death.

Transition to a tone of confusion in your voice as St. Paul confronts this dilemma.

Pause and then proclaim with certainty.

Only, **conduct** yourselves in a way **worthy** of the gospel of **Christ**.

---

because of his commitment to the Gospel. Whether he lives or dies, he believes that Christ will be magnified or exalted so boldly and blatantly in his body that people will take notice. In other words, his physical presence provides a place wherein Christ is seen and glorified in the world—as is the body of every Christian.

Paul's awareness of this reality is so strong that for him "life is Christ and death is gain." His devotion to Christ is so intense that he ponders not just what he should do, but even what he should prefer. He says that he is "caught" between two options

and in the grip of both. On the one hand, he believes that as long as he draws breath, Christ is using him to engage more people. On the other hand, he knows that death is the way to deeper knowledge of Christ and complete everlasting union with him.

Paul's reflections lead to a single exhortation: "*Only*, conduct yourselves in a manner worthy of the Gospel of Christ." The Greek for "conduct," *politeuesthe*, denotes the behavior of citizens who live in accord with the laws of a Greek polis, or city, like Philippi. Its appearance here subtly reminds the Philippians that they are also

citizens of heaven and that the Gospel is the standard for their life.

| GOSPEL | This parable is a long metaphor whose aim is to provoke thought about life in the kingdom of heaven. Jesus uses a common business practice to engage his disciples' interest and adds a twist at the end that challenges their view of divine ways. The parable falls into two parts: in 20:1–7 the landowner hires day laborers and in 20:8–16 he pays them.

The landowner goes out and finds workers between five and six in the morning

---

GOSPEL   Matthew 20:1–16a

A reading from the holy Gospel according to Matthew

Jesus told his disciples this parable:
    "The **kingdom of heaven** is like a landowner
    who went out at dawn to **hire** laborers for his vineyard.
After agreeing with them for the usual daily wage,
    he **sent** them into his vineyard.
Going out about nine o'clock,
        the landowner saw **others** standing **idle** in the marketplace,
        and he said to them, 'You **too** go into my vineyard,
        and I will **give** you what is **just**.'
So they went off.
And he went out again around noon,
        and around three o'clock, and did likewise.
Going out about five o'clock,
        the landowner found others standing around, and said to them,
        'Why do you stand here idle all day?'
They answered, 'Because no one has hired us.'
He said to them, 'You **too** go into my vineyard.'
When it was evening the owner of the vineyard said
        to his foreman,
    '**Summon** the laborers and give them their **pay**,
    beginning with the **last** and ending with the **first**.'
When those who had started about **five** o'clock came,
    each received the **usual** daily wage.
So when the **first** came, they thought that they would
        receive **more**,
        but each of them **also** got the usual wage.

Pause before you begin the parable.

Read all the landowner's commands with a tone of authority.

During the dialogue between the laborers and the landowner, proclaim with vocal expression.

Pause before you begin the command.

---

and again at nine, noon, three, and five o'clock. All of those whom he hires agree to a set and just wage. At the close of day, the landowner instructs his foreman to pay first those who worked the least. As the exhausted laborers who toiled for roughly twelve hours and through the scorching midday heat wait for their pay, they see all the late-comers given the amount promised them. This naturally raises their expectations that the landowner will give them more.

When he disappoints them, they complain, literally: "These last people *one hour* worked, and equal to *us, them you* made." The Greek word order, especially of the pronouns, conveys their anger at and frustration with the landlord. Some scholars suggest that their words reflect the attitude of Christians in Matthew's community who think that they are more religious because they do more. They look down on those who seem to be less dedicated to the kingdom, like the tax collectors whose wealth could be viewed as a divine blessing. These functionaries collect the levies imposed by the hated Roman government. And since their salaries come from what they can amass above the set amount, they frequently gouge the citizenry and became quite "blessed."

Comparison of Jesus' parable with a later rabbinic version of it clarifies the clash between his teaching and the expectations of the disgruntled workers. In the rabbinic parable, a king hires many day laborers and pays one man who worked for only two hours the same wage as the rest. When his coworkers complain, he explains that he paid that man a higher wage because he got more done in two hours than all the other laborers together. We get

Take your time and use good eye contact.

And on receiving it they **grumbled** against the landowner, saying,
　'These **last** ones worked only **one** hour,
　and you have made them **equal** to us,
　who bore the day's burden and the heat.'
He said to one of them in reply,
　'My friend, I am **not** cheating you.
Did you not agree with me for the usual daily wage?
Take what is yours and go.
What if I wish to give this **last** one the **same** as you?
Or am I **not** free to do as I **wish** with my **own** money?
Are you **envious** because I am **generous**?'
Thus, the **last** will be **first**, and the **first** will be **last**."

Pause.

THE 4 STEPS OF *LECTIO DIVINA* OR PRAYERFUL READING

1. *Lectio:* Read a Scripture passage aloud slowly. Notice what phrase captures your attention and be attentive to its meaning. Silent pause.

2. *Meditatio:* Read the passage aloud slowly again, reflecting on the passage, allowing God to speak to you through it. Silent pause.

3. *Oratio:* Read it aloud slowly a third time, allowing it to be your prayer or response to God's gift of insight to you. Silent pause.

4. *Contemplatio:* Read it aloud slowly a fourth time, now resting in God's word.

---

this. It's the way things work in the world. But Jesus' parable is about the way things work in his kingdom.

His three questions provoke disciples to examine where their views lie. The first, "did you not agree to the daily wage?" reminds disciples that at Baptism they agreed to work in the Lord's vineyard in return for all that he promises. The second question, "Am I not allowed to do what I choose with what belongs to me?" specifies the wage as "what belongs to me," or literally "the-*my*-things." The emphatic

Greek pronoun reveals that the disciple's payment consists of unique divine gifts and graces that humans could never attain on their own, such as the constant and caring companionship of the Lord. What more could anyone want? To those who disagree with how God distributes divine gifts Jesus gives a clear directive: "Take what is yours and go."

Jesus' last question shows that failure to immediately "take" and "go" can lead to sin. He asks, "Are you envious because I am generous?" or literally in the Greek, "Is your

eye evil because I, *I* am good?" When disciples find themselves answering yes to this question, when divine goodness and generosity mystify them and rile them up, they could say to themselves something like: "I don't understand this, but I'll just take my blessings right now and move on." E.N.

TWENTY-SIXTH SUNDAY IN ORDINARY TIME

LECTIONARY #136

READING I   Ezekiel 18:25–28

A reading from the Book of the Prophet Ezekiel

Thus says the LORD:
You say, "The LORD'S way is **not** fair!"
Hear now, house of **Israel**:
    Is it **my** way that is unfair, or **rather**, are **not your ways** unfair?
When someone virtuous **turns** away from virtue to **commit**
        iniquity, and **dies**,
    it is because of the **iniquity** he committed that he must die.
But if he **turns** from the wickedness he has committed,
    and does what is **right and just**,
    he shall **preserve** his life;
    since he has turned away from **all** the sins that he
        has **committed**,
    he shall **surely live**, he shall **not die**.

Ezekiel = ee-ZEE-kee-uhl

Pause after the colon, then proclaim with good volume and articulation.
Read with a tone of authority.

Proclaim slowly with a strong purpose.

Transition to a better option: living. Let the congregation hear hopefulness and comfort in your voice.

For meditation and context:

RESPONSORIAL PSALM   Psalm 25:4–5, 6–7, 8–9 (6a)

R. Remember your mercies, O Lord.

Your ways, O LORD, make known to me;
    teach me your paths,
guide me in your truth and teach me,
    for you are God my savior.

Remember that your compassion, O LORD,
    and your love are from of old.
The sins of my youth and my frailties
        remember not;
    in your kindness remember me,
    because of your goodness, O LORD.

Good and upright is the LORD;
    thus he shows sinners the way.
He guides the humble to justice,
    and teaches the humble his way.

READING I   Ezekiel is prophesying to the people of Israel, who are suffering the consequences for centuries of infidelity to the Lord—namely, the loss of their homeland and deportation to Babylon. The people object; "The Lord's way is not fair!" After all, many of them are probably decent people who think that they follow the Lord well enough. The blunt words that Ezekiel puts on their lips are not a quote, but rather an attempt to open their eyes to what their actions say.

He wants them to see that every choice they make either fosters or dam-ages their relationship with the Lord. There is no middle ground. If the virtuous or just turn from doing the right thing, if they treat others in a less than just manner, they (their relationship with the Lord) will die. If, however, they later turn away from doing evil and do what is right and just, they shall preserve their life with the Lord. Humans cannot be perfectly faithful, but they must not persist in doing wrong. The choice is theirs. So are its consequences.

READING II   Thoughts or attitudes play a crucial role in Christian life. In this reading they are conveyed by the Greek word *phroneo*, which can denote to think, to hold or form an opinion, to judge, or to have an attitude or outlook. In the second verse Paul uses *phroneo* twice: when he exhorts the Philippians to be "of the same mind" and to be "united in thinking" one thing. A few verses later he identifies this one thing as the attitude of Christ Jesus.

Militating against a community's uni-fied vision are thoughts that spring from self-interest and vainglory. The Greek for vainglory, *kenodoxia* (*keno*, "empty" +

254

READING II   Philippians 2:1–11

A reading from the Letter of Saint Paul to the Philippians

[Brothers and sisters:
If there is any **encouragement in Christ**,
 any **solace** in love,
 any **participation** in the **Spirit**,
 any **compassion and mercy**,
 complete my joy by being of the **same mind**, with the
  same love,
 united in heart, thinking **one** thing.
Do nothing out of **selfishness** or out of **vainglory**;
 rather, **humbly** regard others as **more** important
  than yourselves,
 each looking out **not** for his **own** interests,
 but **also** for those of others.

Have in **you** the **same** attitude
 that is **also** in **Christ Jesus**,]
  Who, though he was in the form of **God**,
   did **not** regard **equality** with **God**
   something to be grasped.
  Rather, he **emptied** himself,
   taking the form of a **slave**,
   coming in human **likeness**;
   and found **human** in appearance,
   he **humbled** himself,
   becoming **obedient** to the point of death,
   even **death** on a cross.
Because of this, **God** greatly **exalted** him
  and **bestowed** on him the name
  which is **above** every name,
  that at the name of **Jesus**
  every knee should **bend**,
  of those in **heaven** and on **earth** and **under** the earth, **»**

Pause after the colon, then slowly proclaim St. Paul's commands to the Philippians. Use vocal expression as you proclaim. Smile.

solace = SOL-uhs (comfort)

Pause and use good eye contact.

Keep up the energy in your voice.

Proclaim with compassion.

Start with an informational tone and build intensity as you continue reading.

---

doxia, "glory"), denotes the vanity exhibited by those who vaunt their own achievements. Such boasting, even if justified, is useless and divisive. In contrast, the baptized fix their attention on everyone else. They consider others to be more important and their needs to take precedence over their own.

Christ's thinking is the standard for Christian thinking: "Have among yourselves the same attitude (phroneo) that is also in Christ Jesus." Thinking that his divinity is not something to be "grasped" or more "greatly desired" than the Father's will,

Jesus empties (kenao) himself of divine or true glory and takes the form of a slave. He does not seek earthly fame or rank. God's slave spends his time serving others whose concerns and suffering supplant his own. He becomes obedient unto death—not the peaceful passing of an exonerated just man on his own bed, but the painful, humiliating, and public demise of a convicted slave on a cross.

Despite appearances, Jesus' obedience preserved his life. God raised him up and exalted him, giving him a position above all the famous super achievers and

lords of the earth. All knees bending and tongues confessing echoes the language found in a Greek translation (the Septuagint) of Isaiah 45:23. There they convey the acknowledgment of all peoples that Yahweh—the name that Judaism traditionally replaces with "the Lord"—is their God. Paul evokes this passage and proclaims the unimaginable: Jesus, who poured out his life for others and died like a slave, is the ever-faithful God of Israel! The Greek word order conveys the wonder: "The Lord (is) Jesus Christ!" (kúrios Iaesoūs Christòs).

Proclaim slowly with a joyous tone using strong eye contact.

and **every** tongue confess that
Jesus Christ is Lord,
to the glory of **God the Father**.

[Shorter: Philippians 2:1–5 (see brackets)]

GOSPEL Matthew 21:28–32

A reading from the holy Gospel according to Matthew

Pause before you read the question.

Proclaim with good volume and in an informative tone.

Use both vocal and facial expression as Jesus gives the command.

Jesus said to the chief priests and elders of the people:
    "What is your opinion?
A man had two sons.
He came to the first and said,
    'Son, go out and work in the vineyard today.'
He said in reply, **'I will not,'**
    but afterwards **changed** his mind and went.
The man came to the **other** son and gave the **same** order.
He said in reply, 'Yes, sir,' but did **not** go.
Which of the two did his father's will?"
They answered, "The first."

Transition your tone to strong purpose and focus on Jesus' message.

Jesus said to them, "**Amen**, I say to you,
    tax collectors and prostitutes
    are entering the kingdom of **God before you**.
When **John** came to you in the way of righteousness,
    you did **not** believe him;
    but tax collectors and prostitutes **did**.
Yet even when you saw that,
    you did **not** later change your minds and believe him."

GOSPEL This Gospel challenges the complacent, those who presume that things are good enough between themselves and God, to examine the integrity of their discipleship. To the father's command to go out and work in the vineyard, the first son replies literally in the Greek, "I don't want to," but later changes his mind and goes. The second assents to go work but carries on with his usual routine.

The parable reinforces Jesus' insistence that words alone do not prove that one is his disciple. They must be accompanied by action (see Matthew 7:21–23 and 25:1–13). The first son is like the tax collectors and prostitutes, the stereotypical sinners of Jesus' day. They "don't want to" live righteously but change their mind and behavior when they hear the Baptist preach.

The second son is like the religious leaders to whom Jesus addresses the parable. They agree to go work for God but do not. They talk about divine demands and ways but do not live by them because they are inconvenient and require them to change how they spend their time. Jesus warns that those whom they feel superior to are preceding them into God's kingdom.

Jesus' parable is open ended. It challenges its hearers to examine whose will shapes their daily round. Which son are they? Are those whom they constantly criticize walking ahead of them into the kingdom? E.N.

TWENTY-SEVENTH SUNDAY IN ORDINARY TIME

LECTIONARY #139

READING I Isaiah 5:1–7

Isaiah = Ī-ZAY-uh

A reading from the Book of the Prophet Isaiah

Pause before you begin to read the story of the vineyard.

spaded = SPAY-d*d

Let me now sing of my friend,
    my friend's song concerning his **vineyard**.
My friend had a vineyard
    on a **fertile** hillside;
he spaded it, cleared it of stones,
    and **planted** the **choicest** vines;
within it he **built** a **watchtower**,
    and hewed out a wine press.
Then he looked for the crop of grapes,
    but what it yielded was **wild** grapes.

Transition to a personal tone using good eye contact and projection of your voice.

Now, inhabitants of **Jerusalem** and people of **Judah**,
    judge between **me** and my **vineyard**:
What **more** was there to do for my vineyard
    that I had **not** done?
Why, when I looked for the crop of grapes,
    did it bring forth wild grapes?

Proclaim with energy. Continue to build intensity as you read.

Now, I will let you know
    what I mean to do with my vineyard:
take away its hedge, **give** it to grazing,
    break through its wall, let it be trampled! »

READING I In the biblical world, grapes are an annual wonder. Their sweetness breaks the monotony of daily fare and their wine adds a festive note to special celebrations. Isaiah's song about a vintner (the Lord) and a cherished vine (Judah) announces the destruction of the southern kingdom. And yet, the passage conveys far more than an oracle of judgment. The prophet's description of the vine grower's efforts—a detailing that draws readers to feel deeply both his eager anticipation of a good crop and his intense disappointment at finding a rotten one—engenders empathy for the Lord's enthusiastic efforts and hopes for his people.

Readers imagine the vintner spading the soil and removing heavy stones. He uses these to construct a wall to enclose the vineyard and protect it from foraging animals. If his plot sits on a on a hillside, which is likely, he could haul soil up from the valley floor to provide a richer bed for his vines. He then plants the choicest vine that he can find. Not yet done, he builds a watchtower to guard the crop because grapes ripen at the end of the annual five – to six-month long drought. Thieves and passers-by cannot resist their thirst-quenching fruit. Finally, without a jackhammer or dynamite, the vine grower chisels out a winepress in bedrock. Another passage in Isaiah expresses the vintner's loving care for his project: "The pleasant vineyard, sing about it! I, the Lord, am its keeper, I water it every moment. Lest anyone harm it, night and day I guard it" (Isaiah 27:2–3).

When at harvest time he finds only "wild" (or "stinking" or "worthless") grapes, he asks, "What more was there to do for my vineyard?" Not a thing. And so, he decides

Yes, I will make it a **ruin**:
　　it shall **not** be pruned or hoed,
　　but **overgrown** with thorns and briers;
I will command the clouds
　　not to send rain upon it.
The vineyard of the LORD **of hosts** is the house of **Israel**,
　　and the people of **Judah** are his **cherished** plant;
he looked for **judgment**, but see, **bloodshed**!
　　for **justice**, but hark, the outcry!

For meditation and context:

RESPONSORIAL PSALM　Psalm 80:9, 12, 13–14, 15–16, 19–20 (Isaiah 5:7a)

R. The vineyard of the Lord is the house of Israel.

A vine from Egypt you transplanted;
　　you drove away the nations and planted it.
It put forth its foliage to the Sea,
　　its shoots as far as the River.

Why have you broken down its walls,
　　so that every passer-by plucks its fruit,
the boar from the forest lays it waste,
　　and the beasts of the field feed upon it?

Once again, O LORD of hosts,
　　look down from heaven, and see;
take care of this vine,
　　and protect what your right hand
　　　　has planted,
the son of man whom you yourself
　　made strong.

Then we will no more withdraw from you;
　　give us new life, and we will call upon
　　　　your name.
O LORD, God of hosts, restore us;
　　if your face shine upon us, then we shall
　　　　be saved.

TO KEEP IN MIND
Be careful not to swallow words by mumbling. Articulate carefully, especially at the end of lines.

---

to destroy it. The instrument that the Lord will use for this destruction is the Babylonians. The breaking down of the stone enclosure around the vineyard alludes to the typical way that an invading army devastates the agricultural economy of a land. They break down the walls of the terraced hillside so that the soil erodes into the valley below. Weeds and thistles take over the once-precious plot.

　　The last verse identifies the good grapes as the fruits of justice that the Lord seeks from his people. For Isaiah, righteousness is the evidence that God is pres-

ent and acting on earth. The prophet uses puns and the Hebrew *hinneh*, a demonstrative particle which points to something unexpected, to express the Lord's disappointment. "He looked for judgment or righteousness (*mishpat*) but see! (*hinneh*) bloodshed (*mispach*), for justice (*tsedaqah*) but hark! (*hinneh*) the outcry (*tse'aqah*)." The Lord did everything possible to cultivate a people whose lives display the profound joy that comes from choosing to do the right thing in every situation. But, instead of justice, he found bloodshed (a

biblical metaphor for injustice), and the outcries of the oppressed.

READING II　The baptized in Philippi are dual citizens. They enjoy the status and privileges of a Roman colony, and so at all public gatherings acknowledge the current emperor, Nero, as their Lord (*kurios*). The Christian Philippians also enjoy the status and privileges of life in their Lord Jesus Christ, who was crucified by the Romans. Their fidelity, as evidenced by their lifestyle and pursuits, disrupts the comfortable coexistence they enjoy with

READING II   Philippians 4:6–9

Philippians = fih-LIP-ee-uhnz

Comforting words from St. Paul. Take your time proclaiming using a compassionate tone in your voice.

A reading from the Letter of Saint Paul to the Philippians

Brothers and sisters:
Have **no** anxiety at all, but in everything,
   by **prayer and petition**, with **thanksgiving**,
   make your **requests** known to **God**.
Then the **peace of God** that surpasses all **understanding**
   will guard your hearts and minds in **Christ Jesus**.

Pause after each comma. Use good volume and eye contact with each word: *true, honorable, just, pure, lovely, gracious.*

Finally, brothers and sisters,
   whatever is **true**, whatever is **honorable**,
   whatever is **just**, whatever is **pure**,
   whatever is **lovely**, whatever is **gracious**,
   if there is **any** excellence)
   and if there is **anything** worthy of praise,
   think about these things.
Keep on doing what you have **learned** and **received**
   and **heard** and **seen** in me.
Then the **God of peace** will be with you.

Pause and calmly read with a smile.

GOSPEL   Matthew 21:33–43

A reading from the holy Gospel according to Matthew

Pause before you begin the parable.

Use good eye contact and emotion in your voice as you proclaim the story.

Jesus said to the chief priests and the elders of the people:
   "**Hear** another parable.
There was a **landowner** who planted a **vineyard**,
   put a hedge around it, dug a wine press in it, and built a tower.
Then he **leased** it to tenants and went on a journey.
When vintage time drew near,
   he **sent** his servants to the tenants to obtain his produce. ❯❯
But the tenants **seized** the servants and one they **beat**,
   another they **killed**, and a third they **stoned**.

their neighbors who now persecute (not necessarily martyr) them. It is the anxiety that arises from their commitment to Christ, and not merely the worries that attend every life, that concerns Paul.

He writes literally: "About nothing, be anxious." Instead, the community must ask God to provide what they need to be faithful. Their prayers flow from unending gratitude for what God did for them in Christ, and for the unique essential role that God calls them to play in his plan for the salvation of the world. Regardless of how worrisome a

situation seems, a Christian is grateful that God is involved in it.

Paul reminds the baptized Philippians that God, like Isaiah's vine grower, is doing all that could possibly be done in every moment for the peace or well-being of everyone. Though humans cannot perceive exactly what God is doing, they can find signs of it in the murky mix of ideas, philosophies, cultures, practices, personalities, etc. that surround them—when they look for certain tell-tale signs.

They must concentrate, for example, on what is true in statements they hear and

read no matter their source; on what is just for all the people in a situation and not only for those with power to act; and, on what in a human project is worthy of respect and praise, innocent, lovely, and gracious. The community that focuses on these things will grow together in knowledge of God and divine ways.

 Like the vine grower in Isaiah's song, Jesus' landowner planted a vineyard, put up a hedge, dug a winepress, and built a tower. And like Isaiah, Jesus is teaching about God's plan

Again he sent other servants, more numerous than the first ones,
    but they treated them in the **same** way.
Finally, he sent his **son** to them, thinking,
    'They will **respect** my son.'
But when the tenants saw the son, they said to one another,
    'This is the **heir**.
Come, let us **kill** him and **acquire** his inheritance.'
They **seized** him, **threw** him **out** of the vineyard, and **killed** him.

Pause before you ask the question.

What will the **owner** of the vineyard **do** to those **tenants** when
        he comes?"
They answered him,
    "He will put those **wretched** men to a wretched **death**
    and lease his vineyard to other tenants
    who will give him the produce at the proper times."

Proclaim Jesus' words with authority.

Jesus said to them, "Did you **never** read in the Scriptures:
    The **stone** *that the builders* **rejected**
        has become the **cornerstone***;*
    by the **Lord** *has this been done,*
        and it is **wonderful** in our eyes?

Pause before you proclaim this last line.

Therefore, I say to you,
    the **kingdom of God** will be **taken away** from you
    and **given** to a people that **will produce** its fruit."

---

for Israel, but he modifies the prophet's work by shifting the focus from the fruit produced to those given the responsibility for turning it over to the landowner at harvest time. These are the tenants who represent the chief priests and elders to whom Jesus addresses the parable.

The tenants decide to keep the harvest for themselves. Twice they beat up, kill, and stone the servants sent by the landlord to collect it—like their ancestors killed the prophets whom God sent to Israel. Finally, the landowner sends his son thinking they

will respect him, but they kill him too, thinking to acquire the vineyard for themselves.

Jesus' question precipitates his point: "What will the vineyard owner do to those tenants when he comes?" The chief priests and elders condemn themselves when they say literally, "the wicked he will wickedly destroy." God will take away the oversight of the Kingdom from them and entrust it to new tenants who will ensure that God gets the fruit at harvest time. Jesus is the cornerstone of the new tenants, of those who respect him and believe that the Father

raised him from the dead, and that he will one day collect the fruit of their labor.

This parable is more than a justification for Christianity. It warns those who are responsible for tending God's people—a responsibility shared by all the baptized in some way—that they are provisional caretakers of a divine project. E.N.

TWENTY-EIGHTH SUNDAY IN ORDINARY TIME

LECTIONARY #142

READING I Isaiah 25:6–10a

A reading from the Book of the Prophet Isaiah

Isaiah = Ī-ZAY-uh

Proclaim with energy and authority.

> On this mountain the LORD of hosts
>   will provide for **all** peoples
> a **feast** of **rich** food and **choice** wines,
>   juicy, rich food and pure, choice wines.
> On this mountain he will **destroy**
>   the **veil** that veils **all** peoples,
> the **web** that is woven over 2 nations;
>   **he will destroy death forever.**

Pause, then slowly read this line.
Proclaim with an informational tone.

> The **Lord GOD** will wipe **away**
>   the tears from **every** face;
> the reproach of his people he will remove
>   from the whole earth; for the LORD has spoken.
>   On that day it will be said:

Transition to a tone of happiness. Smile.

> "**Behold our God**, to whom we looked to **save** us!
>   **This** is the LORD for whom we looked;
>   let us **rejoice** and be **glad** that he has **saved us**!"
> For the hand of the LORD will rest on **this mountain**.

READING I The thrice repeated "on this mountain" sets out Isaiah's main points in this reading. Its first appearance marks Mount Zion in Jerusalem as the site of the royal banquet that will celebrate the Lord's future final victory and enthronement over all people and kingdoms that oppose him. The fare of this feast is the best imaginable in Isaiah's day. Its food is rich, full of oil, which is essential for good health. Its wine is fine, aged in its dregs and then filtered.

Secondly, on this mountain the Lord will destroy, literally "swallow up," death and its power to inflict suffering on the human race. The image of the Lord God wiping away "the tears from every face" portrays the tender unbiased love that God has for every person and displays the universality of his reign. The Lord will also remove the disgrace that Israel suffers for its infidelity to the covenant.

Finally, on this future day, people will point in awe at the Lord who at long, long last has come. They will exclaim literally: "Let us go wild with joy and be glad that he has saved us." Let us party because the powerful hand of the Lord is resting "on this mountain," protecting all who come there from evil.

READING II For Paul, Christ is more than an imaginary companion, a ghostlike form of Jesus of Nazareth. The risen Christ, no longer restricted to a human body, pervades all creation and encompasses all that exists. After Paul meets him on the road to Damascus, the two of them are inseparable. Christ's interests and concerns replace his own. As he puts it in his letter to the Philippians, to live is Christ (1:21), and he feels taken hold of by

RESPONSORIAL PSALM   Psalm 23:1–3a, 3b–4, 5, 6 (6cd)

R. I shall live in the house of the Lord all the days of my life.

The LORD is my shepherd; I shall not want.
  In verdant pastures he gives me repose;
beside restful waters he leads me;
  he refreshes my soul.

He guides me in right paths
  for his name's sake.
Even though I walk in the dark valley
  I fear no evil; for you are at my side
with your rod and your staff
  that give me courage.

You spread the table before me
  in the sight of my foes;
you anoint my head with oil;
  my cup overflows.

Only goodness and kindness follow me
  all the days of my life;
and I shall dwell in the house of the LORD
  for years to come.

For meditation and context:

READING II   Philippians 4:12–14, 19–20

A reading from the Letter of Saint Paul to the Philippians

Brothers and sisters:
I **know** how to live in **humble** circumstances;
  I know **also** how to live with **abundance**.
In every circumstance and in **all** things
  I have learned the **secret** of being well **fed** and of going **hungry**,
  of living in abundance and of being in need.
I can do **all** things in him who **strengthens me**.
Still, it was kind of you to **share** in my distress.

My **God** will fully **supply** whatever you need,
  in accord with his glorious riches in **Christ Jesus**.
To our **God and Father**, glory **forever and ever**. Amen.

Philippians = fih-LIP-ee-uhnz

Proclaim this reading using a personal tone.

Read with gratefulness.

Using good eye contact, proclaim this last line as if you are in prayer.

> **TO KEEP IN MIND**
> Pause to break up separate thoughts, set significant statements apart, or indicate major shifts. Never pause in the middle of a single thought. Your primary guide for pauses is punctuation.

Christ (3:12). And in Galatians 2:20, he no longer lives but Christ, who loves him personally and gave his life for him, now lives in him.

Paul's witness in this reading flows from his experiences with the risen Lord. For him, and for the baptized who immerse themselves in and live only for Christ, normal human preoccupations like food and the comfort, security, and convenience of their living situation and work environment are of secondary importance. Whatever one's circumstances may be—whether of plenty or privation—they are not merely

adequate. They belong to the "all things that are working together for their good" to accomplish God's purposes (Romans 8:28).

When Paul writes that he can do all things in Christ, he means that Christ empowers him to put forth whatever spiritual and physical effort their mission together requires. Other Christians, like the Philippians who provide for him while he is imprisoned, are often the evidence of this support. Their gifts are also a way to share concretely in the hardships that he endures for his call and thus strengthen the bond between them.

Paul prays that God in turn will supply whatever the Philippians need "from the glorious riches in Christ Jesus," that is, from grace that surpasses every type of human aid. All this needing and supplying manifests God's active involvement on earth. "Amen" is the "so be it" of Paul's ancestors and now of his new community in Christ.

GOSPEL   In this parable, Jesus provokes thought about the kingdom of heaven by comparing it not only to "a king who gave a wedding feast for his son," but also to everything that follows.

GOSPEL   Matthew 22:1–14

A reading from the holy Gospel according to Matthew

Proclaim with good volume and articulation.

Pause before you begin the parable.

[**Jesus again** in reply spoke to the chief priests and elders
    of the people
  in parables, saying,
  "**The kingdom of heaven** may be likened to a king
  who **gave** a wedding **feast** for his **son**.
He dispatched his servants
    to summon the invited guests to the feast,
    but they **refused** to come.
A **second time** he sent other servants, saying,
    'Tell those invited: "**Behold**, I have prepared my banquet,
    my calves and fattened cattle are killed,
    and everything is ready; **come to the feast.**"'
Some ignored the invitation and went away,
    one to his farm, another to his business.
The rest laid hold of his servants,
    mistreated them, and **killed** them.
The king was **enraged** and sent his **troops**,
    destroyed those murderers, and **burned** their city.
Then he said to his servants, 'The feast is **ready**,
    but those who were invited were **not** worthy to come.
Go out, therefore, into the main roads
    and **invite** to the feast **whomever** you find.' »

As you continue to read, keep up your energy with expression in your voice.

The story falls into two parts and a closing statement. The first and longest part describes a series of invitations and the reactions they set off (22:1–10) and the second a judgment scene (22:11–13).

The account of the first invitation and the response that it meets are terse. "He dispatched his servants to summon the invited guests to the feast, but they refused to come." Jesus dwells the longest on the second invitation and the events that follow it. This time the king sends other servants to those formerly invited. He instructs them to emphasize the high qual-

ity of the feast prepared; he slaughtered the choicest animals of his herd—the calves and the fattened cattle. His "everything is ready; come to the feast" conveys his excitement about the event and his anticipation of the wonderful time that he will have with his guests.

Some of those invited a second time snub his invitation and return to business as usual. The rest lay hold of the servants, abuse, and kill them. Formerly eager and excited, now the king is enraged. He sends troops, destroys those murderers, and burns their city. (Many scholars see here an

indictment of the religious leaders who rejected Jesus and an allusion to the destruction of Jerusalem by the Romans in AD 70) Having found none of those formerly invited to be worthy, the king again sends out servants commanding them to invite "whomever you find."

Of the banquet, Jesus describes a single brief scene—the exchange between the king and one person who is not wearing a wedding garment. Because the king was so intent on filling his banquet hall, his concern about the attire of one guest surprises and evokes interest. The salutation

To keep the attention of the congregation use strong eye contact.

Pause before you read the king's command, them say it with authority.

The servants went out into the streets
    and gathered **all** they found, bad and good alike,
    and the hall was filled with guests.]
But when the king came in to meet the guests,
    he saw a man there **not** dressed in a wedding garment.
The king said to him, 'My friend, how is it
    that you came in here **without** a wedding garment?'
But he was reduced to **silence**.
Then the king said to his attendants, '**Bind** his hands and feet,
    and cast him into the **darkness** outside,
    where there will be **wailing** and **grinding** of teeth.'
Many are invited, but **few** are chosen."

[Shorter: Matthew 22:1–10 (see brackets)]

"friend," which occurs thrice in Matthew, never bodes well for the one so named. In Matthew 20:13, the landowner uses it to address a worker who labors the longest and complains because he does not receive more than the others. And in Matthew 16:50, it's the label that Jesus gives Judas after the traitorous kiss in the garden. In this passage, the king's use of "friend" alerts readers that the man improperly clothed is in trouble. The precise meaning of the wedding garment is not clear. But in the context of Matthew's Gospel, it likely represents the lifestyle that a disciple weaves as he or she puts Jesus' teachings into practice and bears fruit.

The guest's punishment for his presumption, like the murder and destruction meted out to earlier invitees, seems disproportionate. The king could simply order his attendants to escort the man out. But no! He commands them to bind his hands and his feet and hurl him out of the lighted feast into the outermost darkness. While those inside celebrate, he lies outside with others who are "wailing and grinding their teeth," a metaphor for eternal punishment in Matthew. The king's extreme responses remind the baptized that the quality of their discipleship determines their unending rejoicing or mourning. Should they die today, what "garment" will they be wearing for the last judgment? E.N.

TWENTY-NINTH SUNDAY IN ORDINARY TIME

LECTIONARY #145

READING I   Isaiah 45:1, 4–6

Isaiah = Ī-ZAY-uh
Cyrus = SĪ-ruhs
Proclaim with good volume and with a tone of authority.

A reading from the Book of the Prophet Isaiah

Thus says the LORD to his anointed, **Cyrus**,
 whose right hand I grasp,
subduing nations before him,
 and **making** kings run in his service,
opening doors before him
 and **leaving** the gates unbarred:
For the sake of **Jacob**, my servant,
 of **Israel**, my **chosen** one,
I have **called you** by **your** name,
 giving you a title, though you knew me **not**.
I am the LORD and there is **no other**,
 there is **no GOD** besides me.
It is **I** who arm you, though you know me not,
 so that toward the **rising** and the **setting** of the sun
 people may **know** that there is **none besides me.**
I am the LORD, there is no other.

Clearly proclaim the reading and take your time.

Pause before you begin the Lord's words. Use good eye contact.

READING I   Second Isaiah reminds Israel that the Lord rules not only over them but over all nations and is the only God. These claims must have seemed absurd to his hearers because in their day a god's rank is reckoned by the nation-status of its people compares to others. That Israel is landless and living in exile in Babylon seems to prove that Babylon's god, Marduk, is more powerful than the Lord. And yet, the biblical prophets insist that the Babylonians are merely the instrument the Lord uses to punish Israel for its infidelity. Now, Second Isaiah, preaching toward the end of the exile (c. 553 BC), announces that their sentence is complete. The Lord is calling Cyrus, an ascendant ruler in Persia, to conquer the Babylonians and allow the exiles to return home.

To engage Israel's attention, the prophet uses a piece of propaganda that Cyrus circulates as his armies approach the city of Babylon. In it he claims that its patron god, Marduk, designates him "the ruler of the world." This politicking proclamation came to light in 1879 when archeologists discovered the "Cyrus cylinder," a type of "printing press." The message was etched on a solid stone tube and printed when it was rolled over wet clay tablets which were then dried and distributed.

Second Isaiah claims that the Lord, not Marduk, is behind Cyrus' success. Cyrus is the Lord's "anointed" (in Hebrew, *messiah*). The Lord "grasps his right hand," a gesture like one in a Babylonian ritual where the grasp of a god's hand (on a statue) validates and empowers a sovereign. The Lord also gives Cyrus a "title," probably "Shepherd" (see Isaiah 44:28), which is a common designation for rulers in the biblical world. All this is evidence that the Lord, as the prophet

For meditation and context:

RESPONSORIAL PSALM Psalm 96:1, 3, 4–5, 7–8, 9–10 (7b)

R. Give the Lord glory and honor.

Sing to the LORD a new song;
  sing to the LORD, all you lands.
Tell his glory among the nations;
  among all peoples, his wondrous deeds.

For great is the LORD and highly
    to be praised;
  awesome is he, beyond all gods.
For all the gods of the nations are things
    of nought,
  but the LORD made the heavens.

Give to the LORD, you families of nations,
  give to the LORD glory and praise;
  give to the LORD the glory due his name!
Bring gifts, and enter his courts.

Worship the LORD, in holy attire;
  tremble before him, all the earth;
say among the nations: The LORD is king,
  he governs the peoples with equity.

Thessalonians = thes-uh-LOH-nee-uhnz
Silvanus = sil-VAY-nuhs

Proclaim in a tone of authority. Use good eye contact and projection.

Transition to a tone of gratitude. Make the reading sound personal.

Say this with focus and a firm purpose.

READING II   1 Thessalonians 1:1–5b

A reading from the first Letter of Saint Paul to the Thessalonians

Paul, **Silvanus**, and **Timothy** to the church of the **Thessalonians**
  in **God** the **Father** and the **Lord Jesus Christ**:
  grace to you and **peace**.
We give thanks to **God** always for **all** of you,
  remembering you in our prayers,
  unceasingly calling to mind your **work** of **faith** and **labor**
    of **love**
  and **endurance** in **hope** of our **Lord Jesus Christ**,
  before our **God and Father,**
  knowing, brothers and sisters **loved** by God,
  how you were **chosen**.
For our gospel did not come to you in word **alone**,
  but **also** in power and in the **Holy Spirit** and with
    much conviction.

---

repeats four times in the last verses, is the only God.

READING II This letter, written in AD 50–51, is the earliest writing in the New Testament. In its opening verses, Paul reminds the Thessalonians of how Baptism expands their existence. Their individual lives are now intertwined—in Christ—with the members of their community, as well as with Christian communities in other places. All the baptized also live within God—the Father, Son, and Holy Spirit. The Father is Israel's Lord, who

called Cyrus to be his messiah more than five hundred years earlier, and the Father of Jesus Christ. (*Christ* is a title from the Greek that translates the Hebrew *messiah*.) The Holy Spirit is present and powerfully at work in every place where believers proclaim the Gospel.

The identifying characteristics of these communities are faith, love, and hope. These gifts, which manifest their shared life with God, require effort. Faith must be demonstrated by action. Love is a labor which is often inconvenient and fraught with difficulties. The hope that

Christ lives and will return needs constant nourishment.

GOSPEL In the parables from the past three Sundays, Jesus tells the religious leaders that they are in danger of losing the Kingdom of God. Angered by his warning, the Pharisees plot to trap him in speech and discredit him. They don't confront him themselves but send their disciples and some Herodians to do so. The collusion of the Pharisees, who in general dislike being under Rome's power, and the Herodians, who support the

GOSPEL   Matthew 22:15–21

A reading from the holy Gospel according to Matthew

The **Pharisees** went off
   and **plotted** how they might entrap **Jesus** in speech.
They sent their disciples to him, with the **Herodians**, saying,
   "Teacher, we know that you are a **truthful** man
   and that you teach the way of **God** in accordance
      with the **truth**.
And you are **not** concerned with anyone's opinion,
   for you do **not** regard a person's status.
Tell us, then, what is your opinion:
   Is it **lawful** to pay the census tax to **Caesar** or **not**?"
Knowing their malice, **Jesus** said,
   "**Why** are you testing me, you **hypocrites**?
Show me the coin that pays the census tax."
Then they handed him the **Roman** coin.
He said to them, "Whose image is this and whose inscription?"
They replied, "**Caesar's**."
At that he said to them,
   "Then repay to **Caesar** what belongs to **Caesar**
   and to **God** what belongs to **God**."

Pharisees = FAYR-uh-seez

Begin with an informative tone.

Herodians = her-OH-dee-uhnz
Pause before you begin the question.
Use expression in your voice.

Pause before Jesus' question. Choose to address the Pharisees in a calm tone.

Say this line using good eye contact.

Roman agent in Galilee, Herod Antipas, is surprising. Perhaps their perception of Jesus as a common enemy unites them.

Those sent address Jesus as "Teacher," a title which in Matthew indicates that they are not his disciples. They flatter him that he is truthful, that what he teaches about the way of God accords with the truth, and that he is rightly indifferent to people's opinions and worldly status. Then they set the trap, a question that seeks a yes or no answer: "Is it lawful to pay taxes to Caesar or not?" If Jesus answers yes, he will offend some of the Pharisees and the Jewish nationalists, like the zealots, who resist Roman rule. If he answers no, he will offend the Herodians and risk their labelling him a rebel.

Seeing their malice, Jesus throws some truth at them: they are hypocrites. And instead of giving them a simple yes or no, he asks them to do something: to show him the Roman coin used to pay taxes. One of them digs out a denarius and hands it to him. He keeps their attention focused on the coin by asking whose image and inscription it bears. When they answer "Caesar's," they fall into his trap.

Jesus' final words are pithier in Greek than English translations of them can be. He says, "Therefore, give back *tà Kaísaros Kaísari* (the things that belong to Caesar to Caesar) and *tà toū theoū tō theō* (the things that belong to God to God)." The things of God—that's what Jesus knows and wants to talk about. Amazed and silenced on this topic, his challengers depart. E.N.

THIRTIETH SUNDAY IN ORDINARY TIME

LECTIONARY #148

READING I   Exodus 22:20–26

Exodus = EK-suh-duhs

Pause before you begin. Proclaim using a tone of authority with good volume.

Articulate your words and use good eye contact.

Pause and then read with firmness and conviction in your voice. Take your time.

extortioner = ek-STOHR-shuhn-*r

Say this last line slowly with emotion in your voice.

A reading from the Book of Exodus

Thus says the LORD:
"You shall **not molest** or **oppress** an alien,
  for **you** were once aliens yourselves in the land of **Egypt**.
You shall **not** wrong any widow or orphan.
If ever you wrong them and they cry out to me,
  I will surely **hear** their cry.
My wrath will **flare up**, and **I** will **kill** you with the sword;
  then your **own** wives will be widows, and your
    children orphans.

"If you **lend** money to one of your **poor** neighbors among
    my people,
  you shall **not act** like an **extortioner** toward him
  by demanding interest from him.
If you **take** your neighbor's cloak as a pledge,
  you shall **return** it to him before sunset;
  for this cloak of his is the only covering he has for his body.
What else has he to sleep in?
If he **cries** out to me, I will **hear** him; for **I am compassionate**."

READING I   Many Israelite laws also appear in the legal material of the peoples with whom they mingled. For example, the commandments "You shall not steal" and "You shall not kill" are common in most societies, and "an eye for an eye . . . " appears in the Old Babylonian Code of Hammurabi that is dated to the eighteenth century BC, around five centuries before Moses. But biblical laws have an added dimension; they present life from God's point of view. Their purpose is to reprogram humans and persuade them to live by divine standards and priorities.

Especially important to the God of Israel is the way that people treat each other.

The first law in this reading forbids molesting and oppressing foreigners. Because they are often unfamiliar with the mores of a new place and not fluent in the language spoken there, foreigners are frequently victimized and their well-being endangered. The Hebrew behind the word *oppressing* conveys the crowding or pressing in of tormentors on their prey. The reason that Israel must not bully foreigners is that they too experienced how difficult an

immigrant's life can be when they took refuge in Egypt.

The second law forbids doing wrong to "the widow or orphan." In the biblical world, these groups are vulnerable because they have no man to protect them and advocate for their rights. By extension, they represent all those in society who have no one to look out for them. In this law, the Hebrew repeats three verbs in different forms to underscore the consequences of one's decision to wrong another. The text reads literally, "If *wronging* you ever *wrong* them, and *crying out* they *cry out* to me,

For meditation and context:

RESPONSORIAL PSALM   Psalm 18:2–3, 3–4, 47, 51 (2)

R. I love you, Lord, my strength.

I love you, O LORD, my strength,
  O LORD, my rock, my fortress,
    my deliverer.

My God, my rock of refuge,
  my shield, the horn of my salvation,
    my stronghold!
Praised be the LORD, I exclaim,
  and I am safe from my enemies.

The LORD lives and blessed be my rock!
  Extolled be God my savior.
You who gave great victories to your king
  and showed kindness to your anointed.

READING II   1 Thessalonians 1:5c–10

Thessalonians = thes-uh-LOH-nee-uhnz

Pause before you start proclaiming. Use good volume and eye contact.

A reading from the first Letter of Saint Paul to the Thessalonians

Brothers and sisters:
You **know** what sort of people we were among you for **your** sake.
And you became **imitators** of us and of the **Lord**,
  receiving the word in **great** affliction, with **joy** from the
    Holy Spirit,
  so that you became a **model** for **all** the believers
    in **Macedonia** and in **Achaia**.

Keep up your energy.

Macedonia = mas-eh-DOH-nee-uh

Achaia = uh-KAY-uh

For from you the word of the **Lord** has sounded forth
  not only in **Macedonia** and in **Achaia**,
  but in **every** place your faith in **God** has **gone forth,**
  so that we have **no need** to say anything.

Proclaim with intensity.

For they themselves **openly declare** about us
  what sort of reception we had among you,
  and how you **turned** to **God** from idols
  to **serve** the living and true **God**
  and to **await** his **Son** from heaven,
  whom he **raised** from the **dead**,

Proclaim with a tone of gratefulness.

  Jesus, who **delivers us** from the coming wrath.

---

hearing I will surely hear their cry." The motivation for not breaking this law is that the wrongdoer will die and his family will experience the harm that he did to others.

The last law reveals that in God's view empathy for people overrides commonly accepted business practices. Here, when a man's cloak is taken to guarantee a loan, the lender must return it to him when he needs it! What a crazy way to conduct business—for a mere human, certainly. But not for those who see even the smallest travails of others' existence with God's compassionate eyes.

READING II   The Thessalonians learned about Christ and decided to commit themselves to him because they were inspired not only by Paul's teaching but especially by the way that he conducted himself when he was among them. They are impressed by how the Gospel shapes his lifestyle as well as how it molds his view and treatment of others. They are riveted by the coexistence of suffering and joy that they see in him. Though he was recently thrown out of Philippi and will soon be driven out of Thessalonica, he remains profoundly happy.

The Thessalonians too suffer and rejoice as they break away from the unbelieving majority who worship false gods. News of their faith and their unusual community spread the Gospel. It travels so effectively along the east-west Roman thoroughfare that passes through their city, the Egnatian Way, that Paul writes, "we have no need to say anything."

GOSPEL   A frequent topic of scholarly discussion among the Jews of Jesus' day is which of their 613 laws is the greatest. For Hillel, an early first-century AD

GOSPEL Matthew 22:34–40

A reading from the holy Gospel according to Matthew

When the **Pharisees** heard that **Jesus** had silenced the **Sadducees**,
  they gathered together, and one of them,
  a scholar of the law, **tested** him by asking,
  "**Teacher**, which commandment in the law is the **greatest**?"
He said to him,
  "You shall **love** the **Lord**, your **God**,
  with **all** your **heart**,
  with **all** your **soul**,
  and with **all** your **mind**.
This is the **greatest** and the **first** commandment.
The **second** is like it:
  You shall **love** your **neighbor** as **yourself**.
The **whole law** and the **prophets depend** on these
    two commandments."

Proclaim using good volume.

Pharisees = FAYR-uh-seez

Sadducees = SAD-yoo-seez

Pause before you ask the question.

Read with emotion in your voice and with good eye contact.

Proclaim the second commandment with the same energy as the first, with firmness and clarity.

---

rabbi, it was: "What is hateful to you do not do to your neighbor; that is the whole Torah, while the rest is commentary on it." In today's Gospel, the Pharisees send one of their Torah experts to seek Jesus' opinion. This man's address of Jesus as "Teacher" in Matthew's Gospel shows that he is not a true disciple. Jesus' demonstrates his own expertise in Torah; his response combines two Old Testament laws which, unlike the ones that prohibit behaviors in today's first reading, require active loving.

Jesus' greatest commandment is a quote from the Shema (Deuteronomy 6:5), a passage that Jews pray several times a day to remind them to love the Lord their God with "with all your heart, with all your soul, and with all your mind." Those who obey this command commit their whole being—their unique personality, thoughts, emotional reactions, strengths and weaknesses, everything that makes them who they are and that distinguishes them from everyone else—to God.

Jesus' second commandment, which comes from Leviticus 19:18, links love of God with love of neighbor. Since earth today is a global community, there are a lot of neighbors to care for. Those who obey this command go into action to meet their needs as they do their own. They do not simply refrain from abusing the disadvantaged and vulnerable. Rather, they think deeply about their needs and work energetically to provide them with material and emotional sustenance. E.N.

ALL SAINTS

LECTIONARY #667

READING I   Revelation 7:2–4, 9–14

A reading from the Book of Revelation

Revelation = rev-uh-LAY-shuhn

Take your time and proclaim with good volume.

I, **John**, saw another **angel** come up from the **East**,
  holding the **seal** of the living **God**.
He **cried out** in a loud voice to the four angels
  who were given **power** to **damage** the **land** and the sea,
  "Do **not** damage the land or the sea or the trees
  until we put thc **seal** on the **foreheads** of the **servants**
    of our **God**."

Pause before you read the quote. Make your voice strong.

I heard the number of those who had been marked with the seal,
  one hundred and forty-four thousand marked
  from **every** tribe of the children of **Israel**.

Transition your voice to a tone of calmness.

After this I had a **vision** of a great multitude,
  which **no one** could count,
  from **every** nation, race, people, and tongue.
They **stood** before the throne and before the **Lamb**,
  wearing white robes and holding palm branches in their hands.
They **cried out** in a loud voice:

Continue reading with a tone of awe and wonder in your voice.

**"Salvation comes from our God, who is seated on the throne,
and from the Lamb."**

All the angels stood around the throne
  and around the elders and the four living creatures.
They **prostrated** themselves before the throne,
  worshiped **God**, and exclaimed: »

Pause and proclaim loudly.

READING I The aim of the book of Revelation is to give hope to Christians who are suffering persecution for their belief in the Lamb, the Risen Christ. In this reading, the arrival of an angel who is holding "the seal of the living God," interrupts the opening of the seven seals. These seals symbolically describe events that will signal the "great trial" that will precede the full manifestation of the Lamb's victory at the end of time. The seal that the angel holds is a signet-ring or a small cylinder, which rulers used to sign documents and to mark their possessions.

For example, archeologists have found several stamps or inscriptions of *lemelek* (Hebrew for "belonging to the king") imprinted by such seals on the handles of clay storage jars.

In Revelation, the angel with God's seal commands four other angels, who have been given power to start wreaking the final havoc, to do nothing until the foreheads of "the servants of our God" bear the stamp that identifies them as God's property and protects them from the coming trial. The symbolic number of those sealed, 144,000, represents the remnant of the

twelve tribes of Israel who acknowledge the Lamb. The verses that are omitted from the reading list these tribes.

The next vision is of another group of people that is not limited to Israelites; they come from every community on earth. Before the throne of God and the Lamb, this multitude stands—a posture of praise in early Christian liturgies. They carry palms that people waved in the biblical world to celebrate the return of victorious armies. Here, the countless multitude welcomes the Lamb's return at the end of time.

Read this quote as if in prayer.

**"Amen. Blessing and glory, wisdom and thanksgiving,
    honor, power, and might
    be to our God forever and ever. Amen**."

Then one of the elders **spoke up** and said to me,
    "**Who** are these wearing white robes, and where did they
        come from?"
I said to him, "My lord, **you** are the one who knows."
He said to me,
    "These are the ones who have **survived** the time
        of great **distress**;
    they have **washed** their robes
    and made them **white** in the **Blood** of the **Lamb**."

Pause before you ask the question.

Take your time and use good eye contact.

For meditation and context:

RESPONSORIAL PSALM   Psalm 24:1bc–2, 3–4ab, 5–6 (6)

R. Lord, this is the people that longs to see your face.

The LORD's are the earth and its fullness;
    the world and those who dwell in it.
For he founded it upon the seas
    and established it upon the rivers.

Who can ascend the mountain of the LORD?
    or who may stand in his holy place?
One whose hands are sinless, whose heart
    is clean,
    who desires not what is vain.

He shall receive a blessing from the LORD,
    a reward from God his savior.
Such is the race that seeks him,
    that seeks the face of the God of Jacob.

The members of this crowd wear robes that are washed white in the Lamb's blood. Some of these are the martyrs of the author's day. But, since the final tribulation is yet to come, their number could also include the baptized of every generation. Being washed in the Lamb's blood is not something that just happens to them; they are scrubbed clean as they actively unite themselves to the Lamb's death by laying down their life for others. What a sight this standing, palm-holding, white-robed assembly makes as they wildly praise God because they experience fully his long-promised salvation.

READING II   The concept of "children of God" that appears here reflects that of believers in the Gospel according to John. These are the baptized who, through the work of the Spirit, were born not of blood nor of the will of the flesh nor of the will of man, but of God (John 1:13; 3:5–6).

The first Letter of John contrasts the children of God with the children of the world who follow the devil. The world's children focus on materialistic things and mere human experiences that will not last. But the baptized focus on doing God's will,

on deepening their relationship with their brother, the Son.

Evoking the Hellenistic maxim, "like knows like," John explains that people did not recognize the Son and do not recognize the children of God because humans understand only what they have experienced. So, when the baptized, who were born of the Spirit, are raised from the dead like Jesus was, they will perceive his divinity fully. In the meantime, they must follow his teachings and personal example.

READING II   1 John 3:1–3

A reading from the first Letter of Saint John

Proclaim with tenderness and joy in your voice.

Say slowly with a smile.

Proclaim with renewed energy and good projection.

Read with finality and conviction.

Beloved:
See what **love** the **Father** has **bestowed** on us
    that **we** may be called the **children of God.**
Yet so **we are.**
The **reason** the world does **not** know us
    is that it did **not know him.**
Beloved, we **are** God's children **now**;
    what we shall **be** has **not** yet been **revealed.**
We **do** know that when it **is** revealed **we shall be like him,**
    for we shall **see** him as **he is.**
Everyone who has this **hope** based on him makes himself **pure**,
    as **he is pure.**

TO KEEP IN MIND
Be careful not to "swallow" words by mumbling. Articulate carefully so that every word is clearly heard, especially at the end of lines.

GOSPEL   The beatitudes describe the mindset and prioritize the activities of those who are destined for eternal life in the kingdom of heaven—all the baptized, who are called to be saints. Though many believers downgrade the beatitudes to impossible standards whose goal is to inspire them to be occasionally a little better, Jesus does not come across in the Gospels as an idealist or a dreamer. He is the Son who reveals how those who belong to God's family, and who want to belong to that wildly cheering multitude that will stand before the Lamb forever, must live.

In fact, the only way to understand the beatitudes and to experience the realities that they promise is to reframe our views and reshape our daily round by them. The adventures that ensue are not for the timid, the merely human. They are for God's sealed children who trust that the Son knows what he's talking about and who want to live with him forever.

The first four beatitudes identify attitudes which Jesus' disciples must repeat until they become "default" responses. These are not natural mindsets, but divine ones which must be learned. The first beatitude states the principle that underpins the rest of the list. Because humans have no control over spiritual matters, the disciple must be poor "in spirit"; they depend on God to give them life in the kingdom on earth and in eternity.

Threaded through the beatitudes is Jesus' insistence that righteousness or justice is a certain indicator of the kingdom. His disciples "hunger" and "thirst" to see divine justice manifested in the way that people treat each other. They must not be

GOSPEL   Matthew 5:1–12a

A reading from the holy Gospel according to Matthew

When **Jesus** saw the crowds, he **went** up the mountain,
    and after he had sat down, his disciples came to him.
He began to **teach** them, saying:

> "**Blessed** are the **poor in spirit**,
>   for theirs is the **Kingdom of heaven**.
> **Blessed** are they who **mourn**,
>   for they will be **comforted**.
> **Blessed** are the **meek**,
>   for they will **inherit** the land.
> **Blessed** are they who **hunger** and **thirst** for **righteousness**,
>   for they will be **satisfied**.
> **Blessed** are the **merciful**,
>   for they will be shown **mercy**.
> **Blessed** are the **clean** of heart,
>   for they will see **God**.
> **Blessed** are the **peacemakers**,
>   for they will be called **children** of God.
> **Blessed** are they who are **persecuted** for the sake
>   of **righteousness**,
>   for theirs is the Kingdom of **heaven**.
> **Blessed** are **you** when they **insult** you and **persecute** you
>   and **utter** every kind of **evil** against you **falsely** because
>   of **me**.
> **Rejoice** and be **glad**,
>   for your **reward** will be **great** in **heaven**."

Blessed = BLES-uhd

Pause before you begin proclaiming the Beatitudes. Take your time as you proclaim. Use a different tone with each one. Good eye contact is essential.

Keep up your energy by speaking clearly.

TO KEEP IN MIND
Repetition of the same word or phrase over the course of a reading emphasizes a point. Make each instance distinct, and build your intensity with each repetition.

---

self-righteous and judgmental, but merciful. If they are easily offended they must retrain themselves to react to those who injure them with God's compassion. Having cut their offenders some slack—often a lot of slack—they can be sure that God will do the same for them at the last judgment.

The "clean of heart" picks up on a phrase from the responsorial psalm, where it is a condition for ascending the Lord's mountain. The clean of heart are people who live with integrity, whose behavior reflects their commitment to God and whose interests mirror divine ones. They

are, for example, the peacemakers who not only believe that all people deserve to be treated fairly but suffer to see that they are. Unlike piously placid people who compromise to avoid unpleasantries or dodge dangerous situations and leadership responsibilities, peacemakers are heroic and unrelenting champions of the oppressed. While in the human view, they seem to be troublemakers who disturb the peace, Jesus calls them children of God. Theirs is not an earthly kingdom, but a heavenly one.

The last beatitude requires a lot of retraining for a human. Jesus teaches that disciples who are being insulted, persecuted, and falsely accused of every imaginable evil "because of" him must know that they are blessed! When going through these truly distressing experiences, they must "rejoice"—and lest this pass his hearers by, Jesus adds "be glad"—because their reward from God will be great in heaven. E.N.

THE COMMEMORATION OF ALL THE FAITHFUL DEPARTED (ALL SOULS' DAY)

LECTIONARY #668

READING I   Wisdom 3:1–9

A reading from the Book of Wisdom

The **souls** of the **just** are in the hand of **God**,
   and **no** torment shall touch them.
They **seemed**, in the view of the **foolish**, to be **dead**;
   and their passing away was thought an **affliction**
   and their going forth from us, **utter destruction**.
But they are in **peace**.
For if before men, indeed, they be **punished**,
   yet is their **hope** full of **immortality**;
chastised a little, they shall be **greatly** blessed,
   because **God** tried them
   and found them **worthy** of himself.
As gold in the furnace, he **proved** them,
   and as sacrificial **offerings** he **took** them to himself.
In the time of their **visitation** they shall **shine**,
   and shall **dart** about as sparks through **stubble**;
they shall **judge** nations and **rule** over peoples,
   and the LORD shall be their **King forever**.
Those who **trust** in him shall **understand** truth,
   and the **faithful** shall **abide** with him in **love**:
because **grace** and **mercy** are with his **holy** ones,
   and his **care** is with his **elect**.

Proclaim with good eye contact and volume.

Say slowly with a smile. Proclaim in a tone of hope and joy.

Continue to build the intensity in your voice until the end of the reading.

With a smile, slow your pace on this line.

There are options for readings today. Ask your parish staff which ones will be used.

READING I Today's passage contrasts the views of death held by the foolish and the wise. Fools think that people exist only while they have a body on earth, and therefore for them death is a final lamentable experience. For them, it is a great affliction that people "pass away," and "go forth from us." In contrast, the wise, who also see their loved ones and others die, believe that they continue to exist. Specifically, the souls of those who lived a just life are "in the hand of God"; i.e., God's power protects them from all harm and they are resting in peace.

The author of Wisdom does not yet conceive of immortality as the resurrection of the body that later Christian doctrine will define. This passage presents the human understanding of the afterlife for those who are just at one moment in salvation history, most probably between 50 BC and AD 50.

The author's concept of immortality lies between the Hebrew and Greek views of his day. For him, those who die continue to exist as more than the "shades" or ghost-like forms of the dead who go down to Sheol, the Hebrew underworld. But he does not yet believe that when a person dies the Greek "soul" separates from the body and lives on. In his view, what continues of a person after death is his or her

275

For meditation and context:

RESPONSORIAL PSALM   Psalm 23:1–3a, 3b–4, 5, 6 (1)

R. The Lord is my shepherd; there is nothing I shall want.
or
R. Though I walk in the valley of darkness, I fear no evil, for you are with me.

The LORD is my shepherd; I shall not want.
In verdant pastures he gives me repose;
beside restful waters he leads me;
he refreshes my soul.

He guides me in right paths
for his name's sake.
Even though I walk in the dark valley
I fear no evil; for you are at my side
with your rod and your staff
that give me courage.

You spread the table before me
in the sight of my foes;
You anoint my head with oil;
my cup overflows.

Only goodness and kindness follow me
all the days of my life;
and I shall dwell in the house of the LORD
for years to come.

READING II   Romans 5:5–11

A reading from the Letter of Saint Paul to the Romans

Brothers and sisters:
Hope does **not** disappoint,
because the **love** of **God** has been **poured** out into our **hearts**
through the **Holy Spirit** that has been **given** to **us**.
For **Christ**, while we were still **helpless**,
died at the **appointed** time for the ungodly.
Indeed, only with **difficulty** does one **die** for a **just** person,
though perhaps for a **good** person
one might even **find courage** to die.
But **God** proves his **love** for us
in that while we were **still** sinners **Christ** died for us.
How much **more** then, since we are now **justified** by his **Blood**,
will we be **saved through him** from the wrath. »

Pause before you begin and take a deep breath.

Speak slowly, with energy in your words as you proclaim.

relationship with God, and this relationship consists in the just acts that he or she performed on earth. Without these, there is no bond that can continue after death.

The just, God's "holy ones" or "saints," do not merely refrain from unrighteous acts. They toil for justice on behalf of others who are less fortunate than themselves or who are oppressed. Though many of his contemporaries interpret human suffering as divine punishment, this author sees it as the way

that God tests the just to discover if they are worthy to share life with him forever.

The simile of gold tested in the furnace reflects a common business practice. When buyers paid with metals for goods or services rendered, sellers or providers of services melted them down to remove impurities and to confirm their supposed value. For example, in one of the Amarna Letters, written in the fourteenth century BC and discovered by archeologists in 1887, a Babylonian king writes to another ruler that

"the twenty minas of gold" that he sent "were not pure, for when it was put in the furnace, only five minas were produced."

Wisdom also describes the just as whole-burnt offerings. In contrast to other animal sacrifices that are partially returned to the offerer to be enjoyed with his family, these are consumed on the altar as a sign that the offerer gives them completely to God. The sufferings that the just endure are the flames of the sacrificial fire that consume them during their earthly life, carry-

Using good eye contact and speaking clearly are essential in this reading.

Indeed, if, while we were **enemies**,
  we were **reconciled** to God through the **death** of his Son,
  how much **more**, once **reconciled**,
  will we be **saved** by his life.
Not only that,
  but we **also** boast of **God** through our **Lord Jesus Christ,**
  through whom we have **now received reconciliation**.

Or:

Pause before you read this added blessing.

READING II   Romans 6:3–9

A reading from the Letter of Saint Paul to the Romans

Brothers and sisters:
Are you **unaware** that we who were **baptized** into **Christ Jesus**
  were baptized into his **death**?
We were **indeed** buried **with** him through baptism into **death**,
  so that, just as **Christ** was raised from the dead
  by the glory of the **Father**,
  we **too** might **live** in **newness** of **life**.

Pause and then ask the question. Use good eye contact and volume.

For if we have grown into **union** with him through a **death**
    like his,
  we shall **also** be **united** with **him** in the **resurrection**.
We know that our **old** self was **crucified** with him,
  so that our **sinful** body might be done away with,
  that we might **no** longer be in **slavery** to **sin**.
For a **dead** person has been **absolved** from sin.
If, then, we have **died** with **Christ**,
  we **believe** that we shall **also live** with him.
We know that **Christ**, raised from the dead, **dies no more;**
  death **no** longer has **power** over him.

Speak slowly so the congregation can follow and understand St. Paul's words.

Pause before you proclaim the last line.

ing them upward toward God. And as they breathe out their last breath, God takes them to himself.

READING II | Paul seems frustrated that Christians expect to experience the resurrected life fully on earth. They do not understand why, since they are baptized into the Risen Christ, they suffer, why life is not always pleasant and gratifying. Paul asks them, are you oblivious that we were baptized into Christ's death? Do

you not understand that you live buried together with and in Christ, so that you will be raised with him and experience the fullness of his resurrected life when he returns at the end of time?

It is the old self, Paul elaborates, the slave to sin who is buried with Christ. And Christ now guides and shapes the life of the baptized. This shift of power from the sinner to Christ is a process. In this letter, Paul compares it to a shoot being grafted onto an olive tree. The Christian is the shoot that

becomes something new as it fuses with Christ, the tree. The sap of the tree pumps its life through the shoot until the two become united (Romans 11).

Belief that they are baptized into Christ's death, and belief that Christ defeated death once and for all—that is, that he cannot die again—makes this union possible. In case we still don't fully grasp this, Paul concludes, "death no longer has power over him." Nor does it have power over those who have already died and are

GOSPEL   John 6:37–40

A reading from the holy Gospel according to John

Jesus said to the crowds:
    "**Everything** that the **Father gives** me will come to me,
    and I will **not reject** anyone who **comes** to me,
    because I came down from heaven **not** to do **my** own **will**
    but the **will** of the one who **sent** me.
And **this** is the **will** of the **one** who sent me,
    that **I** should **not lose** anything of what he **gave** me,
    but that I should **raise it** on the **last** day.
For **this** is the will of my **Father**,
    that **everyone** who **sees** the **Son** and **believes** in him
    may have **eternal life**,
    and **I shall raise him up on the last day.**"

Proclaim in a tone of authority in your voice.

Pause before you say this line.

Proclaim with firmness and certainty.

TO KEEP IN MIND
Making eye contact with the assembly connects you with them and connects them to the reading more deeply. This helps the assembly stay with the story and keeps them engaged.

buried with him. In other words, the real death, for the Christian, occurs at Baptism. Physical death is only a change that allows them to experience fullness of life in the Risen Christ.

GOSPEL   When the Son of God became a human being, he manifested clearly the divine grace, mercy, and care that attend God's holy ones in the book of Wisdom. In this Gospel, the evangelist takes a step back and reveals that God draws or "gives" people to the Son. In other words, those who come to Jesus do not do so on their own initiative.

And Jesus, realizing how important they are to his Father, whose will he always follows, rejects none of them. It is also the Father's will that he not lose any one of these who are chosen to be his brothers and sisters, that is, that he raise all of them up on the last day. E.N.

THIRTY-SECOND SUNDAY IN ORDINARY TIME

LECTIONARY #154

READING I   Wisdom 6:12–16

A reading from the Book of Wisdom

> **Resplendent** and **unfading** is wisdom,
>   and she is readily **perceived** by those who **love** her,
>   and **found** by those who **seek** her.
> She hastens to make herself known in anticipation
>   of their desire;
>   whoever **watches** for her at dawn shall **not** be disappointed,
>   for he shall **find** her sitting by his gate.
> For taking **thought** of wisdom is the **perfection** of **prudence**,
>   and whoever for her sake **keeps** vigil
>   shall quickly be **free** from **care**;
> because she makes her own rounds, seeking those **worthy**
>   of her,
>   and graciously **appears** to them in the ways,
>   and **meets** them with **all solicitude**.

Articulation is important in this reading. Be sure to say each syllable and word ending clearly.

Do not rush. Take your time. Smile as you proclaim all that wisdom does for us.

solicitude = suh-LIS-uh-tood (kindness)

TO KEEP IN MIND
Use inflection (the high or low pitch of your voice) to convey attitude and feeling. High pitch expresses intensity and excitement; low pitch expresses sadness, contrition, or solemnity.

READING I   In the book of Wisdom, Lady Wisdom is intimately related to God. She is described as the divine breath or spirit, a pure outpouring of the glory of the Almighty, the mirror of divine power, and the image of divine goodness. She pervades all things, and especially loves people. She passes into holy souls in every age, changing them into friends of God (Wisdom 7:22–27). Today's reading describes her as shining or transparent and shows how eager she is to make herself known to those who love her.

Those who recognize the value of Wisdom's companionship are always on the lookout for her, like lovers ever alert for glimpses of the beloved. They watch for her at dawn, the symbolic time that salvation occurs in Scripture (see, for example, Exodus 14; Psalm 5, and the Resurrection accounts). They count on her to help them navigate the events of the day.

Wisdom, for her part, waits at the gate of those who seek her, delighted each day to set out with them on new adventures. She is "in their head," helping them to reframe encounters and situations that arise from God's point of view. When they worry, her advice calms them.

She is constantly on the move, making her own rounds through the ordinary places that people pass, seeking to introduce herself to those who are worthy of her. She graciously reveals herself to them as they proceed along the "ways," "the beaten paths," the stages of human growth that lead to maturity which, here, is life lived wisely.

READING II   This earliest of Paul's writings and oldest of New

For meditation and context:

RESPONSORIAL PSALM   Psalm 63:2, 3–4, 5–6, 7–8 (2b)

R. My soul is thirsting for you, O Lord my God.

O God, you are my God whom I seek;
  for you my flesh pines and my soul thirsts
  like the earth, parched, lifeless and
    without water.

Thus have I gazed toward you in
    the sanctuary
  to see your power and your glory,
for your kindness is a greater good than life;
  my lips shall glorify you.

Thus will I bless you while I live;
  lifting up my hands, I will call upon
    your name.
As with the riches of a banquet shall my soul
    be satisfied,
  and with exultant lips my mouth shall
    praise you.

I will remember you upon my couch,
  and through the night-watches I will
    meditate on you:
you are my help,
  and in the shadow of your wings I shout
    for joy.

READING II   Thessalonians 4:13–18

A reading from the first Letter of Saint Paul to the Thessalonians

[We do **not** want you to be **unaware**, brothers and sisters,
  about those who have **fallen asleep**,
  so that you may **not** grieve like the rest, who have **no hope**.
For if we believe that **Jesus** died and rose,
  so too will **God**, through **Jesus**,
  bring with him those who have fallen asleep.]
Indeed, we tell you this, on the word of the Lord,
  that we who are **alive**,
  who are **left** until the coming of the Lord,
  will surely **not** precede those who have fallen asleep.
For the **Lord** himself, with a word of command,
  with the voice of an archangel and with the trumpet of God,
  will come down from heaven,
  and the **dead** in **Christ** will rise **first**.
Then we who are **alive**, who are left,
  will be **caught** up together with them in the clouds
  to **meet** the Lord in the air. »

Thessalonians = thes-uh-LOH-nee-uhnz

Proclaim with good volume and authority in your voice.

Start to build intensity in your voice.

Pause before you begin this line.

archangel = AHRK-ayn-jihl
Continue to build the intensity in your voice.

Testament works suggests that when Paul wrote it, he and many Christians expected the imminent return of the risen Christ. When members of the community die before this event, others worry about what happens to them. Paul reassures these mourners that their beloved dead are with the Lord who will bring them back when he returns.

Paul uses apocalyptic imagery, "the voice of an archangel . . . the trumpet of God coming down from heaven," to convey symbolically the divine plan. In contrast to the more familiar idea that the dead "go up" to heaven to be with the Lord, in this passage the Lord comes down from there. During his descent, the dead and those still living will be caught up (the passive form indicates divine agency) together "in the clouds." They will meet the Lord "in the air," a term which scholars think denotes the earth's atmosphere. It must be borne in mind that Paul is not talking about a physical place. He speaks analogously about a reality that, because it is divine, is beyond complete human understanding—namely, the reality that somehow all believers will one day always be together with the Risen Lord.

The death of their brothers and sisters provides an opportunity for Christians to display their certain hope to those around them. Though they naturally experience deep sadness when a loved one dies, and cannot help but grieve, Paul does not want them to mourn like unbelievers, who do not expect to see their loved ones again. For believers, the dead are merely "sleeping" for a short time. Like the living who wake up each day, they will rise when Christ returns, and all will live together.

The comfort that the baptized have to offer each other is more than pious plati-

Pause and smile as you say this line.

Thus we shall **always** be **with** the Lord.
Therefore, **console** one another with these words.

[Shorter Form: 1 Thessalonians 4:13–14]

GOSPEL   Matthew 25:1–13

A reading from the holy Gospel according to Matthew

Pause before you begin to tell the parable.

Jesus told his disciples this parable:
    "The kingdom of heaven will be like ten virgins
    who took their lamps and went out to meet the bridegroom.

Use good eye contact as you proclaim.

Five of them were **foolish** and five were **wise**.
The foolish ones, when taking their lamps,
    brought **no** oil with them,
        but the wise brought **flasks** of oil with their lamps.
Since the bridegroom was long delayed,
    they **all** became drowsy and fell asleep.
At midnight, there was a cry,
    '**Behold, the bridegroom! Come out to meet him!**'
Then **all** those virgins got up and trimmed their lamps.
The **foolish** ones said to the **wise**,

Put expression in your voice as you read the words of the foolish and wise virgins.

    '**Give** us some of your oil,
    for our lamps are going out.'
But the **wise** ones replied,
    '**No**, for there may not be **enough** for us and you.
Go instead to the merchants and **buy** some for yourselves.'
While they went off to buy it,
    the bridegroom came
    and those who were **ready went** into the wedding feast
        with him.

---

tudes or even profound formulas. It is their deep conviction that the bond they share with and in Christ is so strong that death cannot separate them. Since Christ died and rose, there is—in him—a seamlessness between the physical and spiritual worlds which allows the dead to remain somehow connected with the living.

GOSPEL | This parable is from Jesus' "eschatological discourse," the section of the Gospel where Matthew gathers Jesus' teachings about the end time, especially the final judgment. It com-

pares the kingdom of heaven to ten virgins who go out to meet the bridegroom and to all that happens as the tale unfolds. The women's fates display the two, possible eternal destinies that await Jesus' disciples: they will either be with him or not.

Their mission is to welcome the bridegroom with lamps lit. Since there is no scheduled time for his arrival, the wise ones bring flasks of extra oil but the foolish ones do not. The bridegroom is long delayed (like Jesus' return). All the virgins fall asleep and awake in the middle of the night hearing the cry that the bridegroom is coming.

The foolish virgins see that their lamps are going out and presume that the wise will share their oil. At first glance, the refusal of the wise to do so seems uncharitable and unchristian. But the oil, in this passage, represents something that cannot be shared; each person must provide it for himself or herself.

While the foolish go off to purchase oil, the bridegroom comes and the wise go into the wedding feast with him. The detail, "Then the door was locked" has a haunting finality. Too late, the foolish arrive and say, "Lord, Lord, open the door for us!" Just as

Then the door was **locked**.
Afterwards the other virgins came and said,
   'Lord, Lord, open the door for us!'
But he said in reply,
   'Amen, I say to you, I do **not** know you.'
Therefore, **stay awake**,
   for you know **neither** the day nor the hour."

Proclaim with a loud, firm voice.

earlier they expected their coworkers to do their job, now they expect the Lord to ignore their negligence and let them in. Imagine their shock when they hear his voice behind that door saying, "I do not know you."

"Know" here means to recognize someone from having experiences with them. In other words, Jesus is saying to the foolish, "We never did anything together." He made this point earlier in the Sermon on the Mount, saying that those who merely profess to be his disciple, those who are saying "Lord, Lord" but not doing the Father's will, shall not enter the kingdom of heaven. Even disciples who prophesy, drive out demons, or work miracles in his name could hear him say, "Never did I *know* you" (Matthew 7:21–23).

The evangelist tacks a warning onto Jesus' parable that exhorts disciples to stay awake because the Lord could return at any moment. "Staying awake" or "watching" in Matthew does not mean to wait passively for the Parousia; it entails action. Disciples must be about the work that the Jesus wants to be doing with them. This parable warns that there will come a time when it's "too late" to do anything. Those who claim to be his disciples could, like the foolish virgins, find themselves standing for all eternity, watching the light from their lamps—lamps lit too late—bounce off that door that will never open again. E.N.

THIRTY-THIRD SUNDAY IN ORDINARY TIME

LECTIONARY #157

READING I   Proverbs 31:10–13, 19–20, 30–31

A reading from the Book of Proverbs

Proclaim this reading with good volume and eye contact using a slow but steady pace.

When one **finds** a worthy wife,
  her value is far **beyond pearls.**
Her husband, **entrusting** his **heart** to **her,**
  has an **unfailing prize.**
She brings him **good**, and **not evil,**
  all the days of her life.
She obtains wool and flax
  and **works** with **loving hands.**

Smile as you read.

She puts her hands to the distaff,
  and her fingers ply the spindle.

distaff and spindle = tools for spinning fibers into yarn or thread

She **reaches** out her hands to the **poor,**
  and **extends** her arms to the **needy.**
Charm is deceptive and beauty fleeting;
  the woman who **fears** the LORD is to be **praised.**

Pause before you say this line.

Give her a **reward** for her labors,
  and let her works **praise** her at the city gates.

READING I This poem, which concludes the book of Proverbs, praises a wife who embodies wisdom. In other words, to see her is to see one who embodies wisdom. The opening verse reads, "An 'esheth chayil, who can find one? More than precious stones (pearls or corals) is her value." The Hebrew phrase, 'esheth chayil, is translated variously as a "worthy wife," a "capable wife," or a "valiant woman." In the book of Ruth, the Moabite woman by that name who provided for her mother-in-law, is recognized as an 'esheth chayil (Ruth 3:11). And in Proverbs 12:4, an 'esheth chayil is the

crown of her husband, in contrast to a disgraceful wife who is like a rot in her husband's bones. Today's passage from Proverbs portrays the 'esheth chayil as extremely industrious, competent, resourceful, and powerful.

Many verses of the poem extol her value to her husband. If he relies on her in all things he will find that he "has an unfailing prize." Like wisdom itself in the book of Proverbs, she is trustworthy and through all the stages of their life together brings her husband good things or advantages.

The repetitions of her busy "hands" or "palms or fingers" depict her industriousness. With "loving, willing, or eager" hands she spins the wool and flax that she searched for and found. She puts her hands to the distaff and either works the spindle with her fingers or rolls it between her palms. She then weaves material from the spun woolen and linen fibers and sews garments to clothe her household and to sell for profit. She also extends her "palm" to the poor, welcoming them and offering them aid, and her "hands" to the needy. Her concern for others reaches beyond her

283

RESPONSORIAL PSALM   Psalm 128:1–2, 3, 4–5 (1a)

R. Blessed are those who fear the Lord.

Blessed are you who fear the LORD,
   who walk in his ways!
For you shall eat the fruit of your handiwork;
   blessed shall you be, and favored.

Your wife shall be like a fruitful vine
   in the recesses of your home;
your children like olive plants
   around your table.

Behold, thus is the man blessed
   who fears the LORD.
The LORD bless you from Zion:
   may you see the prosperity of Jerusalem
   all the days of your life.

Thessalonians = thes-uh-LOH-nee-uhnz

Proclaim with firmness and conviction.

READING II   1 Thessalonians 5:1–6

A reading from the first Letter of Saint Paul to the Thessalonians

Concerning times and seasons, brothers and sisters,
   you have **no need** for anything to be **written** to you.
For you yourselves **know** very well that the **day of the Lord**
      will come
   like a **thief** at night.
When people are saying, "Peace and security,"
   then **sudden** disaster **comes** upon them,
   like labor pains upon a pregnant woman,
   and they will **not** escape.

Transition to a tone of hope.

But you, brothers and sisters, are **not** in darkness,
   for that day to overtake you like a thief.
For **all** of you are **children** of the **light**
   and **children** of the **day**.
We are **not** of the night or of darkness.
Therefore, let us **not** sleep as the rest do,
   but let us **stay alert** and **sober**.

TO KEEP IN MIND
Read the Scripture passage and its commentary in *Workbook*. Then read it from your Bible, including what comes before and after it, so that you understand the context.

own household. Like Woman Wisdom in Proverbs, she is interested in the well-being of the people she encounters. In some of the verses that have been left out of this reading, she is shown evaluating a field, buying it, and planting a vineyard. She "girds herself" with strength. This girding is an idiom for people preparing to go to work or a soldier getting ready for battle. The woman's arms are strong from physical labor. Based on parallels from the biblical world, her lamp "that does not go out at night" is probably a metaphor for the prosperity that results from her industriousness.

While most people admire superficial traits, like charm that can deceive and beauty that swiftly fades, this poem declares that truly praiseworthy is the valiant woman. She is shaped by wisdom, which as the opening verses of Proverbs declare, begins with "the fear of the Lord" (Proverbs 1:7). People should talk about her and those like her at the "city gates," the place where one catches up on the news in the biblical world.

READING II In this reading, Paul is not warning believers about a

terrifying future event but encouraging them to keep the faith in the present. "The Day of the Lord" is a metaphor that was used by the Hebrew prophets for the eventual full manifestation of Israel's God to the world. Paul applies this prophetic metaphor to the Parousia. He teaches, as Jesus taught his disciples (Luke 12:39), that Christ would return when no one expects him, like a thief at night.

The baptized believe this, but most of the Thessalonians do not. These short-sighted neighbors put their faith in the "peace and security" that they enjoy as

GOSPEL   Matthew 25:14–30

A reading from the holy Gospel according to Matthew

[**Jesus** told his disciples this parable:
  "A man going on a journey
  called in his servants and **entrusted** his **possessions** to them.
To one he gave **five** talents; to another, **two**; to a third, **one**—
  to **each** according to his **ability**.
Then he went away.]
Immediately the one who received five talents went and **traded**
    with them,
  and made **another** five.
Likewise, the one who received two **made** another **two**.
But the man who received **one** went off and dug a hole
    in the ground
  and **buried** his master's money.

["After a long time
  the master of those servants came back
  and settled accounts with them.
The one who had received five talents came forward
  bringing the **additional** five.
He said, 'Master, you gave me five talents.
See, I have made five **more**.'
His master said to him, 'Well done, my good and
    faithful servant.
Since you were **faithful** in **small** matters,
  I will give you **great** responsibilities.
Come, **share** your master's **joy**.']
Then the one who had received two talents also came forward
    and said,
  'Master, you gave me two talents.
See, I have made two **more**.'
His master said to him, 'Well done, my good and
    faithful servant. ➤

Pause before you begin the parable. Use strong eye contact as you read the story.

Keep up your energy and use vocal expression in the dialogue between the servants and the master.

citizens of a free city in the Roman Empire, a status that depends on their loyalty to its emperor. Paul declares that they will experience Christ's return as a disaster from which they cannot escape.

He urges believers to manifest their belief that Christ is coming back by their lifestyle and pursuits. He calls them to live as "light's children" and "day's children" for they do not live in darkness. Nor are they "of the night" or "of darkness." They must not "sleep" as the unbelieving rest of humanity does. They must not be intoxicated and sidetracked by comfort, ease,

and entertainment. They must not, metaphorically, snooze their life away. Paul exhorts them to stay sober and alert, to work together to shine the light of Christ's peace and the security that only Christ can bring into the dark, slumbering mass of humanity around them.

GOSPEL   The tale of the talents is another kingdom parable from Jesus' eschatological discourse. Matthew places Jesus' telling of it two days before his passion—the supreme example of "using one's talents" for the

kingdom—begins in Jerusalem. The master in the parable represents Jesus, who "goes on a journey" when he dies and returns "after a long time" at the Parousia. A "talent" represents more than our modern definition of an inborn trait. Here, it is a huge allotment of divine goods that God entrusts to Jesus' disciples.

The servants who receive five and two talents strategize how to use them to benefit their master. They take initiative as well as risks. Both double the talents and hear the exuberant "Well done!" or "Excellent!" of the master who is ecstatic about what

Since you were **faithful** in **small** matters,
    I will give you **great** responsibilities.
Come, **share** your master's **joy.**'
Then the one who had received the **one** talent came forward
        and said,
    'Master, I knew you were a demanding person,
    harvesting where you did not plant
    and gathering where you did not scatter;
    so **out of fear** I went off and **buried** your talent in the ground.
Here it is back.'
His master said to him in reply, 'You wicked, lazy servant!
So you **knew** that I harvest where I did **not** plant
    and **gather** where I did not scatter?
Should you **not** then have put my money in the **bank**
    so that I could have got it back with **interest** on my return?
Now then! **Take** the talent from him and **give** it to the one
        with ten.
For to everyone who **has**,
    more will be **given** and he will grow rich;
    but from the one who has **not**,
    even what he has will be **taken away.**
And **throw** this useless servant into the **darkness** outside,
    where there will be **wailing** and **grinding** of teeth.'"

[Shorter: Matthew 25:14–15, 19–21 (see brackets)]

Proclaim this part in a tone of anger and frustration.

Transition to a tone of a teacher, explaining what will happen to everyone's talents.

Proclaim this last line in disgust.

TO KEEP IN MIND
As you prepare your proclamation, make choices about what emotions need to be expressed. Some choices are evident from the text, but some are harder to discern. Understanding the context of the Scripture passage will help you decide.

they did for him. He calls them "good and faithful," words that every disciple hopes to hear at the last judgment.

Jesus talks longest about the one-talent servant because most Christians are like him. He wants to jar these believers out of their complacency before it's too late, to persuade them to do the work for the kingdom that he assigns them. The servant's speech reveals a common narrow view of God; God is "demanding," or "rough," or even "cruel." This servant is so afraid of the master that he puts the talent in the safest place he can think of—a hole in the ground.

Now he is relieved to hand it back over, satisfied that he will escape the master's wrath and certain that he proves himself a good and faithful servant.

Imagine his shock when he hears the master call him evil and indolent. With these words, Jesus teaches that laziness can cost one the kingdom. He adds that loafers are useless for God's purpose because, in Matthew, they bear no fruit. At the last judgment, they will be cast into the outermost darkness where, with other apathetic Christians, they will lament and regret their inertia, hopelessly severed from the Lord's joy for all eternity. They did not work for the Lord on earth. Now they can idle away eternity. E.N.

OUR LORD JESUS CHRIST, KING OF THE UNIVERSE

LECTIONARY #160

READING I   Ezekiel 34:11–12, 15–17

A reading from the Book of the Prophet Ezekiel

Thus says the Lord GOD:
   I myself will **look after** and **tend** my sheep.
As a shepherd tends his flock
   when he finds himself **among** his **scattered** sheep,
   so will I tend my sheep.
I will **rescue** them from **every** place where they were scattered
   when it was cloudy and dark.
I myself will **pasture** my sheep;
   I myself will **give** them **rest**, says the Lord God.
The **lost** I will **seek out**,
   the **strayed** I will **bring back**,
   the **injured** I will **bind up**,
   the **sick** I will **heal**,
   but the **sleek** and the **strong** I will **destroy**,
   shepherding them rightly.

As for **you**, my sheep, says the **Lord GOD**,
   I will **judge** between **one** sheep and another,
   between rams and goats.

Ezekiel = ee-ZEE-kee-uhl

Proclaim with good volume in a tone of authority.

Transition to a tone of compassion. Articulate your words.

You want the congregation to listen to this part of the reading. Pause after each comma for emphasis.

Say this last line using good eye contact and a firmness of tone.

READING I   On this last Sunday of the liturgical year, the Church turns its attention to that time when life as we experience it on earth ends and eternal life begins. The first reading and the Gospel declare the certainty of a final judgment where people will hear their eternal destiny. The second reading assures the baptized that Christ is alive and reigning and that the divine plan for humans to enjoy God's life forever is moving toward its fulfilment.

Ezekiel prophesies to God's people shortly before and after the Babylonians conquered Jerusalem and Judah, around six hundred years before Christ. At that time, some fled from the invading army while others were deported throughout the victor's empire. In the previous century, the northern kingdom, Israel, suffered the same fate at the hands of the Assyrians. These scatterings became known as the Jewish diaspora. In Ezekiel, the Lord lays the main responsibility for them at the feet of the kings—i.e., the shepherds, of Israel and Judah, who failed to care for the flock by maintaining justice for all.

This reading announces that the Lord will come in person to tend his flock: "Look! I, I myself will . . . take care of them." "I, I myself will pasture my sheep . . . I, I myself will give them rest." A technical prophetic formula, "the oracle of the Lord" (translated here as "says the Lord God") marks the announcement as "official" and "irrevocable."

The list that follows describes the condition of the scattered flock and what their Shepherd will personally do for them. The hopelessly lost, those incapable of finding their own way back, and those who went astray, he will search for until he finds them and brings them back. The "shattered," an

For meditation and context:

RESPONSORIAL PSALM Psalm 23:1–2, 2–3, 5–6 (1)

R. The Lord is my shepherd; there is nothing I shall want.

The Lord is my shepherd; I shall not want.
  In verdant pastures he gives me repose.

Beside restful waters he leads me;
  he refreshes my soul.
He guides me in right paths
  for his name's sake.

You spread the table before me
  in the sight of my foes;
you anoint my head with oil;
  my cup overflows.

Only goodness and kindness follow me
  all the days of my life;
and I shall dwell in the house of the Lord
  for years to come.

READING II 1 Corinthians 15:20–26, 28

Corinthians = kohr-IN-thee-uhnz

A reading from the first Letter of Saint Paul to the Corinthians

Proclaim in a tone of firmness and conviction.

Brothers and sisters:
Christ has been raised from the dead,
  the firstfruits of those who have fallen asleep.
For since death came **through** man,
  the **resurrection** of the dead came also **through** man.
For just as in **Adam all** die,

Keep energy in your voice. Take your time. You want the congregation to follow and understand what Paul is saying.

  so **too** in **Christ** shall **all** be brought to **life**,
  but each one in **proper** order:
  Christ the **firstfruits;**
  then, at his coming, those who **belong** to Christ;
  then comes the **end,**
  when he **hands over** the kingdom to his **God and Father,**
  when he has destroyed **every** sovereignty
  and **every** authority and power.
For he must **reign** until he has put **all** his enemies under his feet.

Pause before you say this line.
Clearly speak this last line.

The **last** enemy to be destroyed is **death.**
When everything is **subjected** to him,
  then the Son himself will **also** be subjected
  to the one who subjected **everything** to him,
  so that **God** may be **all in all.**

---

intensive form of the verb "break," he will bind up. The weak or sick he will make strong again.

The tone changes sharply when it comes to the sleek and the strong; these the Lord will destroy "with justice" (Hebrew *bemishpat*). The meaning of this final phrase, which is translated as "shepherding them rightly," is that the Lord will tend to the well-being of all members of the flock, seeing that they get what they need and deserve. The last verse reminds God's people that they, like their leaders, will be judged for their covenant fidelity.

READING II Paul teaches that Christian faith and hope are based on Jesus' being raised from the dead. He calls Christ the first fruits of those who have "fallen asleep" (the Greek verb form emphasizes that they are "still sleeping"). In this passage, the first fruits are not so much an offering as a pledge or guarantee of "the crop" of believers who will be harvested at the end of time.

Paul's comparison of Adam with Christ is of the first man, who represents all humanity, with the last man, who is Christ. The first man (all humans) must die, but the

last man died and was raised up from the dead—as will be all those who are baptized into him. They shall certainly be "brought to life," but in the proper order, that is, in God's order. First, Jesus was raised, then he will return to earth, at which time all the dead will be raised up, and then literally, "the end" will occur, or "the last thing" will be the risen Christ handing the kingdom over to the Father.

The Corinthians, like the baptized today, live between Christ's Resurrection and his (second) "coming" or "arrival," in Greek, his "*parousia*." The image of Christ

GOSPEL   Matthew 25:31–46

A reading from the holy Gospel according to Matthew

Jesus said to his **disciples**:
 "When the **Son of Man** comes in his glory,
 and **all** the angels with him,
 he will **sit** upon his glorious **throne**,
 and **all** the nations will be assembled **before** him.
And he will **separate** them **one** from another,
 as a shepherd separates the **sheep** from the **goats**.
He will place the **sheep** on his **right** and the goats on his **left**.
Then the king will say to those on his right,
 'Come, you who are blessed by my Father.
Inherit the kingdom prepared for you from the **foundation**
  of the world.
For I was **hungry** and you **gave** me **food**,
 I was **thirsty** and you **gave** me **drink**,
 a **stranger** and you **welcomed** me,
 naked and you **clothed** me,
 ill and you **cared** for me,
 in **prison** and you **visited** me.'
Then the **righteous** will answer him and say,
 'Lord, **when** did we see you **hungry** and **feed** you,
 or **thirsty** and **give** you **drink**?
When did we see you a **stranger** and **welcome** you,
 or **naked** and **clothe** you?
When did we see you **ill** or in **prison**, and **visit** you?'
And the king will say to them in reply,
 'Amen, I say to you, **whatever** you did
 for **one** of the **least brothers** of mine, **you did for me.'**

Proclaim in a tone of authority.

Pause before you say this line.

Proclaim in a tone of compassion.

Use expression as you read the questions.

Pause and then say with gentleness and using good eye contact.

---

putting all his enemies under his feet draws on Psalm 110:1, which was read during enthronement rites for a king of Israel or Judah. The psalm itself borrows images from the biblical world that show a ruler who is seated on his throne, using the heads of vanquished enemies for his footstool. The risen Christ will rule until all his enemies are under his feet, the last of these being death. In "the end," when everything is subjected to God, divine life will permeate and enliven all that exists.

GOSPEL This parable, which follows those of the wise and foolish virgins and the talents, concludes Jesus' discourse about the end times. In it, the Lord, who is referred to as the Son of Man, a shepherd, and a king, presides over the final judgment "of the nations." The metaphor that Jesus chooses for this reckoning is a shepherd separating animals at the end of a normal day in the Mideast. There, mixed flocks of sheep and goats are a common sight. Both animals are useful. The sheep provide wool and thus clothing, the goats the dietary staples of milk and

cheese. Goat hair is also the preferred material for tents because it shrinks in the heat and allows air to ventilate these dwellings during the hot dry season, but swells when the rains come, tightening the weave and keeping residents dry. In the parable, for whatever reason, the sheep represent those who will enjoy eternal life and the goats those who will suffer eternal punishment.

The lack of clarity about the identity of "the nations" and "the least" results in two main lines of interpretation for the parable. In one of these, "the nations" who are

accursed = uh-KERST
Transition to a tone of disgust and frustration.

Then he will say to those on his **left**,
  '**Depart** from me, you accursed,
  into the **eternal fire** prepared for the devil and his angels.
For I was **hungry** and you **gave** me **no food**,
  I was **thirsty** and you **gave** me **no drink**,
  a **stranger** and you **gave** me **no welcome**,
  naked and you gave me **no clothing**,
  ill and **in prison**, and you **did not care for me**.'
Then they will answer and say,
  'Lord, **when** did we see you **hungry** or **thirsty**
  or a **stranger** or **naked** or **ill** or in **prison**,
  and **not minister to your needs?**'

Transition to a tone of firmness.

He will answer them, '**Amen**, I say to you,
  what you did **not do** for one of these **least** ones,
  you did **not do for me**.' ·
And **these** will go off to **eternal punishment**,
  but the **righteous to eternal life**."

TO KEEP IN MIND
Pause to break up separate
thoughts, set significant statements
apart, or indicate major shifts.
Never pause in the middle of a
thought. Your primary guide for
pauses is punctuation.

---

assembled before the Son of Man's throne are all non-Christians who will be judged by the way that they treated "the least ones," that is, Jesus' disciples or perhaps Christian missionaries. In the second interpretation, which is more widespread in tradition, both "the nations" and "the least ones" refer to all people who will be judged by the way they treated each other. The first explanation garners more support from the immediate context of Matthew's Gospel, the second from other biblical passages, like "You shall love your neighbor as yourself."

There is no lack of clarity, however, about the criteria for the judgment. Called today "the corporal works of mercy," the list is repeated four times. Each repetition reinforces Jesus' insistence that how people treat others, especially those in need, is how they treat him. The question asked by all who are judged, "when did we see you?" displays the difficulty that humans have in comprehending Jesus' point. You can almost hear the "goats" thinking: "If I'd seen you thirsty, Jesus, I'd have certainly given you a drink! Had you come as an immigrant to my country, I'd have surely welcomed you!" In despair, they sigh, "If only I had known!" Well, now we know. E.N.